THE ROAD TO SUCCESS

Published by CelebrityPress®, Orlando, FL.

CelebrityPress® is a registered trademark.

Printed in the United States of America.

ISBN: 978-0-9975366-2-1
LCCN: 2016942368

This publication is designed to provide accurate and authoritative information with regard to the subject matter covered. It is sold with the understanding that the publisher is not engaged in rendering legal, accounting, or other professional advice. If legal advice or other expert assistance is required, the services of a competent professional should be sought. The opinions expressed by the authors in this book are not endorsed by CelebrityPress® and are the sole responsibility of the author rendering the opinion.

Most CelebrityPress® titles are available at special quantity discounts for bulk purchases for sales promotions, premiums, fundraising, and educational use. Special versions or book excerpts can also be created to fit specific needs.

For more information, please write:
CelebrityPress®
520 N. Orlando Ave, #2
Winter Park, FL 32789
or call 1.877.261.4930

Visit us online at: www.CelebrityPressPublishing.com

THE
ROAD TO
SUCCESS

CelebrityPress®
Winter Park, Florida

CONTENTS

CHAPTER 1

YOUR ROADMAP TO SUCCESS

BY JACK CANFIELD

All you need is the plan, the road map,
and the courage to press on to your destination.
~ Earl Nightingale

Success is possible in every area of your life—job and career, financial, health and fitness, relationships, fun and recreation, sports, politics and service. From my work with millions of people in more than 50 countries I have discovered that there actually is a "science of success." There is a set of universal principles and techniques that all but guarantee that anyone who knows and applies them can achieve anything they want. Obviously, there is only going to be one Super Bowl champion each year, and only one gold medalist in each of the Olympic sporting events. But what is also true is that you don't get into the top tier of any field or profession if you don't apply these principles and strategies.

My intention here is to outline the core principles that, if applied in the right way at the right time in the right sequence, will take you from where you currently are to where you want to go in life—a roadmap to success. Like all roadmaps, GPS systems, and digital navigation systems, all you have to do is follow the directions. And one of those principles is to respond to feedback. I recently downloaded an app called WAZE, and what I love about it is that I continually get feedback from those people who are ahead of me on the road I am travelling—not only telling me where there are traffic jams and accidents, but it also reroutes me to avoid those obstacles. My intention is that this chapter will help you avoid some of the traffic jams and potholes along your journey to success and get to where you want to go faster and with less effort. So let's get started.

1. DECIDE WHAT YOU WANT

In order to get what you want, you must first decide what you want. Most people foul up at this crucial first step because they simply can't see how it's possible to get what they want — so they don't even let themselves want it. Don't sabotage yourself that way! What scientists now know about how the brain works, is that you must first decide WHAT you want, before your brain can figure out HOW to get it.

Be Willing to Dream Big Dreams

> *It doesn't take any more effort to dream a big dream*
> *than it takes to dream a small dream.*
> ~ General Wesley C. Clark
> Former U.S. Supreme Allied Commander of European Forces

As soon as you commit to a big dream and really go after it, your creative mind will come up with the big ideas needed to make it happen. You'll start attracting the ideas, people, opportunities, and resources (including money) that you need into your life to make your dream come true. Big dreams not only inspire you, they also inspire others to want to play big, and to help you succeed as well.

Set Goals That Will Stretch You

Another value in giving yourself permission to go after the big dreams is that big dreams require you to grow in order to achieve them. In fact, in the long run, that is the greatest benefit you will receive from pursuing your dreams — not so much the outer trappings of fulfilling the dream (an expensive car, impressive house, lots of money and philanthropic opportunities), but who you become in the process. As we all have seen many times over, the outer symbols of success, can all be easily lost. Houses burn down, companies go bankrupt, relationships end in divorce, cars get old, bodies age and fame wanes, but who you are, what you have learned and the new skills you have developed, never go away. These are the true prizes of success. My mentor, self-made multimillionaire W. Clement Stone, advised, "You should set a goal big enough that in the process of achieving it, you become someone worth becoming."

Service to Others
Something else you'll discover is that when your dreams include service to others — accomplishing something that contributes to the well-being of others — it also accelerates the accomplishment of that goal. People want to be part of something that contributes and makes a difference.

Turn Your Dreams into Goals and Objectives
Once you are clear about what you want, you must turn each item into a measurable objective. By measurable, I mean measurable in space and time — how much and by when. For instance, if you were to tell me that you wanted more money, I might pull out a dollar and give it to you, but you would probably protest, saying, "No, I meant a lot more money — like $20,000!" Well, how am I supposed to know unless you tell me? Similarly, your boss, your friends, your spouse, your brain — God, the Universe — can't figure out what you want unless you tell them specifically what it is. What exactly do you want, and by what specific date and time do you want it?

2. BELIEVE IN YOURSELF: USE POSITIVE SELF TALK

The second strategy that you must employ in order to achieve all of your dreams is to develop an unshakeable belief in your worthiness to have what you desire — and in your ability to achieve what you set out to accomplish — from financial abundance and a fulfilling career to dynamic health and nurturing relationships.

Ultimately, you must learn to control your self-talk, eliminate any negative and limiting beliefs, and maintain a constant state of positive expectations.

Control Your Self-Talk
Researchers have found that the average person thinks as many as 50,000 thoughts a day. Sadly, many of those thoughts are negative — "I'm not management material." ... "I'll never lose weight." ... "It doesn't matter what I do, nothing ever works out for me." This is what psychologists call victim language. Victim language actually keeps you in a victim state of mind. It is a form of self-hypnosis that lulls you into a belief that

you are unlovable and incompetent.

In order to live your dreams, you need to give up this victim language and start talking to yourself like a winner — "I can do it!" ... "I know there is a solution." ... "I am smart enough and strong enough to achieve anything I want." ... "Everything I eat helps me maintain my perfect body weight."

You Are Always Programming Your Subconscious Mind

Your subconscious mind is like the crew of a ship. You are its captain. It is your job to give the crew orders. When you do this, the crew takes everything you say literally. The crew (your subconscious) has no sense of humor. It just blindly follows orders. When you say, "Everything I eat goes straight to my hips," the crew hears that as an order: "Take everything she eats, turn it into fat and put it on her hips." On the other hand, if you say, "Everything I eat helps me maintain my perfect body weight," the crew will begin to make that into reality by helping you make better food choices, exercise more often and maintain the right metabolism rate for your body.

This power of your subconscious mind is the reason you must become very vigilant and pay careful attention to your spoken and internal statements. Unfortunately, most people don't realize they are committing negative self-talk, which is why it is best to enlist another person — your accountability partner — in monitoring each other's speaking. You can have a signal for interrupting each other when you use victim language.

Use Affirmations to Build Self-Confidence

One of the most powerful tools for building worthiness and self-confidence is the repetition of positive statements until they become a natural part of the way you think. These "affirmations" act to crowd out and replace the negative orders you have been sending your crew (your subconscious mind) all these past years. I suggest that you create a list of 10 to 20 statements that affirm your belief in your worthiness and your ability to create the life of your dreams. Here are some examples of affirmations that have worked for my students in the past:

I am worthy of love, joy and success.
I am smart.
I am loveable and capable.
I can create anything I want.

I am able to solve any problem that comes my way.
I can handle anything that life hands me.
I have all the energy I need to do everything I want to do.
I am attracting all the right people into my life.

3. BUILD ON YOUR STRENGTHS AND YOUR UNIQUE ABILITIES

Everyone is born with a unique set of talents and abilities — what I refer to as your areas of brilliance or your genius. There are certain things you do that are easy for you, that you love to do, and from which you get feedback that people receive value from them. In fact, you probably do these things you do so easily and so well that you feel almost embarrassed or guilty about taking money for them.

For me, my core genius lies in the area of teaching, inspiring, motivating and empowering people in workshops, trainings, teleseminars, and coaching. I love to do it, I do it well, and people report that they get great value from it. Another core genius is compiling and writing books. Along with my *Chicken Soup for the Soul*® co-author Mark Victor Hansen, Janet Switzer and others, I have written, co-authored, compiled and edited more than 175 books—46 of which have become *New York Times* bestsellers.

Take time to determine what your core genius is and begin to focus more of your time on it. Begin to delegate the tasks that are not your core genius to other people who love to do those tasks. I believe that you can trade, barter, pay for and find volunteer help to do almost everything you don't want to do, leaving you to do what you are best at — and which will ultimately make you the most money and bring you the most happiness.

4. BUILD AN AWESOME DREAM TEAM

One of the most critical elements of living your dreams is having your own "Dream Team." It is a powerful way to support your dreams and bring unlimited resources to your professional and personal life.

Sometimes called a mastermind group, your dream team is two or more individuals that voluntarily come together to creatively put their energy behind a definite purpose — increasing each other's income, building a business, raising their kids better, or solving a social problem. Within your mastermind group, you benefit from the other members who empower you and draw out your full talents, resources and abilities. They trigger you, stimulate you and motivate you to become all you are capable of being. As part of a dream team, you use blended mind-power in action to obtain your desired result.

Creating Your Dream Team

In forming your Dream Team, start by carefully enrolling another friendly, on-purpose, like-minded individual. Start by meeting together and then adding other selected, unanimously agreed-upon individuals who will work in total harmony for the good of each other and for the good of the group.

1. Your Dream Team should consist of 4-8 people (most people find that 6 is the ideal number).
2. Meet weekly or twice a month (in person, by conference call, Skype, or Google Hangouts) for an hour to an hour and a half. This meeting must be held sacred as a life-enhancing priority. The meetings should be upbeat, enriching, encouraging and beneficial to each individual and the group's purposes. We always start our meetings with a prayer or an invocation. You could also start with an inspiring story.
3. Each member must agree to play full out — to openly share ideas, support, contacts, information, feedback, and anything else that will help advance the individual and group goals.
4. Start by having each member share something positive and good that happened since the last meeting.
5. Next, have each member share an opportunity or problem they have experienced since the last meeting, and then ask for whatever support they would like on it. This can include brainstorming ideas, addressing limiting beliefs, and suggesting people to contact. Appoint a timekeeper to make sure that everyone gets the same amount of time. This is important if you want your Dream Team to last. Everyone must get value at every meeting or people will begin to drop out. Also make sure to end on time.
6. Have everyone commit to one or more action steps they will take before the next meeting.
7. End by sharing appreciations and acknowledgements with each other.

5. VISUALIZE AND AFFIRM YOUR DESIRED OUTCOMES

You have within you an awesome power that most of us have never been taught to use. Elite athletes use it. The super rich use it. And peak performers in all fields are now starting to use it. That power is called visualization. The daily practice of visualizing your dreams as already complete can rapidly accelerate your achievement of those dreams. Visualization of your goals and desires accomplishes four very important things.

1. It activates your creative subconscious mind, which will then start generating creative ideas to achieve your goal.
2. It programs your brain to more readily perceive and recognize the resources you will need to achieve your dreams.
3. It activates the law of attraction, thereby drawing into your life the people, resources, and circumstances you will need to achieve your goals.
4. It builds your internal motivation to take the necessary actions to achieve your dreams.

Visualization is really quite simple. You sit in a comfortable position, close your eyes and imagine — in as vivid detail as you can — a movie of what you would be looking at out through your own eyes if the dream you have were already realized. Imagine being inside of yourself, looking out through your eyes at the ideal result. See it in as much detail as you can create. Add in any sounds you would be hearing — traffic, music, other people talking, cheering. And finally, once you have created the image, do your best to generate in your body the feelings—gratitude, happiness, joy, excitement, abundance, peace—that you think you will feel when you actually achieve your end results.

When you have finished this process — it should take less than five minutes — you can open your eyes and go about your business. If you make this part of your daily routine, you will be amazed at how much improvement you will see in your life.

Create Goal Pictures

Another powerful technique is to create a photograph or picture of yourself with your goal, as if it were already completed. If one of your goals is to own a new car, take your camera down to your local auto

23

dealer and have a picture taken of yourself sitting behind the wheel of your dream car. If your goal is to visit Paris, find a picture or poster of the Eiffel Tower and cut out a picture of yourself and place it into the picture. You can make an even more convincing image using Photoshop® on your computer.

Create a Visual Picture and an Affirmation for Each Goal

I recommend that you find or create a picture of every aspect of your ideal dream life. Create a picture or a visual representation for every goal you have — financial, job and career, relationships, recreation, new skills and abilities, things you want to own, and so on.

When we were writing the very first Chicken Soup for the Soul® book, we took a copy of the New York Times best seller list, scanned it into our computer, and using the same font as the newspaper, typed Chicken Soup for the Soul into the number one position in the "Paperback Advice, How-To and Miscellaneous" category. We printed several copies and hung them up around the office. Less than two years later, our book was the number one book in that category and stayed there for over a year!

Index Cards

I practice a similar discipline every day. I have a list of about 20 goals I am currently working on. I write each goal on a 3x5 index card and keep those cards near my bed and take them with me when I travel. Each morning and each night I go through the stack of cards, one at a time, read the card, close my eyes, see the completion of that goal in its perfect desired state for about 15 seconds, open my eyes and repeat the process with the next card.

Use Affirmations to Support Your Visualization

An affirmation is a statement that evokes not only a picture, but the experience of already having what you want. Here's an example of an affirmation:

I am happily enjoying my two-week vacation in Maui watching the sunset over Ka'anapali Bay.

Repeating an affirmation several times a day keeps you focused on your goal, strengthens your motivation, and programs your subconscious by sending an order to your crew to do whatever it takes to make that goal happen.

Expect Results

Through writing down your goals, repeating your affirmations and using the power of visualization, you can achieve amazing results. Visualization and affirmations allow you to change your beliefs, assumptions, and opinions about the most   important person in your life — YOU! They allow you to harness the 18 billion brain cells in your brain and get them all working in a singular and purposeful direction.

Your subconscious will become engaged in a process that transforms you forever. The process is invisible and doesn't take a long time. It just happens over time, as long as you put in the time to visualize and affirm, surround yourself with positive people, read uplifting books and listen to audio programs that flood your mind with positive, life-affirming messages.

Repeat your affirmations every morning and night for one month without missing a day, and they will become an automatic part of your thinking. They will become woven into the very fabric of your being.

6. ACT TO CREATE IT

The thing that most separates winners from losers in life is that winners take action. If you want to live your dreams, not only must you decide what you want, turn your dream into measurable goals, break those goals down into a plan of specific action steps, and visualize and affirm your desired outcomes — you must start taking action. I recommend making the commitment to do something every day in at least three different areas of your life that move you in the direction of your dreams. If one of your goals is physical fitness, make a commitment to do some sort of exercise — aerobics, weight training, stretching — four to five times a week for a minimum of twenty minutes. I read recently that if you simply go for a 30-minute walk four times a week, that would put you in the top 1% of those people getting physical exercise in America! If your goal is financial independence, start saving and investing a portion of your income every month with no exceptions. If your goal is to write a book, write for a minimum of one hour every day.

Don't Let FEAR Stop You

Most people never get what they want because they let their fears stop them. They are afraid of making a mistake, looking foolish, getting ripped off, being rejected, being hurt, wasting their time, and feeling uncomfortable. Remember this—all fear is self-created by imagining catastrophic consequences that have not yet happened. It is all in your mind. One solution is to replace any fearful thought or image with a positive thought or image. Another powerful new technology to release any fear that you might have is tapping. Developed by Gary Craig, tapping consists of tapping on 9 acupressure points on your head and upper body while focusing on your fear. It is amazing how powerful this simple technique is in disappearing fear (even phobias you've had for years) in often as little as 5 to 10 minutes, you can learn how to use tapping from the book I coauthored with Pamela Bruner—Tapping into Ultimate Success. It also contains a 90-minute DVD illustrating Pamela and I guiding several students through the technique. You can get the book at Amazon.com

Rejection Is a Myth
One of the biggest fears that stops people from asking for support, guidance, advice, money, a date, a job, the sale, or anything else is the fear of rejection. In fact, it's been known to literally paralyze people. They become tongue-tied and refuse to reach for the phone or get up and walk across the room. They break out in a sweat at the mere thought of asking for what they want.

I have come to realize that the whole concept of rejection is false — that rejection doesn't really exist. Think about it for a moment. If you asked someone to join you for dinner, and they said no, you could tell yourself that you had been rejected, but it is all in your mind. But think about it. Did you have anyone to eat dinner with before you asked them? No! Did you have anyone to eat dinner with after you asked them? No! Did your life really get worse? No. It stayed the same!

Act As If
One of the secrets of success is to start acting like a success before you are one. Act as if. If you had already achieved your dream, what kinds of clothes would you be wearing? How would you act? How would you treat others? Would you tithe a portion of your income to your church or favorite charities? Would you have more self-confidence? Would you take more time to spend with your loved ones?

I suggest that you begin to do those things now. When I decided that

I wanted to be an "international" consultant, I immediately went and applied for a passport, bought an international clock that told me what time it was anywhere in the world, printed business cards with the words "International Peak Performance Consultant," and decided I would like to first go to Australia. I bought a poster of the Sydney Opera House and placed it on my refrigerator. Within one month, I received an invitation to speak in Sydney and Brisbane. Since then, I have spoken and conducted trainings in over 40 countries.

You may not be able to fill your closets with expensive Italian suits and designer clothing, but why not invest in one or two really great outfits, so that when you do need them, they are there. When you dress like you've already made it, you will look the part, and successful people will naturally be attracted to you and invite you to participate with them.

Start acting as if you already have everything you want. Most people think that if they have a lot of money, they could do the things they want to do, and they would be much happier. In fact, the reverse is true. If you start by creating a state of happiness, abundance and gratitude, then do the things you are inspired to do from that state of being, you will end up having all the things you ultimately desire. The Law of Attraction states that you will attract to you those things that match your state of being. If you focus on having gratitude for what you do have, you will feel rich, and you will attract more abundance into your life. If you focus on what you don't have, you will send out a message of lack and you will attract more lack into your life.

7. RESPOND TO FEEDBACK

As you begin to take action toward the fulfillment of your dreams, you must realize that not every action you take will produce your desired result. Not every action will work. Making mistakes, getting it almost right, and constantly experimenting with new approaches to see what happens are all part of the process of eventually getting something right.

Thomas Edison is reported to have tried over 2,000 different experiments that failed before he finally got the light bulb to work. He once told a reporter that, from his perspective, he had never failed at all. Inventing the light bulb was just a 2,000-step process! If you can adopt that attitude, then you can be free to take an action, notice what result you get, then adjust your next actions based on the feedback you have received. The faster you can make mistakes, learn from them and take action again, the faster you will become successful.

Ready, Fire, Aim!

Don't be afraid to just jump in and get started moving toward your goals. As long as you pay attention to the feedback you receive and make corrections based on that, you will definitely make progress. Just getting into the game and firing allows you to correct and refine your aim.

Ask Others for Feedback

One of the most valuable questions I have ever learned for soliciting valuable feedback is this:

> On a scale of 1 to 10, how would you rate the
> quality of our relationship during the last week?

Here are a number of variations on the same question that have served me well in both my business and my personal life.

On a scale of 1 to 10, how would you rate...

- our service?
- our product?
- this meeting?
- our performance?
- my coaching/managing?
- my parenting/babysitting?
- my teaching?
- this class/seminar/workshop/training?
- our date/vacation?
- this meal?
- this book/recording/show?

Any answer less than a 10 always gets this follow-up question:

> What would it take to make it a 10?

This is where the valuable information comes from. Knowing that a person is dissatisfied is not enough. Knowing in detail what will satisfy them gives you the information you need to do whatever it takes to create a winning product, service or relationship.

Ask Yourself for Feedback

In addition to asking others for feedback, you need to ask yourself for feedback, too. More than any other source of feedback, your body will tell you whether or not you are living your dream or not. When you feel relaxed, happy and alive, your body is telling you that you are on track. When you are constantly exhausted, tense, in pain, unhappy and angry, then you are definitely off track.

Take time to listen to what your body is saying to you. Take time to listen to your physical sensations and your feelings. They are sending you important messages. Are you listening?

If you are not feeling joyful and alive, start doing those things that make you come alive and feel joy.

8. NEVER GIVE UP: THE POWER OF PERSEVERANCE

After taking action, the most important quality you will need to develop in order to live your dreams is persistence. You must be persistent in your disciplines and habits; perseverant in the face of adversity, hardship and challenge; and determined to achieve your dreams, no matter what.

There will be many times when you will want to quit, give up, and go back to doing something else, but the one quality that will guarantee you success is the willingness to stick with it, to see it through to the end — to refuse to settle for anything less than your dream.

Adversity and Discouragement Is Inevitable

No matter how well you plan and how well you execute your plan, you are bound to meet with disappointments, adversity and failure along the way to your ultimate triumph. Adversity is what gives you the opportunity to develop your inner resources of character and courage. Adversity is a great teacher. It will test you and make you stronger. But you have to hang in there and not give up.

More than 4000 years ago in China, Confucius wrote, "Our greatest glory is not in never falling, but in rising every time we fall." As long as you know there will be times when you will fail, then you will know that failing is simply part of the process. Just take it in stride and press on — no matter what. And just when you think things are never going to change, press on a bit further, and that is when the tide will turn.

On my journey to living my dreams, I found the following facts very encouraging: The average millionaire in America has gone bankrupt or out of business 3.5 times on his or her way to becoming a millionaire, and there are now over 10.1 million millionaires in America. The Deloitte Center for Financial Services estimates that nearly one out of every 11 American workers is a millionaire. If financial independence is part of your dream, you too can fail your way to success if you simply stay the course.

9. CELEBRATE YOUR VICTORIES AND GIVE THANKS

If you do stay the course, you will eventually begin to realize all your goals. Once that happens, you need to do two things:
>   (1) celebrate your successes, and
>   (2) express your gratitude to everyone — including God — who helped you along the way. Let's take a look at some ways to do that.

Celebrate Your Victories
In order to justify all of the sacrifice and persistence that is required to create the life of your dreams, you have to enroll your family, your friends, your colleagues and co-workers, your employees, your clients and, most importantly, yourself to pay the price. In order for them to do that, there need to be payoffs along the way. Every time you reach a milestone on the path to ultimate success, and every time you achieve a major goal, you need to celebrate by doing something fun and nurturing.

Your Inner Child
It is important to reward your inner child, as well. Every time you work hard to meet a goal, the part of you that just wants to have fun has to sit still and be good. However, just like any kid, if it knows it will be rewarded later with a treat, it will hang in there with you.

How can you reward your inner child?
- Take a 20-minute walk after an hour or two of concentrated work
- Go for walks in the morning with your spouse
- Take 20 minutes to listen to music and daydream
- Take most weekends totally off
- Take several weeklong vacations throughout the year
- Get regular massages

- Engage in daily meditation, exercise and yoga
- Take music lessons
- Go to movies, concerts and plays
- Listen to comedy on CDs, SiriusXM Radio and the Comedy Channel
- Listen to motivational audio programs when driving

Have an Attitude of Gratitude

Take the time to thank every one that helped you achieve your goal. Write them a letter, call them, send them a card or an email, or send them a gift. It can be as simple as a hug and a thank you — to something as elaborate as letting someone use your summer vacation home for a week.

The Power of Acknowledgment

When you take the time to thank someone, they feel acknowledged for their contribution and will be more likely to want to help again.

Thank Your Higher Power

Finally, it is important to thank God, or however you perceive the Higher Power, for all of the abundance that comes into your life. Start with the little stuff — another day of life, healthy children, a sunny day, people who love you, family and friends. Be thankful for the birds, your pets, the clothes you have and the food you eat.

And be especially thankful for any additional blessings that come into your life. Take time each day to say a prayer of thanks when you first arise, before meals, and again at night before bed. Having an attitude of gratitude opens up the channels for even more abundance to flow into your life. The more grateful you are, the more you will attract to be grateful for.

10. GIVE SOMETHING BACK

A great philosopher once said, "Whatever you want more of, first give it away." If you want more love, first give away more love to others. The same is true for money. The best way to ensure an ongoing flow of abundance into your life is to share with others the wealth you have already received. I am a big believer in tithing — giving away 10% of your income to your church and/or favorite charities and causes. I believe that it does indeed come back multiplied. This has been demonstrated in my life and the lives of *Chicken Soup for the Soul*® readers over and over again.

My *Chicken Soup* co-author Mark Victor Hansen and I have been tithing for years and believe it is one of the major factors of our phenomenal success. Along with Peter Vegso, our original publisher at Health Communications, Mark and I have given away millions of dollars to more than 70 charities and non-profit organizations. We also distributed nearly 150,000 copies of *Chicken Soup for the Soul*® and *Chicken Soup for the Prisoner's Soul* to inmates in all of America's prisons.

If you have never tried tithing, give it a three-month trial and see what happens. Remember that, when you are giving, like attracts like. The more you give, the more will come back to you. If need be, start with one percent of your income, time, energy or effort, and then slowly build up to ten percent.

Tithe Your Time, as Well as Your Money

You can tithe your time, as well as your money. If you are uncomfortable tithing ten percent of your income, try tithing ten percent of your time. You can make a huge difference in so many areas of your community by giving of your time. There are numerous schools, churches, and other non-profits that are all clamoring for help.

****

The roadmap I have covered here is the essence of what I know works and what I have seen proven to work time and time again for individuals from all walks of life. You have the opportunity to create the life of your dreams, and you now have a proven road map for success — but it takes determination, planning resolve and effort on your part to actually travel that road. Remember, the only two things that will create the future of your dreams are the decisions you make and the actions you take—today! Don't wait. Get started today.

About Jack

Known as America's #1 Success Coach, Jack Canfield is the CEO of the Canfield Training Group in Santa Barbara, CA, which trains and coaches entrepreneurs, corporate leaders, managers, sales professionals and the general public in how to accelerate the achievement of their personal, professional and financial goals.

Jack Canfield is best known as the coauthor of the #1 New York Times bestselling *Chicken Soup for the Soul®* book series, which has sold more than 500 million books in 47 languages, including 11 New York Times #1 bestsellers. As the former CEO of Chicken Soup for the Soul Enterprises he helped grow the Chicken Soup for the Soul® brand into a virtual empire of books, children's books, audios, videos, CDs, classroom materials, a syndicated column and a television show, as well as a vigorous program of licensed products that includes everything from clothing and board games to nutraceuticals and a successful line of Chicken Soup for the Pet Lover's Soul® cat and dog foods.

His other books include *The Success Principles™: How to Get from Where You Are to Where You Want to Be* (recently revised as the 10th Anniversary Edition,) *The Success Principles for Teens, The Aladdin Factor, Dare to Win, Heart at Work, The Power of Focus: How to Hit Your Personal, Financial and Business Goals with Absolute Certainty, You've Got to Read This Book, Tapping into Ultimate Success, Jack Canfield's Key to Living the Law of Attraction*, and his recent novel—*The Golden Motorcycle Gang: A Story of Transformation.*

Jack is a dynamic speaker and was recently inducted into the National Speakers Association's Speakers Hall of Fame. He has appeared on more than 1000 radio and television shows including Oprah, Montel, Larry King Live, the Today Show, Fox and Friends, and 2 hour-long PBS Specials devoted exclusively to his work. Jack is also a featured teacher in 12 movies including *The Secret, The Meta-Secret, The Truth, The Keeper of the Keys, Tapping into the Source*, and *The Tapping Solution*.

Jack has personally helped hundreds of thousands of people on six different continents become multi-millionaires, business leaders, best-selling authors, leading sales professionals, successful entrepreneurs, and world-class athletes while at the same time creating balanced, fulfilling and healthy lives.

His corporate clients have included Virgin Records, SONY Pictures, Daimler-Chrysler, Federal Express, GE, Johnson & Johnson, Merrill Lynch, Campbell's Soup, Re/Max, The Million Dollar Forum, The Million Dollar Roundtable, The Entrepreneur Organization, The Young Presidents Organization, the Executive Committee, and the World Business Council.

He is the founder of the Transformational Leadership Council and a member of Evolutionary Leaders, two groups devoted to helping create a world that works for everyone.

Jack is a graduate of Harvard, earned his M.Ed. from the University of Massachusetts and has received three honorary doctorates in psychology and public service. He is married, has three children, two step-children and a grandson.

For more information, visit: www.JackCanfield.com

CHAPTER 2

BE YOUR OWN BEST PEACOCK

BY MARIE BAÑUELOS

Everyone is born with an instinct of success, and ability to make it, but only the ones who think out of the box succeed.
~ Unarine Ramaru

Name the fears that are holding you back. It's the equivalent of flooding the boogeyman with light.
~ Gina Greenlee, *Postcards and Pearls: Life Lessons from Solo Moments on the Road*

IT STARTED HERE

I progressed in education starting with being a high school dropout. I wasn't stupid; I was bored. I married at 16, had a child at 17, and remained a bored housewife until I divorced at 24. The big question was "Now what?" I was a single parent and on welfare. Not a great place to be.

I was known as the black sheep in my family. I never quite fit into the traditional Italian old-country family. I was **independent** (finally), stubborn in my beliefs, *didn't do-what-I-was-told*, always way **outside the box**, and fairly fearless. But I did get through community college and the universities in record time (without a high school diploma) just because I worked hard and didn't accept the Dean's comment I couldn't do it. I did do it. I was not afraid to try and do what others hadn't. I

35

also received a clear secondary teaching credential at the same time. Another thing I wasn't supposed to be able to do.

DO IT ANYWAY

I was known as the weird teacher. I did innovative things, I experimented with instruction, I refused individual seats in the classroom and had tables because, I knew to succeed, working together was the key. Students had affirmations they said every day loudly before class instruction (of course I warned my neighboring teachers). These things were in a time when none of these strategies were even thought applicable. My students flourished. Yep, I always thought out of the box.

I started to move up the ladder quickly. I was a constant learner and always experimented with better ways to accomplish goals. I tried new things no matter how hard and sometimes failed but kept risking by experimenting with new ideas. I became an administrator of Athletic Programs at a comprehensive high school when females were not in those positions and not administrators in secondary education. I wasn't a coach, but I knew how to manage the legal and program issues. I was good at analyzing the core of problems and finding solutions. I knew how to work with coaches and get the best from them.

Then I learned about sexual harassment, the glass ceiling, and the fight for promotion. Administrator in charge of athletics was not a job I truly wanted or even desired; it was a job the district designed to get me into administration. I thought long and hard about accepting. I knew I would suffer and spend many nights crying because of the way I would be treated; the disrespect I would have to go through would be grueling. I felt a little afraid but when did that stop me? I also knew I had to do that job to learn. As I look back now, it was probably the job that taught me the most about administration, people, laws, and management. There was something in my heart that told me do it anyway even through the pain. That was an extremely important lesson for me and that lesson made me brave and strong so I could stay true to myself.

I was determined, a little different than most, and had competencies that others could not ignore. I very quickly went from Administrator in charge of athletics to Assistant Principal, Principal, to County Office Administrator, to Assistant Superintendent, to Director of all Programs and Staff Development in a large school district, to Superintendent of Schools.

STAY TRUE TO YOURSELF

I was still myself through all the trials; stubborn, did what I felt was right even when opposed, researched constantly to find better solutions, included all staff in building a successful organization (even when the hierarchy couldn't understand why I would include "those" people). And I really cared for people and their feelings. I respected not only what they were but what I knew they could be. After all, I had lots of experiences that showed me how painful and lonely it was when not respected, supported, or believed in for who I was. I did it all anyway.

I believed in what I was doing in my career, and I also knew the "line" that I would not cross to move forward. That was the hardest lesson I learned and what also made me the most successful. Being female in a mostly male-dominated profession in secondary schools was a tough road to walk successfully. Education is political. To get to high positions, many times, it is who you know, what you are willing to do, and especially what you are willing not to do to make employees and Boards happy. I was known as a Warrior fairly soon after becoming a District Administrator. I told the truth, did not accept what was not researched, expected professional growth of all staff, and did not cross my ethical line. The last was the hardest and had the biggest cost.

I kept my skills sharp, constantly sought out new learnings, constantly read business books, not educational books because they were too narrow for managing an organization made of flesh and blood parts. I improved my "soft" skills: understanding motivation, emotions, satisfaction, need for recognition, and people needs. I sought out learnings in legal matters, planning, evaluation of plans, selling plans to others, all the while training others to do what I could do.

I was always described as a weird and very different administrator. But these were good things. I did not run a top-down organization, very different than the "normal" organization. I was driven by success not by what was always done before me. I made my ethical line very clear to Boards; I didn't lie, I shared all information unless it was personnel matters. I followed the law. I was above board in all dealings. I expected all staff to work as a team and build their skills, and I did not cross my ethical line. Sometimes the Boards were not so happy about those things.

KNOWING WHEN IT IS TIME TO MOVE ON

Not crossing my ethical line resulted in me leaving one administrative position because the boss was abusive to women. I do not allow anyone to abuse me or my staffs, so I resigned. Why resign? Because the Board wanted me to cross my ethical line. I would not cross it. I did not have a job when I submitted my resignation but, before I left, I was recruited by another district and secured a multiple-year contract as a result. They found me because of my reputation and skills.

The second time I left a position was when the Board was committing horrendous crimes against my staff, the students, and the organization. I took action to protect staff, fought hard to change what was illegal, and spent many an evening totally hating the job. My health was suffering. This was a battle that I could not win. I resigned and then participated in a Grand Jury investigation and was totally vindicated by the Grand Jury Report. I knew I had to leave but I could not leave without helping the organization change. I provided the Grand Jury evidence of Board misconduct and evidence of nepotism, creating a hostile work environment, and misappropriation of funds. The Grand Jury also found the Board at fault for "losing a highly qualified superintendent." The county took over to make changes by mandate.

Could I have stayed in these awful positions? Yes, but the cost would have been deadly. My health was struggling. To save an organization from the politics and the management from people "in power" is most times almost impossible. I had very hard decisions to make. After all, I am stubborn, willing to do what scares me, but not stupid. I could not give in to what they wanted (couldn't cross my line) so I no longer fit. One staff member cried when I left and it made me feel so guilty because I always cared deeply for my staffs. I gave all staff a book that helped me, A Peacock in the Land of Penguins, A Fable about Creativity & Courage by BJ Gallagher Hateley and Warren H. Schmidt (a business book). It told the story of a Peacock in the land of penguins and how the Peacock did not fit in no matter how much it tried. The Peacock could not be a penguin. The Peacock was a Peacock and always would be; the Peacock had to leave to be happy. I had to leave. I couldn't cross my line and couldn't be other than I was. These were the right and best decisions in my life. Those decisions led me to better places and continual growth.

LESSONS LEARNED

As I look back and move forward, there are five concepts I use to coach others to reach their goals. They are simple but take dedication even through hard times. They take guts and energy. The payoff for them is a life fulfilled and successful. If money is your only goal, they may not work for you. Money can be a product of using them, but won't guarantee riches.

I. Be true to yourself:

You can't be a Penguin if you are a Peacock. You can try, but you will always fall short. Be the best Peacock you can be. Learn, explore, think outside of the box. If you don't fit, go to a place where you do. Your happiness and success depend on it.

II. Be honest and upfront:

If you are political, this might not work for you. If you want to build trust and loyalty it will work great. Honesty does not mean say whatever comes out of your head through your mouth. Honesty are those things that are thought out carefully, considered, and as true as you can know them. Sometimes it means telling the truth even when it goes against the grain. It means admitting your shortcomings.

III. Know your ethics and integrity LINE:

Know yourself. Really know yourself. Identify what you believe (usually demonstrated by how you act). Identify what will do and won't do. That is where you draw your line. Being on your side of the line is where your happiness lies. If you cross that line, it wasn't your line after all. Be more honest with yourself.

IV. Use fear as an indicator of a new adventure and do it:

It is exciting to do something a little scary. I think that is why many like rollercoasters or bungee jumping. Doing something scary means we have no experience with it. Do it as long as you have a guarantee it won't kill you or cross your line. These are the things that will lead to discovery, learning and success.

V. Always think out of the box:

First know what the box is then get out of it! This is where your true success lies. Being innovative and creative, doing what others hadn't thought of and making it work makes you the best thing since sliced bread. This is the future. This is being cutting edge. This is how you take an organization where it has never gone before. It's okay if it is scary; do it anyway. The payoff is huge.

THE PRESENT

I have retired twice and still haven't made it stick. I just love the work too much to stop. I love seeing people take leadership and create miracles in their fields, not always in education. I get to coach adults and share my experiences. I get to listen to ideas and explore them with others, I don't know others' answers but I do know how to help others find their own answers.

I am again teaching others, but now adults, how to use their own abilities. I get to share what little I do know from research and experience. I figure this high school dropout is destined to be in education the rest of her life. How's that for Karma? I don't know a better way to be my best Peacock.

Big ideas come from forward thinking people who challenge the norm, think outside the box, and invent the world they see inside rather than submitting to the limitations of current dilemmas.
~ T.D. Jakes

About Dr. Marie

Dr. Marie Bañuelos is a graduate of the University of La Verne, California, with a doctorate in Organizational Leadership. Marie coaches working administrators and has coached over 100 schools in school improvement, staff relations, and reducing resistance and stress while going through change. She donates her time to the Western Association of Schools and Colleges to accredit high schools, adult schools, private schools and prison schools.

Marie has a unique style that is inclusive of all staffs in schools and districts. Her most important advice to schools that are going through difficult times is, "Schools are machines made of flesh and blood. If you break the cogs in these machines, they cannot be fixed as easily as metal." Marie's humanistic style unites staff and leadership to helps schools through difficult times of change.

Marie began her growth journey with Jack Canfield in the 1980s. She participated in workshops that Jack Canfield led for other organizations. When Canfield began his own business, Marie participated in Jack's programs and later managed support personnel for Canfield's workshops for over five years, and contributed to Canfield's "Self Esteem in the Classroom" curriculum.

Marie provides schools and district with workshops on building relationships, problem solving, team building, goal development and action planning. Marie also assists schools and districts to analyze new school legislation and develop ways to meet the new state requirements while still building strong teamwork in times of regulations. Marie helps schools to identify avenues for self-governance and team decision making for what is best in their communities.

You can connect with Marie at:
- ed.coaching4excellence@gmail.com
- http://coaching-for-excellence.com

CHAPTER 3

BEING GROUNDED IN THE CORPORATE WORLD
—HOW SPIRITUAL AWARENESS EXEMPLIFIES SUCCESS

BY DANNY KHURSIGARA

The best way to predict the future is to invent it.
~ Alan Kay

The corporate environment creates challenges for everyone who is actively submersed into it. There are stressful moments, times of uncertainty, and tough deadlines, just to name a few. It can all weigh on your mind and create turmoil if you don't embrace awareness of your situation. Being self-aware, listening to your intuition, and spiritual grounding can exponentially contribute to your success in facing the myriad challenges of today's constantly changing world. Over the years, developing a sense of centeredness has helped me remain a bit more grounded in the corporate world.

With corporate life comes moments that you aren't always prepared for. One of the most challenging and yet highly rewarding things I've had to do was move around the world—a lot! These are exciting new places that are wonderful to experience, but at times can be tough on us, as a family. Moving from country to country takes a certain mindset and you must possess the ability to assimilate and adapt positively; especially when you're out of your comfort zone. Ultimately, being able to thrive in multiple cultural environments is an excellent education in itself. One of my biggest takeaways is that people are intrinsically the same regardless of where they come from.

As life evolves you need to evolve as a person and a spiritual being. Not just from a financial and career perspective, but to become the best version of you.

My corporate life has provided well for us as a family, but has also opened up a gateway to a wonderful fusion with my desire to help others. I embrace the opportunities I have to coach and mentor others, because they offer me the opportunity to help others create practices that will bring them harmony and fulfillment in both their personal and professional lives. For they are intricately linked.

MY SEVEN (7) 'SUCCESS' HABITS

These practices I'm going to share, I find, are essential to helping me keep my perspective and calmness in times when I feel as if the world around me is not calm. I believe they can help anyone who is willing to apply them to their own life. Simple practices applied consistently over time will often produce profound results.

1. **Living with gratitude.**
   There have been many times when I've taken my life for granted, only to have something happen that froze me in my tracks. Through those "wake me up" moments, I was able to see all the things that I had to be grateful for in that moment—not just in the future. This lends to greater contentment and better perspective for challenges that must be faced.

2. **Power of prayer and meditation.**
   For me, this is transformational. By taking time to do this daily I feel centered and inspired. Unexpected opportunities and ideas flow through at any time, urging me to take inspired action. Where I am matters not, because I recognize when intuition and inspiration is calling upon me. Trust your intuition even when the odds are against you.

3. Visualizing your desired outcome.

This is something that I've been doing for over fifteen years, but only recently became more aware of its powerful potential (through working with Jack Canfield, my mentor). I use this to see myself in the roles I want to be in with work, and the relationships that I want to experience and cultivate. I make these as vivid and real as possible. In time, they always become a reality.

4. Being aware of self-talk.

We can be outwardly positive, but filled with negative thoughts, doubt, and defeating self-talk. Through what we think and say to ourselves we impact our outcomes. By paying attention to what we're thinking and feeling we can create beliefs that transcend fears. This can have a profound impact on the choices and the decisions we make at any given point in time. Remembering this will keep you focused, calm, and more centered. Doubt your doubts before you doubt your faith.

5. Acting on a vision.

In my career, specifically, this is very important because I move nearly every three years and my jobs are extremely demanding. There is always an agenda or bigger vision that needs to be fulfilled. By taking action and having a clear vision that people are aligned to, a better culture is created. If I were to ask any of my team what our vision is, they would be able to answer without contemplation. The vision for our best year yet was: From Good To Great. It was posted in numerous places to offer a daily reminder that the actions we take should never be to play catch-up, but to move ahead with focus, clarity, and a winning attitude. When people are aligned to a single vision great success can be achieved.

6. A healthy body is a healthy mind.

No matter how busy you are, do something! I experience the benefit of this in my life. When we are physically fit, it impacts our self-esteem and mental fitness, as well. Investing in this is smart, as well as kind to ourselves. Nobody wants to face health issues that could have been prevented with some self-care; especially when it's self-care that enhances the quality of your life.

7. Acknowledge and appreciate others more often.

When we get busy, appreciation often goes to the wayside. Never forget your colleagues, friends, family, and mentors who play a role in your life—whether significant or small. Spend more time with people who inspire and empower you than you do with those who wear you down. Being more mindful of appreciation makes a powerful difference because it brings out the best in others. And in return, you receive it back. This all makes for a better environment that will create better outcomes.

The more grounded we are in life the more assured we feel, sparking our better selves to come out as well as creating a better leader for others to learn from. Regardless of how much resistance or challenge you get from the outside world, try not to be focused on your current reality. Instead, focus on your divine unfoldment, your vision, your dream. Over time, this will do wonders.

LIVING WITH HIGH INTENTION AND LOW ATTACHMENT

The statement of living with high intention and low attachment resonates with me deeply. It reminds me of a point in my career where things were seemingly rough for me—even with my level of awareness and positive life vision. I just couldn't quite place my finger on what was wrong to resolve it—no matter what I did.

At this time in my life I was moving quite a bit. Back in 2007, I was going from Tokyo to the Philippines as COO and CFO with my banking position. Within nine months of a move, the bank had decided to exit that market and we had to wind down our businesses within very tight timeframes, and there was no certainty as to what came next for me. This was new and uncomfortable. I felt like hell had broken lose.

My job in this "exit strategy" was tough and complex to varying degrees. I was clearly out of my comfort zone, and in some ways, felt like I was in the twilight zone. From a rather well-defined routine role, my assignment dramatically changed to something more complex and demanding (i.e., migrating the assets and liabilities to an international acquirer, winding down two legal entities and selling the local subsidiary in the local market). Yet, at the end of it all, one looming reality existed: I would soon be running myself out of a job.

Being unemployed at a young age wasn't in my game plan. My game plan was to successfully complete my assignment and to take a step up into living and working in a big regional location. Feeling that this wasn't going to happen was very disappointing. Anger and denial had beset me. Without realizing it, I was living in a state of victim consciousness. I felt it and my family felt it, which did not help the situation.

Finally treading for something solid on which to grasp, I contemplated and meditated on what I was experiencing, and soon made a conscious decision that if I saw the experience through – a better future would emerge. With an urgent impatience to succeed, I decided on doing what was asked of me by the organization and detached myself from the outcome.

*I realized that I did not have to be attached to what
my success looked like. I just needed to intend it.*

Through me stepping out of my comfort zone and performing the best I could with a solid team behind me, we were able to exceed organizational expectations and achieve a great result. With the organization's support, I was offered a new position within the company—that of Chief Operating Officer for Hong Kong and Taiwan. Making that conscious decision to 'detach from the outcome' was a turning point in creating a favorable outcome.

In hindsight, I realized had I remained in my low vibrational-victim consciousness state, filled with self-defeating thoughts and energy, this outcome couldn't have happened. I would have self-sabotaged. Instead, I ended up in a very good place. Our choices define us and shape our outcome.

LIVING WITH PURPOSE—LEANING INTO THE SIGNS AND SYMBOLS THAT GUIDE YOU
Hints to help guide us to exist everywhere.

Regardless of the challenges life throws at us, I believe that my life has been quite fortunate. Born to the two most wonderful parents, my brother and I were brought up in a caring and close knit family environment, and today I'm surrounded by my wife and three daughters—who I love and gain strength from. However, deep inside, despite all of this, I've always sensed something was missing, but I had no idea what it was. Maybe it was luck or maybe the universe just grew more determined to guide me toward recognition of what was missing, because the journey to find it has really been quite incredible. For you, it's a reminder to always pay attention to what is happening around you. It does have significance.

First, I realized that no matter how much I willed it, I could not answer the question, "Why am I not fulfilled?"

Working in banking, I am a natural strategist, evaluator, and analyzer. Not being able to answer this seemingly simple question was starting to wear me down. One day I had to take a bus home from work (my wife usually picked me up) and I was looking out the window with thoughts running through my mind at the velocity of a bullet train. There on the street was a huge banner that read: Ask and you shall receive. I must have seen that a million times before, but on that day the statement struck me differently. Later, in my meditation I asked what must I do to feel more fulfilled.

Next, a few months later I was at a bookstore with my family and a book just happened to fall in front of me—the universe willing me to read it.

Now, I'm not a big reader, which is unlike many people who seek better meaning in their lives. I enjoy movies. So when this book titled The Secrets of the Light by Dannion Brinkley landed in front of me, I reacted differently than I normally might. I picked it up and began reading. For fifteen plus minutes I was sitting on the floor of the book store and was a good twenty pages into this book. I was drawn in so I purchased it. This story was about a man who had two near-death experiences, in which he went to the light and was returned to life on earth. His story was so powerful to me in an inexplicable way. I just knew I had to reach out to him. The day came when I called Dannion up. While dialing his number I was thinking, but what am I going to say to this man? It turned out that I didn't need to say anything. I introduced myself and he said, "I was waiting for your call. What took you so long?" I was blown away. From there, I realized I have a larger vision and a grander plan to work toward a divine unfoldment that I had not known thus far.

Gradually, I was able to see the signs that the universe does put out there for us.

To me, there are signs everywhere and I didn't always believe that, writing off things such as number sequences reoccurring as coincidence. With this new awareness, I began to pay attention to number sequences that I'd been seeing, the exact same sequences appearing over long periods of time. For example, seeing 555 appear daily everywhere I looked for period of over 2 months. I intuitively felt my attention being drawn to this, and was now curious as to what they may mean. My intrigue guided me to Doreen Virtue's number interpretations. 555 meant huge life changes are rumbling. Stay positive and centered in prayer and affirmation to ensure favorable outcomes. The sequence kept showing up and within a matter of weeks I was asked to move to Shanghai for a new position. This is just one example. To some, this may seem farfetched and they discard it as coincidence. I get that, as I had been that person, but today I assure you that it has been incredible to acknowledge these existences. It has assisted in my journey to fulfillment, and being truly grounded in something bigger than just myself that also nourishes the soul.

Someone once said, "The reason why angels can fly is because they hold themselves lightly." This idea resonates with me and everything that I focus my mentoring and coaching on, as well as the choices I make for my career and personal life. When we keep things light and allow them to unfold the way they should, we let go of the strong arm of over-attachment and the cruelty of intense scrutiny. We are taking action without forcing a wrong or unwise destiny to become our reality. I have drawn strength from this belief.

Today, I believe we all have the ability to influence on a larger scale than just the business in front of us or the personal evolvement of our lives. I believe that by finding a way to create the "sweet spot" that can exist between the corporate world and a spiritually-grounded life takes success and personal growth to the next level. My purpose, which is to inspire and empower others to become successful through leading happier, and more fulfilling lives—by becoming the best version of themselves—is opening up doorways.

New awareness is taking me to places that are far beyond what forced will could ever have guided me toward.

About Danny

Danny Khursigara is a Senior career banker and a Certified Success, Life and Executive Coach, Speaker, and Trainer. Through the experiences of his distinguished corporate career, he has served in various capacities, including Chief Operating Officer and Chief Financial Officer for Fortune 500 financial institutions. He is an international business leader with over fifteen years of experience in multiple locations across Asia Pacific, within Financial Markets, as well as the international and consumer banking world. His expertise extends to significant strategic change management through market growth cycles, business growth and contraction, risk and control management, financial management, and client engagement.

Starting as an accountant for PWC, Danny has performed COO and CFO roles with oversight in the retail, commercial, wholesale, and investment banking sectors. These opportunities have allowed him to live in some of the most exciting cities in Asia Pacific, including Tokyo, Manila, Hong Kong, Karachi, and Shanghai. His employments include ABN AMRO Bank, Royal Bank of Scotland, Standard Chartered Grindlays Bank, and ANZ (Australia & New Zealand Banking Group).

Danny specializes in cross-cultural engagement and leadership, Executive coaching, and high performance team coaching, and motivational speaking in corporate settings, universities and TEDx. His proven track record in business includes stellar results in: risk-and-control turnaround, integration and, divestment of merged or acquired businesses across dispersed geographies.

Despite having much of his career focused in the corporate world, Danny has a much greater calling in mind. His purpose is to inspire and empower others to become successful through leading happier and more fulfilling lives, and becoming the best version of "themselves."

As a qualified Life and Executive Coach, Speaker, and Trainer who has been mentored by Jack Canfield—co-author of *Chicken Soup for the Soul* series and *The Success Principles*—he is endlessly passionate about helping to develop the human potential that all people have. Today, Danny is also a Best Selling Author with Jack Canfield, having contributed a chapter to his book *The Road to Success*. He spends a large component of his time coaching and mentoring others, using his relevant industry experience and insight into becoming successful with great potential to inspire and move others forward in their lives' goals. His strategies are time-tested and effective; his keynote talks and coaching sessions leave attendees with inspiration and calls to action to become the best version of themselves. He continues to believe in experiential training and coaching that lends to transformational breakthroughs in key areas of their life – including career, finance, relationships, health and well-being, "me time", personal growth, and contributions to society.

Having been born in Pakistan, Danny belongs to the Zoroastrian (Parsi) community and presently lives with his wife and three daughters in Shanghai. He believes in being a universal citizen, treating everyone alike with no distinction in ethnicity, culture, faith, and nationality. Danny practices meditation and enjoys a good workout & listening to music. He loves to travel, (particularly fond of white sand beaches), experiencing different cuisines, and meeting new & interesting people.

To reach Danny you may email him at sundans6@yahoo.com, visit his website, www.PathtoPurposedk.com, or find him on LinkedIn, www.linkedin.com/in/danny-r-khursigara-1118785.

CHAPTER 4

FROM BAGS TO RICHES

BY GARY DUVALL, CRPC®*

Fierce winds shoved me from side to side as I stumbled forward around the side of a three story apartment building in the early morning darkness. A Midwestern thunderstorm was blowing hard with gusts coming from one direction and then another, as I delivered newspapers in plastic bags to the local residents. Torrential rain coming down in sheets rudely slapped me with no remorse, as if my presence inside a mighty force was an insult to it. Usually my delivery run was completely silent as the city slept, but the strong winds combined with pouring rain filled the darkness with the threatening and ominous roar of nature's fury. Rumbling thunder closing in from the distance put me on edge and sudden sharp eerie whistles from the shifting gales tearing at the roof top cornices added to my foreboding. The shocking event that happened next changed my life forever!

IT WAS A DARK AND STORMY NIGHT!

It was a dark and stormy night, but not only because of the weather. Bad weather seemed like a minor inconvenience to my real problems. I was depressed, bitter and angry because of the dire straits I was in. My career after graduating from college had been on the fast track with four corporate advancements within five years. A corporate recruiter had placed me in that fourth job, a coveted position with a major industry player in the Mid-West. I had moved my family halfway across the country from the beautiful Rogue River Valley in Oregon to Nebraska to take advantage of the opportunity. In less than a year, there was a

*Chartered Retirement Planning Counselor℠ and CRPC® are registered service
  marks of the College for Financial Planning®.

"corporate restructuring" and I was unemployed. There I was with a wife, a young daughter, and a brand new mortgage in an unfamiliar city. I quickly learned what "overqualified" meant, when my extended resume of progressively responsible specialized professional experience, advanced education and extensive training became the reason employers chose to hire others instead of me. My wife had been a full time homemaker, but took a part time job while I searched for work. Looking back and analyzing it, I discovered our household income dropped below the poverty level the previous year when I wasn't working.

Through sheer determination and persistence, I pieced together a couple of low paying jobs. One was delivering newspapers starting shortly after midnight. I made very little money throwing papers because I drove my car, purchased my gasoline, and paid for the bags I was required to use. During the day I worked as inbound telephone sales representative for a company that provided a subscription service that delivered information electronically through a computer system, about the commodity markets. That job paid just above minimum wage. With those two jobs and my wife's work, we barely made ends meet.

That fateful night, I didn't even bother to wipe the water dripping off my face anymore. The thunderstorm seemed like the least of my worries. Water was pouring over the top of the overloaded rain gutters, creating unusual three story waterfalls at the end of each apartment building. These waterfalls blew apart in the wind and reached the ground like the rest of the rainy deluge. Drenched from head to toe, with a fresh supply of plastic bagged newspapers under my left arm, I was reaching for the doorknob on the metal fire door at the entrance to the next apartment building WHEN IT HAPPENED!

A BOLT OF LIGHTNING!

A blinding blue flash of lightning slammed my eyelids shut and the simultaneous explosion of thunder was so loud the ground shook underneath me. Instantly frozen by fear, I stood motionless with my hand cupped in the shape of the doorknob a few inches away. Appearing like one of those people who stand perfectly still imitating a statue, I counted the seconds and listened to the remaining sound of the thunder. The thunder continued for another seven seconds as it seemingly retreated to the top of this monstrous thunderhead. I estimated the top of this dangerous storm cloud was about 35,000 feet directly above my head.

Coming to my senses, I threw open the door and began my ascent up the stairs delivering my papers in an adrenalin fueled state of terror. My heart was pounding, my lungs were panting and my legs felt like rubber. I was mumbling in a whisper with each breath "I've got to get out of this job!" like some mentally deranged person. "I must find a way to dump this route!" grumbling up the stairs and down again. "I really need to find something else to do!" By the time I had finished delivering the papers at this location, I had calmed myself and started imagining what it would be like to do some kind of work indoors safely protected from the weather.

A FLASH OF INSPIRATION!

The rain and the sound of thunder were subsiding as I made my way across the concrete parking lot to return to my car. Suddenly in mid step, a plan for creating a new business that would replace the paper route job flashed into my mind. In that split second, I conceived an entire marketing, sales and delivery system to sell the same subscriptions I was selling at work, but operate as an independent sales contractor earning straight commissions. I knew the company already had field sales representatives all over the country, including the state of Oregon. A clear vision of working from the warm, dry, safety of my home and making much more money filled my mind.

Excitement and enthusiasm replaced the fear and anxiety I had been feeling for months. As I finished my paper route that morning, I went over and over this remarkably detailed business plan that seemed to instantly jump into my head. It seemed so logical and flawless that I presented the idea to the Western Regional Sales Manager later that day while at work. He liked the idea and authorized me to start immediately. Within a few weeks I became that company's top producing commissioned sales rep in the country, working part time! Dropping the paper route, I ran my new business from home and my income took off. I found another inbound call center job with a different company for the "extra" income and benefits like health insurance, 401k, holiday, vacation and sick pay, etc. Now I was doing the restructuring and had taken control of my destiny!

Within a year I was able to sell our house and moved my family back to the Rogue Valley. Shortly after my return to Oregon, I was hired into Management with a well-known financial institution and proceeded to build an outstanding career in financial services. A few years later, I restructured my career again and became a Financial Advisor earning an excellent income while helping others achieve their financial goals.

DISCOVERING TRUE RICHES

Experiencing those stormy times in the past created the opportunity to discover a path to the true riches of life. The priceless intangibles such as the love of family and friends, sound physical health (including working in a safe environment), service to others and living in harmony with my spiritual beliefs rose to the top of my personal priorities. It also became obvious that having plenty of money facilitates the enjoyment of the true riches better than suffering through the struggle, worry and misery of having inadequate financial resources.

I also discovered something more. I had been "shocked" into a state of mind from which I became aware of an idea that empowered me to transcend and transmute my dismal personal situation into something much greater. After I returned to Oregon, I became determined to acquire the secret of recreating destiny-changing thoughts at will. I found the answer, but it was not what I previously imagined!

At first I wondered if the mind would only produce truly great ideas when pressured by some exceptional external event. However, I learned that everyone has outstanding thoughts much more often than they recognize. In fact, you and I have potentially great ideas multiple times each day! These impulses of thought are sometimes so subtle that we often don't pay attention to them and they get washed away in the flood of thoughts passing through our minds. The four step method I now use to capture important and relevant thoughts is so effective and valuable, I consider the acquisition and use of this process a form of great wealth and wisdom in itself! To make sure I never forgot this powerful formula, I gave it a special name.

TRANSCENDENTAL TRANSMUTATION!

On that blustery night so long ago I drove down the same street as I did so many times before. Yet *Everything Was Different*! My anger, bitterness and negative attitude had completely vanished. Instead, I was filled with optimism, enthusiasm and excitement. I was driving down the same street, but it had suddenly turned into the road to success.

As I outline this simple process to employ success principles and bring your own creative ideas to life, I'll use the "dark and stormy" night experience as an example. The key is to learn to recognize, relate, assimilate and apply any successful idea, practice or technique you become aware of to achieve your desired outcome.

Step One: Information

Recognize useful concepts, methods and strategies as you encounter them. Also be mindful of ideas that quietly occur to you, sometimes when you least expect them to appear, and capture them by writing them down. Write, type or record the idea into something the eye can see or the ear can hear. Doing this instantly converts the intangible impulse of thought into physical reality and launches the whole process. Proactively seeking the valuable information can help you move forward from where you are to where you want to be. For many years I had studied the laws of success from books, seminars and audio visual programs in addition to my formal education. A few months prior to conceiving my new business concept I had taken the initiative to purchase and complete a mail order course on commodity trading. I was searching for a way to increase my income and I thought I may be able to profitably trade commodities someday.

Step Two: Understanding

Once you recognize useful information, relate how you may be able to use it to your advantage, particularly how it can be used to benefit others. I had taken the time and effort to understand the laws of success and also learned about the fundamental and technical indicators used in trading in the commodity markets. As a result, I understood the detailed information contained in the commodities information service I was selling at work, and was outselling my colleagues on the job. Becoming a top salesperson didn't help my income initially because I was paid hourly, but I became prepared to recognize an opportunity no one else at that company had ever thought of!

Step Three: Knowledge

After understanding the information, assimilate it by converting it into knowledge. Remember, necessity is the mother of invention, but repetition is the mother of retention. During the storm, I clearly envisioned working indoors which became my definite major purpose at the time and I had a burning desire to make it happen. I inadvertently exercised the power of autosuggestion with repeated emotionally-charged affirmations and triggered my creative imagination. This was possible only because I had laid the foundation of acquired knowledge through my previous studies.

Step Four: Wisdom

Applying knowledge effectively is practical wisdom. As the storm was fading, I recovered my composure and began to relax into the mindless routine of delivering my newspaper bags. Suddenly, I remembered that the author of the commodity trading course recommended specific commodity brokerage houses for students to do business with. I already had permission to contact those brokerages because I had purchased the course! It occurred to me that many of their clients would probably purchase the commodity information service I was selling at work if they knew about it. Instantly, my plan to become a commission sales person and distribute my employer's brochures through the brokerages was born. I began as soon as possible to implement the plan.

PREPAREDNESS + OPPORTUNITY = SUCCESS!

Fortunately, you don't need a bolt of lightning or any other extreme external event to capture your flashes of inspiration, creative ideas or emotional motivations. You increase your awareness of your valuable thoughts and insights when you practice constant vigilant attention more often. In other words, make a habit of observing and noticing your thoughts. Habitually prepare for achievement by actively seeking out the practices, methods and strategies shared by others that have been proven effective. When you regularly search and ask for this information you will find it. If you become relentless in pursuing such wisdom, it becomes attracted to you and you will then see opportunity when others see only obstacles and adversity. The process of Transcendental Transmutation enables you to acquire and utilize information that is presented to you from both internal and external sources with four clear steps. You accelerate your journey on the road to success when you recognize information, relate to it and understand it, assimilate it to knowledge and then exercise your wisdom by applying your knowledge to accomplish a specific goal.

About Gary

Gary Duvall helps his clients try to create, grow and protect their personal and family financial independence. Before graduating from Rogue River High School, Gary had already become an avid student of success philosophy. He turned this passion into a lifetime avocation of learning how to enjoy health, wealth and wisdom, and recently coined the phrase "Transcendental Transmutation" to describe the process of accomplishment. Living most of his life in the Rogue Valley, Gary has served as a Student Manager, VISA Division Manager, Purchasing Agent, Merchandise Manager, Operations Manager, and Sales Manager for various businesses. He re-entered the Financial Services profession in 1992, and for over 16 years has served the members of Rogue Credit Union as a trusted Financial Advisor through CUSO Financial Services, L.P.*

"Money is meant to bring value to your life, not the other way around." Gary is fond of saying. The decisions people make should be based on sound logic, and beneficial to their core beliefs and values. Gary has a reputation for making sometimes complex topics easily understood, and is known for 'not talking over your head.' Gary helps his clients manage their investment portfolios containing mutual funds, annuities and other investment and insurance products.

He is now entering his 30th year of marriage to his wife, Carol, who also graduated from high school locally. They both remain close to their daughter Calley who turned 28 this year, and is employed in the medical field in the Rogue River Valley. Perhaps because Gary and Carol were born in the greater Los Angeles area and arrived in Oregon with their parents as teenagers, they both love the creeks, streams and rivers that flow through the mountains and valleys of Southern Oregon. The nearby Pacific Ocean coastal area and mountain lakes are favorite vacation spots. They have fountains that run throughout the summer in their back yard. Their three cats and one dog like to drink from those fountains when they are not chasing each other. Even their golf balls seem to find the water on every course. There are others who evidently like the water more, because when Gary goes fishing the fish end up staying in the lake after he leaves.

Gary is a graduate of Southern Oregon University with a Bachelor of Science in Business Administration. He holds the Chartered Retirement Planning Counselor^{SM} (CRPC)®** designation from the College for Financial Planning®. Gary is a Qualifying and Life Member of the Million Dollar Roundtable (MDRT), The Premier Association of Financial Professionals®, with 14 consecutive qualifying years.*** He is a Past President of the National Association of Insurance and Financial Advisors (NAIFA) Rogue Valley.

Gary Duvall, CRPC®**
Financial Advisor
CUSO Financial Services, L.P.
at Rogue Credit Union
(541) 622-7325 | 541-770-3710 (fax)
gduvall@roguecu.org

*Non-deposit investment products and services are offered through CUSO Financial Services, L.P. ("CFS"), a registered broker-dealer (Member FINRA/SIPC) and SEC Registered Investment Advisor. Products offered through CFS: are not NCUA/NCUSIF or otherwise federally insured, are not guarantees or obligations of the credit union, and may involve investment risk including possible loss of principal. Investment Representatives are registered through CFS. The Credit Union has contracted with CFS to make non-deposit investment products and services available to credit union members.

**Chartered Retirement Planning Counselor℠ and CRPC® are registered service marks of the College for Financial Planning®.

***Membership in the 2016 Round Table is based on production equal to or greater than $93,000 in eligible commissions paid or $186,000 paid premium earned or $160,000 in annual gross income during 2015. An individual becomes a Qualifying and Life member when approved for the 10th year of membership.

CHAPTER 5

WHEN WE FIND PERSEVERANCE, WE EXPERIENCE SUCCESS

BY DAVID AUER

With ordinary talent and extraordinary perseverance,
all things are attainable.
~Thomas Foxwell Buxton

We are born with a great many things; however, perseverance is not one of them. It doesn't just exist and while understanding it may be more natural for some, everyone needs a commitment to perseverance in order to experience professional accomplishments and many times, personal achievements as well.

For many of us, we think of the words passion and purpose as the "big P words" in this world. Perseverance should be added to that list, because without it, we seldom connect to our passion and purpose. You have to have what it takes to get there.

IT ALL BEGINS WITH A GOAL

In the beginning...there must be a goal that is worth you pursuing.

I don't recall there ever being a time in my life when anyone really engrained in my mind that I had to have focus and commitment to achieve the outcomes I desired in life. So, thankfully, I just grew into awareness about this from the time I was a kid onwards. I credit a portion of this to the fact that my family moved a lot. And with each move, starting over is a part of it, which meant that each and every time I had to set a basic goal, which was to make new friends where I was at. To do this, you need to be steadfast. You don't always find your best friends right away. It takes time, effort, and patience. But eventually, you'll make great connections.

Starting anew is never easy, particularly if you are not guided by a plan that you are going to put into action to achieve. It takes perseverance to see it through, because every day is not always going to be an easy day. Having this gumption is particularly important when you're not the guy who is the best at everything you do naturally. I was the guy who had to work hard and without a strategy, I'd be spinning circles or quitting. There were two things, aside from friendship, that I really applied myself to so I could find success: athletics and academics.

- I was not the most gifted person athletically. Yet, I loved to play sports and wanted it to be a part of my life. I'd work really hard and train with a specific goal in mind—to eventually make the varsity squad or #1 team for my preferred sports, which were baseball and football. There were no days of rest if I wanted to achieve this goal. It required action to see results. And I did.

- Academically, I was not a straight A student. This was in part because I spread myself thin with everything I loved to do—sports, Boy Scouts, developing friendships—and also because I was never that guy who just loved the classroom or homework. Yet, I knew that education was part of the pathway to success that my ambitions and goals would require some day—so I found ways to make sure that my grades, while not perfection, were not dismal, either.

Without perseverance, high school would not have been the great experience that it was for me. It wouldn't have given me the chance to recognize my pathway in college as quickly as I did.

When I first went to college I chose an engineering major. After just one semester, I was on the brink of dropping out, not having a clear path for success or a real connection with the plan. But dropping out would have stopped me dead in my tracks for the type of success I knew that I wanted my life rooted in. Instead of giving up when I reached that road block, I switched majors and ended up in Accounting. It suited me better and I had the perseverance to see it through, because I had the vision of how it would be good for me and my life. Plus, I enjoyed it—enough to even get my Master's degree in it. Now I was the good student and after succeeding in my goal, I found a wonderful new opportunity as a result. I continued on to go to Law School so I could become a Tax Attorney. Without perseverance, I would have been the "drop-out" – maybe going back some day to earn a degree, or maybe not.

For the past thirty years, I've tried to be the best tax attorney I can be for my clients. This commitment and the need for further education, learning, and experiences didn't just stop after I began working. It continues on, day after day, year after year. Tax laws change daily and I need to demonstrate the perseverance to keep up with these demands in order to best serve my clients.

My approach and success is interesting to people. A common question that I get asked is, "How did you make sure you stayed on track, David?" The answer—by setting up goals and constantly evaluating them. It all begins with a goal! The steps I take are:

1. **Set a formal goal.**

   This should range from a one-year to a three-year goal. You want it to be as specific as possible so you know exactly what achieving it entails, and how to gauge if you are progressing as you need to in order to recognize success of the goal.

2. **Think of any and all obstacles that may stop you from achieving the goal.**

   This is different than focusing on the positive only like many people suggest. However, there is excellent reasoning behind thinking about what may stop you. First of all, you won't be surprised when it suddenly appears. Second of all, you can begin thinking of specific ways that you may be able to solve or circumvent the obstacle or roadblock. Being proactive is a wonderful complementary quality to having perseverance.

3. **Develop an action plan to overcome the roadblocks and obstacles.**

   By setting an action plan into place that includes daily, weekly, and monthly action steps, you are showing your commitment and focus to your goal. Fewer unanticipated surprises are highly beneficial because they allow you to approach the unexpected with more confidence and sounder solutions. And better yet…with practice and time, this step becomes increasingly easier!

PERSEVERANCE IS GREATLY ENHANCED BY DEVELOPING GOOD DAILY HABITS

I am wired to set new and bigger goals on a consistent basis. This is how I am and the older that I've gotten, the further I've reached . . . the larger my goals are. Why? There are two main reasons:

1. **My confidence grows.**
   This is what happens when you set goals and achieve them. They become easier to visualize, learn from, and experience success in.

2. **I have gained experience by achievement.**
   Once I have achieved something, a new goal is put in place—often one that is an extension of the goal I just accomplished, and many times, even more rewarding. When we learn there is a pleasant surprise in the process—a reward or benefit we hadn't even considered—we become excited, often surpassing our original marker in expectation and results.

DEVELOPING THE PERSEVERANCE MINDSET

Effort will only release its reward after it sees that you refuse to quit—that you are exercising perseverance to accomplish your goals.

Shocker—becoming successful requires change. I do not know of anyone who has become successful without changing. Staying in one place doesn't change anything. Change isn't typically easy, of course, and it requires us to push ourselves outside of our comfort zone. As a result, we need to tap into our perseverance that we learn over time as we reach for and achieve our goals.

Here are some of the lessons about perseverance that I have used my entire life, and that have proven themselves as necessary for success in our goals:

- **Be patient**

  Perseverance is a big thing; you need to be patient because it does not just happen overnight. You cannot take it off the shelf and drink it or eat it. You have to grow with it and in its spirit.

- **Have the right attitude**

  With an attitude that allows you to get upset or frustrated each time you encounter resistance or problems of any sort, you will struggle to learn perseverance. Be joyful and excited about obstacles and roadblocks, because every one that you overcome means you are one step closer to your goal. Attitudes of frustration and negativity cannot help you move forward. A positive perspective is always better.

- **Success requires repetition**

  Most people who make mistakes will make the same one repeatedly if…they did not change the patterns that lead to that same mistake. In order to avoid repeating mistakes you must repeat good habits that lead to victories. Perseverance helps give you the internal fuel to do that. New habits that are grounded in sounder outcomes and beliefs will likely lead to better results.

If we're not cautious, we can also digress in our perseverance—it can lead us downward instead of upward. This is most likely to happen when we turn it on and off, not always using it to get our best results out of life. It's a lot like physical exercise and you have to go through the routine in order to reach the goal—you can't run a race without the training, you don't just exercise for a week and take a month off and truly believe you will improve.

PERSEVERANCE MUST CONSTANTLY BE WORKED ON AND IN THE FOREFRONT OF OUR MINDS

When I was in my 20s, I ran a few triathlons—an event that requires biking, swimming, and running of various lengths, depending on what type of triathlon you pick. It's an accumulation of all three times combined that determines where you finish in the race. I wanted to finish well and I had to put my all in to even finish at all. They are not easy! As I trained toward this ultimate physical experience, I got shin splints. If you've never had them, consider yourself fortunate. They are painful and they are a result of stress that is put on them through repetition. I'd been training hard so they were my reward? What!

Thankfully, quitting was not an option for me. Instead, I realized that by continuing to train and allowing my bones to recover through motion, I could keep moving forward. I had to overlook the pain, but it was a roadblock in my process to successfully completing my goal. Movement and action kept me going, not becoming passive because "it hurt." I realized that if I'd given up running because of those shin splints I would have accomplished nothing, but remembered a failure. That did not set well with me. It shouldn't with anyone!

IF YOU DON'T "USE IT" YOU'LL "LOSE IT"

Perseverance is just like our mind. We must work it every day in order for it to be at its best.

I have had to make sure my perseverance was intact every time I've ever set a new goal in life, whether it was as a child or as an adult who is trying to make sure that I give my best to the world I live in—both family and clients. To do this, I must remember: there is no straight line to success. It's a journey of peaks and valleys—those obstacles and roadblocks—that often get in your way. If you practice perseverance, those things won't blind you. Rather, they'll inspire you to move on.

Being aware of what you are actually doing in order to keep your perseverance working for you will take you a long way. I always remind myself to:

- **Maintain self control and practice perseverance on a daily basis**
  Whether it's an action step toward a goal or just a reminder of how good habits are necessary to cultivate success, I am always mindful of my state of mind.

- **Associate with likeminded people**
  It's important to surround yourself with people who will support you as you overcome obstacles. People who "get where you are coming from" can always be inspiring to help you "get to where you want to go."

- **Keep your eye on the final prize**

  Keeping your goals and why they are important to you in front of you is necessary. It's the reminder that helps you remember why your goal is important and what you've already acknowledged needs to be done to achieve it. You've shown perseverance to get as far as you are—now it's time to keep yourself enveloped in it until you cross the finish line and direct it toward the next thing that will bring you fulfillment.

SET YOURSELF UP FOR SUCCESS EVERY DAY

"Success is no accident. It is hard work, perseverance, learning, studying, sacrifice and most of all, love of what you are doing or learning to do."
~ Pele

Bottom line: perseverance leads to character. Our character that we develop by not giving up helps us to develop strength to face obstacles. And it's our attitude mixed with perseverance that allows us to believe and think . . . I can conquer this and I won't give up. It's a hopeful message, and hope turns into confidence in having a greater faith in our abilities to finish the race and complete our goal. It's the most amazing cycle of success that you can put yourself into.

About David

David Auer is the Founder of Auer Tax Group, a national tax planning law firm, Blue Ocean Strategies, a business strategic planning group, and The Advanced Planning Group, a collaboration of multi-disciplinary advisors focused on tax, estate, asset protection, and business succession planning strategies for successful business owners, professionals, and high networth investors all over the world.

David has over 30 years of experience as a CPA attorney, earned his BSBA and MS in Accounting from Oklahoma State University, his JD (Hons.) from the University of Oklahoma College of Law, and his LLM in Taxation from New York University School of Law. He has the Personal Financial Specialist (PFS) and Chartered Global Management Accountant (CGMA) designations with the American Institute of CPAs. David is a Fellow with the Esperti Peterson Institute and a member of the Order of the Coif, Wealth Counsel, and The American Association of Attorney-CPAs.

David lives in Tulsa, Oklahoma with his wife, Julie, and their three children, Ellen, John and Emily.

CHAPTER 6

THE ROAD TO NICHES

BY VICTORIA COLLIER, ESQ.

Business success is a journey. The roads you choose will lead to success or failure or both. The more you can narrow the path, the more successful you may be. The more willing you are to create new paths, the wealthier you will be.

Never once did I think I was smart. Rather, I spent my entire childhood trying my hardest just to reach average. Average athlete in basketball and track, . . . average grades, . . . and average looks. It was easy for me to spend so much effort into being average because I was extremely shy and did not have many friends. I was close to a few kids, but like in sports, I was usually playing second string. Standing out was not my goal – I just wanted to be in the game.

I took myself out of the game when I was 17 and moved out of my parents' house while still a senior in high school. Finishing school on time while working full time at a national burger chain did not leave room for notable excellence academically. I did learn a lot of life experiences. For example, when the electricity went out at my new home, a trailer in a trailer park, I didn't even know what a fuse box was, much less where to find it and what I would be looking for to get the lights back on. Following, my girlfriend almost broke up with me when the hinge fell off the kitchen cabinet and I didn't know how to fix it. She rightfully accused me of not being able to do anything for myself and being dependent on others.

69

JACK-OF-ALL-TRADES, MASTER-OF-NONE

These experiences prompted me to want to learn as much as I could about everything to "take care of myself." That concept was buttressed by hearing from others about others that "he is a Jack-of-all-trades" which sounded inspiring at the time. A man that can do it all. I found further support for that when I enlisted in the United States Air Force and became a structural specialist (carpenter and mason) in the civil engineering squadron. An airman was coveted if he could assist the plumbers, electricians, or sheet metal specialists. So, of course, I tried to learn as much as I could in those areas, too. After three years of that and realizing that being a five-foot-four female who only weighs 100 pounds would not take me far in a labor career, I cross-trained to be a paralegal. As before, I was encouraged to learn all areas equally, which included military justice prosecution and defense, personal property claims, and tort claims arising out of sonic booms. I was a "utility" player and climbed the military rank ladder because of it.

It was not until I was a civilian and an adult that I learned the second half of the saying, "Master-of-None." Ouch. That was not at all inspiring. I realized that I was the poster child for that saying. I had learned how to be self-sufficient, but I was just maintaining my average status flying under the radar of excellence. The reason I joined the Air Force was to "get an education and become someone great." Sure, I accumulated awards to include Airman Below-the-Zone, Sharp Shooter with the M-16, and the Commendation and Achievement Medals, but as a person, I was still just as camouflaged as my uniform.

INTRODUCTION TO NICHE PRACTICES

After spending six years enlisted in the United States Air Force, I landed a job as a paralegal in a boutique medical malpractice law firm in a small town in South Georgia where many lawyers were considered general practitioners. I learned from my boss that "general practitioner" was the equivalent of "I'm desperate and will take any case that walks in the door." I didn't want to be desperate; I wanted to be deliberate. Deliberately successful. But how?

Before enlisting in the military, one of the many jobs I held was as a nurse's aide in a nursing home and providing one-on-one care for home health care patients. I realized that I loved taking care of senior citizens. My father was a single dad from when I was two years old and I spent a lot of my formative years with my grandparents. They moved out of state when I was six and then my grandpa died when I was 10 and my grandmother when I was 20. I didn't realize how much I missed them until I worked at the nursing home and providing private care. Thus, when I was progressing through law school, I searched for a type of law that would satisfy my passion to help senior citizens.

MY FIRST ROAD TO NICHES

To my delight, Elder Law was a budding area of concentration. In 2002, there were only five true, full-time elder law attorneys in Atlanta, Georgia, where I became number six. Just 14 years later there are no fewer than 15 and the number keeps growing. Like buying a house at the right time in the market, I got into this practice at the right time.

The Elder Law niche essentially consisted of Medicaid eligibility planning, non-taxable estate planning and probate, and guardianship hearings. A sub-niche within elder law that was created included special needs planning for adults between the ages of 18-64 who would benefit from Medicaid services. I witnessed successful elder law attorneys further distinguish themselves from the pack by niching within the niche. I wondered how I could do that.

A NICHE WITHIN A NICHE

When planning for seniors to obtain Medicaid, a means-tested program for the indigent, I met a client who was too poor for Medicaid. You may wonder, "How could that be possible?" Once on Medicaid, all of the client's monthly income would go directly to the nursing home to share in the cost of her care. Unfortunately, she had a house with a mortgage that had to be paid each month. The house also had noteworthy equity. The house had been for sale for over four years without a nibble. Had this client accepted Medicaid she would not have had the income to pay for both her care and her mortgage. The house would have gone into foreclosure and she would have lost all of her equity. Thus, she was too poor to get Medicaid.

What was the solution? A virtually unknown Veteran's Benefit called

Improved Pension specifically designed for wartime Veterans and their widows. My client was the widow of a Veteran and could receive up to $924 of tax free income per month to pay for care. That was just enough so she could avoid Medicaid and still cover her mortgage.

MONETIZING THE NICHE

This one client transformed my law practice! That was in 2003. By 2006 I was teaching lawyers across the nation about this new opportunity. By 2008, I was the recognized national expert on VA Pension Planning. I created a two-day training program that lawyers paid premium prices to attend. Once the economy really tanked and lawyers were reluctant to spend money on travel, I turned my live training into a home/office study course that my website could sell 24/7 while I slept and ran my law practice. In this way, I was able to help thousands of lawyers and so many more seniors and Veterans (or widows).

ANOTHER NICHE WITHIN A NICHE IS BORN

Unfortunately, VA benefits are a form of government assistance, like Medicaid. When the national budget is in crisis, the government slashes benefits making it more challenging to qualify, which in essence, can reduce the market base of clients. In 2014, I knew it was time to change with the times and niche again to sustain a healthy business and continue to help seniors.

A trend I was noticing by listening to my younger clients (late 60's – early 70's) was that they wanted to create a plan to protect their assets for long-term care without purchasing traditional long-term care insurance. I found a gap between estate planning (death distribution planning) and crisis VA or Medicaid planning. People who needed more than just wills and trusts but not yet ready for care.

Therefrom emerged a new niche -- Financial Care Planning -- wherein insurance products used to leverage assets to pay for care are incorporated as part of an estate plan. For example, a widowed client who is 72 years of age has a strong desire to remain in his own home to receive care if and when he needs it, and if not, to leave a financial legacy to his daughter. His assets were approximately $450,000, which would be depleted in about 56 months when receiving 24/7 home health care. By using a life insurance product with a long-term care rider, his $450,000 increased to $1,100,000 for care, dramatically extending the length of time he could receive care at home and maintain his quality of life. My clients love these creative, tax-incentivized planning options. Naturally, I am involved with coaching other attorneys in this new niche who are keenly aware that this is the next big niche for elder care attorneys because it blends so well with estate, VA and Medicaid planning.

How do you create a niche you would love to succeed in?

FOLLOW THESE EIGHT STEPS TO SUCCEED WITH NICHES:

1. Decide what you love that you want to make money at. As my story clearly shows, I love old people and it is my passion to ensure they age with quality of life no matter what their ability or disability is. They have contributed so much to our world and this is my way to give back to those who paved the way for me and my family. Who and what is your passion?

2. Research to find out who is doing it already. I was not the first elder law attorney. In fact, there were already 3,200 nationally and five locally. That was a healthy number to see that the industry was credible, yet still had a ton of opportunity to grow. Where is the opportunity within your specialty?

3. Is this something the market wants or needs, or both? Yes, in my industry there are 10,000 people turning 65 every day for next 15 years and living longer than ever before. This suits well for estate planning, financial services planning, and crisis planning for long term care through veteran's benefits or Medicaid. What are your market demographics?

4. Is your specialty favored or not; is there any controversy around it? There is much controversy around government benefits planning (saving people's money and still qualifying for government assistance) to aid the traditional middle class. On the financial planning side, certain financial products, like annuities, can be

controversial. Controversy creates curiosity and conversation and opportunity.

5. Has anyone written books about your topic? If someone else has written on the topic, then you likely have a market for your specialty. In my industry, there were books written on a national level, but not locally until I did. Thus, I wrote a book called 47 Secret Veterans Benefits for Seniors: Benefits You Have Earned but Don't Know About, that I currently sell on Amazon.com.

6. What are possible sub-sets? For Elder Law: Medicaid, VA, SNT, Guardianship, fiduciary litigation, financial care planning. Think of all the services or products you could offer and think of derivatives to niche separately.

7. Can you offer a different angle to the same market? Financial care planning helps to "empower not impoverish" seniors - a totally different message than, "let us shelter your money and get you Medicaid."

8. Have a mentor. Since the year after I started my law firm, I joined a group that was led by a man who owned a successful elder law firm. He became my mentor and has remained so throughout the years, to include when niching into financial care services. I could not have done any of this alone. Find someone you admire who is successfully doing what you want to do and invite them into your world. You may have to pay for the association, but it will be well worth the investment.

About Victoria

Victoria Collier, Esq. has been helping lawyers find their legal niche within estate planning since 2006. Being a paralegal in both the United States Air Force and also in the private sector, Victoria learned from her mentors that being a "jack-of-all-trades" and a "generalist" would only bring boredom and burnout.

Since establishing her own law firm, The Elder & Disability Law Firm of Victoria L. Collier, PC, exclusively to assist individuals planning for the second phase of their life, Victoria has created niches within niches and coached hundreds of other attorneys to do the same. It is Victoria's goal to help other professionals find their passion and create profit. Victoria's client base ranges from lawyers to authors to work-from-home mothers.

Victoria knows how to work hard and smart. She moved from her parents' house at age 17, still in high school, while working full time. After graduation, Victoria moved from Houston, TX to Dallas, TX, knowing only one person. Victoria worked several jobs simultaneously to support herself until she enlisted in the USAF at age 19. Victoria was trained as a carpenter and mason, being only one of two females in a shop of almost 50 men.

Three years later she cross-trained and became a paralegal, prosecuting and defending military personnel. After six years of honorable service during the Desert Storm era, Victoria entered the civilian workforce in South Georgia as a paralegal working with people with disabilities. Inspired to do more, at the age of 29 Victoria enrolled in law school at the University of Nebraska – Lincoln, College of Law. Upon graduating, Victoria opened her own law firm focusing on estate planning, disability planning, and elder care planning.

In 2006 Victoria began educating lawyers across the nation on the special benefits available to senior veterans who were disabled. She not only became the national expert in VA Pension Benefits laws, but she created a fast-growing niche within the estate and elder care planning profession. Due to the changing atmosphere of elder care, Victoria is once again creating a niche in elder law and coaching lawyers on how to incorporate long-term care planning through the use of financial products within their law practice.

Victoria is the author of the top selling book, *47 Secret Veterans' Benefits for Seniors, Benefits You Have Earned But Don't Know About!*; *47 Secret Marketing Strategies for Veterans Benefits Attorneys*; and *Paying for Long Term Care: Financial Help for Wartime Veterans: The VA Aid & Attendance Benefit, Georgia Edition*. Victoria has also co-authored the following books: *Blooper Episodes in Estate Planning and Elder Law: Lessons From Prime Time TV, Georgia Edition*, with Debbie J. Papay; *Don't Go Broke in a Nursing Home, Georgia Edition*, with Don Quante; *Protect Your IRA: Avoid the 5 Common Mistakes*, with David J. Zumpano, CPA, J.D.; *Running Through Life's Lessons*, with Jackie Clark; and *Getting to Baby: Creating your Family Faster, Easier and Less Expensive through Fertility, Adoption, or Surrogacy*, with Jennifer Collier.

You can contact Victoria at:
- Victoria@ElderLawGeorgia.com
- www.ElderLawGeorgia.com

CHAPTER 7

FROM ROCK BOTTOM TO ROCK STAR

BY TIFFANY BALLARD

The "mishaps" and "mistakes" in life offer us the greatest insight as to how we can grow above and beyond our circumstances.

When a lost soul has a child, that child is likely to be a lost soul, too. I came into this world with a tremendous amount of potential, just as we all do, but circumstances did not land me in an environment where I could recognize that easily. This was the way that it was and my mother, as much as she wanted better, couldn't quite get there when I was young. She struggled with addiction and eventually I did too. She had challenges establishing good, solid relationships and I ended up carrying those same struggles, as well. She was in and out of my life at times, just as I often felt like an observer of my own existence on occasion.

All of these tragic early events were significant, and logically I did not want them, yet I ended up deeply involved in them even as I grew into a young woman. I was no longer the "helpless child," I had become an active participant. My direction in life wasn't looking very good. By the time I was fourteen, I ended up getting sent to juvenile hall for nine months due to the choices I made. It was harsh, but not farfetched from what anyone would have expected of a young girl like I was at the time.

AND THEN I TURNED FIFTEEN...

When it's time to change our course in life, no one can make that happen besides us.

It wasn't without a serious commitment to change that change came. I was sick of turning into what everyone else thought I'd inevitably end up being. And I am the first one to admit that being in juvie actually saved my life. Without it, there was a good chance I would have been the next statistic of someone to die from a heroin overdose.

With my days in detention behind me, I began to look ahead. My mother had eventually lost custody of me, but she gained it back when I was sixteen so I went back to live with her. However, I had two positive things working in my favor. First were goals. Second were wonderful grandparents and immediate family members who, in my earlier years, did the best they could for me. They made a huge difference and contributed in giving me something positive to focus on. I finished high school at the age of sixteen and began college early. It was a lot of work, but I was vested in my success. The drive I had led to my mom and I joking about how I was actually the one raising her, not the other way around. It's those little bits of laughter that give you strength to keep moving toward that "better day." And with each good choice, every day can get better.

Yes, life was getting interesting in a different way than it ever had before, not only because of my academic goals. It was in my approach and philosophy about life that the most significant changes were taking place. My ability to tap into my intuition and past experiences to make better choices was on the rise. This is when I realized something so filled with self-empowerment that it changed my perspective and gave me endless drive. Everything we achieve comes from how we react and respond to the conditions that are taking place in our lives, not despite them. Without the rollercoaster childhood I encountered, I likely would not have developed the drive and ambition that I did, much less the appreciation for the human condition and the innate ability to conquer obstacles and barriers that define our lives.

WE ARE ALL INFINITE BEINGS HAVING A HUMAN EXPERIENCE

Life is 10% what happens to us and 90% how we react to it.
~ Dennis Kimbro

When we become aware that as humans, we make mistakes and live in imperfection, the awareness of recognizing this enables us to understand the fact that we can conquer anything that our mind perceives as "something holding us back." We can turn it around and make it into something that is "helping us now and in the future." We enable ourselves to live the joyful, abundant life that we all deserve to live. You see? It's all in our perception, our thinking, and how we choose to react that really matters. By sharing my life story in combination with the concept I just mentioned, is how I have successfully bounced back, time and again, and now have the rewarding privilege of helping several people from many different walks in life.

- For every "low" – I've experienced a thrilling rush that inspired something great.

- With every "setback" I've encountered – I was able to find a way to turn it around and use it to move further ahead than I'd been before.

Obviously, the ability to turn the perceived negatives into positives does not happen for everyone as naturally as it has for me—yet—with persistent determination, anyone is capable of doing so. How? Through the two Ps: Passion and Purpose. When we identify our passions and come into realization of what our purpose in life is, things begin to click and we gain a valuable perspective of the peaks and valleys of our lives.

We all have different directions we must take to discover our purpose and passions. Our past experiences are the landscape along the way, but in the end, we must and will become the masters and experts of our own destiny. This is not easy to do, of course, but there are qualified people like myself who can help assist you with this process. It is worth taking the time to put into action the required work involved to help you get there. I am living proof of this and am living a dream life that might not be mine, if not for a few nightmare circumstances that I redirected.

LIVING POSITIVE

We will never be able to plan for a perfect life. Unfortunate things will happen to us. It is in our response to these situations that we determine their true impact.

There is no way that life is always going to go smoothly—even for those who strive to have control of their environments and their outcomes. We'll always have to deal with various events that we struggle with, obstacles to overcome, and people that challenge us. When we are facing these things, we have two choices:

1. Take the mindset that we are a "victim." When this happens we'll fall into the pity party and embrace that victim mentality, rendering ourselves helpless to what we can do to learn, grow, and move on from what has happened. **Lots of people make this choice, but I help people see the benefits of taking choice number two.**

2. Take on the mindset of being a "survivor." Survivors get back up when the world weighs them down and tackles them flat to the ground. They assess their situation, acknowledge their emotions, and then start working toward solutions and take-away lessons from what has happened. **We can all choose to be a *survivor!***

Admittedly, at first I survived just because I was determined to do so, and I didn't always get the value in the surrounding lessons. Once I started purposefully living my life and participating in the activities that I am most passionate about, I did. I saw that there were lessons in absolutely everything that happened to me. After going through and analyzing a lifetime of experiences—addiction relapses, a failed 12 year marriage, a still-birth pregnancy, and many other chaotic events that took place—I've been fortunate and am grateful. I've experienced many good things in life, as well, such as having a successful modeling career, success in business, and getting to travel all around the world. But my favorite thing is recognizing the unique gift I have in my ability to relate to and connect with others intuitively, and making good use of it to inspire others to take action in purposefully "living" their lives.

THE SEVEN LESSONS

Today, I have Seven lessons that I've created and use when I coach, mentor, and support others who are going through tough transitions. I help them realize that by turning their "undesired events" into the stories that define their lives, they can accept their incredible potential.

1. **Know that everyone in life experiences hard times on many different levels.**

   We may not always see others' past or present challenges, but they are there. Knowing that you are not alone and having empathy for what others may be going through will take you a long way. Reach out to inspiring sources. For me, I found healthy role models and influential leaders that I knew could inspire me in some way, including Jesus, Gandhi, Buddha, Jack Canfield, Dr. Wayne Dyer, Louise Hey, etc. The point is to consistently keep learning, growing, and keep getting inspiration.

2. **Live, breath, and memorize the movie, "The Secret."**

   This movie (and book) has changed lives, including mine. It's so powerful and I'll never forget the first time I saw it back in 2004, it drew me in and I instantly became fascinated with the Law of Attraction. As I learned it and practiced it, my life began to work for me, which sparked another level of change in myself that was magical.

3. **Use positive affirmations.**

   We cannot get enough positive affirmations, and when properly applied, they can create miracles, as they continue to do in my life. Find small mantras you can repeat or write throughout the day. The key to making affirmations work for you is through "gratitude." You must be thankful for what you are affirming as if it has already taken place, and feel gratitude towards it on every level. I personally write mine out every morning and I always end the sentence with, "Thank You." An example of a great positive affirmation is: Success and prosperity follow me everywhere I go, Thank You!

4. **Commit to a daily "brutally honest" session with yourself.**

   You can try to be a certain way for everyone around you, but you cannot deceive yourself for long. Be honest and assess where you are at with everything in your life. Define what you're not happy with in your life or with yourself and admit it! Find ways to get yourself on a more solid ground. I recommend these measures to help assist you with assessing how to be truly and "accurately" honest with yourself:

- Look deep within yourself— compare and contrast where you're at in your life compared to where you want to be. Ask yourself why. Keep a journal of all this, as well as recording any and all your thoughts, feelings, motives, reactions, etc.
- Seek professional help or consult with an expert— don't be shy to do this.
- Find an accountability person to confide in— don't choose someone who is just a "yes" person, but someone who can help you sort through your problems and help guide you to your solutions – such as a mentor, coach, or close friend.

5. Meditate and strengthen your intuition.

I cannot stress enough the importance of regular and consistent meditation. Our intuition lets us know what to do and tells us the choices that are best suited for us, but the only way to be able to receive this crucial guidance from our higher self is to go within. As Dr. Wayne Dyer portrays, "Prayer is like us talking to God, and listening to our intuition, that voice inside us, is like God talking back." The more we meditate, the more "in tune" we are to our intuition, the more we are able to receive the clear, necessary guidance within ourselves that we need. This takes time and practice and I've gotten a tremendous amount of insight and guidance using Jack Canfield's 7 Tips to Strengthen Your Intuition and Take Soul-Inspired Action. Maybe you can too!

6. Surround yourself with good people and help others!

Being around people whom we admire, can learn from, and that help us grow in some way is necessary. It is essential to be in the presence of others who you learn from, who help you grow, and who possess the qualities of someone you'd like to emulate. To put it roughly: by previously hanging out with my heroin dealers, there was no way I would have tapped into what I know today. We all need support and encouragement from the right voices and the right sources. Seek it out! Plus, the day will come—if it isn't here already—where you are that source of inspiration for someone else.

7. Develop a routine or system that works for you.

Through everything you are learning about yourself and finally recognizing as your reality, you can begin creating a system that will help you move forward, address any emotional issues or lingering feelings properly, and keep you on track. This will also help you get back on track when you fall. We all fall sometimes, even me! What's important is how you pick yourself back up, and having an established system to utilize that works best for you, making the "awareness" process much easier.

These Seven steps have proven to me to be advantageous over and over in my life. **I am constantly mindful of them, and using them in my daily life has become a habit, but more than that, it's my personal checks-and-balances system.** You cannot talk the talk without walking the walk with these seven steps. Will they work for everyone the same way they work for me? No, but anyone can draw from them to come up with their own plan and number of steps. Maybe you only need 6, or maybe you need 8. Only you will know.

TODAY...

Driven by creating a community that is "Purposefully Lovin' Life & Livin' It Up!"

I've learned so much and continue to learn through each action I take and each individual that crosses my path. In order to reach as many people as I can, I've created **tiffanyteeworld.com**. Through this resource I am able to share my life with others so they can see first hand the "real and raw" me, how I live my life, handle situations, find guidance, and where they can learn more about living life on purpose both through myself, as well as others.

As we all improve as individuals, we can slowly start improving the world around us. Today, I am so grateful and continue living my life on purpose, and know that there is no one stopping me from enjoying an abundant, rewarding life, except myself.

And to me, practicing life "awareness" and understanding ourselves is the real "Road To Success."

About Tiffany

Tiffany Ballard is an Intuitive Soul Strategist, Transformational Healer, and Facilitator for Conscious Living. She owns and Operates the Strategic Social Media Marketing Company, Savvy Social Now, and is Founder and Creator of Tiffany Tee World, her passion project, which focuses on exploring higher consciousness with the objective of bringing deeper awareness to the world and those who occupy it. Her greatest satisfaction comes from helping others realize their fullest potential, finding their hidden gifts, and breaking free from limiting beliefs that keep their "true higher self" hidden; so they can become who they really are and live a meaningful life that is accompanied with love, success, and abundance. Tiffany commits herself to influence personal excellence, happiness, love, and compassion to the world and to whomever crosses her path in life.

Far and above the 16 years of literary background and practiced knowledge in the Personal Growth and Development field, her personal life challenges and triumphs have given her the hands-on understanding and expertise necessary for being an effective advocate of pushing through fear and failure to become more victorious. The significant mental, and emotional challenges she has had to endure, and the strategies to overcome these hurdles, has given her tremendous insight and wisdom into what motivates us as conscious beings and the peculiar, infinite spirits we all are. Tiffany is a real-life survivor, having encountered much trauma, but has learned from every situation with grace and gratitude, turning each adverse experience she encounters into an opportunity for soul growth, and an experience she can benefit from.

"We truly do have the authority to create the life we rightfully desire. A life that is purposeful, meaningful and fulfilling. Mastering our life challenges starts with self-awareness," explains Tiffany. *"We cannot assume to change that of which we are unaware. Our personal quest as human beings on this earthly realm is all about ultimately becoming conscious of what is now unconscious within us, in search of our inner selves on the soul level. Self-awareness is the greatest powerful resource we have to bring about change in our lives. Otherwise we are merely reacting, unconsciously analyzing, judging and interpreting, without really comprehending the big picture. As we enhance our awareness, we see with better clarity the dynamics at play, which provide us with the precise information we need to consciously choose what's best for us. I have made a promise to myself to continuously challenge myself, learn, and grow each day. Besides, I can only offer my assistance based on the level of awareness and life-learning success that I, myself, have acquired throughout and on my own personal journey."*

While most people are terrified to step out of their comfort zone, to start their dream business, to love themselves, to love a stranger, to leave a toxic environment, or to invest in their own self-improvement; Tiffany delivers a message that permeates your inner being and lights a fire within you to live life to the absolute fullest and to chase down everything your soul desires.

Websites-www.TiffanyTeeWorld.com / www.SavvySocialNow.com
Contact-Tiffany@Tiffanyteeworld.com

CHAPTER 8

CREATING AN ENTREPRENEURIAL WORKPLACE

BY MICHAEL LEVIN

"We'd like you to help us create a more entrepreneurial workplace." This was a request I received from a client several years ago. I frequently customize trainings and workshops to meet my client's needs. In this case it wasn't about customizing. I would need to completely develop this workshop from scratch.

With my companies, and as a senior executive during my corporate career, I have always tried to create an entrepreneurial environment. I had never formalized a process though and was intrigued by my client's request. Developing a workshop around this topic I felt was not only important, but formalizing a process could help transform how companies drove initiatives and change within their organization.

I told him I'd create the workshop and would need their support. I didn't have a clear vision at that time as to what the workshop would entail and how to maximize its impact. His team needed to understand this was a pilot. And they needed to help me develop the program. He agreed.

I understood where his request came from. He knew my background. I've been a serial entrepreneur, even during my corporate career. I have trained Entrepreneurs and spoken before Entrepreneur Groups as well as graduate classes at Universities. I've had the opportunity to share what

I know on numerous TV and radio shows around the country along with having my own radio show, entitled "How to Take a Product to Market." His company valued and embraced entrepreneurism and he felt they could use my assistance getting their company to the next level.

My first significant venture was at the age of 18. A friend and I started a teenage discotheque. We had leased the oldest building in the town of Livermore, California, an old firehouse. We completely renovated the building. At the time, we had no idea what a big deal this venture was.

We caused quite a scuttle as the neighboring businesses didn't want us to open. Many signed a petition to that effect. We did, however, have support of Livermore teenagers and their parents.

Our disco was big news in the community. On numerous occasions, my partner and I found our pictures on the front page of the paper. At the City Council meeting to vote for our approval, we had a standing-room-only audience.

The pressure from the community helped get our discotheque approved. We had a run for a while as the city hotspot for its youth. I joke that I got my Master's Degree before my Bachelor's as this experience was much more difficult and provided a far greater education than my collegiate experience that followed.

Since then I have launched numerous companies. When I was earning more from my ventures than my corporate career, I became a full-time entrepreneur.

I remember my Uncle, who always worked for others in traditionally-run companies, telling me he wished he had started his own business. I asked him what type he would have liked to open. He told me it didn't matter as long as it was his own.

I understood what he meant. The passion isn't necessarily about the industry or the product. It's about the solution you provide and feeling passionate about what you offer. It's about having something that is your own. I've had businesses in consumer products, software, health and wellness, and the automotive industry amongst others. My passion wasn't necessarily for the industry I got involved with or the product. I just felt strong about the opportunity and the solution we provided. I also liked feeling more in control of my own destiny, even if at times I was tempted to go for the security of a regular paycheck.

With my ventures I have tried to create an entrepreneurial environment. I wanted each person on the team viewing themselves as the owner of their piece of the business. I've also found it was difficult for many employees to embrace the role.

I've heard the same from numerous companies I've worked with. The leadership team wants to see the employees take a greater role and higher level of responsibility. They want them to be more entrepreneurial, feel more empowered and be willing to both embrace and lead change.

Why is it so difficult to create this environment? I believe there are several reasons. When I have researched the needs of the employee, the information I have found indicates why. First, when you look at the basic needs of most employees, being entrepreneurial or empowered isn't on top of the list. Security, being able to support themselves and their families, ranks far higher. So does safety, recognition and feedback, being compensated equitably and an opportunity to grow.

The question becomes for many employees: "Why should I take the risk?" Why should they make decisions and take ownership if it could put their career and job at risk? Isn't it safer for them to be led by others, follow instructions and if things go wrong, let others take the blame? "I just did what I was told." "It wasn't my fault." These can be perceived to be a safer stance.

What is the motivation for employees to be entrepreneurial? This issue doesn't just apply to line staff. I have personally found this to be the case with senior executives as well. Over the years, I have brought in leaders from many companies including Fortune 500 firms to be part of my organizations. They claimed a desire to be business owners. What I found, and they did as well, is when they had to be self-motivated and self-disciplined, when they weren't getting a paycheck, when they didn't have a boss, they couldn't do it.

So how do you overcome the natural conflict of the needs of the employee versus the needs of the employer, and create an entrepreneurial environment? There is one key employee need that does fit. Employees want the opportunity to develop and grow. Part of that development includes new learning opportunities and the chance to significantly contribute to solving company issues and challenges.

As a leader, your role is to give them that opportunity while satisfying the rest of the needs of the employee. They need to feel safe and secure. They need to feel heard. They need to feel as though they can contribute, make recommendations, and lead initiatives while feeling it won't jeopardize their ability to take care of themselves and their family.

Having your staff feel heard is a significant challenge as well. It can be done but it's not easy. Even if you feel like you've created an open environment, it's difficult to get them to share everything. They don't for a few reasons. One comes back to "Why take the risk?" The second is even if they tell you what they feel, they don't feel like you'll listen.

I had an interesting experience with one of my companies that emphasized for me how difficult this can be. My partner and I fostered a very open and communicative environment. We were very proud of our culture. Our team was loyal to us and we had built a very strong company. We created a collaborative environment and our door was open. We shared company financials with the team and they had incentives tied to our success.

We met with them regularly to get their feedback and input. This included meeting them in the field along with taking them to lunch individually and asking for their ideas. Our business was in the automotive industry. While we were easily the industry leader, we had a significant amount of competition whose primary means of competing was to undercut us price-wise. Due to these pressures, we were at a stage where it was difficult to increase our staff's pay. Many had been with us for a number of years and we wanted to take care of them.

As a pilot, we helped one of our senior staff develop their own business. They'd be able to contract themselves back to us as well as others and dramatically increase their income. We tutored and helped them set up their business.

We had fully equipped vehicles to provide our service. When our staff member purchased a vehicle to start his business, it was significantly different than ours both in terms of type of vehicle and set-up. We asked him why he never told us about his idea as we liked it better. He said because he felt we wouldn't have listened. We were stunned.

We found out why he felt this way. We helped other members of our staff start their own business. When they purchased and set up their vehicles, each had different versions of what our first contractor had done. We also changed out all of our vehicles with similar layouts to theirs. We thought we clearly listened. The perspective of the staff member who piloted the program though was because we hadn't done "exactly" what he did we hadn't listened. His perception, versus our perception, was eye opening to us.

This however had nothing to do with his feelings or respect for us. This same individual showed us how he and the rest of the team felt. Around the holidays he came to my partner and me. He said that he and the team wanted to thank us for all we had done for them over the years. We had always sponsored a company holiday party. He said he was going to host the party and the team was paying for it. All we needed to do was show up. It was quite a lesson for us. We learned no matter how much your team likes and respects you they may still be unwilling to fully share all of their thoughts and ideas. They feel they may not be heard despite how much you feel you listen to them and act on what they said.

Back to my client who wanted me to develop the Entrepreneurial Workshop. I knew I had to work through all of these factors. How do you get employees to feel safe? To feel heard? To be willing to not only embrace change but also lead change.

I put together what I felt was a strong curriculum and also felt it could be improved. We had broken this initial workshop into two days. I made a request of the attendees. At the end of the first day, I asked for volunteers to stick around and make any adjustments to Day Two's curriculum to maximize the impact of the workshop. I told them I'd be willing to throw out what I had developed and start over. Several members of the workshop took me up on my offer.

They provided great feedback and I made several changes. We came to agreement on key company initiatives. We then divided into teams to leverage what they learned during the workshop to take those initiatives and develop executable action plans. We'd secure leadership support, including budgets. This way the workshop could help pave the way for each participant to lead change within the organization.

Some of the projects in this initial workshop went very well. Some could have gone better. I've learned a lot since then. To me, strong leadership habits and creating entrepreneurism is counterintuitive to what we inherently do. Much has to be learned and sometimes unlearned in order to have the impact and outcome that both I and my clients desire.

I've developed a series of training modules that now lead up to the Entrepreneurial workshop. I realized in order to have full impact, it was necessary to train Leaders and Managers in a variety of areas including communication skills and protocols along with understanding and gaining alignment as to what makes great Leaders and Managers. Learning how to gather input, give feedback, delegate effectively, train and develop staff, on-board new Managers, ensure proper performance and development plans are in place, along with other key leadership skills, helped dramatically improve the outcome of the entrepreneurial training.

I've also learned from my own experiences this is a journey, not a destination. There will be steps forward and backwards. There is always going to be room for improvement, to embrace more change and to learn from experience.

After putting my curriculum together, I was working with a client. We were conducting one of the initial workshops. I was training at one of their satellite facilities where I find it's typically more challenging as they can feel isolated from headquarters. This company inspires a great deal of loyalty and has a very senior team. We were conducting an exercise in which I take the team through a four-step process I developed to work through challenges and problems. The participants pair up and practice the process. There was an odd number so I paired up with one of them. He was one of the more senior people.

When we started working through a problem, he initially started by what happens traditionally. He was blaming others, in particular at headquarters, saying "they" were the cause of the problem. I began asking him questions, going through my process. I asked him, within his span of control, what could he do to help solve the problem? We continued to go deeper and work through the process. He had a number of great ideas.

At the end, we all debriefed and I asked what each got out of the exercise. He said that he had never realized how big a part of the solution he could be. He recognized he would identify problems but hadn't taken the ownership to see how he could contribute to solving those problems. Those are the moments that create the greatest satisfaction for me. I believe if we make individual breakthroughs they will lead to team breakthroughs and then company breakthroughs.

A veteran member of the National Speakers Association once told me she appreciated that with respect to Public Speaking, I work without a net. What she meant was I use my own material, I don't stand behind a podium and I rarely use PowerPoint. I leave myself exposed and she felt that took courage. As an Entrepreneur, I have sometimes worked with a net and sometimes without. Sometimes I've had a job while I got my venture off the ground. Sometimes I found investors. At times, it was my house and savings on the line.

I believe the key to creating an entrepreneurial environment is to embrace employee ownership while giving them a net. Your employees can be inspired to lead and drive change while feeling safe, secure and heard. It's not something that happens easily. I also know the incredible reward and success it means for companies, its Leaders and Managers, and their teams when it's embraced. I've personally seen it in my own businesses as well as my clients. Once you experience this environment, you'll never go back.

About Michael

Michael Levin is President and CEO of Custom Solutions Inc. He is the author of *Sitting on the Same Side of the Table: The Art of Collaborative Selling* and *How to Take a Product to Market*.

He has launched both product and service companies and turned them into multi-million dollar entities. His products, including those he has patented, have been sold in every major retail drug, grocery and mass chain in the country. His patented products have been featured in *O Magazine*.

Michael now shares his knowledge and processes through training and coaching in the areas of Sales, Leadership and Management, along with Presentation Skills. His clients range from Fortune 500 companies to small and midsize manufacturers in a wide variety of industries.

Michael's personally developed sales process helps companies learn how to turn traditional presentations into high impact conversations that not only create more business but more profitable business. His unique leadership training helps his clients create an "Entrepreneurial Environment in their Workplace." His curriculum helps employees learn how to lead and drive critical initiatives along with greatly enhancing communication and an environment that embraces change.

He has personally appeared on TV and radio shows around the country sharing his knowledge. He has appeared on Home Shopping Network numerous times and has also been featured in *Entrepreneur Magazine*.

Michael's corporate career was with Pepsi Cola, running divisions in San Francisco and Oakland, California along with Reno, Nevada. He also developed their Northern California training program.

Michael is a graduate of CSU Chico with a Degree in Marketing. He is a former board member for the Institute of Management Consultants and volunteered for years at the Contra Costa Crisis Center. He lives in Northern California.

You can connect with Michael at:
- mlevin@csicconsultinginc.com
- www.csiconsultinginc.com

CHAPTER 9

POTHOLES, DETOURS AND BUMPS IN THE ROAD

BY MARTA ZARRELLA

The road of life, for most human beings, is not a super highway. No one gets from where they are to where they want to be in a self-driving vehicle, directed by GPS, which is navigation programmed by the Universe or God. Nope! More often than not, when you hear stories about some of the world's most successful, accomplished or inspiring people, the opposite is true. Their road was full of challenges and often required a number of detours and restarts.

I know mine is. I have been called "inspiring," "resilient" and most recently a "Phoenix Rising." I am always humbled and grateful to hear that. What I do now as an award-winning writer with newspaper and magazine stories as well as a novel under my award winning belt, is to help people write the stories of their lives. I am an author, coach and editor. I still have the pleasure of writing articles and stories for print publications, usually about the amazing people who populate our world. I love human interest stories. My clients – all incredibly successful in their careers – have overcome unbelievable challenges. My story, as 'inspiring' as it might be, pales in comparison to stories that I get to write.

One client, in his golden years, was born in Hungary to a Jewish family. When he was a young boy, Jews were gathered up and put into camps. So, his family went into hiding in a basement. Because he was small and stealthy, my client went out in the dark of night and found food for his family to eat in their underground hiding place. He found a dead horse once, and as hungry as he was, it looked good enough to eat. For many weeks he snuck out and carved pieces of horsemeat, always carefully reburying the horse in the snow. His family cooked the 'sweet tasting' horsemeat over small candles and fed themselves that way for most of the winter.

Years later, early in his working life, he stumbled upon an uprising in the town square of Budapest. He was in the area hoping to meet his father for lunch. Instead he met two armies firing at each other, oblivious to the innocent citizens trying to get to and from lunch. My client climbed over 'a pile of dead bodies and jumped, head first, through a window.' His head broke the glass, he bled – a lot – but he lived. That did not deter his goal of getting to America where he could find a job and make a life. Today, at 89, he has two PhD's in Engineering Physics and Applied Physics, an impressive resume, and a number of patents and awards. He is still consulting, playing tennis, driving too fast and enjoying the company of a beautiful lady. He is often called away from his beautiful million-dollar home in the hills of Los Angeles to serve as 'expert witness' in complex law suits. I am in awe of his good natured, humorous look at life, and his drive and desire to be of service to others at 89. When asked, "What is it that gives you such a positive outlook and zest for life given what you have experienced?" His answer is, "what else would I be doing all these years."

Another client as a little girl, watched members on both her mother and father's side of the family deteriorate from Alzheimer's disease and learned not long ago that she, too, would likely walk down that same agonizing path. She had been feeling out of sorts with no definitive reason for what ailed her after many medical tests. She chose to participate in a research study through the healthcare system that employed her husband. One day, she opened an email and read the results of the DNA swab she sent to the researchers. That email told her she had two copies of the ApoE 4 allele (known as the Alzheimer's gene) which meant that she had a 91% chance of developing Alzheimer's. Only two percent of the population has this genetic status. Because she was a registered nurse in her early career, and because of her family history, she knew that was not good news. In her mid 40's she knew what she had to look forward to and spiraled into depression and was diagnosed with PTSD. Her marriage suffered while she dealt with her new reality.

—The journey through PTSD, finding the right therapist to help her cope, and taking control of her new reality was not easy. One day, after a conversation with her husband, she decided to become a victor and not a victim. With his love and support, she started a 501(C)(3) non-profit dedicated to raising funds and awareness for Alzheimer's research. She is proud to be an "Alzheimer's Lab Rat" as a participant in ground-breaking research. Her personal experience of living with this genetic status has been highlighted in the New York Times and featured in a PBS News Hour segment discussing how Alzheimer's disease researchers seek better prevention with early detection. Her story and mission have been shared with numerous media outlets. She is co-authoring a book inspired by her story with one of the country's leading medical experts on Alzheimer's and Dementia. When asked what motivated her to dedicate her life to the disease that will forever change it she stated passionately, "What else should I be doing?"

As for me, like so many, I survived sexual abuse in the hands of a caregiver. I was around three when it began. We think it ended when I started school. I knew I wanted to move away from that painful place, so I worked very hard to put myself through college and got a Bachelor of Business Administration. I went to work for a major international corporation two weeks after graduation and worked in Information Systems and Accounting in two states and three companies, moving from entry level Information Systems Assistant to Strategic Planning Director in a short twelve years (which included two maternity leaves).

What I am most proud of during that stage of my career, is earning the Pinellas County Florida American Business Woman's Boss of the Year when I managed an office of 35. It was a union shop and 32 of my employees were card-holding union members. I was the youngest person in that office (barely 30) and was nominated by the oldest person in the office who was 64. I was also the youngest nominee and beat out several male executives to earn that honor. Helping people find the best within themselves is what makes me happy.

I wanted to raise my own children instead of entrusting them to a nanny, so when my third child was born, I left Corporate America. Eventually I became a computer teacher at a private school in Florida, where my children attended pre-school. I helped create a state-of-the-art computer lab back in the early 1990's. That computer lab catapulted them to become one of the most sought-after schools in the area. And now, in mid-life when many of my friends are starting to travel and do all those things they've been planning all their lives, my world was changed completely by a catastrophic loss during one of those famous California wildfires.

My family of five lost everything but what we threw in our vehicles and took with us, plus a few things in one outdoor shed that did not burn. Our catastrophic loss happened as my three kids were graduating from high school. Life's double whammy — losing every material possession at the dreaded 'empty nest' period of life. Wow! That kind of life event makes you take personal inventory, in doing so, my husband and I realized our life goals were no longer all that similar. We decided to part ways. Consequently, I had to start from scratch after being a stay-at-home Mom and community volunteer for many, many years. I took what had been a hobby that I loved and was being recognized for, and turned it into a thriving career in a few short years. When people ask how I could do what I have done after losing so much? I say, "My writing has helped people heal, grow, or succeed including myself – so why not?"

What is it that makes some people turn bumpy roads into the ride of their life?

I believe the there are five *main* reasons why some people are more resilient and successful than others. Those reasons are: knowing their "core values" and "core competency." Other important attributes are the desire to learn and a sense of purpose and gratitude.

So, what are core values and why are they so important? Values are those guiding principles that dictate our choices, our behavior in other words. My core values are integrity, compassionate empathy, and passion. I need to be honest, care about others and do things from a place of passion, not because it's a habit, it is easy or simply to make a buck. Other 'value' words are responsibility, professionalism, community, honesty, respect, loyalty, accountability, innovation, freedom, and so on.

I recently attended a workshop where presenter Greg Montana and his wife Tamara talked about 'Heart Virtues.' Greg described our behavior as being directed by our beliefs and our beliefs in turn being influenced by our values. Our values might come from our employer — many companies have stated "core values" — from our church, community or family. He calls "values" our external motivators. Greg suggests that we also have a Heart Virtue, the core value of our heart in other words.

Our heart virtue is ours and ours alone, it is developed over time, by the events of our lives. It also influences our core values when it is just us making decisions about life, away from work, church, community or family.

When a person knows themselves enough to understand what their heart virtue-inspired core values are, they are generally driven to do from a place of passion and purpose. That drive is powerful! Maybe that is what we call 'resilience?'

My 89-year-old client's core values are learning, hard work and making things better. In 2005 and 2010 while working for Boeing, he developed patents for a unique full-size test facility to simulate the loading of air cargo, advanced robotic cargo decks and loading systems for military aircraft, lightweight military cargo restraint system, military rescue vehicles and load distribution systems of military cargo deck conveyors. He did not survive what he survived in his youth to get to America and be mediocre. He was also named a Who's Who in the World. He has passion and purpose and he knows himself very well.

My Alzheimer's client has the core values of compassion, purpose and responsibility. She cares about people, as most nurses do. She feels a responsibility to help others not go through what she went through as a family member watching loved ones struggle with the debilitating and destructive effect of Alzheimer's Disease and the compassion to 'donate' herself to research and her story to awareness. She wants to help the Alzheimer's community find a cure by 2020. She has passion and purpose and has come to know herself very well also.

The secret weapon for navigating the potholes, detours and bumps in the road of life, for me, is this. Take a really good look inside, get to know yourself honestly and deeply. I have known many, many people who hate their jobs, it doesn't matter how big their home or bank account. I know miserable rich and poor alike. I also know people who, like me, have found personal and financial success doing what we love. Know your heart virtue, your core values and core competencies (also called skills and strengths). Look for the lesson in every challenge, failure or obstacle and learn from it, don't use those things as excuses, and live a life of passion and purpose.

To your success!

About Marta

In 2014, with a robust list of people seeking her help to write, coach writing, or edit their written work, Marta Zarrella incorporated her business. M.P. Zarrella Books, Inc. provides writing, editing, coaching and publishing services. She also has the pleasure of writing newspaper and magazine articles about the interesting people in her community of Ramona, California.

In 2003, her first work, a poem called *With Dignity and Strength*, was published. A few years later in October of 2007, the family's home was completely destroyed by the devastating Witchcreek firestorm. All of Southern California, it seemed, was in flames. At the time, son Richard was a freshman at University of California, Santa Cruz, son Robert was in his first year of Community College in San Diego, and daughter Kathryn was a Senior in High School. The healing process after such a catastrophic event goes very deep. Zarrella and her husband of 29 years decided that life had taken them in very different directions - an amicable divorce was finalized in 2010. Every member of the family had to adapt to a number of significant life events.

Single now, she needed to significantly grow her income, so Marta began writing for a local newspaper, a magazine, as well *Examiner.com*, producing content for both an equestrian and a wine page. At the same time, she was processing her thoughts about loss and change in what has become her first published award winning novel, *A Tangeled Web, Rejecting Technology's Assault on Mother Nature*. The book was truly inspired by Marta's life, her work, and her interests.

A native Texan, Marta graduated from the University of Texas, El Paso in 1979 with a Bachelor of Business Administration. Two weeks after graduation, she moved to San Angelo, Texas and began her career with General Telephone and Electronics (GTE Corporation – Verizon since the 1990's). For twelve years she worked in Accounting and Information Systems in Texas and Florida, eventually 'retiring early' as Director of Strategic Planning for GTE Data Services. Marta had the distinct pleasure of forging a path for Part Time Professionals with GTE/Verizon Corporation, piloting a Part Time Salaried Employee program after the birth of her second child. When their third child was born, Marta chose to become a stay-at-home Mom. Knowing the life of a full-time working Mom, raising her children was the next goal.

By 2012, she was a busy freelance writer and submitted her work to the San Diego Press Club Annual Excellence awards. The prestigious competition processes over 4,000 entries. In her first year she won First and Second Place in the Magazine category. In 2013, a piece on the Boston Marathon bombing earned first place in *Breaking News*. She began submitting her novel to writing competitions as well. It, too, earned recognition each time. Zarrella likes to challenge herself by holding her work up to the best in the industry. Writing is her third career, what she has been preparing for all these years.

CHAPTER 10

MARIO BLACK SHEEP

BY MARIO MAZZAMUTO

The Black Sheep's Path to Greener Pastures

For most people, the road to success starts in high school, with good grades, good attendance, and good manners. My freshman year I punched a teacher. Yeah, I guess I am a black sheep.

There are a lot of people following the road to "success." Our parents, schools, peers, and media reinforce the right way to get there, and define what success should look like. This book has many great ideas to help you get on THE road. But traffic, detours, or lost directions can take you off the road, and leave you on your own to find where you need to go.

That teacher? He totally had it coming. I was at school, talking to friends between classes, on the road my parents and teachers had mapped out, and the teacher tackled me. The bully teacher belligerently assumed a drama class prop was a weapon, and thought he was "bravely" defending the school from a little kid. I thought a crazy grown-up was attacking me, so I beat him up. Of course, I was expelled from school, and taken off the road to success.

Black sheep are different. Not bad or good, but certainly distinct. They stand out from the flock.

I went off the road to success and drove myself down the highway to Hell. I rebelled. I fell in with a tough crowd, ran around with gang members, dealt weed, and tried to be a bad boy. I was really good at doing the opposite of what society expected of me. The thing is, I came from a good family, working class Italian roots, with strong grandparents from both sides of the family in my life. I played sports, ate family dinners, and respected my elders. My actions brought shame on my family, they were disappointed in me. I am not a thug, I am a black sheep.

My stint as a 'wannabe' gangster was short lived. I saw rock bottom. The kids I ran with had broken families, no goals, and a dangerous lifestyle. Their dads and brothers were in and out of jail, and a few in prison. They lived in dirty homes with empty pantries. They were 18 years old and failing tests in my 9th Grade reform school classes. Alcohol and drugs drove both their career goals and leisure activities. This lifestyle was not for me. I was not sure what I wanted, or how I would get there, but I knew I could not follow this road either. I am a black sheep.

Ironically, the Godfather is one of my favorite films. I have seen real gang-life, and it is shabby and dim. But in the Godfather I think maybe something in Francis Ford Coppola's vision spoke to me. When he was small, Vito Andolini, the future Don Corleone, was thought to be dumb and simple. Similarly, Francis Ford Coppola shares, "I was always the black sheep of the family and always told that I was dumb, and I had a low IQ and did badly in school." It is not always easy for the little black lambs, but eventually they grow in to black rams.

After long, heartfelt discussions, my parents agreed the best thing for me would be to drop out of school, go to work, and get my GED on my own. So at age 14 I joined the work force. I went to work for my dad in construction, and when I was 18 took on more jobs in the building trades. Young, fit, and hardworking, I was assigned many grueling and dangerous tasks in, under, and over job sites. I worked hard, learned a lot, made money, and soon I had a new car and bought a house and had a steady girlfriend. I became a licensed real estate appraiser at 21 and never looked back. These were not my initial goals, but came along the way as I was working towards making ME better.

Are you a black sheep?

Society reinforces traits and outcomes they see in themselves. These are the flock of white sheep, who want to sustain and promote a consistent social identity. The safe route. Go to school, get a job, get a mortgage, have a family, and retire at 65. That road satisfies 90% of society. But these are goals in and of themselves for the flock members. Black sheep veer from that plan and have their own goals and method of attaining them.

Don't confuse a goal with the means of attaining a goal. A black sheep's goal may not be to "go to school," but rather to learn about life, or a hobby, or area of interest. A job is not a goal in and of itself, but a means to express oneself and make money to provide for happiness. A spouse and family are not end goals; what is important to the black sheep is finding the love of their life and sharing goals together. This often includes a house and family, but might just as well be to travel, or build a business, or anything else together.

And retirement? White sheep plan for the day they can end 40 years of the grind to finally retire and start enjoying their life. If they are young and healthy enough to still enjoy it. A black sheep loves their life and has a balance they would happily enjoy forever.

White sheep worry more about success than the road to get there. Don't be a white sheep!

How to be a black sheep

This book is full of great advice. If you are a black sheep, you will read, pick and choose the bits that apply to you, do whatever the 'heck' you like, and get on with your own brand of success. Most readers will be white sheep, looking for advice from other white sheep on how to make friends and influence people (no offense to Mr. Carnegie!). But white sheep can learn from the black sheep's attitude and approach to success. Black sheep are not always black. They can be purple, or teal, or plaid. The important thing is to embrace your individuality (and the uniqueness of others) to let our differences be the driver towards success. Not our sameness.

Music executive Simon Cowell appreciated the unique artistry of Stefani Germanotta, and saw how she would change the music industry: "I want people to understand that from the minute Lady Gaga arrived, she created a new set of rules: being different is good; embrace it."

It is easy to be a white sheep. So easy that wolves can do it pretty well. It is not easy to be a black sheep, to stand out from the herd, to be identified as different. The black sheep is unique on the outside, but we all are unique on the inside, and can choose to let that uniqueness shine. Let your guard down, take a step away from the flock, and project your uniqueness. Be a black sheep.

SEVEN WAYS TO BE A BLACK SHEEP

1. Be Happy.

Black sheep are OK being happy, and do it on their own terms. This happiness does not come at the expense of anyone else's. On the contrary, happiness for the black sheep is despite what anyone else thinks. This especially applies to careers.

Though I didn't like school or homework, it turned out that I love learning and solving interesting problems. I am now a life-long learner who reads all the time, either a web article or a book. And for work I grew from appraising homes to buying and renovating them. These complex problems are interesting to me, make me happy to do, and I profit from them.

Do what you love, love what you do, and everything else will follow.

2. Be Courageous.

Every fool is unique, but is ignorant of it. The Black Sheep is unique by definition, and bravely owns his or her distinctions. People are drawn to those who are different and interesting. Sometimes the Black Sheep is teased for being different. But by embracing who you are and being comfortable in your black wool, people will appreciate you for your differences. A wise man once said, "To be yourself in a world that is constantly trying to make you something else is the greatest accomplishment." That man was a champion of self-reliance, a critic of societal pressures: Ralph Waldo Emerson.

Share your confidence and uniqueness with others, and use it to inspire others and to expand your sphere of goodness. Let your bravery embrace your friends and family, your co-workers, as well as yourself. That makes you a leader.

3. Be Grateful.

Appreciate what you have, and for what others offer. I really appreciate my elders, and those more experienced who have wisdom to share. Even in my wildest days as a teen hellion, I respected my grandparents and learned from my bosses. Gratitude opens your heart to reality through humility. It helps you sort your place in the Universe. I constantly take stock of where I am, the people in my life, what I have, and am grateful for it. It is impossible to be grateful and fearful at the same time. Gratitude is the best way to be courageous.

4. Be Chill.

There is something about the herd mentality that keeps white sheep on edge, always looking at the other sheep around them for assurance. Black sheep stand out from the flock, so they don't sweat the trepidations of the crowd. Let your own drive and potential re-assure you as you work toward your goals. Like Walt Disney said, "The more you like yourself, the less you are like anyone else, which makes you unique." Everything worked out for Walt, who was always looking to the next challenge.

Things are either OK, or else you will figure out a way to make things OK. It is that simple. If you cannot figure out something, break it down into smaller chunks you can sort out as you go. Anything is scary if it is big enough. My wife's terrier is super cute, but if it were 400 pounds it would be terrifying. Don't get stressed out by goals that appear to be too huge.

5. Be Balanced.

Too much of anything is bad thing. You can drown internally from drinking too much water! Remember that King Midas guy? He really got tired of his family whining all the time so he turned them to gold, then he got lonely and regretted it. Or something like that.

White Sheep tend to work too much for the sake of working. Working and making money are not ends in and of themselves. They are means to accomplish other goals that balance out work, like travel, or home comforts, or fun with family. The Black Sheep enjoys sleeping in, a cold beer, a good book, or a workout, or a nice steak without guilt when they are part of balance.

Work and play. Family, friends, and solo reflection. Candy and cardio. There is literally nothing in your life that does not need balance.

6. Be Consistent.

Habits and routines will round out all the above. You are what you think and do. If you are vegetarian except for bacon, that is at least consistent. If you are only on the wagon when your kids are around, that is not. Something like that.

That was only six. So What? I am a black sheep, I got the job done in six instead of seven. The seventh item is to go do something you want to do. Don't follow the flock.

NOW WHAT?

We are all still sheep, and our wool still keeps us all equally warm, so what's the big deal? The white sheep follow the flock, but they are more worried about their role, or the perception of their roll, within the flock. Black sheep tend to the flock by not worrying what they think. The world would be a much happier place if we all let our herd-mentality guards down and stood out a bit.

"Everybody is a genius. But if you judge a fish by its ability to climb a tree, it will live its whole life believing that it is stupid." Albert Einstein said that. If you were going to be the next Albert Einstein, you should have figured it out by now. So no, you are not a secret Einstein. That guy was a black sheep from a future planet who understood the DNA of the universe before DNA was even invented. But you still have vast potential you should tap to excel as a black sheep.

Do what makes you happy, think outside-the-box. Build an income and lifestyle based on what you love to do, not what you have to do.

Don't be afraid to think for yourself, act for yourself, choose for yourself. You will not accomplish anything if you worry about the flock. But if you focus on your own happiness, and by extension the happiness of those you care about, you will accomplish more and the flock will be better off.

And most importantly, don't let the flock get you down. You cannot help being a black sheep any more than they can help being white sheep. But you can choose to be the best damn black sheep you can be.

You know you have a little rebel inside itching to come out. Be Happy, have fun and embrace your black sheep!

About Mario

Being a Black Sheep turned out OK for Mario Mazzamuto. He is currently in his early 30s, married to the woman of his dreams, and has two amazing kids. Despite punching out of high school at age 14, he worked hard and studied hard to become his own boss by 21.

Success for Mario is working really hard through Thursday, then spending a three-day weekend at Disneyland with his family. Success for him is earning a buck, playing with the kids, reading a few chapters, snuggling down all night. Using balance as a measure of success, Mario has been very successful for many years. He is happy, and it makes even the white sheep jealous.

Mario was born and raised in the San Francisco Bay Area, coming from a large Italian family that has strong roots in his home town of Martinez, CA. His parents are both immigrants, making him a first generation American. He has built a thriving real estate appraisal company, San Francisco Bay Appraisal. He also is a real estate investor who personally manages the construction and renovation of his projects. This has allowed him to grow a real estate management and investment company with properties all around Northern California. Mario is also a certified life coach helping others find balance as a black sheep.

As part of his work/life balance, and his pursuit of happiness, he enjoys working with others on their goals for real estate, business, life, or balance. As a black sheep, he will not tell you what success is, but he will help you get there on your terms. He has gone through similar struggles to your own.

You can reach Mario Mazzamuto at his office, at: SFBayAppraisal.com, or via his personal website: MarioMazzamuto.com.

CHAPTER 11

BUILDING YOUR OWN ROAD TO SUCCESS: PETER DIAMANDIS' QUEST TO CHANGE THE WORLD

BY JW DICKS & NICK NANTON

It's been our honor in recent years to be able to work with space pioneer, physician, engineer and entrepreneur Peter Diamandis, founder of the X Prize Foundation as well as co-founder of Singularity University, Space Adventures Ltd., International Space University, Planetary Resources, Human Longevity Inc., and the Zero-Gravity Corporation.

Last year, we were grateful to get permission to tell his story in our Emmy Award-winning documentary on Peter's life and work, *Visioneer*; now, in this exclusive excerpt from our new book, *Mission-Driven Business*, we're proud to be able to offer this illuminating interview with Peter – and how his passionate commitment to his mission enabled him to create exciting new challenges that have engaged the entire scientific community, as well as such private sector legends as Richard Branson and Tony Robbins.

Among the many, many honors he's received, Peter Diamandis was recently named one of Fortune magazine's "50 World's Greatest Leaders" – and with good reason. Armed with an unshakeable belief in his cause, Diamandis spearheaded private industry's entry into space exploration, despite a lack of significant money and resources.

Peter likes to say, "The best way to predict the future is to create it yourself." To that, we'd like to add, "The best way to experience success is to be committed to your passion."

In Peter's latest best-seller, *Bold: How to Go Big, Create Wealth and Impact the World* (co-written with Steven Cotler), he discusses at length the importance of having an MTP (Massively Transformational Purpose) – which is the equivalent of being Mission-Driven in our book. We asked him to speak a little bit more about his own personal MTP and how it spurred him on:

I grew up inspired by the Apollo program and by Star Trek. My heart and soul really connected with that, and I feel very lucky to have had that inspiration. However, I grew up in a family that was very much a medical family and urged me to become a doctor. I remember one day telling my mom I wanted to be astronaut and her response was, "That's nice son, but I think you need to be a doctor." She said it in a very caring way, and I ended up pursuing medicine to make my family happy - but also, because I realized if I wasn't a fighter pilot, the next career that had the highest acceptance rate in the astronaut core was a physician. So I rationalized that and went that route.

But the passion of wanting to go into space never left me. When I went through MIT, when I went to Harvard Medical School, I got to meet a lot of astronauts, and I realized after some time that my chances of becoming one were relatively low because of the acceptance rate. Even if I did get accepted, did I really want a career as a government employee? I'd only get a chance to fly once or twice in my career, and I'd have to do what I was told. That wasn't what I wanted for myself. I ended up channeling that frustration into building a series of entrepreneurial efforts in the space arena and, finally, starting the XPRIZE foundation.

For me, space was my guiding star, it inspired me, it woke me up in the morning, it ultimately drove me to start a dozen space companies. My mission and purpose in life has been to open the space frontier and make it accessible to humanity. I've added to that mission and purpose.

In 1995, Peter founded the X Prize Foundation, which offered a $10 million prize for the first entrepreneurs who could successfully launch a private aircraft into space. Here, he discusses how he analyzed the incentive competition that motivated Charles Lindbergh to perform the first solo flight across the Atlantic, a contest that announced it would award the winner $25,000 – and how he realized that he could put the principles of that early 20th Century competition to work nearly a century later.

As I read Lindbergh's story, I made notes in the margin. I was amazed by how much money the teams were spending to win $25,000, some as much as $100,000. I remember totaling it up at the end, and being astonished that it was nearly $400,000 or 16 times the prize purse. Equally incredible was the fact that Lindbergh appeared to be the least qualified guy to win the competition given his short flying career at the time. I was fascinated by the idea that by offering up an incentive competition, a winner was automatically selected and financially rewarded.

I thought about that prize and its implications. A $25,000 purse commanded $400,000 in team expenditures and ultimately gave birth to today's multi-hundred billion-dollar aviation industry. And, as I finished reading Lindbergh's book, I started thinking about a prize to promote spaceflight and wrote down in the margin, "XPRIZE???"

My thinking at the time was that perhaps a prize could be used to develop private spaceships for the rest of us. I had long since given up on the idea that I would actually travel to space as a government astronaut. But...if I could create a prize to encourage the creation of a new generation of private spaceships, perhaps that would be my ticket to space. Since I had no idea who would be my prize sponsor, I used "x" as a place holder, and thus the origin of the name XPRIZE.

A few months later I wrote up my XPRIZE idea. I then wrote an article that appeared in National Space Society magazine and was invited to give testimony in Congress about it. The year was 1994. It was during this testimony that I first met Doug King, who was about to become president of the St. Louis Science Center. One evening, over dinner, we started discussing the XPRIZE; Doug said, "You have to come to St. Louis. St. Louis is where you'll find the funds to support this vision."

Once the fourth largest city in the United States, St. Louis had descended to number 40, and was eager to regain its reputation as an aerospace leader. So, with my good friend and partner Gregg Maryniak, I traveled to St. Louis and met the one person that Doug believed could raise the capital, Alfred Kerth, who was one of the great thinkers and promoters of St. Louis. In my first meeting with him he got so excited he stood up and shouted: "I get it. I get it. Let's make this happen."

We met that evening at the Racquet Club for scotch and he laid out his vision. We would create the NEW Spirit of St. Louis organization that would follow in the footsteps of the original. The New Spirit of St. Louis (or NSSL) would be a group of 100 St. Louisans who contribute $25,000 each to provide the seed capital to launch XPRIZE.

On March 4th of 1996, we held another meeting at the Racquet Club, at the same table where Lindbergh himself had raised his original $20,000. That evening we raised about $500,000 from twenty St. Louisans who pledged to join NSSL. About two months later, on May 18th, we used that seed funding to boldly announce the $10 million prize competition - albeit without actually having the $10 million in place!

That day, hundreds of press outlets reported on the story and gave credibility to my idea. People got it; people believed it and it was a brilliant launch. But the hard work was just beginning - the work to fund not only the $10 million purse, but also the operation of the foundation itself. As bullish as I was, pitch after pitch failed to turn up a title sponsor. I presented to well over 150 CEOs, CMOs and philanthropists, everyone from Fred Smith of FedEx to Richard Branson of the Virgin Group, but the audacity of the prize and the chance that someone could die in the attempt, stalled our search for a sponsor.

The New Spirit of St. Louis Organization added members slowly $25,000 at a time and it was those funds that allowed us to continue operations. These funds helped us continue along but ultimately were not enough to fund the purse. It was then that two friends of mine told me about the idea of a 'hole-in-one insurance policy', the notion that one could buy an insurance policy to underwrite the prize.

Here is the way it worked.

We had to set an end date to the competition. We selected December 31st, 2004. We would buy an insurance policy and pay a multimillion dollar premium. If someone were to win the prize by making the two flights to space within two weeks before that deadline, then the insurance policy would pay the ten million dollars. If no one pulled it off, then the insurance company would keep the premiums. We were basically placing a large Las Vegas bet.

Of course, the insurance company would also be betting that the efforts of Diamandis and his supporters would come to nothing – and that nobody would come knocking on their door to actually collect the $10 million prize. So the insurance company did the necessary legwork to assure themselves that no one would succeed at the XPRIZE mission.

The insurance underwriter hired a consultant to evaluate all the teams registered for the competition. They approached companies like Orbital Sciences, Lockheed and Boeing only to verify that they did not intend to compete. The big players were somewhat dismissive of the idea that a start-up entrepreneur could build a private spaceship and fly to space.

Luckily the insurance underwriter took the bet. All I had to do now was come up with a three-million-dollar premium payment. The problem was that I didn't have three million. What I did instead was negotiate with the insurance company a series of progressive payments. The XPRIZE foundation would make a $50,000 payment every month for a year, and then make a $2.6 million balloon payment at the end of that year. The insurance underwriter was effectively giving us runway to raise the funds. They didn't feel they had anything to lose - their expectation was that they would take our money and never have to pay anything out.

The first couple of $50,000 payments we made from funds we had raised. I made the next payment personally - and then we were out of money. Every month for the rest of that year-long period, Gregg and I would need to go and raise the money. It was not an easy task. I remember many Monday mornings knowing that I only had five days left to raise $50,000 or the competition was over.

Of course, the biggest challenge was being able to manage that $2.6 million due at the end of the year. If we had so much trouble raising $50,000, how would we manage an amount 52 times as large?

It was at this point that I met my guardian angel, who came to me in the form of a magazine article. I was in my Santa Monica apartment on a Saturday afternoon, catching up on some reading when I flipped through a copy of a Fortune magazine issue featuring the "Wealthiest Women under 40." One of those women was named Anousheh Ansari and as I read her write-up, I stopped dead in my tracks. I read it over and over again in disbelief.

"It is my dream to fly on a sub-orbital flight into space," Ms. Ansari was quoted as saying.

Yes, Anousheh, like me, had grown up watching Star Trek *and dreaming of becoming a space explorer. As I read further I learned that Anousheh, her husband Hamid, and brother-in-law Amir Ansari had just sold their third company called Telecom Technologies to Sonus Networks for over a billion dollars. That was when I knew I had found our sponsor.*

We flew down to Dallas to meet Anousheh, Hamid and Amir. We presented the XPRIZE vision and expressed our great desire to have them underwrite the purse and the operations of our first prize. According to Anousheh, they were sold within the first 10 minutes. I waited two days to hear from Hamid who called to say yes, that they would do it, that they would fund the operations and fund the remaining insurance payments. Shortly thereafter we announced the purse had been fully funded, and was now being re-named the Ansari XPRIZE, named in their honor.

Now, the only question was, could anybody win this before the December 31st, 2004 deadline?

Of course, there was still a major piece of red tape that Diamandis had to cut through – and the way he accomplished that impressive feat was surprisingly easy. But only because, once again, someone had responded to the power of his mission and wanted to be a part of helping it come to fruition.

In 2003, a year before the prize was to be awarded, in a meeting with Marion Blakey, the FAA administrator, and Patti Smith the associate administrator, I explained how the current FAA rules did not allow for private spaceflight. In order for the competition to be won in the U.S., the rules would have to changed, or teams would need to fly from outside U.S. territories. In her southern drawl the Administrator responded with, "Well then, we'll just have to change the rules, won't we?" True to her word she worked with Patti Smith to write regulations that ultimately allowed for private spaceflight to blossom.

The XPRIZE was to be collected only after two spaceflights had been accomplished – and the deadline was coming up fast. It wasn't until six months before the time would be up, on June 21st, 2004, that the first space flight was attempted. As it wasn't carrying a full load of three passengers, it didn't count as one of the actual flights required to win the prize, but it proved to be an invaluable and successful trial run.

The first official qualifying flight finally came three months later on September 29th – and the date for the second and final qualifying flight was set for October 4th, the anniversary of the USSR's launch of Sputnik, the first satellite ever to fly into space launched in 1957.

It's hard to fathom how much work went into reaching the October 4th 2004 milestone. That day has been, and always will be, a special day for me. I remember leaving my Santa Monica apartment at 2:00 AM and driving 2 hours out to the Mojave Desert to meet up with my team. Through the night tens of thousands of people descended from around the world to be there for the historic event. With me that day were my mom and dad, my soon-to-be wife, Kristen and all of my closest friends. What I remember most vividly besides the ocean of people who had gathered, was the lineup of close to one hundred satellite news trucks camped out to watch and see whether Burt Rutan and Paul Allen could win the $10 million Ansari XPRIZE.

In the pre-dawn hours, the carrier airplane WhiteKnightOne was being fueled and SpaceShipOne was being readied. The pilot on this X2 flight was Navy fighter pilot and SpaceShipOne test pilot Brian Binnie. Brian would go on to become our Charles Lindbergh. A tall, thin man with a generous attitude and a strong supporter of XPRIZE over the years, we could imagine no one better to carry the torch of commercial space on that day.

Just after sunrise, WhiteKnightOne's twin Williams FJ44 jet engines carried SpaceShipOne from the Earth's surface on an hour-long ascent to 60,000 feet. Our high-magnification TV cameras watched from the ground and broadcast the image to both the TV stations and large Jumbotron screens for the crowd to see. Edwards Air Force Base, a mere 50 miles away, watched the spaceship's flight on its radar, helping us measure its exact altitude to determine if we had a winner.

It was a magical moment when Brian's voice boomed out over the loudspeakers "Release, release, release." Seconds later SpaceShipOne was released from WhiteKnightOne, then a few seconds later its hybrid engine ignited and Brian was thrown back into his chair as multiple Gs hurled the ship upwards towards space. Brian flew a picture perfect flight. The vehicle not only exceeded the 100 kilometers required to win the $10 million but shattered the X15 altitude record set some 40 years earlier.

The winning of the XPRIZE was, of course, a pivotal point both in the advancement of Diamandis' mission as well as its ultimate expansion. The event ended up bringing many important and influential people into his orbit, people who were energized by his ambitions and, even more importantly, his ability to transform those ambitions into reality.

Another vivid October 4th memory was having the XPRIZE capture the coveted Google Doodle real estate. On the Google homepage, soon after the winning flight was completed, was an image of SpaceShipOne flying over the Google logo, next to it a small flying saucer with two green aliens observing the flight. That Google Doodle later lead to my addressing a room full of 4,000 Googlers at the Googleplex on the Ansari XPRIZE, and a subsequent lunch with Larry Page, Google co-founder (then co-President and now CEO). During that lunch I presented an impromptu invitation for him to join the XPRIZE Board of Trustees (which he happily accepted).

His participation, along with Sergey Brin, Eric Schmidt, Wendy Schmidt, Elon Musk, Jim Gianopulos, Arianna Huffington, James Cameron and other notable figures who subsequently joined the XPRIZE Board of Trustees breathed new life (and capital) into XPRIZE, fueling our commitment to use prizes to take on the world's grand challenges and create large-scale incentive competitions where market failures existed.

What motivates these kinds of prominent business leaders and influencers to work with Diamandis and join in his mission? He sums it up in one word.

Passion.

I think having my true passion shine through when I'm on the stage, or when I'm communicating, brings people to me. It's about speaking from my heart. It's being authentic in what I truly believe and having that come through. Whenever I don't...it fails. Whenever I do, people gravitate towards it.

It's that we have common aspirations, passions and interests to do big things in life. Google co-founder Larry Page once said something to the effect of, "I have a simple metric, a question I use now that says, "Are you working on something that can change the world, yes or no." It's the experience of most successful people in the world that, when you revolutionize one industry, you're not satisfied ever again with incremental change, you're looking to do big and bold things in life. So you're attracted to people who do equally big and bold things.

As Diamandis said earlier, his initial space mission has led him to embrace other important pursuits in which technology has the potential to solve pressing world problems. The more he can do to make that happen, the more he will do.

It was only after I had some success with space that I expanded my mission beyond that. I went into a larger orbit, if you would, beyond just the grand challenge of space and into even bigger challenges. If you can take on private space flight, you can take on a lot of other seemingly-impossible goals. I don't think it's the case that you have to have only one mission in your life, I think it's important to have something that you build on and grow with.

We are entering a point in history where entrepreneurs are now capable of doing what only the largest companies and governments could do before. Forty years ago, only a government could build a spaceship. Today, a small team of 30 engineers powered by exponential technologies can do it. In the same way I believe that there is no problem that cannot be solved, that entrepreneurs powered by technology can take on any challenge and find a solution, I believe that we've entered a day and age where we can stop complaining about problems and start solving them. That's how you can impact the lives of a billion people.

But finding that initial MTP (Massively Transformational Purpose) is something that I think is ultimately one of the most important first steps any entrepreneur, any CEO needs to take on. Whenever I talk to people now, I say, "Do you know what you would do in life if you didn't have to work, if you had all the time and energy and resources in the world? Do you have a mission? Do you have a purpose in life?" That's one of the most fundamentally important things.

Peter Diamandis doesn't just talk about thinking big and doing big things – he actually finds the ways to turn intangible ideals into reality. By kickstarting the movement towards private entrepreneurs taking on mankind's biggest challenges, he's opened up many more potential pathways to progress than have ever existed before.

So - how can you challenge and change the world? How can you create a mission that will attract the rich and powerful to your side – and engage the imagination of millions?

It's a tall order – but it's also a guaranteed recipe for building your own Road to Success!

About JW

JW Dicks Esq., is a Wall Street Journal Best-Selling Author®, Emmy Award-Winning Producer, publisher, board member, and advisor to organizations such as the XPRIZE, The National Academy of Best-Selling Authors®, and The National Association of Experts, Writers and Speakers®.

JW is the CEO of DNAgency and is a strategic business development consultant to both domestic and international clients. He has been quoted on business and financial topics in national media such as the *USA Today, The Wall Street Journal, Newsweek, Forbes, CNBC.com*, and *Fortune Magazine Small Business*.

Considered a thought leader and curator of information, JW has more than forty-three published business and legal books to his credit and has co-authored with legends like Brian Tracy, Jack Canfield, Tom Hopkins, Dr. Nido Qubein, Dr. Ivan Misner, Dan Kennedy, and Mari Smith. He is the editor and publisher of the *Celebrity Expert Insider*, a monthly newsletter sent to experts worldwide as well as the quarterly magazine, *Global Impact Quarterly*.

JW is called the "Expert to the Experts" and has appeared on business television shows airing on ABC, NBC, CBS, and FOX affiliates around the country and co-produces and syndicates a line of franchised business television show such as: *Success Today, Wall Street Today, Hollywood Live*, and *Profiles of Success*. He has received an Emmy Award as Executive Producer of the film, *Mi Casa Hogar.*

JW and his wife of forty-three years, Linda, have two daughters, three granddaughters, and two Yorkies. He is a sixth generation Floridian and splits his time between his home in Orlando and his beach house on Florida's west coast.

About Nick

An Emmy Award-Winning Director and Producer, Nick Nanton, Esq., is known as the Top Agent to Celebrity Experts around the world for his role in developing and marketing business and professional experts, through personal branding, media, marketing and PR. Nick is recognized as the nation's leading expert on personal branding as *Fast Company Magazine's* Expert Blogger on the subject and lectures regularly on the topic at major universities around the world. His book *Celebrity Branding You®*, while an easy and informative read, has also been used as a text book at the University level.

The CEO and Chief StoryTeller at The Dicks + Nanton Celebrity Branding Agency, an international agency with more than 1800 clients in 33 countries, Nick is an award-winning director, producer and songwriter who has worked on everything from large scale events to television shows with the likes of Steve Forbes, Brian Tracy, Jack Canfield (*The Secret*, Creator of the *Chicken Soup for the Soul* Series), Michael E. Gerber, Tom Hopkins, Dan Kennedy and many more.

Nick is recognized as one of the top thought-leaders in the business world and has co-authored 30 best-selling books alongside Brian Tracy, Jack Canfield, Dan Kennedy, Dr. Ivan Misner (Founder of BNI), Jay Conrad Levinson (Author of the Guerilla Marketing Series), SuperAgent Leigh Steinberg and many others, including the breakthrough hit *Celebrity Branding You!®*

Nick has led the marketing and PR campaigns that have driven more than 1000 authors to Best-Seller status. Nick has been seen in *USA Today, The Wall Street Journal, Newsweek, BusinessWeek, Inc. Magazine, The New York Times, Entrepreneur® Magazine, Forbes, FastCompany.com* and has appeared on ABC, NBC, CBS, and FOX television affiliates around the country, as well as on CNN, FOX News, CNBC, and MSNBC from coast to coast.

Nick is a member of the Florida Bar, holds a JD from the University of Florida Levin College Of Law, as well as a BSBA in Finance from the University of Florida's Warrington College of Business. Nick is a voting member of The National Academy of Recording Arts & Sciences (NARAS, Home to The GRAMMYs), a member of The National Academy of Television Arts & Sciences (Home to the Emmy Awards), co-founder of the National Academy of Best-Selling Authors, a 16-time Telly Award winner, and spends his spare time working with Young Life, Downtown Credo Orlando, Entrepreneurs International and rooting for the Florida Gators with his wife Kristina and their three children, Brock, Bowen and Addison.

Learn more at:
- www.NickNanton.com
- www.CelebrityBrandingAgency.com

CHAPTER 12

SUCCESS: DO IT RIGHT

BY JOSEPH A. CARPENTER,
CARPENTER FINANCIAL SERVICES

It was the early 1970s, a time when children still cherished the wisdom of their elders. While others were playing ball outside, I was the kid who was always around while adults were doing their projects. I loved to watch and learn, and there was something about people taking control of their projects and giving it their all that made me take notice.

So when my grandmother's sister, Aunt Anna, came up to me and said, "Joey, you still want to do that lemonade stand?" I was all in and ready to go. It would be unlike any other that has ever existed—maybe ever—because it had an Italian flair. My stand offered meatballs, homemade pasta, fresh-cut French fries, fried chicken, and, oh yes, lemonade. People came to see, they stayed to buy, and then enjoyed camaraderie while they ate. That was one of my most important early lessons:

1. When you are going to be an entrepreneur, be different and take risks.

From about the time I was five or six, I really liked to do hands-on work. My grandfather, Nanu Tony, was the son of Italian immigrants, and they knew about hard work, doing things right, and overcoming the odds. My grandmother, Nana Gloria, had a similar perspective—she took pride in everything she did with her hands. It was her work.

She used to iron everything, including all of her family's handkerchiefs.

She would iron each one when it was all opened and out flat. Fold it in half and iron again. Fold it in half and iron again. The result was a crisp handkerchief that was presentable for its purpose. It was so perfectly starched it could even stand on its own.

There was no room in her world for doing anything less than perfect. And if you did…well, plan on starting over again.

I watched her spend hours crocheting Afghans for the family. If the start wasn't perfect, you might as well forget about it, she'd tell me. I remember watching her rip apart her handiwork to begin anew—over and over. She'd spotted some tiny imperfection.

Doing something slowly, carefully, and meticulously was a better choice. I remember helping Nanu Tony replace boards on his back porch one hot summer day. He set aside his everyday suit coat and tie and created the tongue and groove planks, spending hours sawing and sanding each board. The other grandkids had long since left to play, but at seven years old, I was transfixed. I wanted to learn more. I stood by, watching the entire process, and must have seen him measure each board twenty different times and saw it down, little by little. But it paid off. When he was ready to slide it into its spot—it was perfect. No need for a do-over.

They taught me that **patience is part of success**. The quickest person in the race isn't always the most successful one. That person who can go at the right pace and gain a wealth of knowledge and wisdom along the way will end up further ahead.

Some people may have found their attention to detail overwhelming, but for me, it was a way of life. It was part of their fabric—and therefore part of me. That was another foundational lesson that I learned in life:

2. It is a waste of time to not give everything you do your best effort.

By the time I was twelve—just to relax—I had taken on the task of cleaning my father's vehicle. It was actually calming to me. I enjoyed taking care of the family car. I took pride in making things look new again. And thoughts came to my mind when I got involved in the process. These thoughts were productive, inspirational, and helped give me a direction of what I might want to do someday.

My father, Sam, was a CPA and his clients took note of how his vehicle was always sparkling and spotless. "Where do you get that detailed?" they'd ask. He'd smile and say, "My son Joey does it." It was the onset of my car detailing business—Joey's Wash & Wax—and while it came about quite by accident, it truly was a family business. Referrals from Dad. Valet service from my brother because I wasn't old enough to drive. And waxing and detailing from me! I felt this great sense of purpose from it all. I was offering a service that other people appreciated and needed.

I realized it right then: I was an entrepreneur. And I loved it. These lessons that I'd learned through being around my grandparents and parents had stuck. I had developed their ethos and a bit of each of their personalities.

And you guessed it, another lesson was under my belt:

3. Perform a service that other people need, do it in a high quality manner—and watch your business grow.

Car detailing helped carry me through college, and I also saw an opportunity to expand. In the early '80s the Pennsylvania Lottery became popular. I decided to open a lottery stand. In the spirit of my experience in "stand" businesses, I decided that to be successful it would take more than just the lottery alone. I added magazines, gobs, pop, cigarettes, candy, Cabbage Patch Kids, and whatever else was in demand at that time or would draw attention from passersby. I watched the stand grow for four or five years successfully before I decided it was time to move on.

My brother Sam suggested that with my business acumen and strong analytical skills, I could have a promising career as a financial advisor. I wasn't afraid of hard work or learning new things. The idea for a new career appealed to me—even though the stakes now were much higher. I had a family with a wife and four children, depending on me. Together, we prayed for direction and guidance.

I approached my new business with the same exacting standards I had learned from my family. Working in numbers requires expertise and precision—the same level of perfection needed to crochet an Afghan or line up tongue-and-groove boards. The drive behind the lemonade stand, the car detailing business, and the lottery stand was focused on a new endeavor. The push to do it right, every time—a push that might bother other people—was part of my DNA.

Being laid back goes against my natural grain. I am so comfortable in who I am and how I help others that I couldn't imagine any other way. I am happy, and I get things done.

Even though I've been recognized consistently as a Premier Advisor—and I'm humbled each time—I still approach every client as my most important. I remember starting out with a single client and have been amazed at how it's grown over the last twenty-six years. But to me, it's not about how big the business has become. I measure my own success by understanding my clients' needs, creating solutions for each of them and their families to realize the education, lifestyle, and the retirement they deserve.

Seeing people as individuals is just like seeing homemade macaroni as an individual noodle.

Stick with me—I assure you that I have a point. My mother, Josephine, and my Nana used to make homemade macaroni. I'm not certain if you've ever seen this process, but it is quite meticulous.

Mix all the ingredients and let the dough rest under the kitchen towel. Roll out the pasta and then wrap it around a wire, roll it again and slide it off. Then you cut it into sections and put a slight curve to it. By now you likely have gotten the "precision" message. It carries over into homemade macaroni, as well. Those macaronis would be lined up in a row like soldiers, ready to march off. Even though each and every macaroni appeared to be the same length, curve, and width, in reality they weren't. Not an easy task. What's the lesson?

4. No two people are exactly the same. Treat them as an individual, each of whom deserves your time, respect, and perfection, just like the homemade macaroni.

The world of finance, the place I'm so blessed to have found my calling, has been incredible for me, as well as my family. Through good intentions, a never-ending desire to learn and give my best, and embracing opportunities, I have helped families discover smart strategies and found real financial solutions tailored to their needs. To me, that's success. Johnstown, PA isn't the largest area, but I'm blessed to call it home. The region's economic struggles make me even more driven in what I do. Everyone—regardless of where they call home or how much they make—deserves top-level financial services.

There are times when I feel like a throwback, a guy who maybe landed in the wrong generation. But I realize that I am where I'm meant to be. The lessons I learned are timeless, my actions based in trying to be the best I can be. All of this stems from the inspired lessons from my parents and grandparents. I see how these life principles have helped me gain the life and opportunities I have today. My wife, Christine, is such a blessing and my children continue to amaze me, as well as my granddaughter. However, my obligation to offer my best extends further than just my immediate family. Through service to others—whether through financial guidance, investment strategies, or mentorship—this calmness comes over me. I feel the connectedness and it is a source of daily inspiration.

TWO FINAL LIFE LESSONS

The two final life lessons—ones I continue to rely on as I go about my work every day—have become so ingrained in my psyche that I call them my mottos. They'll be on my tombstone one day and part of the legacy I hope to leave behind.

These two lessons are built on what I learned as a child. Back in high school, I created this art project and it simply had the word "D.A.D." on it. No one got what it meant besides me. It was an acronym: desire, ambition, and determination. Those three words carried me far, but they won't take anyone all the way. There's more to this story than what we can do on our own. Sheer determination is powerful; combining it with strength outside yourself is far more powerful.

D.A.D. now is **G.O.D.A.D: God, Opportunity, Desire, Ambition, Determination.**

Now, it is always God first. God gives you the 'O'—opportunity—but you have to be tuned in enough to see it. You still must have the desire to follow through with the opportunities. You have to keep the ambition and the determination, because it's not going to be easy.

By putting God first, I look to him as the guide to help me with my desires, ambitions, and determinations. This is the foundation of everything that has become so meaningful in my life, including my family and career. Adding those letters to the motto made all the difference.

Being a Christian has been the single most impactful shift in my life. Intertwining my goals and life with God—the one who gave it to us— has given me so much clarity and purpose. I've always seen the path, and it is a lot easier to walk because of my relationship with him. Have I ever tripped? Of course. We all have, and that's part of the journey. But when we trip, we get back up. Then...we learn our lesson, if we're open to learning. Life is bigger than "just us."

It's also smaller than just us. There is no magic bullet to success. Success is an accumulation of actions. *Success is doing 100 little things right, each and every day.*

That's my other guiding light—one I learned from my parents and grandparents, and it's the final lesson I want to share with you. Remember the handkerchiefs, the boards, the 12-year-old making every inch of a car spotless. In business and in life, every single action has an impact. Stay positive. Stay patient. Stay committed. Always be kind to everyone you meet. Focus on doing what generates value and be genuine while doing so. When you do what is right and do it with the best of your ability with the right intentions, I can guarantee you good things will happen.

DO ONE THING, DO IT RIGHT !

About Joe

For more than 26 years, Joe has advised clients in the Greater Johnstown, PA area. Carpenter Financial Services began with Joe's father, Samuel C. Carpenter, over 60 years ago when he established the business as a Tax and Accounting firm. When Joe and his brothers began working at the family business, they quickly realized that there was a lack of information for clients who were looking for an entire wealth management experience. This gap caused clients to seek advice from multiple professionals and was a confusing process for all involved. To better serve our clients, Joe and his family expanded Carpenter Financial Services into the practice we have today as a wealth management company that offers customized comprehensive financial services.

Joe's mission is to help his clients reach their retirement goals using his business acumen as a Chartered Retirement Planning Counselor, Certified Senior Advisor and Certified Fund Specialist. Joe is a Premier Advisor through H.D. Vest, one of the top broker/dealers in the nation, and has received the H.D. Vest Excellence Award for multiple years. This honor recognizes the top 75 advisors in the nation based on annual production who exhibit professionalism, leadership and commitment to their clients. Met Life Premier Partners Club has honored Joe and his team with many service awards for the quality and client satisfaction prevalent at Carpenter Financial Services. Joe has also been recognized by the Prudential Masters Council for commitment to retirement income solutions and Scudder Executive Council for outstanding client service. Locally, Carpenter Financial Services has repeatedly been voted Simply the Best Financial Firm for Greater Johnstown.

Keeping the family traditions alive, Joe still keeps current on tax laws through continuing education and extensive research so he may accurately advise his clients with complete financial solutions. Joe was selected to be a mentor to other financial advisors throughout the United States and shares his knowledge and expertise with next generation of financial advisors. He has also shared his understanding of the financial world with a number of publications, including *Accounting Technology, National Underwriter Life & Health,* and *Practical Accountant,* as well as the local Johnstown *Tribune-Democrat.*

Joe and his wife Christine reside in Johnstown, PA and have four children; Joe Jr., Lauren, Alyse, Christiana and one granddaughter, Mira. In his spare time, he enjoys spending time with family, traveling, skiing, ice skating, and reading.

CHAPTER 13

TEAM POWER: USING STRENGTHS TO GAIN SUCCESS IN REAL ESTATE

BY JONATHAN LAHEY,
BROKER/OWNER OF RE/MAX FINE LIVING

In Real Estate, just like in life, you must have the right attitude and mindset to create distinction.

My story is not dissimilar to many out there that want to begin a career in Real Estate. I started off slowly, working another job at the same time. Truthfully, the main reason I even got there was because since I was in my early twenties I had a goal to become an investor. I achieved that, buying many properties to either rent or renovate and sell again. Through these experiences, I gained a wealth of knowledge. **I had suddenly become the guy who people asked their real estate questions to.** That's when I thought, hey, maybe I am not meant to be in IT only; perhaps I also have a home in Real Estate.

In 2005, I earned my real estate license and decided to focus on being a Listing Agent. Meeting people and helping them fulfill their needs appealed to me, and like many new Realtors, I longed to make a difference…and to make it big. Before I knew it, 2010 came along and I was doing "okay," but I definitely hadn't made it big.

I'm a fairly attuned guy and I instantly started to think about why I hadn't grown more successful and was only able to manage 4 or 5 closings per year. The answer: I wasn't committed. Did I want to commit? Every thought and instinct in me knew that I did. That's when I came up with a plan, and through less challenging work than one might think, my tides shifted. **My business grew at an amazing pace, enough that I no longer had to work in IT, as well.** I was 100% in—a committed Realtor.

The Three Big Questions that Guided Me

Anyone can plot a course with a map or compass; but without a sense of who you are, you will never know if you're already home.
~ Shannon L. Alder

The Real Estate industry is just as much about human connections as it is about paperwork and extensive knowledge about how to structure a deal that works and closes. There were three questions that I really took to heart when I began my pursuit to go from single digit closings per year to something substantially more.

1. **I asked: "What is my why?"**
   If we don't know "why" we are doing what we are, how can we really commit to giving it our best. Many Realtors, myself included, start out with the most basic "why" answered—the need to survive. But it takes more than that to go to the next stage. For me, the "why" was that the feelings that I received when I helped other people achieve their goals with investment properties or home ownership—it was incredible. Seeing their success helped to inspire my success.

2. **I asked: "What do I know?"**
   Our "what" is our goal and that is what changes everything, because goals require action. I began to visualize what my plan would be, how I would get there, and exactly what it would look and feel like. It took life inside of me and through that, my goals were put into place and my process of achieving them began.

3. **I asked: "Who is knowledgeable about what I want to achieve?"**
   There will always be someone who has experienced success than can help you to achieve the same thing. That's why I am such a firm believer in finding mentors and coaches to help you bring out

the best potential you have. For me, men such as Craig Proctor and Todd Walters have had a significant impact, because they have experienced the success that I have wanted to see in my life. And through their mentorship, I was able to go from just a handful of transactions in a given year to 110+. That was in just the first few years after I committed to giving Real Estate my best efforts.

By implementing what my mentors taught me my business grew exponentially. Seeing how effective it was created this amazing shift within me and I began seeing different outcomes were possible for all Realtors who wanted to commit to the industry, but weren't quite sure how to do so in the proper manner. *It's an old fashioned concept I connected with, but it delivers results that appeal to the modern world.* It's called "Team Work".

Team Work Lifts Up the Real Estate Industry

Individual commitment to a group effort—that is what makes a team work, a company work, a society work, a civilization work.
~ Vince Lombardi

I had a specific vision to be the owner/broker of my own Real Estate company, which is what I have achieved with Re/Max Fine Living today. As I'd evaluated what could help me take that next, rather significant, step, I looked around me. There were all these really gifted Realtors, each loving different aspects of the industry, and they were doing "okay." Yes, I remembered that quite well, but I wanted them to be doing great.

I knew my passion—networking. Everything about meeting people, inspiring them to pursue their Real Estate ambitions as either a Realtor or a buyer/seller resonates deeply within me. It's the human side of the industry and it will always have to be a part of it in some way. Sure, consumers can find out more things online about a property than they ever could before, but ultimately they are going to need someone to guide them through the process. Why can't that someone be an actual team—a devoted, intelligent team?

Personally, I am never overly enthusiastic about all the paperwork that comes with Real Estate transactions. I get its necessity, of course, but I know that it is not my strength. However, it is other peoples' strength in the industry. Some love the organization that comes with doing paperwork, keeping track of all the specifics of a transactions, and other aspects of it. If you're the guy like me, realizing that it's beneficial to add someone to your Real Estate team who excels in paperwork is not only smart, but exciting. It's a winning idea:

Realtors who use their strengths deliver better customer satisfaction and find more personal fulfillment.

Today, my team has a motto: *We Have Happy Clients.* This is what we need to remember day in and day out. It reminds us of why we are here and is a statement that portrays a big part of my core values and also the core values of my team, too.

The phrase "happy clients" is one that is over-used and under-accomplished, in my opinion. Everyone likes to say they go out of their way to make clients happy, but can they really prove it? My team makes sure we are demonstrating how absolutely sincere we are with this statement and the proof is in:

- **60% of our business is referrals and repeat clients.**
  This is the fruit of our commitment and our team focus on our core values leads to better experiences for our clients—they are important to not just one of us, but to each and every one of us.

- **There are no doubts in our clients' minds that we are taking care of them.**
  Real Estate transactions can be easy, but they can also be very complex, depending on what's involved. Or…something can happen at the last minute. The response becomes everything. Very recently, we had a transaction where we were representing the seller. The buyer thought they were getting a furniture item in transaction and brought it up at closing, but that had never been part of the deal—only an assumption the buyer somehow came up with. Now, this deal had to close, as the seller had a new property to buy. We resolved it with some logical thinking, which was giving a slight reduction in our commission to help the buyer feel they were being taken care of (who were not our clients) and the seller saw that we were vested in their outcome. I don't recommend that you always give commissions away—as they are hard earned—but I can tell

you this with all certainty:

It is much more affordable to keep current clients than to try and connect with potential new clients.

- **Our clients are usually pretty excited to see us again—just because.**
  When you spend 3-4 months with clients working on their transaction you become close. You learn about their families, know about their careers, and a variety of other things. You're so happy for them and excited for them to close on their transaction, and they do. Then…you miss them because you realize that they've become an attachment of your family. My team does a few different things to keep that connection intact and let our clients know that they are still appreciated and in our hearts. We have a few different newsletters for them, one monthly and a different quarterly one, but more than that, we have a party. In specific, a *Friends and Family Appreciation Party*.

These events are fun and wonderful and everyone is invited. Our past clients come to these, as glad to catch up with us as we are to see how they are doing. We notice how the kids grow the way friends might who don't see them often. It's nice, but what makes it even more unique is how we encourage those few people to attend that didn't necessary believe their transaction met their expectations. We want them to know that they are equally important to us and that they have access to an abundance of people who did have a great experience. What do most agents do? They sweep "those clients" under the rug. That's just not us, because it doesn't align with our core values.

Welcome to Your New Home

You can have everything in life you want, if you will just help enough other people get what they want.
~ Zig Ziglar

Today, I see no better way in my life to serve others than by extending an invitation to those Realtors who are ready to take a step forward toward their success in this industry that has been so amazing for me. There is so much potential out there for so many Realtors, yet they are stuck for one reason or another. Maybe they know why, maybe they do not. I want to help them figure this out. It's time for me to be the mentor that helps someone else out.

Being a mentor is an honor, of course, but it is also a big responsibility. You have an ethical obligation to do your best and your heart should guide you to do even better. Because as Zig Ziglar suggests—through helping others we can all achieve what we want in life.

Realtors who have a desire to stand apart amongst the large number of Realtors that are out there are finding that my team is a team they can rally around. There are some things that are expected from them, of course, which are:

- They understand that their word is everything. Without that, what do you have, really?
- They are committed to their service to others, knowing that rewards will come from providing the best services possible.

When a Realtor feels "maxed out at their current place" it makes sense to find someplace new where there is no brick wall in front of you and there is a group of vested, successful Realtors who want you to succeed too! This is where my role as mentor really takes form. The steps are eye-opening, as well as transformational.

1. We sit down together and dissect their business.
Through thoughtful conversation and success-based solutions, we determine what they are currently doing that makes them money. From there, we find a pathway to improve on that by understanding where it comes from and what it entails.

2. Take what already works from good to great.
It's seldom a matter of committing more time to the parts of the business that are not your strengths if you want to go from good to great. Usually, it's evaluating how to take what does work wonderfully for you and increase on that. For example: if your last ten closing were referrals, how do you expand on that? There are ways to become more strategic about every step you decide to take toward your success.

Teamwork builds camaraderie, which is what leads to sustainability and long-term success that benefits everyone.

As Re/Max Fine Living expands and stands apart in our competitive Real Estate market, we grow more excited about our team approach to success. When everyone is benefiting you know that you've created something that is aligned with a genuinely good purpose.

About Jonathan

Jonathan Lahey is the CEO and Team Leader of the award-winning real estate team, The Lahey Group, and the Owner of RE/MAX Fine Living, located in Rockville, MD. Since choosing to focus on real estate, Jonathan has consistently finished in the top 1% in the nation as a realtor selling over 100 homes per year.

In rising to the top of his field, Jonathan Lahey has become a national resource for many others in the real estate industry. He's been the featured speaker at national real estate conferences, has been interviewed on several coaching calls, and has appeared on marketing panels alongside other top real estate producers in North America.

Jonathan is a member RE/MAX's The Chairman's Club and The Diamond Club, as well as the RE/MAX Hall of Fame. Jonathan has also received the Coveted Quantum Leap Award for Marketing Excellence for having made the most significant gains and the Million Dollar Award, awarded to those agents who grossed over One Million Dollars in commission in one calendar year.

When Jonathan is not out selling homes, Jonathan focuses on teaching and coaching other real estate agents make a quantum leap in their real estate business. Jonathan was a featured guest on *Success Today* which will be airing on FOX, CBS, ABC, and NBC affiliates across the country this Spring.

CHAPTER 14

WHEN COLLEGE IS NOT AN OPTION: 10 STRATEGY TIPS FOR HIGH SCHOOL STUDENTS TO FIND SUCCESS

BY CHANDRA WORTHINGTON

The very first awful childhood memory I have is the one of a man taking a fork that I had given him and dragging it down one side of a woman's face. Scarring her for life. That memory has always stuck with me since I was about five years old. I remember them both yelling at me. One said get a knife and the other said to bring a spoon. I was confused and didn't know what to do. I thought about it for what seemed like an eternity and decided instead to get a fork.

Childhood and domestic abuse, molestation, low self-esteem, lack of family support, lack of money, brokenness, arrested, no direction, no friends, shyness, people walking over me, bullying, racism, fights, peer pressure, suicidal, loneliness and many hurtful situations like these is what I experienced before graduating from high school. Most people call these roadblocks, stumbling blocks, obstacles, life-ending problems, humps, etc. I simply call them tests. I could have committed various crimes in an effort to be seen and heard, but I didn't. It just wasn't in me to indulge in revenge. At least not in a negative way. You know the saying, let your haters be your motivators.

Why am I telling you this? Because I believe me getting through those tests helped to prepare me for the obstacles I would encounter later on my journey. Believing in God, karma and forgiveness is how I managed to successfully pass my tests. Now, I'm not perfect and no I haven't always turned the other cheek.

So in everything, do unto others as you would have them do unto you.

I started working when I was fourteen years old by cleaning other people's homes. By the next summer, I was working in the tobacco fields and tobacco warehouses. I didn't start working because I wanted to, but because I had to. By the time I was sixteen, I was purchasing my own school clothes as well as my sister's. I worked an assortment of rat race jobs, such as a hotel maid, newspaper delivery girl, restaurant cashier, cleaning crew member, hammock maker, dishwasher, waitress, t-shirt screen printer, assembly line worker and many more. Now many of these jobs don't exist today and although most of us wouldn't consider these opportunities, each job that I got, I considered a blessing. I worked hard at each and always gave my best. By the time I was 24, I had three children to support.

With the help of a person whom I think was an Angel sent by God, I entered college at the age of 25, graduating three years later with a Bachelor in Computer Science and a minor in Accounting. Programming is what I learned, but Technical Support is where I began my journey in Corporate America and entered a new era of a different kind of rat race. Now I come from a dysfunctional family, like so many others. So I never had the advice of anyone on what to do to get ahead. I just knew to work hard.

When I graduated I started earning $11 an hour. I came out of school with about $60,000 in student loans. (Stay with me here.) So with three children, life necessities such as rent, food, gas, clothes, housing, insurance and just regular life emergencies, maintenance on your car, flat tire, oil changes, daycare, school supplies, clothes, etc. It becomes really hard to see how you are going to pay on a student loan by only making $11 an hour. I still believed in working hard and learning in order to advance, but soon realized that moving up meant continued struggle! I had no idea the amount of struggle or type of struggle I was headed for. For the average Black, we are already fighting an uphill battle. And not all of the struggle is the fault of others. Sometimes we as Blacks are not willing to help one another. I guess when I moved to Atlanta, Georgia from Greenville, North Carolina I thought things would be different. I mean there were so many people and everyone I ran into always said if I needed anything they would help. But being the naïve person that I was, I realized a lot later that most of that was polite talk. I simply couldn't tell the difference between the fake and the real. I just knew to keep working. But to get the decent wage increases I had to change jobs frequently. The IT world is very competitive, but it is even more competitive for Blacks. Most of the time, I am the only representation of my color in a meeting or on a project.

Back then most of the promotions were based on seniority. So I had to wait until a person was promoted, quit or died. Do you know how long waiting takes???? Waiting takes a very long time and I was so impatient. In the meantime, I'm still trying to find a way to make the money that I believe that I'm entitled. I never wanted to be anyone's manager. It's my opinion that managers judge. And I'm not a judgmental type of person. But the most eye-opening thing that I learned is that relationships are what get you to the money in Corporate America. Everything is based on who you know and not what you know. I needed to get to know someone, but being shy and not having the time to stay after work and drink socially, my chances for advancing were looking like slim to none.

So while Corporate America was taking its sweet time in deciding if I was worthy of promotions, I tried outside of Corporate to earn extra money. I tried working with companies like Primerica, Avon, Mary Kay, etc. I tried starting from scratch designing and printing t-shirts, resume design, tech support, rebuilding old computers, flea market, smoothie/coffee stand, writing a fiction book (never finished), etc. Life just kept catching up… Corporate America was working the heck out of me. I was now working more hours a week and only getting paid for forty and I had thrown my back out from lifting huge dinosaur computers. But I kept working hard. Kept coming in early and working late at night at home – trying to find what I could to make extra money.

Eventually I found success in Project Management. I got into the field after researching it on the Internet. I didn't want to manage other people, so the normal management route was not going to work for me. But I needed to increase my income and challenge myself with something new. I started in the field in 2004 after being laid off for seven months. I only applied for positions pertaining to project management and I did that because I felt if I took a position in LAN/WAN or Network Engineering I would be on the waiting list for advancement for the rest of my life. Project Management allowed me to grow and push my boundaries for excellence. It fit my personality and I love the field, but I must admit it, like most jobs, this field definitely comes with challenges. But in the end, the pros outweigh the cons.

What I believe helped me to become successful, that may also help you are the following ten strategy tips:

Tip 1: Channel Your Vision and Define Your Scope

See your vision. Write your vision. Scope out the details of the what, where and how of your vision and when it will come to fruition. You cannot let any test or obstacle no matter the size or number keep you from your dream. You have to move forward and if you keep looking behind you, you won't be able to pay attention to what is going on in front of you.

Tip 2: Identify Your Objectives

Manage your vision by creating goals and setting dates to each. Your vision is too large to try to implement in one piece. So chunk it down into smaller pieces. Keep the list short. The longer the list, the longer it will take to achieve and you will quickly lose focus.

Tip 3: Don't Get Caught Up in the System

Sometimes we have to work a regular job in order to make our visions come true. So don't get caught up in the current work system and believe you can work at one company until you retire. Working for a company these days does not mean you will have longevity. Companies are laying off and overworking those who remain behind, creating low morale and stressful work environments. Instead go into the workforce with a goal in mind of gaining experience for the passion in which you want to make a living at.

Tip 4: Contract You

Do not work as a permanent employee unless you absolutely must. When working as a perm employee, often times the pay will be low, overtime is expected (unpaid) and politics get in the way. In the end you become stressed and this prevents you from making progress. As a contractor (no loyalty is needed because you're ignored and most internal topics are not discussed around you). This makes it so much easier to come in and do your job. As a contractor you earn more money and get paid for every hour worked. Negotiate for the highest rate, as in these days, companies are doing even crazier things to ensure board members will get paid high dividends. Such as making it mandatory for contractors to take time off with no pay and reducing the agreed-upon hourly rate by as much as 10% in the midst of your contract – and your consent is not needed.

Tip 5: Keep Your Business Your Business

Keep your ideas to yourself – for lots of reasons, but mainly because you don't want people to deter you from the path you are walking. Whatever your vision is, don't share it with others unless you need help in getting it completed. This is where you find out who your real friends are and those who are not. Friends support even if they cannot be of assistance.

Tip 6: Expand Your Vision into Multiple Streams of Income

Identify opportunities where you have multiple streams of income. When I say multiple streams of income, I do not mean working two nine-to-five jobs. You need to identify products that can create cash flow without you having to trade your time for a dollar. When working for an employer, regardless of whether it is as a permanent employee or contractor, you have to be available to that company for those hours and that limits the amount of income you can earn.

Tip 7: Embrace Loss & Failure

When doing something new it creates a certain level of risk with the possibility of loss. Loss comes in many different forms, i.e., friends, money, job, time, etc. Learn to accept risk and be ok that at times you may fail or others may fail you. The sooner you embrace the loss, the quicker you can continue down your path. I experienced a two-year loss of income in 2008. The best lesson I learned during this time was to use the time to define what else I could do well and to save better because nothing is forever. But most importantly, I realized I had to learn to create opportunities for myself and not depend on a company to look out for my best interest.

Tip 8: Focus on Careers Where Skills are Interchangeable

There are a few jobs out there that do not require a college degree and still pay very well. Project Management is one of those fields. It has an interchangeable set of skills, so that it's used in almost all career choices. You can break into fields like this by starting off at the lowest position and working your way up. In this case from Project Coordinator to Project Manager.

Tip 9: Keep Yourself Motivated

No one can motivate you, but you. If you feel like you don't have the strength to keep moving, call upon God or your preference of faith. Pray and believe that what is for you is for you and that no weapon formed against you shall prosper.

Tip 10: Ask for Advice

Let go of your pride and ask for help when needed. Associate yourself with people who are positive and be open to receiving help from strangers. You never know when an angel is being sent your way.

The most important lesson that I learned during my journey is that many of the people I worked with or encountered are getting paid high salaries and do not have a college degree, and I wondered why did I get one and get into debt, if I had to work harder than others who had less credentials and experience. Some of them are in executive management positions and never had any professional training or higher education learning. I say this to you so that you know that you do not have to have a college degree to get a high-paying position. You just need to shift your focus and start paving your road to success while you are still in high school. Your high school should be focused on getting you educated in fields that pay high salaries, but where the skills are universal. The skills you need to learn will need to be able to be utilized in more than one field.

There will be many tests in which you will have to face throughout your life. You don't have to pass them with flying colors, but you do have to pass them.

Most importantly, no matter the number of tests, you must believe in yourself.

If you don't, no one else will.

About Chandra

Atlanta-based Chandra Worthington currently serves as Founder and CEO of the project management consulting firm In the Box Management Solutions and Designs, LLC (MSD).

MSD offers an online program to assist new project managers in producing deliverables equivalent to those who have been in the field for several years. Her company also partners with high school systems to offer project management training programs to help decrease the number of students entering into low paying wage jobs, focusing specifically on those not college bound. Chandra has always enjoyed helping others and she and her family make it a tradition to help those in need as often as possible. Growing up, one of her dreams was to find a way to help the homeless and, with that being the end goal, she created a solution that will help in reducing the number of people who may become homeless due to unfortunate circumstances.

With four children of her own, Chandra realized that not every child will attend college and each child learns at his/her own pace. When a student chooses not to attend college, this creates issues for everyone involved in their lives. Chandra's solution is to partner with the public school systems and re-evaluate the skills that are currently being taught to students and to bring those skills more in line with those required of higher paying positions via a two-year program and internships.

Chandra has a proven track record of leading both onshore and offshore work teams, while leading and managing diverse projects for both Fortune 100 and Fortune 500 companies. Among Chandra's specialties, she works with clients to provide solutions in IT Life Cycle Management and as an IT Infrastructure Program Manager, while providing savvy team leadership and business continuity acumen.

In 2005, Chandra was certified by the Project Management Institute and is a Lean Six Sigma Green Belt. She has over two decades of diverse senior-level and entrepreneurial career experience in the Information Technology industry. Her former roles include Senior Project Manager for Bank of America, Program Manager/ Senior Project Manager for SunTrust Bank, Senior Project Manager for TMX Finance, Consultant Program & Project Manager for Home Depot, Senior Project Manager for eTrade and Project Manager/Developer & Consultant with Heritage Unlimited/Avery Dennison.

She is the co-chair of the Luxury Committee of the Women in Technology organization focusing on high school girls in the STEM program. Chandra has worked with great motivational speakers such as Steve Harvey and Lisa Nichols and organizations such as True Colors. In her spare time, she enjoys karaoke, bowling, cooking, listening to great music and spending time with her family and friends.

You can connect with Chandra at:
- chandra@intheboxmsd.com
- www.twitter.com/virginbluprint
- www.facebook.com/virginblueprint

CHAPTER 15

MENTAL CONDITIONING FOR SUCCESS

BY DR. DRAYTON PATTERSON

On Friday May 13, 1977, Baseball Hall of Fame owner, Bill Veeck of the Chicago White Sox, arranged for me to have a personal tryout with the team at Comiskey Park. Known for his controversial promotions, my tryout was on "Anti-Superstition Night", where mirrors were broken, fans would walk beneath ladders, and "dancing gypsies" would cast spells on the opponent. Wanting to display my pitching skills and not being superstitious, I jumped at this opportunity. Before the tryout, Mr. Veeck asked, "What is it that you want Drayton?" A simple question, but I was baffled as to how I should reply. He asked again, and I mumbled something unintelligible. He raised his voice looking at me directly and asked, "What do you want Drayton?" I quickly replied, "I want to play in the Major Leagues with the White Sox." We began to converse, and it was apparent that Mr. Veeck knew what I wanted, but more importantly, he wanted to know if I understood the trials, the sacrifices, and the long road from having a Major League tryout, to becoming a Major League baseball player. Basically, my "mental-makeup" was being evaluated along with my self-concept, self-esteem, short and long term goal-setting knowledge, as well as my ability to cope with the peaks and valleys experienced along the road to attaining success.

Having a positive self-concept and high self-esteem play a larger role than many realize in attaining success, whether it be career-related, for monetary gain, or to improve interpersonal relationships. When combined with developing the ability to set appropriate goals and utilize critical thinking strategies which aid in our ability to make good decisions, the likelihood of becoming successful markedly increases. We have all heard about "The Four D's" being determination, dedication, discipline, and desire which can aid in our becoming successful, or "S+S=S" (Sweat + Sacrifice= Success), which supposedly can lead us to success. But how do we begin the process of conditioning ourselves for success?

AN INTEGRATIVE MODEL

An Integrative Model to aid in one's success can be utilized to mentally condition and prepare individuals to become competent, healthy, happy, and successful people. Two primary components of this model for success include the enhancement of our self-concept and self-esteem. Our self-concept is based on how we view the facts about ourselves or what we perceive about ourselves to be true. This perception of self may be accurate or inaccurate, but most importantly, it is an accurate perception of what "we" believe about ourselves to be true. The following steps can be taken to achieve an accurate self-perception. This "introspective housekeeping" is sometimes difficult, but necessary:

1) Become more aware of your Sense of Purpose. Determine what you want to achieve or want to attain. What do you desire? What is your passion? What have you accomplished?

2) Set appropriate short, intermediate, and long term goals. Goals must be attainable and unify your thoughts with your actions. Most successful people set very specific goals, and work diligently to stay on task and realize their goals

3) Develop your Sense of Identity. Identify your personal values and morals, explore who you are as a person and your family background. Does your sense of identity or purpose contradict your short and long term goals? Creating an awareness of who we are as human beings is essential to our success.

4) Strengthen your Sense of Belonging. Some may underplay this in one's journey to success, but think about the individuals who go to extremes to "belong" to an organization that has similar goals and values. Think about your friendships and career and community-

related associates....are they in alignment with your personal belief system and the goals that you desire to attain?

5) Increase prosocial behavior (activities helping others). Showing kindness and caring towards others and realizing that the world does not revolve around your personal desires is healthy for everyone. This creates a "win-win" situation because we help others and we become caring human beings resulting in positive reactions in others. This results in our self-conception (self-concept) becoming positive, which elicits us having positive feelings (self-esteem) about ourselves. Being kind makes us feel good!

6) Assessing your Personal Competence (personal strengths and weaknesses) when viewing your life, can aid to your success. Honest self-evaluation....."looking within," is important for everyone to succeed.

7) Efficient problem solving leads to increased feelings of self-efficacy and empowerment. Once realizing that you have this ability, your confidence level and feelings of personal competence also rise.

Systematic problem solving involves:

   a) Acknowledging a problem exists.
   b) Determining what the problem is.
   c) Focusing on what YOU want to happen. What is Your Goal?
   d) Looking at the possible solutions to the problem.
   e) Exploring the possible consequences of each solution to resolve the problem, (some may be appropriate and some inappropriate).
   f) Choosing the best possible solution, making an effective plan to implement that solution.

Upon feeling confident in your ability to implement successful critical thinking and problem solving strategies in your career, interpersonal relationships, finances, etc., chances of becoming successful in these areas improve markedly.

SELF-TALK, SELF-SABOTAGE, FEAR

The words you speak to yourself and others have the power to "build-up" or "tear-down." Positive self-talk leads to positive actions that place yourself in a position to perform in a productive fashion. With athletes, "I'm going to throw this ball on the outside corner at the knee," or "I'm going to kick this football between the middle of the uprights for a field-goal," are examples of positive self-talk that can give you a positive mindset. Negative self-talk can lead to a negative frame of mind where you subconsciously program your behavior to perform in a manner similar to the way that you speak to yourself. For example, an office employee saying, "I'm never going to get a promotion," may alter the effort and behavior needed to attain the promotion. This type of self-talk leads to negative actions, placing us in a position for failure.

An example of negative self-talk which led to self-sabotage, involved a client who stated, "I'll never be promoted." This employee reported that she dressed casually, never disagreed with her supervisor when thinking of more efficient ways to complete tasks, had average attendance, brought "doughnuts" for office employees, and would "work late... sometimes." It was explained to this employee that it appeared as if her boss nor co-workers took her seriously as a potential leader, and that her responses and actions within the workplace made it appear that she did not take herself seriously as far as being promoted to a position of leadership. After being challenged to become more assertive, give opinions in meetings, come to work earlier and stay later working on projects, dress for success (not wearing jeans and tank-top shirts), and discontinue bringing doughnuts for co-workers, this employee reported that co-workers and supervisors initially were surprised with the change in her demeanor and actions, but later treated her as an equal and began to ask for her opinions. After six months of attitudinal and behavioral adjustments combined with positive self-talk, this employee's self-esteem and self-concept improved, resulting in her being promoted within this corporation.

MENTAL CONDITIONING FOR SUCCESS

The saying "never judge a book by its cover" is very popular because this is something that most people do on a daily basis. I have witnessed in business, educational systems, and on the athletic field, where first impressions gave individuals "labels" that either they were never able to erase or took them years to erase. Make your first impressions as positive as possible. Constantly remind yourself "who you are and what you stand for" (sense of identity and purpose). Without a sense of purpose, you have no sense of who you are as a person and have no idea of how to attain the goals that you want to accomplish. Negative labels are acquired when not hustling in sports, failing to act or dress appropriately and professionally at work, or when educators consistently show ineffective classroom management skills.

Your desired success can be "self-sabotaged" by being lackadaisical in your efforts and failing to utilize positive self-talk, which reminds you of your personal sense of purpose and identity. When speaking with clients, I often ask if their personal mission and purpose in life is in alignment with the mission of their workplace. If their personal purpose (as an individual), organizational purpose (employer), and task purpose (completing assignments) are not in alignment, the likelihood of success is diminished.

Most of us understand the concept of "fear of failure." Who wants to fail? I have known several individuals who will do most anything not to be viewed as a failure (by self and others). Some individuals may say that, "nobody can out-work me!" The problem with this attitude is that sometimes people get so involved with the concept of "working hard" for long periods of time, that they forget to "work smart" and remain focused on their goals and sense of purpose that will help them maintain success or achieve success to a higher degree. This thought process can also lead to losing sight of other facets of life that are extremely important to being a successful person (familial and personal relationships, taking care of personal health needs, etc.).

But what about having a fear of success? After a promotion, a great presentation, an excellent work evaluation, an outstanding game on the athletic field, one may think, "How can I possibly top that?" Anxiety, tension, and fear can enter your mind and body. Instead of fearing success, embrace the fact that you now have a history of experiencing success, you have now proven that you can be successful and you can repeat your history of success. Make adjustments to your goals that are appropriate and attainable. Do not think of your success as a burden to always perform at high levels, but as an opportunity to accomplish different tasks in your life that will make you happy as a whole person...

not only as an employee. This holistic thinking allows us to view ourselves as someone who also needs to be a successful spouse, partner, parent, sibling, friend, etc. and not just an employee who is valued by an organization.

When completing my dissertation, a good friend spoke with me about my tendency to push or force events to happen in my favor. She described the concept of "flowing" – filling my mind and body with positive thoughts and visions, having confidence in my ability, knowing that I have a history of always accomplishing a task, and realizing that life is a journey and that I should enjoy the journey and not fear it. "Life is like the seasons, after winter comes the spring" ... such simple lyrics, but meaningful to many who may get "stuck" along the road to success. Success without preparation seldom occurs.

GOAL SETTING FOR SUCCESS REMINDERS

Remember to set goals that are not only reachable and realistic, but empowering and motivating, which will align your actions and attitude with your aspirations, and will "keep you on track" along your road to success. Goals that are clearly defined and easily measured are more easily realized. For example, "I will arrive to work at least 10 minutes early each day and begin to work on my caseload," or "I will complete my work on time or before it is expected each day," are clearly defined and easily measurable goals which will make them easier to attain given they have a specific deadline. Many people make the mistake of setting only long-term goals and quickly lose interest because the reward is far away in the distance. Your goals can be as short as one day or one week, and then you can make your goals one month, three months, six months, one year, three years, or more.

As you reach your goals, monitor your progress carefully and modify as needed. Goals, self-talk, and affirmations can be written down and repeated aloud on a daily basis. Furthermore, you can begin utilizing visualization and imagery as you work towards attaining your goals. Several days before pitching, I would begin to visualize locating my pitches exactly where I wanted them and imagine the sound of the ball hitting the catcher's mitt, smelling the dirt of the mound, etc. These tactics can be utilized to help attain any goal that you desire. For those in leadership roles, you can print on an index card or repeat from memory several times per day, "I will speak and listen to my staff respectfully and listen intently, and be open to their suggestions." This can be done in your office, your car during the morning drive to work, or walking down the hallway. As long as you focus on this task several times a day, you will move towards your goal.

Many people who say "goal-setting doesn't work for me," fail to follow through with many of the steps stated above. They fail to make a "game plan" when setting their goals, as I find many become so focused on the long-term outcome, that they fail to set appropriate short and intermediate goals that are exciting and attainable. Maintaining an appropriate balance in our lives also enhances our passion and motivation in our journey towards success in all aspects of our lives, and maximizes our potential for maximum effort towards our goals and eventual success. This holistic balance of family, career, emotional, social, and physical (proper nutrition and rest) is of utmost importance in becoming a successful human being.

Just as Bill Veeck attempted to gauge my "mental-makeup" (self-concept, self-esteem, ability to set goals, cope with adversity and make good decisions), business professionals, students, athletes, and anyone attempting to attain lofty goals and aspirations, must first begin by participating in some "introspective housekeeping" as they mentally condition themselves for success.

About "Dr. P"

Dr. Drayton Patterson is a professional speaker and a multi-award winning psychologist, and was recently rated as one of the "10 Best Chicago Psychologists" by Thumbtack, a definitive list rated by the Chicago community. Professional consultative services are provided for large and small businesses, school districts, colleges, universities, sports teams, individuals, and athletes. Licensed in Illinois and a Nationally Certified School Psychologist since 1990, Drayton has provided psychological services for children, students of all ages, teachers, and administrators since 1984, has taught and lectured at the collegiate and university level, and is widely recognized for his research in self-esteem and self-concept enhancement.

Affectionately referred to as "Dr. P." and "Dr. Smoke" by athletes, Drayton's pitching career was shortened at the Minor League level due to severe shoulder, back, and knee injuries. However, he has remained active in professional baseball for over thirty years as a professional baseball scout (Major League Baseball Scouting Bureau and Texas Rangers), Sport Psychologist (Texas Rangers and Toronto Blue Jays), served as a minor league pitching coach, third base coach, and was the first Ph.D. Psychologist to manage a professional baseball team (Minor Leagues).

Dr. Patterson's wealth of experience as a psychologist, educator, administrator, and athlete have provided thousands of individuals with information on how they can maximize their full potential to "be the best that they can be." Drayton has traveled throughout the U.S. and beyond, delivering his holistic and positive psychology-based messages that educate and uplift individuals, helping them to realize that everyone has the power imbedded within themselves to succeed and become healthy, happy, peaceful, and prosperous individuals, and that this self-actualization can become a reality.

The founder and former owner/president of Chicago's "Stress Reduction Clinic", Dr. Patterson has spoken to a wide range of audiences including Fortune 500 corporations, the Federal Aviation Administration, professional and amateur sports teams, religious organizations, and many educational institutions throughout the United States. Topics include subjects such as mental conditioning for success, decision making strategies, character development, stress management techniques, cultural diversity, enhancing your self-esteem and self-concept, and coping effectively with adversity.

Published as an author in self-esteem and self-concept enhancement (Master's Thesis and Doctoral Dissertation), Dr. Patterson also wrote a monthly newspaper column, *Winning with Sports Psychology,* was featured in VGM's Career Portraits, written magazine articles, and his poem, *REACH,* was published in *A River of Emotion,*

The International Library of Poetry.

Dr. Patterson is a member of numerous psychological, sports, and educational organizations, and is currently the president of the Zoreda Rone Patterson Foundation (not for profit), in memory of his mother, a former "Teacher of the Year", who passed away in 1993 of ALS. This foundation provides help and recognition to at-risk children, their caregivers, and the chronically and terminally ill.

Dr. Drayton Patterson is available for speaking engagements
and can be reached at: www.reachdrp.com

Facebook: Dr. Drayton Patterson
Google: Dr. Drayton Patterson
Twitter: @docdpatterson23
Email:patterson964@comcast.net
LinkedIn: Drayton Patterson

CHAPTER 16

HOW TO TURN YOUR WEAKNESS INTO A STRENGTH

BY ALGIRDAS KARALIUS

There is not a night that would not be followed by a day. There isn't a life that would not end in death. And there is no weakness that could not be turned into a strength.
~ A. Karalius.

Some people believe that the quickest way to success is to find one's talents, turn them into strengths, and constantly focus on improving them. This applies to all the athletes who dream of becoming champions, as well musicians who want to become famous. Also, most teachers advise their students to stop thinking about their weaknesses and concentrate on developing their strengths. I like this idea. I largely agree with it. However, I would like to tell you a story that made me look at success very differently. I hope that this story will help you discover brand-new strategies and paths to achieving success.

I was born in Kazakhstan, in a family of Lithuanian political prisoners. Therefore, my childhood was spent in a multilingual environment. At home we spoke Lithuanian (my parents' mother tongue). Russian was the language used at school, and in the neighbourhood the Kazakh language was widely spoken. For whatever reason, I started speaking quite late, at the age of four. When I was five years old, my parents decided to send me to school. I was the youngest; everyone else was seven or eight years old. I had little speaking practice, and on top of it all, it turned out that I was a stutterer. When the teacher called me to the blackboard, to pronounce a sentence, I vigorously stomped and the whole class would laugh at me, cracking jokes, like "the scooter won't start today."

To my great surprise, my primary class teacher decided to help me. Instead of developing my strengths, of which neither she nor I had any idea, she decided to focus on turning my weakness into strength. Not only did she invite me to participate in the drama group, but she also gave me one of the main parts in the play Cinderella, where I had to play the prince. Moreover, we had to perform for the entire city. I still remember the time of the dress rehearsal, when I stood in front of the jury of the city administration, trying to say one sentence: "This is all that was left of the evening."

Instead, I was stomping in despair, with my mouth distorted in an agonizing attempt to utter a word. I saw the surprised eyes of the jury, and the main question from the jury to my teacher was, "Why did you give the lead role to a stutterer? Were there no other more talented candidates?" To which my teacher, Tatiana Leontievna Kaplan, said in a calm voice, "Do not worry. You will come to the premiere and will see that everything will be fine. "She said it loudly enough so I could overhear. These words so dramatically stuck in my mind that mysteriously, during the premiere, *my scooter started from the first attempt.* I managed, with dignity, to pronounce my few lines, to a storm of applause from the audience.

My second experience was related to my parents' attempt to send me to a gymnastics school. As a child, I was a rather chunky boy. My first training session, filled with hysterical laughter from other children, was a complete fiasco. I tried to pull up on the bar at least once, but instead my entire body stretched in convulsions, especially my legs that looked like those of a ballerina. My gymnastics coach apparently had a specific sense of humour. He joked, "Perhaps you should take up ballet dancing instead." Which produced even more laughter from the children and tears of resentment and shame on my face. What did I do? For whatever reason, I decided to take revenge on this coach and enrolled in a ballet school. After training there for five years, I danced a solo part on the main stage. Neither my weight, nor lack of other natural traits prevented me from achieving this.

In the environment where I grew up, attending ballet classes was not something worthy of a real "macho" man. I grew up in a very criminal area, where all the hooligans somehow sensed that they could take money or new clothes from me. As this happened quite often, I had developed a fear —almost a phobia. I was afraid of going out or to movies on my own. I could not understand why I was picked on at least two to three times a month, while nobody bothered my friends. I felt like a marked man. What do you think I had to do in this situation?

The desire to protect myself was so great that that it changed my life. I dedicated 15 years of my life to the martial art of Jiu-Jitsu and found my vocation in this area. I became the youngest coach. Later in life I trained special forces troops. What was once my biggest weakness became my biggest strength.

However, success in sports did not equate success in learning. In school, despite my efforts, I experienced learning difficulties. I always failed my tests and exams. My memory would let me down at the worst possible time. Instead of the regular six, I spent ten years in medical school, constantly retaking failed exams. The more I studied medicine, the more chaos it created in my head, and so by the end of my graduation year, I was rather confused. The ONLY reason I finally passed was the promise that I made to never practice medicine. I therefore fulfilled my Hippocratic Oath by never subjecting anybody to my treatment.

Having received a higher education diploma, I had one question in my mind: "What is the reason for my failures?" I thought, "There is something wrong either with my head or with the education system. Maybe the system is the cause?" I was mostly perplexed by the fact that neither at school nor university was I taught how to learn. I decided to answer this question, dedicating twenty years of my life to helping people achieve their goals.

Which training system is the most effective? Because I was a stutterer and had a very socially awkward beginning in childhood, as an adult the very idea of public speaking was a nightmare for me. The whole experience proved that any public speaking occasion resulted in another failure and mockery. I decided to turn this weakness of mine into strength, visiting 60 countries in the process. Very soon, I became the most famous and most popular public speaker in Eastern Europe. Tens of thousands of people attended my seminars in Eastern Europe every year. Among my students were directors of the largest companies and commercial banks. Strange as it may sound, I felt at home when standing alone on stage in full view of a crowd of thousands. How could this happen? Public speaking was the weakest link in the chain of my capabilities.

In conclusion, I would like to add that another weak point for me was foreign languages. I wasted 15 years trying in vain to learn German. As a result, I couldn't say anything beyond a simple hello and goodbye. A weak knowledge of Latin was the main cause of my failures while studying medicine. Latin names of medicines, muscles, and bones were all mixed up in my head. Later, I tried to learn English, both on my own and by attending many courses. I would spend a month and a half in America or England, learning the language in the best schools. However, the results were pathetic. I could not even talk properly with Customs on the border. Finally, I had enough and decided to do something about it. That's why I made a decision to become an instructor in this language and to develop my own method of fast learning, Colibri (Hummingbird).

This method is designed for people like me, with learning difficulties, who had tried to learn the language and quit in frustration. Colibri was a real bombshell. Thousands of people successfully went through the courses, leading me to offer them not only for English, but also for French, Italian, German, and Norwegian languages. While learning foreign languages was my weakest link, teaching them has become my passion and my most successful commercial project. My classes are often attended by professors and tutors of foreign languages, and each time they wonder how such a complex thing as a foreign language can be taught in such a simple manner.

Last but not least, I have had the same recurring dream for 20 years. In this dream I saw my teachers at the Medical Academy attending my classes and writing down everything I would tell them. I would tell them: "There are no incapable students. There are tutors who cannot teach. And all you have to do as tutors, is help your students find their weaknesses and turn them into the most powerful competitive advantage. Write this down — there is no such weakness that you cannot turn into the greatest strength." It was a sweet dream. I have been having it for 20 years.

One day everything changed. The entire faculty of the Medical Academy attended my Colibri seminars, and wrote down everything I told them.

My "cascade method" of training doctors received acclaim, not only in Lithuania but also in some of the largest U.S. medical schools. With this method, you can teach any student or doctor the most complex procedures and prepare these people to act effectively in a variety of settings. There are now several established international scientific laboratories that study the effectiveness of my method using traditional gold standards. Also, I am pleased to hear from the best experts in the world that our methods of accelerated learning help save thousands of lives around the world. Doctors trained in the cascade method make significantly fewer errors, thereby increasing the patients' chances of survival.

What were the conclusions that I have drawn, having lived on this planet for over 50 years? Firstly, there is a strategy that allows the weakest traits to be turned into the strongest ones. Also, there are techniques that allow you to become a professional in a specific field more rapidly. Moreover, these methods offer a guarantee of success. Being trained in the traditional way, you have to spend about 10,000 hours to master the skills, but 80% of people fail at that. 17% become good practitioners, while only 3% become true professionals. You surely agree these statistics are rather dreadful. Bearing in mind the rapidly changing situation in the market and high costs of education, very often, after 10,000 hours spent in the training centres, your profession may become obsolete. The world is changing too fast. Therefore, we need methods of quick learning in order to adapt. Using the four-step "cascade model" of training, 97% of the trainees acquire the necessary skills at least 10 times faster. What are the magic four steps?

Step 1 - MODELLING

Find someone who has already reached the highest level of the skill. When I studied Jiu-Jitsu, I chose a teacher with the 10th rank. To improve my memory skills, I chose Dominic O'Brien, an eight-time world champion in memorization, as my teacher. When I decided to learn how to read faster, I learned from Guinness record holder Howard Berg, the fastest reader on the planet. What were the results of such studies? During the three-day seminar with the master of Jiu-Jitsu, I acquired more skills than I had in three to five years of training with an ordinary coach. With Dominic O'Brien, I easily learned 2,000 foreign words per week. After training with Howard Berg, I became a true bibliophile (there are over 4,000 books in my library) and in one evening I can easily read 10 to 15 books. Then I can conduct a professional seminar on the new topic the following morning.

Step 2 - ALGORITHM

When you are learning something, it is very important to have a good algorithm. A good algorithm is the answer to four questions:

1. What do we have to do?
2. How do we do it?
3. What do we do when things do not go according to plan?
4. Why do we do it this way and not any other?

Unfortunately, most books and textbooks are not an algorithm but simply a declaration.

Therefore, these books are very difficult to apply in real life. In my practice I use a graphic algorithm, Dragon. This algorithmic language was created in the space industry. The main developer of this language is Vladimir Danilovich Parondzhanov. This algorithmic language allows any information from any source to be turned into a clear step-by-step algorithm. Since most of the books do not contain the algorithm, your task is to create such an algorithm yourself.

Step 3 - ALGORITHMIC SITUATIONAL TRAINING

Now that you have an algorithm, your job is to learn by using this algorithm to solve a situation which you may encounter in real life. If you want to become an artist, then you need to find a picture you want to paint with the help of the step-by-step algorithm. If you are a doctor, you have to learn the treatment algorithm for various patients. It is important to exclude the trial and error method from the learning process. You need to be in the success zone 100% of the time you are doing any learning exercises. To achieve this, simply scroll your finger over the steps of the algorithm, read each step aloud, and solve the selected task. You can learn with your friends and colleagues. The roles will change. First you are a student, then a teacher, and then an observer making sure that all the steps are correctly taken. The ultimate goal of this step is to bring a new skill to the level of automatism.

Step 4 - INTEGRATION

Your task now is to integrate the new skills into your daily life. You must turn these new skills into a habit; then you will not need motivation or willpower to use new skills. 95% of what we do every day is a habit. Therefore, success in life is the result of good habits. Using the four-step cascade model, you get three great benefits.

- You reduce training time from 10,000 hours to tens of hours.
- You increase the probability of achieving the goal from 3% with traditional training to 97% with the cascade training.
- You get a huge economic impact.

Life is short, and if we want to try and learn new skills, we must learn how to learn fast. My wish is for everybody to live their lives according to their dreams, so they will not later in life regret wasted years.

About Algirdas

Algirdas Karalius is the most renowned and sought after motivational speaker in Eastern Europe. Born in Kazakhstan in 1966 in a family of political prisoners, he returned to Lithuania at the age of twelve, where he graduated from high school and subsequently from the Kaunas Medical Academy, majoring in Psychotherapy. Later, Algirdas graduated from the Institute of Neuro-Linguistic Programming (NLP) in Canada, learning from the best experts in the field of psychotherapy - Richard Bandler and John Grinder. He devoted 25 years of his life trying to find an answer to questions such as, "What makes successful people different? What do they do differently? What constitutes success?" He specializes in accelerated learning of success models.

For over 25 years he has worked with hundreds of thousands of people in over 15 countries, with tens of thousands of people attending his seminars every year. He is the author of ten books and unique techniques of accelerated learning. His "Colibri" (Hummingbird) method, being the fastest way in the world to learn foreign languages, has become popular in a great number of countries, from Lithuania and the Baltics and Russia to France, Switzerland, England, Spain and America. He also has developed accelerated learning techniques for physicians in cooperation with the Crisis research center in Kaunas, Lithuania. These methods were introduced and are being used now in Kazakhstan, in the Baltic countries, as well as in the Centers opened in the U.S. (New York, Stanford).

It is important to note that the clinics that adopted these methods, such as in Kazakhstan, have succeeded in reducing the rate of neonatal and maternal deaths by 70%.

Algirdas has worked with a number of large companies, such as PepsiCo, pharmaceutical giant GlaxoSmithKline and some of the Scandinavian banks. He has developed revolutionary accelerated learning methods for sales teams that enable employers to implement training academies within their company.

He is the first certified trainer in corporate change implementation program at Harvard Business School. He also developed accelerated learning programs in such skills as drawing and playing musical instruments.

Algirdas also has experience of working with the military, in the training of special operations units. He worked together with a lot of very successful people. Among them are world and Olympic champions, as well as very prominent businessmen.

He considers it his mission to help people believe in their unlimited abilities, and his goal is to equip individuals and companies with accelerated learning skills. His program has got great recognition in Europe. And in 2015, he was nominated by the European organization of quality innovations for the most innovative teaching methods applied in the various fields of activity. He has been happily married for more than 20 years and is a father of two wonderful children. His hobby is extreme sports. He also holds a black belt in Jiu-Jitsu. And he is a lot of fun as a person!

CHAPTER 17

JUST SAY NO. . . LEADING THE WAY FOR AMERICA'S PREVENTION MOVEMENT!

BY JOSEPH P. MIELE AND ANGELO M. VALENTE

A LOOK AT 25 YEARS OF NEW JERSEY'S SUCCESSFUL SUBSTANCE ABUSE PREVENTION

The 1980s brought a new national consciousness about the misuse and abuse of drugs and alcohol. Drug abuse was everywhere and its consequences were far reaching – on the University of Maryland's basketball court, in the streets of New York City, and in homes of millions of American Families. My family was not immune.

In the mid-1980s, programs, initiatives and efforts bloomed across the country to address drug abuse and stop young people from using and abusing drugs. The nation had a new anthem in the fight against drug abuse: "Just Say No," a message introduced by First Lady Nancy Reagan. At the same time, law enforcement introduced the DARE program, and the advertising industry created the Partnership for a Drug-Free America (PDFA). A coalition of advertising executives, the PDFA created the visualization of a brain on drugs with its iconic fried egg Public Service Announcement that stated, "This is drugs, this is your brain on drugs."

Everyone's Problem

During this time period, New Jersey was not immune to the problem of drug and alcohol abuse. Many lives had been ruined. Many families had been destroyed. New Jersey residents needed help.

New Jersey's then Governor Tom Kean, a longtime friend and one of the best governors to serve our state, was in office and appointed W. Carey Edwards Attorney General. Edwards was a man with an insight and understanding of the need to address drug and alcohol abuse straight on. Carey spearheaded legislation, called the "Comprehensive Drug Reform Act of 1987," that was introduced and passed by the New Jersey legislature. This act was designed to enhance and coordinate efforts designed specifically to curtail drug-related offenses, which would therefore lead to a reduction in the rate of substance abuse related crime, and benefit all residents of New Jersey. The passage of this law led to the creation of the New Jersey Governor's Council on Alcoholism and Drug Abuse (GCADA), an office mandated to create and support policy and planning to prevent substance abuse, increase public awareness and education; and, coordinate the Alliance to Prevent Alcoholism and Drug Abuse Programs.

Kean was looking for a strong leader to Chair the GCADA and asked me to consider this request. I accepted, knowing that I could use my years of experience in law, public service and industry to make this council an effective tool in preventing substance abuse, as well as highlight the need for treatment and recovery opportunities for those who were addicted. I understood the importance of the GCADA's mission: to provide grassroots prevention programing through the Municipal Alliance program that appealed to the needs of each specific community. The key to success lay in the reality that the impact of a prevention program on the residents of Bridgeton, in Cumberland County, was vastly different from the prevention program that would resonate with the residents in Jersey City, in Hudson County, or in Cape May, Cape May County. Local committees of concerned residents and local leaders who were responsible for planning prevention programing – such as holding parent education sessions on substance abuse prevention or distributing information to the community - formed the Municipal Alliance program.

The creation of hundreds of municipal alliances was the next step and key to success. Even before the office was staffed, I traveled thousands of miles and visited hundreds of municipalities to encourage local leaders and governments to create a municipal alliance for the prevention of alcohol and drug abuse in their community. I am so proud that today, over a quarter of a century later, more than 90% of municipalities in New Jersey continue to maintain a municipal alliance for the prevention of substance abuse. Choosing an executive director for the GCADA led me to a man who would bring his unique skills to this newly-formed statewide effort.

Riley Regan was selected as the first executive director of the GCADA. He was uniquely qualified for the position. As a recovering alcoholic and drug addict, Regan used his past experiences with drug and alcohol abuse to enhance his work. As the GCADA grew and flourished, it became clear that a missing element in the unification of prevention services existed. That missing element was soon discovered in 1992, when Robert J. Del Tufo, the Attorney General of New Jersey at that time, was contacted by the Partnership for a Drug-Free America. The Partnership for a Drug-Free America was looking to create alliances in each state as a way to penetrate individual, local media market. General Del Tufo immediately reached out to me to see if I would be interested in creating the New Jersey Affiliate of the Partnership for a Drug-Free America.

Successful Leadership Is Rooted In Passion

From my many years and experiences successfully navigating the New Jersey state government, I knew the needs of the Partnership for a Drug-Free America would not be suited for a state government office. I also knew bringing the Partnership for a Drug-Free America's messages would be an invaluable service to the residents of New Jersey. Soon after I created a non-profit organization, the Partnership for a Drug-Free New Jersey, to support the efforts of the Governor's Council on Alcoholism and Drug Abuse, serve as the New Jersey Alliance of the Partnership for a Drug-Free America and most importantly, to provide New Jersey residents with crucial prevention education messages. In 1992, the Partnership for a Drug-Free New Jersey was created as a state anti-drug alliance to localize, strengthen and deepen drug and alcohol abuse prevention media efforts.

Once again, I was in a position where I needed to find someone who was uniquely qualified for the position of Executive Director of the Partnership for a Drug Free New Jersey. This person had to bring a keen understanding of the state of New Jersey as well as a background in advertising and promotions. My search was simple. A few years earlier, I was fortunate to have recruited a young man from the Governor's Office who was working with me in my private companies, who was and still is, an advertising and creative prodigy. I contacted Angelo Valente on the twenty-pound cell phone (we all remember those) that I carried with me on the ride back from my meeting with General Del Tufo, and I congratulated Angelo on being the first Executive Director of the Partnership for a Drug-Free New Jersey, but explained to him that he would be volunteering his services until we developed a strategy and plan for the organization's future. He gladly accepted the position and challenge.

Partnership for a Drug-Free New Jersey and You, Perfect Together... Bringing Together a Dynamic Team

When I first received the call from JP about serving as the Executive Director of the Partnership for a Drug-Free New Jersey, my mind immediately raced with hundreds of ideas and plans. Of course, JP brought me down to reality. We were an organization with no office, no staff and no funding, and our first objective was to change all of these. With regard to staffing, JP immediately assigned his longtime assistant, Diane Higgins, to serve as the office administrative staff. JP also designated a portion of his personal office to me to use at his law firm, Miele, Cooper, Spinrad and Kronberg, to use as the Partnership for a Drug-Free New Jersey headquarters. Finally, the funding: Together, Diane, JP, and I, developed a list of New Jersey corporate leaders and within a very short time, held the first meeting of the Partnership for a Drug-Free New Jersey's Board of Trustees. It should be noted that attendees of this meeting were asked to come and learn about this new state-wide organization, but by the time the meeting concluded they were on board - literally. JP's passion, enthusiasm and determination to not take no for an answer "convinced" all of those in attendance to join forces with us on this endeavor. Today, 25 years later, many of these same original board members still proudly serve the Partnership for a Drug-Free New Jersey.

Necessity is the Birthplace of Invention

Creating a media organization in a state without its own media market, but located between the first and fourth largest in the country, proved that necessity truly is the birthplace of invention.

Starting up this organization in New Jersey caused both challenges and opportunities. Our first and most important challenge was convincing media executives that the messages that we were creating were important enough to be seen and heard in their newspapers and on their radio and television stations, and all of this would have to be done without any cost to the Partnership for a Drug-Free New Jersey.

Without a media market in New Jersey, we had to rely on non-traditional opportunities. We knew our messages targeted families, so now we had to get the message to them – and we knew right where to go, where all families can be found—in the local grocery store.

With the help of the New Jersey Food Council, we were able to convince every grocery store in the state to imprint a substance abuse prevention message on each of their grocery bags. This meant that every mother or father in New Jersey brought a Partnership for a Drug-Free New Jersey message into their kitchen. New Jersey is known as the Garden State, so grocery stores seemed like the perfect fit, but New Jersey is also known for its toll roads, so toll booths seemed like another great place to reach our targeted audience. Working with the New Jersey Turnpike Authority and the Garden State Parkway Authority, for which incidentally, JP served as a Commissioner on both of these Authorities during his public service career, we replicated the messages we used on the grocery bags on hundreds of thousands of litter bags that were handed out at toll booths. We even enlisted Governor Christine Todd Whitman to help spread the message by bagging groceries at her local grocery store, and handing out litter bags at a toll booth as part of media events to promote both of these initiatives. We didn't stop there.

Family – The Anti-Drug

Based on the results of this campaign, we began to understand the impact that family involvement could have on a child's decision to experiment with drugs and alcohol. We embarked on a statewide research project to prove it. At the time, this research project was so groundbreaking that the White House Office of National Drug Control Policy's Deputy Director, Donald R. Vereen, Jr., visited our New Jersey office, and based on the research we presented him, the ONDCP shifted their media campaign to focus more attention on parental involvement.

What New Jersey Makes, the World Takes

This would not be the first time the Partnership for a Drug-Free New Jersey's initiatives received national attention.

Between 2010 and 2015, President Barack Obama, not once, but twice, featured a Partnership for a Drug-Free New Jersey initiative in his annual National Drug Control Strategy Report. In 2010, the Partnership was recognized for its innovative action to prevent opiate abuse. Based on the National Survey on Drug Use and Health (NSDUH) research that found that over 70 percent of people who abused prescription pain relievers got them from friends or relatives, PDFNJ created a campaign targeting one of the main sources – grandparents – by creating the, Who Knew Grandma Kept a Stash, campaign. This campaign challenged New Jersey residents to secure their medicine cabinets to prevent access to these medicines by the young people in their lives. The results of this campaign were so overwhelmingly positive that we received hundreds of phone calls in our office from New Jersey residents asking how they could dispose of their medicine. With the help of the Special Agent in Charge of the Drug Enforcement Administration New Jersey Division at the time, Gerard McAleer, and the New Jersey Attorney General's Office, we created the first-in-the-nation statewide day-of-disposal of unused, unwanted, and expired medicine. On November 9, 2009, we collected over 9,000 lbs. of medicine from residents across New Jersey. Not only did this initiative receive the recognition from the ONDCP, it was replicated by the Drug Enforcement Administration National Headquarters, who implemented a national take-back component of this effort in National Take Back Day.

For PDFNJ, this effort evolved into a national subsidiary, the American Medicine Chest Challenge, that asked every American family to take the five-step AMCC challenge:

(1) take inventory of their prescription and over-the-counter medicine

(2) secure their medicine cabinet

(3) dispose of unused, unwanted, and expired medicine in their home or at an AMCC Disposal site

(4) take their medicine(s) exactly as prescribed

(5) talk to their children about the dangers of prescription drug abuse

Currently, over 1,800 local law enforcement agencies have joined the movement and are listed in the AMCC National Directory of Permanent Collection Sites.

The Right Prescription For New Jersey

Prescription Drugs and heroin continued to be abused in record levels, leading the Centers for Disease Control and Prevention to declare an epidemic. Our newest Board Members, Steve and Elaine Pozycki, and our Chairman, Joseph A. Miele, son of founder, Joseph P. Miele, understood how a prescription for an opiate could lead to heroin abuse. As a result of this perspective, the Partnership for a Drug-Free New Jersey understood how important it was to engage physicians in developing a solution to this epidemic, and with the support of the New York/New Jersey High Intensity Drug Trafficking Area and the DEA-NJ, the Partnership developed a symposium series, hosted by local hospitals to begin a dialogue with physicians on how they can become part of the solution. As a result of these important educational events, over 90% of physicians who attended reported they would alter their prescribing habits.

Messages Matter

PDFNJ messages are currently seen and heard throughout New Jersey and the country on buses and trains, on billboards, on New Jersey Broadcasters Association radio stations, and television. And over the past 25 years, it has generated an estimated 250 million dollars in in-kind advertising, received over 200 awards and recognitions from national, statewide and regional public relations and advertising organizations, and were featured on the Geraldo Rivera Saturday Night Live, Good Morning America, in Time Magazine and Readers Digest, for its innovative, groundbreaking, and creative initiatives and public awareness campaigns. However, what is most rewarding is having families throughout the state of New Jersey thank us for giving them the knowledge and information they need to have a conversation with their children and protect their families.

A Confused Generation

Children are now more confused than ever as the movement to legalize marijuana expands. We need to pause and truly examine both the purported benefits and unforeseen negative consequences this expansion brings. If it is not organizations like ours shining an objective light on this issue, then who will it be?

About Joseph

Joseph (J.P.) Miele's public service career spans more than 50 years, beginning with serving as the youngest first assistant prosecutor in the history of Essex County, New Jersey. He later established a private law practice and was owner of over 20 companies throughout the United States.

As founder and Chairman of the nationally recognized, award-winning Partnership for a Drug-Free New Jersey, established in 1992, J.P. was the driving force behind the creation of the largest Public Service Media campaign in the state's history.

In 1985, J.P. was appointed Chairman of the Governor's Council on Alcoholism and Drug Abuse and, under his leadership, more than 500 Municipal Alliances were formed, consisting of over 50,000 volunteers.

J.P. served as Commissioner of the New Jersey Highway Authority from 1985 to 1990, chairing the Technology Committee which was successful in computerizing the entire Garden State Parkway operations. He also served as president of the Garden State Arts Foundation which provides free theatre performances for thousands of senior citizens, youth, and the disabled.

In 1993, J.P. was appointed commissioner of the New Jersey Turnpike Authority and subsequently served as Vice Chairman of the highest revenue-producing toll road in the country. In 1997, J.P. chaired the Committee for a Smart New Jersey, whose objective was to improve the state's transportation network, improve air quality, and foster economic development. JP also served as Vice Chairman of New Jersey's Constitutional Bicentennial Commission.

JP takes most pride in the Joseph P. Miele Foundation, which has awarded academic scholarships to needy students. To date, over one million dollars has been awarded in scholarship aid.

In 2007, J.P. retired from his public and private undertakings, passing the torch to his son, Joseph Anthony Miele. However, his accomplishments continue to touch many lives, remaining passionate and true to helping those in need.

About Angelo

Angelo M. Valente has served as Executive Director of the Partnership for a Drug-Free New Jersey (PDFNJ) since its inception in 1992 and has led the organization to become the largest, continuous Public Service Campaign in New Jersey's history.

Mr. Valente also serves as Chief Executive Officer of the American Medicine Chest Challenge, a national public health initiative to raise awareness of prescription drug abuse and maintain a National Directory of Permanent Prescription Drug Collection sites. Since 2000, Mr. Valente has served as a Member of the Holy See's Delegation to the United Nations.

Mr. Valente, the youngest person to serve on the Hoboken City Council, also served as a Commissioner of the Hoboken Housing Authority. In 2005 he led the City of Hoboken's sesquicentennial celebration as Co-Chair.

Angelo has served on the Governor's Council on Volunteerism and Community Service, the New Jersey Redevelopment Authority, Secretary to the North Jersey District Water Supply Commission and is a commissioner on the Hudson County Board of Taxation. Mr. Valente is a Member of the Arbitration Committee to the Supreme Court of New Jersey and a Trustee of The Waterfront Project. Mr. Valente is a life-long Parishioner and Trustee of St. Francis Parish in Hoboken.

Mr. Valente has a B.A. from Montclair State University and Masters Degrees from Fairleigh Dickinson University in Public Administration and Seton Hall University in Diplomacy and International Relations.

Angelo Valente is married to Jane Valente. They are the proud parents of three daughters, Hannah, Mia and Marietta.

Mr. Valente credits the unwavering support of the PDFNJ Board of Trustees with the Partnership's success, along with its team: Larry Agne, Christopher Barton, Jeannine Brown, Angela Conover, Diane Higgins, Dina Lobaina, Bill Lillis, Kathy Sansevere, and Greg Startzel. For more information, please contact: Angelo@DrugFreeNJ.org or visit www.DrugFreeNJ.org.

CHAPTER 18

THE 1000-POUND MIRROR

BY ALYSSA AUBREY

In the classic children's fairy tale, *Snow White*, the beautiful but fatally-flawed Queen stands before her mirror and asks "Magic mirror on the wall, who is the fairest one of all?" Each time her faithful mirror replied, "Thou O Queen, art the fairest in the land." But, the day came when the mirror gave the Queen a very different answer, as the mirror never lies. In real life, those of us privileged to own or spend time around horses find ourselves in the company of just such an honest and mystical reflection.

Tizzy, a beautiful 34-year old Appaloosa mare has been retired in my care for several years. You can usually spot her dappled body on the pasture's periphery. A seasoned, shy, sentinel member of the herd with a beautiful face that looks at you with one blue and one brown eye.

From the very beginning, Tizzy's owner wanted her to have a job participating in my youth classes, but Tizzy never seemed interested in joining up. Then one day, Tizzy began banging her hoof on the metal gate that separated her from the paddock as I was readying for the soon to arrive class. Obliging the request, I opened the gate and watched her trot by me, the first one in the paddock. Several of my regular and seasoned program horses joined her a few minutes later.

The bus arrived with a group from a local non-profit, all teen girls who had survived family violence. The last to step off the bus was a 14-year old African-American girl named Jaden. As I greeted her, I noticed that she had one blue eye and one brown eye.

Tizzy let out a call from thirty feet away and came galloping towards the fence where the young girl stood in amazement. Their connection was so apparent, it felt like electricity in the air.

The youth director confided, the girl's mother had been murdered in front of her and she had not spoken a word since that day, almost two years ago. Jaden has been in therapy and regularly participating in this violence prevention group but through it all had remained silent.

Our first activity was a grooming exercise with the horses, (which I use as a metaphor for self-care). Jaden and Tizzy paired up and she began to slowly brush the horse. Tizzy wrapped her neck around the young woman's shoulder, much like horses do with their young.

Moments later we could hear the young girls muffled sobs. Tizzy stood quietly, gently holding Jaden against her warm body, arms wrapped around the horse's neck, her faced buried in the mare's thick mane.

The activities now complete, I asked everyone to gather in a circle and share their experience of grooming the horses. After several comments by both staff and participants, I asked if anyone else in the group had reflections before we moved on.

"I want to say something," the voice stammered. It was Jaden, who hadn't spoken a word in more than two years. She told the group that while Tizzy was holding her, she had remembered being with her mom at her Grandfather's horse ranch in Mexico.

They were celebrating his birthday and Jaden sang Happy Birthday to him. He had put his arms around her and whispered in her ear..."your voice is a gift from God, promise me you will never lose it." Until today she had forgotten her promise. Tizzy, she explained softly...had helped her remember.

I am often asked, what do you do with horses, if you don't ride them? It's true, in the 6500+ clients I've worked with, every bit of horse power has happened from the ground. The story of Tizzy and Jaden underscores the horse's remarkable brilliance and generosity of spirit that can mirror our stories, mend what has been broken and encourage new possibilities for healing and transformative outcomes.

My work for the last 15 years has been in partnership with horses. Together we support developing personal life skills that encourage taking a deeper look at ourselves, our beliefs, our relationships, desire to expand careers, to feel more joy, peace, confidence, serenity, and true purpose.

My clients run the gamut from youth at risk and recovery clients to CEO's and coaches seeking leadership development, companies tracking innovative team building, and organizations facing challenges that often impede successful outcomes.

Each workshop begins by gathering in a circle, our routine for grounding and centering on our day's intention. After a review of housekeeping and agenda for the day, each participant introduces himself or herself and agrees to the Safety/Responsibility Agreement:*

My name is _____, and I agree to be responsible for myself today, which includes my thoughts, my feelings, my behavior, my projections, my assumptions and my actions, thus contributing to the safety of the group.

People are often surprised to learn that in addition to physical or body position around horses, authentic expression is the number one safety rule. It is highly disconcerting for horses (and humans for that matter) to be in the space of incongruent human energy. An example of this might be feeling afraid or confused, or bored, but pretending all is well with a big smile on our face. Humans are the only species on the planet capable of thinking one thing, feeling another and acting still another. It is impossible for horses (or any other animal) to pretend. Horses immediately reflect this "split" by becoming restive, anxious and in extreme cases of suppressed energy (PTSD), horses can become aggressive. The safety agreement reminds us to be congruent, our first cornerstone lesson in being a trusted leader for self and others.

* *The AIA (Adventures in Awareness) safety/responsibility agreement was authored by Barbara K Rector, MA, CEIP-ED. Barbara is credited globally with development practice of psychotherapy with the help of horses (Equine-Facilitated Psychotherapy EFP) in clinical setting of a residential hospital in early 1990.*

Kim is a team leader employed by the largest health care provider in California. She is asked to introduce herself to Charlie Blue Eyes, a black and white paint horse. Kim approached the horse as though she was hailing a cab on the streets of Manhattan during rush hour. The more Kim tried to approach, the further the horse moved away. When asked what the scenario reminded her of, she began to talk about how disconnected she felt from her team. Kim's position required constant email communications, meetings and project deadlines, the workload was daunting. Kim had developed a coping mechanism of moving faster and faster in an effort to stay on top her impossible to-do list. In reality, just like the situation with Charlie, the harder Kim worked, the further away progress seemed to be. As Kim continued to speak about her life in an honest way, Charlie began to walk towards her. Then Charlie took a deep sigh, licked his lips (a sign of relaxation) and moved closer to Kim. In that moment Kim experienced the reward of being present. She was able to connect with herself and Charlie in an authentic way in the midst of being honest and open with her true feelings, something she had not known how to express in her work environment.

In an email follow up, Kim wrote:
"Three weeks out and I continue to process my experience while still trying to wrap my mind around those few moments with Charlie. What became immediately clear was my need to slow down and connect to me. I am happy to report work life and home life are much improved. I'm moving through my days mindfully, remembering to breathe and noticing how my energy affects the people around me. I've made time to connect to each member of my team. Our conversations have been illuminating and productive. Thank you and Charlie so much for a life-changing and life-affirming experience."

My equine coaching and development programs aim at engaging participants in deeply transformative experiences that stimulate powerful insights and ignite sustained growth and leadership effectiveness. In a horse herd, leadership is shared. The lead mare sets the direction and pace for the herd. The stallion protects the herd from predators. Each and every member of the herd is valued; every individual's contribution is essential to the safety, harmony, unity and survival of its members. Horses are highly sensitive to changes in the environment and they are able to give immediate, clear signals when need arises to take action. Trust among the herd members is earned, and tested constantly. It is not a static state. Human teams can draw upon many similarities and experience a new model for effective leadership, collaborative practices and cooperation by studying horses in their natural herd environment.

The white Arabian horse strolls over to Bill, the only participant who expressed a fear of horses in the morning check in. Bill is the chair for a local non-profit. He gives direction to Toyota to move forward, Toyota plants his feet and begins to push into Bill's arm. Bill responds by petting Toyota and telling him what a nice horse he is. Soon after Toyota starts nibbling on Bill's jacket zipper. Bill quickly made the connection that his leadership style is ineffective, often absent of good boundaries, which often includes rewarding unwanted behavior. Bill is not unaware of his habits, he states, "but I've never witnessed the negative impact of my actions before today." Once Bill stopped giving a "mixed message" to Toyota and simply asked him to move, the horse complied willingly.

Since the beginning of recorded history, horses have danced through our dreams, shared our mythology and contributed to our civilization in ways unequaled by any other animal. Together we have ridden into battle, tilled the soil of new lands, explored uncharted territories and engaged in great contests. Kings and commoners have both ridden into history on the back of a horse.

Our Industrial Revolution changed the need for horses as transportation, but up until about 50 years ago, horses were an everyday feature in our human lives. The modern horse signals the emergence of teacher, healer, mentor, guide, coach and mediator at the very forefront of human self-development. The size and power of a horse can be intimidating to many of us. Accomplishing a task such as leading a horse on a walk around the arena in spite of fear, creates an instant and residual sense of confidence, while providing metaphors when dealing with other life-challenging situations. A woman in recovery from cancer will describe the disease itself as a 1000-pound animal. By partnering with a horse (which initially seemed out of the question), the same woman successfully leads the horse over an obstacle marked CANCER! In this process, a troubled spirit is lifted and set free again.

Today thousands of people are learning to clarify purpose and bring authentic expression into work environments and family situations that include corporate leadership training, troubled veterans returning from war, at-risk teens learning to navigate new choices, parenting skills, divorce, recovery from illness, grief and loss, addiction, and even literacy programs. It is an enormous privilege to witness first-hand the horses healing influence.

I deeply believe the lifelong task of our human evolution is to recover the essence of who we are, while simultaneously "shedding the skin" of that which no longer serves our highest expression. These jeweled moments of clarity arrive when our inner thoughts, feelings and stories align with our external experiences. Horses access the wide-open spaces in our human hearts, engage our willingness to rediscover the best parts of ourselves, peel away our masks, our fears and traumas, and unreal expectations by quickening the return to our fullest expression and potential.

This is the ultimate goal of all personal and professional development, therapy and education, and the deeper meaning of success. The lessons of my own life continue to take shape as I experience moments in which thinking, feeling and knowing are all the same, reflected in the 1000-pound mirror of this silent teacher.

About Alyssa

Executive Director Alyssa Aubrey, CEGE, is the Founder and Program Director of Medicine Horse Ranch, an educational experiential learning center incorporating horses in human self-development. Alyssa is a writer, teacher, facilitator, empowerment speaker, money coach, and business consultant with over 30 years of experience as both educator and entrepreneur. She is a Certified Equine Guided Educator (CEGE) and a Certified Money Coach through the Financial Recovery Institute.

Alyssa is a seasoned facilitator with broad experiences that arise from coaching over 6500 clients in equine-guided learning processes. She is compassionate and tenacious with a genuine passion for supporting others as they embark on new directions for discovery, recovery and transformation. She considers the herd of Medicine Horse program horses to be partners, healers, teachers and guides in this powerfully transformative, often spiritually-awakening experience.

Alyssa's current focus is developing eligible candidates to become successful in the field of horse and human interaction. She has developed a nationally-recognized curriculum that includes best practices and core principles for the field, providing hands-on training and development through intern and apprenticeship participation.

After attending Ohio University, Athens, Ohio, Alyssa finished her postgraduate training from Writtle College (U.K.) in Horse Behavior and Psychology, Barn and Stable Management, Equine Feeding and Nutrition and Equitation. Alyssa currently serves on the CBEIP (Certification Board for Equine Interaction Professionals) Board of Directors. She is the 2016 co-chair for WAAT (Women's Association for Addiction Treatment). Alyssa is the US License holder for Horse Dream® and an active member of the EAHAE (International Association for Horse Assisted Education), NAWBO (North American Women's Business Organization) and ICF (International Coaches Federation). She was awarded the AIA Meritus Certification in 2016 for her project of excellence: Medicine Horse Ranch Field Studies Program.

Inspired by colleague Jan Butler Loveless and the success of Jan's Horse and Reader program, Alyssa launched Horse Sense for Readers™, a literacy pilot program in 2011. She received a $30,000.00 grant from the Marin Community Foundation for the project that included nine 6th Grade Latino boys and girls (reading at a 3rd grade level). The goal of the program is academic intervention integrating equine-guided experiential learning, cultural enrichment, expressive arts, career exposure, and horsemanship, riding and family involvement. In only four short months there were dramatic and positive changes in reading comprehension, reading fluency, in writing and academic performance, in self-esteem and confidence, in socio-emotional skills and in handling frustration. These boys and girls also learned horse handling and riding at the walk and jog trot.

Medicine Horse clients include: Leadership Consortium, Apex Leadership, IMPACT Leadership Coaching, Inspiring Success/Executive Coaching, Five Sisters Ranch, Muir Wood Adolescent Treatment Center for Boys, Alta Mira (IOP), North Bay Recovery, Olympia House, Living Reflections, Reflections (IOP), Willow Tree Counseling, Sutter Health, Marin General, Kaiser Permanente, Women's Cancer Awareness Group, Shambhala International, Kohl's Dept. Store, Wells Fargo Bank, Marin Curiosity Club, CASA, The United Way, A Home Away from Homelessness, Boy Scouts and Girls Scouts of America and the Novato Pregnancy Prevention Program.

CHAPTER 19

LIFE'S CHALLENGES: A GUIDE TO UNDERSTANDING OUR LIFE'S PURPOSE AND GLOBAL COMPASSION

BY CATHY WAIDELICH

Through life challenges, we can offer the best inspiration and lessons to those we are blessed enough to reach.

On September 14, 2014, I composed an email to send to a man of great inspiration to me, Mr. Jack Canfield. Part of it read: *What I am currently building has been the most soulful experience of my life—so much BIGGER than me!* Today, as powerful as those words remain to me, they don't adequately reflect the breadth of my journey.

I originally met Jack in 1990 at a conference. I knew he was special and brought him to the university I was working at to train leaders. Then I didn't see him again. I was delighted and happy for him when he became a household name not even three years later with his *Chicken Soup for the Soul* book series. Then in August of 2014, we reconnected at one of his workshops. My life has not been the same since.

Helping others has always been my passion and drive for everything I've accomplished. Taking an approach to my personal and professional life, which are intricately intermingled, I am always mindful that I am dealing with individuals and families, not just a number or statistic to help me reach a goal. Because of this, I am able to offer more meaningful services and develop wonderful relationships. I have been a teacher, counselor, and director of a University Wellness Center, where my team developed a model wellness program for campuses nationwide. Seeing ways to put together ideas that are impactful and people-oriented is a natural fit for me. As life evolved and my callings changed, I gravitated toward real estate. It was another area in which I felt the way I connected with people during important life situations could play a significant role in enhancing their lives.

If we are motivated for the right reasons and guided by the right sources, we will help others - sometimes even despite ourselves.

Real estate was another career that came easy to me. I had this natural insight that allowed me to see the big picture and the small details. Consequently, I built success models that were created around people, not numbers, and it worked. I cultivated success at a rapid rate! I became a Broker/Owner with 30 Realtors, and then the CEO of 100 Realtors. Little did I know it was through real estate that I would learn of something that made me so restless I couldn't sleep at night; something I knew in my heart and soul I needed to do something about. The problem was that Seniors were were falling victim to financial fraud at alarming rates. Why? Because they were polite, kind and trusting. They should be able to trust people who are supposed to be helping them!

Through being compelled to help Seniors, I drew on something incredible that I had played witness to many years earlier. It involved my "Gram," and it was when I was an educator at a university. Gram had visited my Developmental Psychology class and spoke to the students. There she was, as beautiful as could be at 80+ years of age and connecting with these younger students. They adored her! By the end of our class, Gram had been voted best guest speaker on student evaluations. We were all inspired! I remember thinking, *it's the stories of our lives that can help people and guide us to the opportunities that get us closer to reaching our life's purpose - one step at a time.*

THE BIRTH OF A VISION: SERVITUDE THROUGH COLLABORATION

*Through collaboration and empowerment we
can best support and serve others.*

With a newfound energy and focus on helping Seniors gain access to trusted resources and advice for their real estate needs, I left my entire brokerage business behind. It was a bold move, one that many people shook their heads about, but I wasn't swayed. My intuition told me it was the right decision. Although I didn't have the entire plan laid out or all the right collaborators in place, I knew that by doing the right thing, the best people would gravitate toward me. The Law of Attraction is a powerful, effective way to get the best out of life, and it does work. Through sharing my story and knowing I would cross paths with the right visionaries, that is exactly what happened.

Senior Transition Network was the name initially chosen to market this concept. We would connect Seniors with the right housing, bringing assurances to them and their loved ones that their best interests were being served. During this time, I was also able to share this wonderful vision with Jack Canfield, and I found out that he was very interested and saw its potential. Jack had experienced being the concerned relative. It was an "aha moment!" We have all been or will be the one who will ultimately have to help guide and make decisions for the elderly people we love. Jack also shared that his mother-in-law wanted to help people prepare for retirement. She had decided to be a certified trainer to facilitate his Break Through to Success (BTS) workshops, where she would help people develop their vision, mission, goals, etc., for seven different dimensions in their lives. Sadly, she passed away before she could move forward and make her dream a reality. I told Jack that with his permission, I believed my group was supposed to do this. Jack was very supportive and today, I am now a certified BTS trainer. This workshop, based on Jack's Success Principles, is the foundation of the trusted referral and training programs we're building.

While everything I was working toward was exciting, I would be remiss to not mention that it was also quite scary. Fear motivated a great many of my choices, just as much as a desire to help Seniors did. And when fear controls us, we lose sight of the purity of our intents. Sometimes, we might pass on what feels great in our heart and right for our soul for what

191

looks good on a financial statement. We may be inspired by an idea that is complete servitude, but put it on the back burner - after all . . . there is an endless to-do list.

Time forced me to accept that a great vision from the heart and a lot of hard work doesn't necessarily mean that you're creating what you should be. I had to evaluate through daily meditation, reflection and taking highly-needed, deep, calming breaths that while the idea I had was great, it wasn't at the place it should be. I was only halfway there. That's when I felt the BOOM!

BABY BOOMERS: CAUGHT IN THE MIDDLE AND NEEDING A PLACE TO GO

Our quality of life relies on us addressing our physical, emotional and spiritual needs.
There is no need to pick and choose between these three things.

Through meeting Seniors over the years, working with them through real estate, education and the various events that I've played a part in creating for their betterment, I finally saw one thing that existed nearly all of the time - many involved their children/loved ones in these big decisions.

I sparked. . .

I smiled. . .

I found the gap that had eluded me!

None of us see things until we are meant to. The children of these Seniors are part of the Baby Boomer generation, and their lives are unlike any others we've had in history. They are at the center of today's families. They take care of their aging parents and much to their surprise, their grown children are often moving back home. Their life's process is completely different than anyone could have guessed when they were born. WOW! Through serving the Seniors, I saw that we could take that same platform, expand it and help Boomers with all things related to home, health, and finances, and give them access to needed resources. They could go to one source and gain access to a wealth of information from highly qualified experts who are vested in their well-being.

Our group wanted to help Baby Boomers navigate through life. This is how the LegacyCaring™ and the LegacySuccess Academy™ got started.

Realizing this lifted a burden off me that I hadn't even realized was weighing me down. I instantly recalled a conversation that Jack and I had back in March of 2015 where he said "the word" that few people ever want to hear. . . "Patience." Many of us are inclined to think that we don't have time to be patient when we have great things we want to achieve. I don't want to say it's a mistake to ignore the virtue of patience, but you may want to give it a try. It's worth it!

I had to give myself reminders and they worked wonderfully. I said two daily inspirations that were necessary to keep this amazing vibration going in the universe—positive energy that draws the right solutions and individuals to you.

I put Jack and my visions on paper so I could always see them. I also saved them on my computer so they would be present when I worked. Here is what these visions state:

> **Jack:** "To inspire and empower people to live their highest vision in a context of love and joy in harmony with the highest good of all concerned."

> **Cathy:** "To be the online global trusted resource - the ONE place where everyone can find honorable service providers and educators by connecting the most exceptional professionals.

I took Jack's words and created a daily affirmation that kept my energy and connectedness focused on the people I wanted to attract. I would say, "I am feeling patient. It's happening! ALL the resources I need are on their way!" These words kept me grounded while allowing me to recognize that the right things would come my way when they were meant to. It wasn't about what was convenient for my time, but the right time.

Then I waited. Patient. Productive. Ready. I was no longer a "People Pleaser." I knew by moving forward toward my life's purpose every day, all of the trustworthy service providers who had already joined me, would have the opportunity to build their businesses by helping people. I was creating a vehicle to help them move toward their life's purpose.

HAVING FAITH IN YOUR ROLE IN THE WORLD

We can reflect on the reason for our journey when we look
at the timeline of our life.

A misconception many people have is that good things happen to "lucky" people. This is simply not true. I encourage you to take any opportunity you can to connect with and learn from people whom you admire. You're likely to find tragedy, drama, comedy and relationships worthy of a Shakespeare play. The difference in those who reach their purpose and those who wander about, is persistence (they don't give up) and their mindset about achieving it. Do you believe it will happen? Feel it NOW? Are you worthy? The answers to these questions must be "YES" to fulfill your dream.

Even though all the things I have been creating are coming together, in the past, I have dealt with some tough life issues, including: my mother's death when she was forty years old and I was nineteen, and the oldest of six kids, my brother's suicide when he was twenty-two and I was twenty-three, two divorces, being almost fired from a job, bad credit, no money, an eviction notice, people not believing in me and complete disruption. However, I never abandoned my dreams because of life's circumstances. I knew there was something out there that needed me as much as I needed it. This is what happened in 2015:

September 28: I surrendered to a "Higher Power." This is different than giving up.

October 3: I received a message from an Investor.

October 8: We met and there was no doubt in either of our minds that there was something bigger than us happening. We were meant to be intricately connected.

October 12: His resources gave me the ability to build my dream and vision to help millions of people, which was aligned with his dreams for a wonderful life for him and his family. He realized his life's purpose is to help others fulfill their dreams!

In less than two weeks, I had gone from fear to surrender to alignment, because I had learned that it took more than visualizing and thinking about what I wanted. I had to feel that I already had my investor - even before he was technically present. I had become fearless and willing to lose everything, because I knew it was critical to create one universal safe place by connecting the most exceptional service providers. This is one way we can raise the consciousness of mankind and help millions of people take steps toward their life's purpose and make a positive global impact!

The Law of Attraction was heightened! Experts in their fields were sharing their stories and captivating me! Each time someone was vulnerable with me, I was reminded that we are not always what we appear to be outwardly. Not everyone wealthy started out wealthy. Not everyone wise has always made wise decisions. Not everyone who cannot stop smiling like the sunshine has always smiled brightly. I am proud that many of these people have joined our exclusive network.

Life stories and the lessons that come with them have meaning. They are a part of us, and even though we may not have been happy experiencing them, we can look back and see the choices we made: did we play victim or see the gifts that helped us move closer toward our dream? We all have our share of misfortunes, our stories. Jack taught me: E (event) + R (our response) = O (outcome). We control our responses. Realizing that our struggles make us more like everyone else than "all alone," we can support each other in making wise choices.

We need to create the meaning we long for. Through being witness to so many lovely peoples' stories, I can more easily recognize hope and goodness in this world. I can also choose action over passivity.

INTO THE FUTURE
We must become the change we want to see.
~ Mahatma Gandhi

So much is happening and it feels right. The LegacySuccess Academy™ has given me new life and energy, and it is doing the same for others. We are creating a culture unlike any other. We will help people personally and professionally navigate each stage of life and business by connecting them to extensively-screened service providers and educators. When families and companies are on the same page, there is more love, laughter and success. We are creating and building the memories we will carry with us forever. This is the start of a new era of legacies, where we embrace clarity, positive energy and the trusted resources necessary to make healthy, wise decisions - creating Peace-of-Mind for all generations!

About Cathy

Cathy Waidelich is the Founder/CEO, of LegacyCaring™. Cathy was a Managing Real Estate Broker and top producing Realtor for over 10 years, and Broker/Owner of her own real estate company, Market Street Realty, with 30+ Brokers. She has a Master's Degree in Counseling & Education and received her Senior Real Estate Specialist Certification in 2009. It was through her real estate experiences in helping Seniors, that Cathy realized how often Seniors are victims of financial fraud and poor service.

Before real estate, Cathy worked for 15 years at Universities, where she was responsible for thousands of students and hundreds of staff in residence halls. She was also a Director of a University Wellness Center where she and her staff developed the model wellness program for university campuses nationwide. Cathy was a university instructor and taught Psychology classes at Bastyr Naturopathic University. Her Gram, while in her 80s, was a guest speaker for Cathy's Psychology classes. Cathy's Gram inspired her to start LegacyCaring™.

Cathy has been a leader at Master Builders Association (MBA), the largest home building association in the U.S. She was their Education Director and developed the MBA University (model education program for home builders) with 150+ members. During the 2010/2011 holidays, Cathy heard the stats from the Alliance of Aging: "10,000 people turning 65 every day for the next 20 years!" She formed a group within the MBA to assist Seniors with their housing needs. In 2012, Cathy led the first *Senior Day @ the MBA* with Dr. Marion Somers, Senior Psychologist, which launched the idea of LegacyCaring™.

Cathy left her position as CEO/Team Leader at Keller Williams Realty in 2013 to follow her passion and focus on creating a trusted place for Seniors to go for their housing/ real estate needs.

Update: Cathy is a certified Jack Canfield trainer and created the LegacySuccess Academy™ to develop collaborative, holistic trainings based on Jack's *Success Principles.*

LegacySuccess Academy's Training & Enhancement Program is a series of workshops that train people in a company at any stage from start-up to exit, which focuses on the best job/position training PLUS incorporates Jack Canfield's 7 Dimensions of Life: Financial, Business, Relationships, Health, Recreation, Personal and Contribution. Workshops are information, skill-building and/or experiential integrating the mind/ body/spirit connection through, education, inspiration, music and humor, and focus on helping people be proactive in home, health and finances.

Three Tracks: Family, Entrepreneur and Leadership
Pilot: Greater Seattle Area

In addition to loving her work and helping others, Cathy enjoys many activities such as meditating, being an avid reader of growth and development books and nature hiking. Cathy also loves boating & water sports, especially scuba diving.

Cathy is an adventurer and a risk-taker who enjoys jumping out of planes and running off mountains (with a parachute of course!). Cathy loves to dance and admires anyone willing to get on a dance floor and move around. Most of all, she is someone who loves to laugh and to make others feel good.

CHAPTER 20

WHAT IS SUCCESS?

BY LYNN KRUSE

To me, success is a matter of individual decision. Or, I should say "decisions." A sense of success is built by achieving one goal at a time. Being raised by a single Mom, I had a series of babysitters. One of them would pay me to help with the household chores such as folding clothes and dusting. I saved the money to buy my Mom a clock radio, because she hated being awakened by an alarm. Selling Campfire Girl Candy to help pay for a week at camp was a lot of knocking on doors and asking people to buy for the goal of going to camp to learn new skills. Accomplishing skills such as being able to start a fire in the woods with only three matches earned a badge.

After my Grandfather died, my mother inherited money to make the down payment on a house. I wanted her to buy it in the high school district that had the best coach for synchronized swimming. She managed that! The remaining challenge was that I had spent summers with my grandparents in a town of 500 with no swimming pool. I didn't know HOW to swim! For the next two summers, I walked the three miles to the high school to every swimming class the Red Cross offered. By the time I was fourteen, I had finished the lifesaving course and was hired to teach the ten-year-old boys swimming classes at the pool only four miles away! I found I loved teaching, especially the rural kids who had been on a school bus for an hour before they got to the pool. What a fabulous amount of energy and enthusiasm those boys had!

Living only fifty miles from Iowa State University, I decided that I should go there to major in Home Economics. On an assigned career paper in ninth grade, I investigated becoming an appliance tester and demonstrator for a utility company. Then the results of aptitude tests came in. I was the only person in my class to earn a negative score on mechanical aptitude! It was time to change that goal. When something isn't right, one must rethink the situation and try a different solution.

Even though I loved teaching swimming, it didn't pay much. Knowing I wanted to go to college, I needed to start earning money for that goal. My single mother had a two year business college degree and a responsible position with an insurance company. The discrepancy in the pay for women and men was the problem. My mother was supporting a home for her mother and daughter. When young men just graduated from college were hired and brought into the company for Mom to train, they were paid twice her salary. When they went on to other offices for her position, they were paid three to four times her salary! This unjust inequality still exists.

The best job I could get was at a drive-in restaurant a couple of miles from home. I was assigned to work the switch board for receiving orders. Older girls wore uniforms and waited on customers outside in their cars. At closing, the family who owned the restaurant delivered us home. I liked the job, but my mother wasn't happy with the late hours I arrived home.

In the fall, Mom got me a job working as a part-time secretary to one of the agents at the insurance company where she worked. I caught a bus after school to downtown to work and rode home with Mom. The agent was very kind and had three children of his own. The funniest thing he ever asked me to do was to go into a store and buy his wife a baby-doll nightie that he was too embarrassed to be seen buying.

Working after school forced me to give up synchronized swimming. Our swimming team had taken third place at the State Meet the preceding year, but colleges didn't give scholarships for women's synchronized swimming anyway. Since I wasn't working nights and weekends, I was available to play my violin in the orchestra when there were events. There are always tradeoffs! Sometimes we are forced to make decisions without being able to judge just what the tradeoffs are.

Working in an office further convinced me that I was NOT going to be more fodder for the insurance industry! Mom had finally been able to replace the coal-fired furnace with a natural gas one. She let me paint the former coal storage room and convert it into a place to study away from my Grandmother's need to have the television ever louder. I knew I had to get good grades to earn a scholarship, which I had to have to be able to go to college. Mom went to bed after the ten o'clock news, but I was often up until midnight.

My academic advisor suggested that I should attend a four-year liberal arts college rather than a university. Looking at their requirements showed my lack of foreign language credits. It was decided that I should take Latin. To get in the full two years before graduation, I had to pay to be tutored over the summer to earn credit.

My favorite teacher and mentor, Elizabeth Almen White, asked me to befriend a new student from Iran who was struggling with English. The lovely young woman of 16 had graduated from an American high school in Teheran and had come to attend Drake University. The university officials felt she needed more time with English before beginning her college courses. Her mother rented an apartment and stayed until Goli could begin at the university. Through my relationship with Goli, I was included in a group of foreign students who met informally at the home of a woman who had been stationed in Panama and spoke Spanish fluently.

At the insurance office, I had seen pictures of German prison camps and the huge piles of bodies of tortured and murdered people. One of the students came from the area in the Middle East where families were dispossessed of their homes, estates, and lands for the resettlement of the Jews by the Allies. What is fair for one group is so often unjust to another. Most of these young people would go home to arranged marriages, so there wasn't the pressure of much high school and college dating. I was not willing to settle for a "Mrs." Degree, three children, and a desk in an insurance office. I wanted to teach and to travel. It's important to remind yourself of your goals daily and to take advantage of learning opportunities along the way.

During my junior year in high school, I was chosen by the faculty for the Daughters of the American Revolution's Good Citizenship Award.

I gave my study hall time to work in the library and helped coordinate the annual Red Cross Drive under the direction of the librarian. Also at her direction, I had prepared and given speeches to service clubs on the United Nations. The preceding year, I had helped to organize the creative writing club that published an annual magazine of student work. It was probably believed that I could win the state-wide essay contest, but I didn't. It's important to realize that being successful doesn't mean winning everything. When things don't work out as you might wish, think about whether or not there is something you might have done differently to have changed the outcome. Then believe there is a better opportunity out there that will show up when you're ready.

Choosing a college is a difficult task. I was invited to teas for a couple of well-known eastern women's colleges. I was blessed by the home visit of a local graduate of one of them. She advised me that if I really wanted to teach, I would be better served by staying in the Midwest, because the better students in the East attend private schools which offer very low salaries. My college curriculum in the East would not certify me to teach in the Midwest. She was kind enough not to even mention how my lack of familial and financial status would also be great handicaps in her "alma mater."

Because I was at the top of my class in the fifth semester, I was chosen to take a competitive exam at Drake University. I was offered the Phi Beta Kappa scholarship to go there, but I would live at home. I was offered a scholarship and board job at Cornell College. Mom offered to try to help me get my junior year abroad if I would stay home and take the Drake scholarship. I insisted upon going to Cornell. I needed a more "normal" environment. My grandmother and her friends liked to sit on the front porch and assess every date. At Drake, I would hang out with Goli and other foreign students who didn't have the pressure of maintaining grades for a scholarship. I might also continue to be stuck in that insurance office.

At Cornell, I did get stuck in the Alumni Office. The people were great, but I envied those who had no office skills and were assigned to work in the dining halls and kitchens. They lost no study time to do their work. I loved my roommate. She had an older sister who was a junior there, so she knew all the ways of the college. Their father was an architect in the Chicago area. We got along so well that they invited me to go home with them for the summer. I was eager to do this.

My mother had been audited by the IRS. Even though I was away at college and working fourteen hours per week to pay for two-thirds of my board cost, the IRS made her divide her food bills by three instead of two for Grandmother and her. Lack of that qualified deduction reduced the dollars available for college tuition. She had arranged with her boss to give me a job filling in for vacationing employees. If I didn't come home and work, there wouldn't be enough money for me to return to college in the fall. I couldn't transfer my credits without first paying back the scholarship money. The only reasonable solution was to forge ahead with the program I was on and go home for the summer. At least there I could hang out with foreign student friends. Staying focused on your major goal forces you to make many compromises along the way.

At Cornell, I was most blessed to have been assigned to Dr. Walter J. Hipple as my academic advisor. It was his first year at Cornell. He was newly married to Hannah, who had been a secretary at the British Museum in London. About every quarter, they would invite half a dozen of his advisees to their on-campus apartment for afternoon tea. Dr. Hipple would play us one of his records of classical music. His sound system was wonderful! While at Cornell, Dr. Hipple taught in the English Department. I usually got one special, seminar-sized class with him each semester. When the English Department updated its requirements for graduating with a major, Dr. Hipple figured out a schedule for me, so that I could accomplish those requirements in the most economical way. I decided that I wanted to finish college in the shortest time possible. This was a new goal!

When I went home for the summer, I got permission to arrive at work late, so that I could take two classes at Drake University. I did that for two summers and carried eighteen hours at Cornell. When we set a goal, it may seem nearly impossible to accomplish. The help we need and the opportunities appear to make it possible. I was particularly happy to be leaving Cornell midyear with all my requirements for graduation completed, because Dr. and Mrs. Hipple had left for England where he had a Guggenheim Fellowship to do further study.

In the fall of my junior year in college, I was invited on a double date arranged by a sorority sister. My date was a Cornell graduate with a master's in library science and a position with the University of Iowa, which was about thirty miles away. For my twenty-first birthday, he gave me an engagement ring. He bought a lot and planned to build us a new house closer to his work. The head of the education department at the college found me a position filling in for a reading teacher in a small town seven miles from the campus for the semester until I would officially graduate. He also got me an interview and position at a school within five miles of Iowa City. Everything was perfectly arranged. I had a teaching position from January to June to earn the money for the wedding. Our goals were set!

Then I got a telephone call telling me that my fiancé was dating my former college roommate! I walked the seven miles to see my fiancé. I confronted him. He said it was true that he was dating my former roommate. I gave him back his ring.

When life doesn't go according to plan, it's necessary to set new goals!

When I called Mom to let her know the wedding was cancelled, she was relieved. The money I had been saving for the wedding could be spent to go to Europe. Mom said that she would come to visit me the next weekend, so that we could go to travel bureaus to see what might be available.

The following weekend while we were on the sidewalks of a city some thirty miles from Cornell's campus, we saw the head of Cornell's Education Department. I told him that I had broken my engagement and that I no longer wished to be teaching near the University of Iowa, but would prefer to teach in Illinois in the Chicago suburban area. He smiled, nodded and said he thought that would be for the best. The following week, I received a phone call from a school in Illinois offering to interview me on my lunch break at the school where I was teaching. I was interviewed and hired to teach high school English!

My high school mentor, Elizabeth Almen White, had led several National Council of Teachers of English tours of Great Britain. She helped me plan an itinerary. Dr. and Mrs. Hipple invited me to spend my first week in England at their home. Success wears many faces! What appears to be a disaster may be the greatest opportunity! Set goals, achieve them, and celebrate. Success is a lifestyle!

About Lynn

Lynn Kruse's passions are teaching and cultivating international understanding and cooperation. She graduated from Cornell College with an English major and minors in Education and French. Her MA was granted by Marycrest University in Specific Learning Disabilities. Lynn has taught all levels of the secondary schools and spent over twenty years teaching Freshman English in several different institutions.

Since teachers are not well paid, Lynn and her husband saved all of Lynn's salary for the first year and a half of their marriage to buy a house. They bought a duplex, so that the rent would pay the loan on the house. Subsequently, they also bought the next-door duplex.

In America, one makes more money as an entrepreneur and doing the manual labor of caring for and cleaning apartments than one does teaching. Improving and selling those properties, Lynn and her husband were able to get the capital to buy an eighty-acre farm in her husband's home area.

Living in a newer suburban house, they turned at last to their common interest of writing. After several years of struggle and countless rejections, their *Parent Prerogatives* was published by Nelson-Hall. They were interviewed on an ABC morning show in Chicago and did several book signings.

Lynn's next writing effort was two children's books. After several failed attempts to get them published, Lynn let them age in a filing cabinet for years. Discovering self-publishing on the Internet, Lynn decided to make *New Neighbor* and *Zoolatives* available to everyone. In 2011, she self-published a book of poetry, *Transitions*, followed by another named Insights in 2014.

In 1992, Lynn was invited to appear in *Who's Who in Education.* After much hesitation, she decided it was important for others to know that an illegitimate child raised by a single mom could accomplish life goals. Since then, she has been listed in *Who's Who in America* and *Who's Who in the World.*

After attending three workshops, Lynn also completed the year-long Train-the-Trainer Program to teach *The Success Principles* offered by Jack Canfield. She made several presentations to campus and professional groups including one in New York City to the International Convention of Delta Kappa Gamma, a Professional Educators Organization.

Following college graduation, Lynn spent six weeks traveling in the British Isles and France. Lynn visited China and Tibet with Educational Opportunities. Under the auspices of Iowa State University, Lynn did a family stay and studied in Spain. She participated in People to People delegations to Russia and to Egypt. While attending the Oberammergau, Germany, commemoration of Christ's Passion, Lynn's group was housed in a beautiful resort in Austria. In 2015, Lynn attended the International Congress in Edinburgh, Scotland, sponsored by the International Biographical Centre of Cambridge, England. The Centre has awarded Lynn an Honorary Doctorate, the title of Deputy Director to expedite the planning of regional conferences of the Americas, and the Tesla Award which will afford her a web page accessible through the Centre's web site.

CHAPTER 21

AT WAR FOR YOUR MONEY
– DO NOT GET CAUGHT IN THE CROSSFIRE

BY MICHAEL RIEDMILLER

There are two opposite sides that are literally at war and battling for your retirement dollars. On one side are the commission brokers that most likely want you to have all of your money in equities such as stocks, bonds, mutual funds and variable annuities. On the other side are the safe money agents which many times want your money to be in the bank and insurance products. These two different sides compete very hard for your money.

WARNING: The way that an advisor is licensed will likely determine where they want you to invest your money. There are huge potential biases and conflicts of interest because of this. Just think, if you are shopping for a new car and go to the Ford dealership, are they going to try to sell you a Chevrolet? Of course not. If you go to the Lexus dealer, are they going to show you a new Cadillac? Not a chance.

Everyone understands that there are many different kinds of doctors, but for some reason people think all financial advisors are the same. Regarding doctors, there are general practitioners, specialists, surgeons, dentists, chiropractors, eye doctors, foot doctors, etc. It's the same thing in the world of financial services. There are commission brokers (which used to be called stock brokers), financial planners, financial consultants, insurance agents, bankers, accountants, estate planning attorneys, financial coaches, etc.

The reason why I am involved in this industry is because I enjoy helping American Seniors, Baby Boomers and their families to live the life that they have always desired. It's all about helping them to have the very best quality of life. It is very fulfilling for me to see somebody who was previously fearful about their finances, and now has a real plan moving forward with the peace-of-mind that comes from this.

This reminds me of a new client partner that I recently began to work with. They were scared to death of running out of money, and for good reason. If they stayed on the path they had been on (and continued to listen to their current advisor), there was a very good possibility that they would have outlived their money which would have been terrible. After I met with them so I could learn about their specific situation and goals, we were able to work together and put a plan in place in which they are now assured of not running out of money. This gives me a feeling of great joy and satisfaction of being able to make a life-changing impact such as this!

YOUR CURRENT INVESTMENTS

Take a look at your current investments. If the majority of your money is in stocks, bonds, mutual funds and/or variable annuities, then there is a good chance that your advisor is a **commission broker or stock broker** (which is the same thing). There is nothing wrong with this, as long as you are aware of this and it fits into your investment objectives.

If the majority of your money is in the bank you might not be keeping up with inflation, thus your money is losing value every year. If most of your money is in insurance products, then your advisor would be an insurance agent.

QUESTION: Is your current investment portfolio prepared for the next major market downturn (whenever that may come in the future)? As we know things that happen in different parts of the world which we have no control over can have a big impact on the market and the value of your accounts. I hear from many American Seniors and Baby Boomers that do not know the reason why they hold certain investments. This is not good. Every investment should have a specific purpose and fit into your plan.

By the way, it's always head scratching when a person calls themselves a very **"Conservative Investor"** but they have the majority of their money in stocks, bonds, mutual funds and variable annuities. Or should I say, their "current" advisor has all of their money in these investments. In many cases, the best thing would be to change the word "current" to "former" when referring to their advisor.

College Planning is very important since the cost of sending children to college can be some of the biggest expenses that parents will face during their working years. The college that your children or grandchildren attend can have a big impact on the type of career and earnings that they will experience. Proper planning in this area can have a dramatic impact on the quality of their lives and on the amount of your hard earned money that you have to pay. There are proven strategies to reduce these costs.

And how about **Long Term Care Solutions**? This is a big issue since the majority of Americans will need some kind of long term care in their lifetime. I spoke to somebody recently that told me she had asked her current advisor about Long Term Care, and he told her to call an insurance agent because he didn't deal with it. This is a pretty good indication her advisor only operates in the risk management business and is probably a commission broker only.

Another new client partner that I was able to help had the vast majority of their money out of the markets. This fit into their goal of not losing money, but the challenge was that they were not keeping up with inflation. The buying power of their portfolio was being reduced every year. After meeting with them and learning about their specific goals and situation, I was able to put together a plan in which their portfolio will grow when the market is up, and will never lose value when the market is down. They are now able to stay ahead of inflation, safely grow their money and they still do not have to worry about any market losses.

REASONS TO WORRY

Did you know that from 2000 through 2010 has been called the **"Lost Decade of Wealth"**? This is because in May 2010, the stock market was around the same level as it was 10 years prior. If a person had $250,000 in their account in 2000, their account balance would have been at about the same level 10 years later (or even less after fees and other charges were taken out). Factor in inflation, and their buying power would have been reduced even more.

In 2008, the market was down by over 40%. Many American Seniors suffered great losses because of this. If you are younger and feel you can wait for the market to go back up, then this is the "Buy and Hold" strategy (or as some call it, the "Buy and Hope" strategy). For a retiree that needs to live on this money and will be withdrawing some of it from their account, this can have a devastating effect since they will be withdrawing money from a declining account.

Here is a simple example that will clearly illustrate a point. If you have $100,000 and the market goes down 50% and then back up 50%, what is your account balance? Many people reply that their balance would still be at $100,000, but this is **incorrect**. If you start with $100,000 and the market is down by 50%, then your balance is down to $50,000. If the market then went back up by 50%, then your account balance would be at only $75,000. So even though the average return in this example was 0%, the actual real return was a negative 25%. This is why I have people who see their account statements from their current brokerage accounts with their other advisors and ask me why their account balances (the actual dollar value) are going down even though it's showing a positive percentage return.

THERE ARE SOLUTIONS

When you the have proper amount of residual income being paid to you every month and you know it's going to continue for the rest of your life, this changes that way you invest (and you will sleep much better at night, too).

How would you feel to know that the money coming in from Social Security, and also any Pensions or other income would be enough for you to live on and enjoy your quality of life? This could give you a great feeling of peace-of-mind. Then you could have part of your portfolio invested like that 35-year-old that still lives inside of you. That 35-year-old who enjoys the market when it's up, and does not worry when the market goes down. The reason for this would be because a big drop in the market would not affect your monthly income payments. You can be fearless, instead of fearful.

YOUR FINANCIAL PLAN

It's very important to know that with your financial plan, you should have your money in three different areas which all have different objectives. Let's look at those…

1. The first place to have your money would be funds that you have **easy access** to (let's call it "9AM Money"). The returns that you make on it are not important. This would be money at the bank in your checking or savings account. Many people want to have enough money in this category to cover 6-12 months of expenses which they have ready access to.

2. The second place would be money that you have **at risk and invested in the market**. This is money that you hope to grow over time, and you are willing to ride the ups and downs of the stock market. Many people use the **"Rule of 100"** to determine approximately how much they should have in the market. Subtract your current age from 100, and this will give you the percentage that you might be comfortable of having in the market. For example, if you are 65 years old, you might want to have only 35% of your money at risk in the market. This way when the next major market downturn happens, it will not affect your entire portfolio.

3. The third place would be money that you still **want to grow**, but yet **not have at risk** in the market. There are financial strategies and solutions that offer upside growth when the market is up, but no downside losses when the market is down. This can give you the peace-of-mind of having your money not being at risk in the market while still growing it at the same time. Many Baby Boomers like to have 25-50% of their money in this category.

EFFECTIVE PLANNING

(a). What would the retirement of your dreams look like?

(b). What are the things important to you that you would spend your time doing?

(c). Who would you like to help?

(d). Where would you like to travel?

(e). What does your current Financial Plan from your current financial advisor look like? I am not referring to brokerage or account statements.

(f). What does your Risk Reduction Plan from your current financial advisor look like? If you do not have a plan like this, then it could be time to find a different advisor.

Experts advise that effective planning begins **before** there is a big loss to your portfolio, since it can be too late to initiate any worthwhile protection after the fact.

IT IS IMPORTANT TO KNOW

- Every investment should have a **purpose**. If you do not know the specific purpose of an investment, then chances are that it's a bad investment.

- We cannot plan for every single event over the next 20 years of your life. But if you do not have a plan, then you have a **plan to fail**. When you work with me and my firm, we will give you a total plan for today and your future, and then make adjustments as needed on a regular basis.

- There is **no perfect investment**. Every investment has its pros and cons which is the upside and downside. I always review all sides with my client partners so they know exactly how everything works. Many have told me that they have never had an advisor that did this for them.

- If you are confused by your current investments, then the financial advisor you are working with probably does not have a clear understanding for themselves and are not able to communicate everything to you. Or perhaps they do not want you to know everything about it. **Honesty and full disclosure** are vital for all financial matters, period.

Those that are pro-active and take "action" in regards to their portfolio could be better prepared for what might be coming in the markets. It's your money and your future.

People that have the most secure financial plans work with advisors that can help them with both equities and the safe money side. This way they can have a plan based upon their true financial goals and risk tolerance. I believe it is important to bring the competitive worlds of safe money and risk management together. This is the reason why I am **both securities licensed and licensed for multiple types of insurance.** With these different licenses, I strive to avoid bias and conflicts of interest as I enter into the planning that I do with my client partners.

It is now more important than ever to work with a firm that has a thorough understanding about changing tax laws, investment strategies, and the basics and perils of probate courts, wills and asset preservation for their heirs through trusts. I believe strongly in the team concept of working with dedicated professionals. Attorneys, accountants and financial professionals are invaluable in managing client's affairs. This requires a **broad-based, balanced approach to estate planning** which many other financial planners do not offer.

I work with my client partners to build a **"Total Plan"** so they have enough money coming in each and every month in addition to the proper amount of money in the bank and in their investment accounts. This is all based on their lifetime dreams, financial objections, goals, risk tolerance and much more. **I believe that your plan should be the same!** You have worked hard for the money you have in retirement – a proper plan is one that caters to your specific needs and goals. If you do not have a **Total Plan**, I hope that this chapter will help get you on the path to living the retired life you deserve and bring a little more clarity to the most important stage in your life, where every little bit counts.

About Michael

Michael Riedmiller is a Financial Advisor and College Planner with Pro Wealth, and an Investment Adviser Representative with Royal Fund Management, LLC, a SEC Registered Investment Adviser.

In order for Michael to be able to act in the best interests of his clients, he is both Securities-Licensed for equities and Insurance-Licensed for life, annuities, sickness, accident and health. This allows him to put together a "Total Plan" for his clients based upon their true financial goals and risk tolerance. He believes very strongly that it is important to bring the competitive worlds of safe money and risk management together.

Michael is passionate about building long-term relationships with his clients to help them achieve their important life goals and financial objectives. This has been accomplished through the right financial strategies which best serves each person's situation. The cornerstone of this strategy is a solid foundation of education and real world application of knowledge and experience. He strives to create tremendous value within these relationships by carefully listening to clients and understanding what is truly important to them.

Helping people to build a safer and more secure retirement plan and assisting families with college planning are things that Michael is passionate about. He finds many people that either do not have a plan in place, or do not know the reason why they have certain investments. He advises and helps his clients with investments both in and out of the market. Michael works very closely with his Professional Financial Teams in building the best plan that is customized to fit the specific needs of each client.

Michael is committed to delivering outstanding professional service to his clients and always acting with honesty and integrity. As a Financial Professional, he has a fiduciary responsibility to:
- Always act in the best interest of the client
- Exercise a high standard of client care
- Complete confidentiality
- Presenting accurately and in full all information essential to making informed decisions
- Recommending only financial products and services that are in the best interest for each client's needs
- Loyalty and integrity in all relationships
- Continually enhancing his knowledge and skills
- Regular contact and review

He attends several industry training and educational events every year from top experts in finance and retirement planning. He is actively seeking additional investment strategies so he can continue to deliver the kind of results his clients have come to expect in this constantly changing world and market. Michael has read hundreds of books on the subjects of investing, business, finance, success and entrepreneurship.

Michael and his wife, Carisa, have been married since 1995 and live in Nebraska. They have three children and enjoy spending time with family and friends, traveling, snorkeling in the ocean, hiking in the mountains, biking and meeting new people. Some of their favorite places they have traveled to include Hawaii (Maui, Oahu, Big Island), San Diego, Santa Barbara, Carmel, Colorado, Chicago, Florida, Cancun, Jamaica and the Dominican Republic. The kid's activities include basketball, baseball, tennis and cheerleading.

You can learn more about Michael Riedmiller at: www.ProWealthTeam.com
You can contact him at: mikeriedmiller@gmail.com

CHAPTER 22

COURAGE: YOUR FIRST STEP ON THE ROAD TO SUCCESS

BY MARGARETA KULL

What is success? Cutting the ribbon to the new offices of a business you've built from scratch? Never having to say "yes" to jobs you don't believe in? Showing your kids the new Sustainability Award you've received? Or hearing your partner whisper "I love you for who you really are"? Whatever your definition, one thing is to success what oxygen is to a flame. Without courage - success is hollow or out of reach. How do we grow our courage and keep its flame alive in a world full of fear?

I remember it like it was yesterday. I was in third grade. I must have been about nine. On the other side of the schoolyard a group of kids had gathered around Marie, a girl from my class with thick, brown-framed glasses. Her back was pressed to the fence and a tall, blonde boy, Peter, loomed in front of her, prodding her slyly and making snide comments as the others erupted with laughter around him.

I kept looking around me. "Maybe a teacher will come along" I thought, but I knew I was on my own. In between me and the group other children were playing, laughing, clapping. "Can't they see what's going on?" I thought. "Can't they feel the tension?" I was sad and angry. Afraid. My stomach a knot. My legs jelly. "What if I ask them to stop, but they don't?" I remember thinking, "What if they turn on me?"

Long term-success is built on courage – for ourselves and the planet

It's no accident we talk about being 'frozen' by fear. Fear does freeze us. When fear takes over it steals our future and numbs our limbs - unable to voice our true opinions or make the decisions we really want to make. Over my long years of business experience, I've seen how commonly fear limits our horizons, blinding us to essential, strategic, long-term issues and leaving us lurching from Quarter to Quarter. Volkswagen's recent fiasco is a great example: When the company admitted in 2015 that it had cheated on carbon emissions tests for eleven million cars, two-thirds was wiped off its market share in two days. Clearly for many VW decision makers, the fear of not meeting their short-term results outweighed the fear of failing to create long-term success, a sustainable planet - and a lasting legacy for the company.

Did some of the VW managers feel in meetings as I felt in the schoolyard all those years ago? I'm sure they did. And Volkswagen isn't alone. All across our planet citizens don't have to imagine a world run by fear – sadly, for many, it's routine: Feeling we 'have to' say yes to things we don't believe in, work under stress with no proof if it's even effective, stifle new ideas for fear of how they might be received. The sad truth is that for many businesses and governments fear is the rule not the exception, and whilst this remains so – for our children and our planet – any road to success is blocked.

Make friends with your fear

So how do we face down our fears – and become the leaders we really want to be? Courage starts by admitting we're afraid. And that takes guts. Fear thrives on shame and secrecy. Fear feeds on fear. Most toxically of all - fear is subconscious. We're often not even aware of it. Admitting we're afraid is nothing to be ashamed of. Fear is natural. It's often a sign we want something to be different. So look out for it. Sense it. Notice it. When you do – admit to yourself: I am afraid. Now you can begin. Your road to success starts here.

Fear: Is it always what it seems to be?

The next step is to reflect on what it is I am really afraid of. Fear is rarely what it seems to be. Let's go back to the schoolyard for a moment. Looking at it now, I realize that there was more there than just adrenaline-fueled panic. These were my classmates, my peers. Deeper than any physical fear, I was afraid of them rejecting, ignoring or humiliating me, and that I would just not be able to handle that.

Fear has three faces, know what you're up against

What I've learnt in my *The Human Element*® training has been confirmed by many years training organizations: The vast majority of our fears boil down to three powerful universal fears – which few of us are aware of. Many of us spend our entire professional lives protecting ourselves from these - without even knowing it.

1. **We're all afraid of feeling ignored**
2. **We're all afraid of feeling humiliated**
3. **We're all afraid of feeling rejected**

– Sometimes we're afraid of all three

Let me guess – when you read these you were a little disappointed. "Oh! Is that it? Is that all?" That reaction shows how subconscious these fears are. When we look at them consciously they can seem pretty harmless. But the subconscious pictures our fear summons up really scare us: We avoid raising difficult, strategic issues because we fear our team would dismiss us. We avoid challenging colleagues who don't follow through because we're afraid we'll be criticized ourselves in front of the team. We avoid giving co-workers frank feedback because we fear they'll like us less. Subconsciously, these three fears can feel like 'life-or-death.' We fear that what is happening could destroy us: Destroy the picture we have carefully built up of ourselves, our career and our relationships – leaving us feeling exposed, vulnerable and worthless.

Stop > Reflect > Act

When we drag these three subconscious 'beasts' into the light, it's astonishing how much they can shrink. We underestimate how powerful consciousness is. It's important to remember: Fear's not all bad. Fear is essential to our survival. We're not trying to 'overcome' it here - that would be impossible. We're facing it, and learning to manage it better. Facing down our physical reactions to fear takes practise. But our courage grows stronger every time we do it.

FLEX YOUR COURAGE MUSCLE: A THREE-STEP ACTION PLAN

1. STOP
When you begin to feel yourself reacting strongly in a situation:
- Stop.
- Be curious.
- Consciously evaluate your feelings and what's going on.

2. REFLECT
Reflect honestly on your fear. Find out the real reasons for it. Get it into perspective. Ask the following questions:
- *Is your fear here connected in some way to you feeling ignored, humiliated or rejected? How?*
- *How likely is it that what you are really scared of will actually happen?*
- *If it did - what could you choose to do then?*
- *What do you really want to do, here and now?*

3. ACT
- Do it.
- Act on your reflections.
- Make the decisions you actually want to make.
- Do what you really want to do.

Reflection is at the heart of courage: Prioritize it
Why do so many managers avoid consciously reflecting on their reactions? "I'm too busy" they tell themselves, or, more honestly, "What would my team think if they saw me staring out the window doing nothing?" But consciously reflecting is like training. Growing courage is like training a muscle, we need to keep flexing it or it dies. The more we flex and stretch it the stronger it gets.

How courage delivered millions in seconds
One of my clients improved the results of a negotiation by several million dollars – just by flexing his courage muscle and asking himself – what is it I'm really afraid of here? The answer surprised him. Deep down he was afraid that if he insisted on the right price the client would no longer like him, and maybe reject him. He told me: "I stopped, took a

breath and reflected. I asked myself: Do I really need this person to like me in this situation? No, my goal here is to get the business. I breathed, flexed and focused on this goal. It took 30 seconds at the most. When I went back into action the result was a totally different negotiation. I won respect, and the deal. I have a completely different relationship with the client now."

Small acts of courage have a big, big effect

For most of us courage begins with small steps, not epic acts. Courage isn't just scaling a mountain or rescuing children from a burning building, even though these take courage. Neither is courage technology-driven, in fact, look below the surface of even the most sophisticated tech. company, and you'll see it's courage that drives innovation. No. The courage I admire most is often found in 'small' acts – that deliver big change: Saying "enough" to the school bully, making the decisions we know are truly best for our business, opening up to strategic issues we know need to be talked about, hitting the green receiver and taking that tough call, saying "yes" and "no" when and where we really want to.

- **Courage is** not being "fearless" – courage is owning up to our fear, honestly reflecting on what it's really all about – and then doing what we believe in despite it.
- **Courage is** making the decisions we want to make, and being the leaders we want to be. And it gets easier the more we practise it.
- **Courage is** what enables us to be happy on our terms, in our way. Likewise, without courage, success is never on our terms, in our way.
- **Today's courage is** the sum of all the small acts of courage we performed in the past.
- **Tomorrow's courage** will be the sum of all the small acts of courage we started today.

Courage is listening to your inner voice

Even as a child I knew deep down that I was going to live life on my own terms. It was in my blood. In the Big State economy of 1970's Sweden, entrepreneurs like my parents, Brita and Åke, were rare. In a country that distrusted and suspected small enterprise they were their own bosses: their arms open, their hearts big, their days long... And they believed passionately in giving their kids the same tools and independence. They weren't afraid of hard work. They weren't afraid of risk. If you thought things through and did the right thing there was no reason why you should fail. Unbeknown to the other kids in the schoolyard that day, that is who they were up against.

I passionately believe that we all have an inner voice that never lies. Courage is listening to that voice, no matter how loudly our fear tries to drown it out. There comes a time for all of us when everyone and everything lets us down – but that small, inner voice will always be there, the voice of our values, our ethics, our true self. I can't really remember what compelled my nine-year-old self to resist the fear flooding her system that day, but I am sure that inner voice whispered not only "This is wrong." but "What would mum and dad want me to do?" Because something in me paused, and listened. And after a few seconds, that felt like an eternity, I strode across that yard:

"That's enough now Peter! What are you doing? You can see she doesn't like it! Come with me Marie," and arm-in-arm we marched away, adrenaline flooding through us as the crowd, shamefaced, parted – not a voice raised, not a punch thrown.

How quiet and undramatic it turned out to be! I know now, my whole attitude to fear somehow shifted. Somewhere inside me I began to realize that whilst fear is – well, frightening - that doesn't mean I need to follow it. It wasn't a 'heroic act,' I didn't feel 'courageous,' I was still afraid of Peter, and of being frozen out by the class. But there was a quiet confidence inside me now, I knew my mum and dad would be proud.

It was a quiet, cloudy day in a tiny schoolyard in the Swedish countryside, but somewhere inside me I'd taken a small, crucial step towards being a leader.

And today, you can too.

About Margareta

From highest vision to bottom line, from individuals to businesses to the whole planet – one thing drives success: Courage. Margareta Kull is an international trainer, public speaker and executive coach challenging people in power to grow their courage and become courageous leaders. Training executives and high potentials in a range of multinationals, she is recognized as one of the top transformational leaders in Europe. In 2015 she was honoured to be made a member of the Association of Transformational Leaders in Europe, created by Marie Diamond and Jack Canfield.

Margareta is the CEO of Kull Leadership AB, which she founded in 1995. The company's team of trainers, coaches and inspirers challenge managers, executives and decision makers in multinationals in the construction, pharmaceutical, consulting and IT industries. She has trained leaders from over 15 countries to make more courageous decisions. Her own management background is in the financial, global telecommunications industry and international advertising agencies, after graduating with an MSc in Business, Economics, Marketing and Finance from Gothenburg University in Sweden.

Read the book COURAGEOUS LEADER

Margareta's first book, *COURAGEOUS LEADER: Increase Your Impact by Facing Your Fears* will be published in the early part of 2017. In it she draws on 20 years' in-company experience to offer decision makers techniques on building courage and a courageous culture within individuals, teams and whole organizations. Using cases from science, technology and politics as well as business, *COURAGEOUS LEADER* is essential reading for good managers looking to become great leaders, and all decision makers committed to driving positive, sustainable change for the planet.

A divorced mother of three courageous young women, Margareta walks the talk and practises what she preaches: Her training, speaking, executive coaching and writing draws extensively on her own story and her own journey towards a more courageous and fulfilled personal and professional life. She has two remaining ambitions: 1) to leave the world a better place, and 2) to die knowing she's lived the life she truly wanted to live. One thing connects both, and yes, of course-

It's courage.

Connect with Margareta at:
- www.kulleadership.com
- info@kulleadership.com
- https://www.linkedin.com/in/margaretakull/
- https://www.facebook.com/kulleadership.se

For more information on the upcoming book, please go to:
www.courageousleaderbook.com

CHAPTER 23

TWELVE LESSONS IN TWELVE MONTHS OF REAL ESTATE

BY RODRIGO HURTADO

If you are not willing to risk the unusual, you will have to settle for the ordinary.
~ Jim Rohn

How does one measure success, when the road to success is littered with failures? Or, should I say learning. The answer lies in how you choose to define the moment.

After being an educator for eleven years, I found myself deeply fulfilled and deeply broke, unable to pay all of the bills that a family of four has. I had spent years living an unbalanced life that had culminated in my inability to afford the lifestyle that I had been blessed with, and now with a new baby our financial situation looked bleaker as each day passed by. This brings me to the first lesson that I learned in my journey to succeeding in the world of real estate investing.

Lesson 1: What you don't know can and will hurt you.

The opportunity of doing real estate investing had always been there, just like it has been for you. I just didn't know anything about it, so I couldn't see it. Frustrated and unable to find a solution to my family's financial challenge, I took massive action and purchased an expensive ticket that I couldn't afford to see one of my mentors, Tony Robbins, in Dallas.

Lesson 2: You must be willing to take massive action, anything less will yield an unwanted outcome.

After a weekend of transformation, my mindset had changed and I began to see opportunity where before I had overlooked it. I registered for a short seminar about real estate investing. That same day my wife had bought a lottery ticket. Needless to say, we didn't win the lottery, but I was blown away by the seminar and purchased the three-day seminar that was being sold. I was filled with excitement and a sense of relief because I had found a solution to our financial challenge.

Lesson 3: If the financial reward is great, it will not be easy; otherwise everybody would be doing it.

The room was packed with aspiring investors. The information was phenomenal and my mind was overloaded. My last minute guest and I decided to join forces, go full out and start our business. The tools that were presented seemed powerful and the strategies seemed fool-proof. On top of that, we were taking massive action. I had two challenges to overcome, bad credit and no money. What could possibly go wrong?

Lesson 4: Be ready to hear the word "no" more than you've ever heard it before. Therefore, you must know without a doubt that you will be unwaveringly passionate about your reason why you've decided to do this, because your perseverance will be tested again and again.

As a new real estate investor, I had to learn everything from the very basics of real estate to sales and marketing to running and operating a business with little to no money. However, my unwavering belief that I was going to be successful was more powerful than any obstacle I could ever encounter. Which led me to understand that time is our most valuable non-renewable resource that we have. Money can come and go, but once time passes it's gone for good. This led me to learn my next lesson in real estate.

Lesson 5: Visualize your outcome with such unwavering faith that you can burn the boat, and be absolutely certain that you've made the right decision. Then, you must follow through.

My time was being swallowed up by my job, and I was torn by my commitment to my students and my urgent need to get my business rolling. I was sleeping 3 hours a day, working on my business at night and any time I could create for it. With the absolute certainty that we would be very successful, I burned the boat and retired from my job as a teacher. With a massive debt, I decided to bet it all on myself knowing that I possessed the skills and will to be successful. However, before I made that decision, I learned the next lesson that is critical to your success in real estate.

Lesson 6: Leverage other people's knowledge and experience because you must have coaches, mentors and be a part of a community.

There are too many pitfalls in real estate, so unless you have someone to guide you through the countless questions that you will certainly have, you could leave yourself exposed and be out of the game as quickly as you got into it. Not every coach and/or mentor is created equal, so make sure that they are the right fit for you, because they will be the ones that will help you take your business to the next level. I found a local company that has brought so much value to my business, from mentorship and coaching to education and systems, to build my business. Another tremendous asset was the mastermind weekly meetings that allowed for me to continue my education, make me accountable and be a part of a community of like-minded investors that are action-takers. Becoming a part of this community led me to learn the next critical lesson to having success in real estate.

Lesson 7: Learning is great and important, but success will only come from taking action because that's where experience resides.

Fear is such a powerful force in our lives that we allow it to dictate our outcomes. Too many of us are consciously and subconsciously limited by our fears. We fear the unknown, so in order to break that fear down, we study the information by taking classes, going to seminars, reading books, etc. All of these activities are important and necessary, but ask yourself, "How many times have you learned something new and then never applied it?"

We all have drawers and notebooks full of notes with a wealth of knowledge that if we ever applied it, we'd breakthrough to another level. That's a challenge that many investors have to overcome. That is the clichéd "paralysis by analysis."

Our minds get so overloaded with knowledge plus there are so many great resources out there that we end up becoming "wannabe" real estate investors, when in reality we are just students limiting ourselves because we feel that we must know everything first before we can apply it. The outcome we get when applying this strategy is one of little results, because the strategy confuses inaction with learning. We have been programmed since our early schooling that you should get penalized for mistakes, so many respond by limiting their actions unless they know how to do it correctly. The truth is that our first reaction is likely wrong, so if you allow the fear of the unknown, the fear of rejection, the fear of being wrong, the fear of failure and even the fear of success to keep you hostage, then you will be one of the 95% of real estate investors that gives up. This led me to uncover the next critical lesson on the road to success in real estate investing.

Lesson 8: Mistakes are blessings in disguise, if you learn from them.

Mistakes must be viewed as our stepping stones to success. The mistakes you make will bring insights that are not taught in the seminars or webinars. We made the mistake of acquiring a house from a big wholesaler company that was covered in mold instead of mildew, so our projected $60K profit was wiped out just like that. We lost our non-refundable earnest money because we had to back out of the contract, but it became a mistake that allowed us to stay in business. Now I know exactly what mold looks like and smells like. Another mistake was not being flexible, thus causing the deal to fall apart over small differences instead of finding creative ways to bring value to the negotiation. Finding your road to success requires you to be unyielding in your determination to get to your desired outcome; however, if one road is blocked, look for another road, and if that road is blocked as well, look for another way. Remember that it's not about the destination; it's about the person that you become to get there. Like Jim Rohn said, "Never wish life were easier, wish that you were better." Mistakes are the tools that will get you there. One of the most important lessons that I uncovered on the road to success ties in with the experience that mistakes bring about.

Lesson 9: Commit to being consistent.

With consistency you develop your skill sets, and the only way to do it is by doing. Like in any business, lead generation is the life blood of your business. However, 48% of investors quit after the first contact with a prospect, yet only 2% of deals happen on the first contact. 72% stop after the second contact, yet only 3% of deals happen on the second contact. 84% have given up on a prospect after the third contact, yet only 5% of deals happen on the third contact. By the fourth contact, 90% have given up on the prospect. By simply being consistent, you have already eliminated the vast majority of your competition. You are now in the 10% that has 80% of the seller market available to you. What are some other benefits that consistency will bring to your ultimate success?

Your constant practice and action are building your confidence and momentum. By the time you get to that market that's full of opportunity, your skill set has greatly improved. Your ability to communicate and build rapport with sellers will give you an advantage over your competition that will blow them out of the water. You transform yourself from being an amateur investor to becoming a professional investor. Life begins to adjust to your commitments, not the other way around. You become powerful in your skills, and you begin to become fearless because you know that you are going to win. You are now a host to your success.

Lesson 10: Uncomfortable is good, comfortable is bad.

If you are thinking about getting started in real estate or any business because you believe with absolute certainty that you can and will create your own path down the road to success, then be ready to live permanently out of your comfort zone. The most common answer to questions about real estate is, "it depends." The reason is that every opportunity will come with unique challenges and plenty of the unexpected. Therefore, you have to condition yourself to be able to withstand the transition from the comfort zone to being out of the comfort zone via the panic zone. The panic zone will test your resourcefulness which is one of the critical skills that is needed to be successful in real estate.

At one point, I found myself with $8.00 dollars left in our account for my family of four to live on, and through determination and massive action we overcame the challenge. At another point, we found ourselves with three weeks left before we completely ran out of money and unable to pay for food and shelter. Yet, throughout those very uncomfortable experiences I was able to breakthrough because I have been conditioning my mind, body and spirit in order to get myself into peak state. It's in your peak state that solutions will be found. It's in your peak state that your abilities and skills will align with the universe. It is in these moments of great trial and tribulation that requires you to be fearless, direct your focus and experience your greatest most powerful self. It is where your why, as long as you are so passionately willing to do whatever it takes as long as you act based on your core values with integrity, that will guide you through the bumps and potholes of the road to success. None of this is possible in your comfort zone.

Lesson 11: You must build a team that aligns with your core values.

The moment you decide to become an active real estate investor, you become a business owner. When you are at the three-day seminar, the instructor tells you who the key people are that you will need on your team. Right of the bat you realize that the business you are now undertaking is not really real estate. You are in the building relationships business. You cannot succeed by going solo on the venture. Therefore, you have to become a great leader that can inspire your team. You do this by building a team aligned with the core values that will guide your business. It is in your purpose, core values and mission statement that you set the sail that can withstand market changes and the unexpected, that without a doubt will occur. In business, if you don't have problems, then you really don't have a business. Your job is to find solutions to those problems, and those solutions are found in the team that you build. To quote John Maxwell, "People buy into the leader before they buy into the vision." The team must be nurtured and their work must be valued. In order to make it on the road to success, you need to find the leader inside you, because that's where the final critical lesson to your success in real estate resides.

Lesson 12: It's not about you; it's about the massive value that you bring to those you serve.

In the beginning of your real estate investing career, you may find that the biggest challenge you face is aligning your skill set with the massive value that everyone that you come into contact with will require you to bring. As you take massive focused and consistent action, you will begin to develop into a deal maker. You will lose your fears and become this confident, powerful investor that creates value by structuring deals that are win-win-win-win. You will master the art of influence by connecting deeply with who you talk to by getting them to do something for their own reasons. You will ask powerful questions that will reveal the wants and needs of those you serve. You will be able to contribute to the community by rebuilding it, assisting families that are struggling with challenges that life throws at them, as well as creating beautiful homes for new families. You will also develop the critical skill of influencing yourself. You see, the road to success in real estate investing is really the road to transforming your life. To quote Tony Robbins, the man who provided the environment that allowed me to believe that I could overcome any challenge, "I challenge you to make your life a masterpiece. I challenge you to join the ranks of those people who live what they teach, who walk the talk."

Do you have the courage to be successful in real estate?

About Rodrigo

Rodrigo Hurtado is a professional real estate investor in the Dallas, Texas area. Rodrigo is behind Ultimate Vision Investments, LLC and iWillMakeYourHousePayments.com LLC. Rodrigo has done a variety of real estate deals from wholesaling to fix and flips, short sales and owner finance transactions.

Rodrigo believes that home ownership should be attainable for all those who are rebuilding their lives but are unable to purchase a home traditionally. Rodrigo believes that real estate should be a partnership between buyers and sellers, so his business aims to provide massive value in the acquisition and selling of real estate.

Rodrigo has a Master's degree in Conflict Management and Dispute Resolution from Southern Methodist University in Dallas, TX as well as a Bachelor's degree in Communications – Advertising from Southern Methodist University. He is a member of The Real Alliance and received the honor of being Investor of the Year in 2015. Rodrigo was a middle school teacher in Plano, TX for 11 years where he taught AP Spanish, a leadership class and established a peer mediation program.

Rodrigo is married to his beautiful wife of 10 years, Miriam. He has two children, Amelie and Oliver.

You can contact Rodrigo at:
- ultimatevisionllc@gmail.com
- www.facebook.com/Ultimate.Vision.Investments.llc

CHAPTER 24

HOW TO BE HAPPY, SUCCESSFUL, AND UNDERSTOOD AT WORK

BY SARAH E. BROWN, Ph.D.

The happiest I can remember being vocationally was the year I worked on my master's degree in mathematics and taught college-level courses. It was also one of my most productive times. I completed my thesis in record time, solving a mathematical problem that had languished unsolved for years. I taught undergraduate-level calculus, inspiring a few others to love math the way I did. I had a real sense that I had made a contribution to the field of mathematics and to real people (my students) all at the same time.

My career then went off on one tangent after another, until I came full circle to understanding what I unconsciously knew about myself that year in graduate school. In the process, I came to a different definition of success. My Road to Success took over 30 years. What I learned could make your Road to Success a 30-day journey.

I have always had an affinity for numbers, and I always did well in math at school. I planned to earn my Ph.D. in mathematics and teach at the university level while doing theoretical mathematics research. So I was thrilled when, at age 21, I got a fellowship to work on my master's degree and began teaching introductory calculus classes. I rode my bike approximately two miles onto the campus at Wake Forest University every day, rain or shine. I can still feel what it felt like to have the wind on my face, and I remember that I was always a bit rosy-cheeked when I arrived at my own little office. I imagine that my hair was pretty crumpled from my helmet, but I don't think that ever bothered me. I do vividly remember how filled with energy I was at that point each day.

I had total control to plan my days. I know now that freedom and control over my time is critically important to me. I spent an hour or two bouncing ideas off my thesis advisor, like a conceptual ping-pong game, strategizing various approaches to this unsolved mathematical conundrum. This gave me my "fix" of just enough human contact to then retreat to my private little office, where behind closed doors, no one bothered me as I researched, thought on my own, and wrote papers on the results.

About noon, I would stop and go for a run. There was a big, beautiful park with wooded trails, and I would run several miles all by myself. These runs cleared my head and got my energy going again. They also served to help me shift gears for the rest of the day.

In the afternoon, I taught calculus. This is a subject I knew extremely well, so preparation was a breeze. I loved interacting with the students, all of us focusing on what to me were fun puzzles to solve. I doubt all those students thought the subject was as fun as I did, but I know my passion for the subject came through to them and made the class more enjoyable.

My days that year were filled with activities I loved: research, writing, and teaching; a limited amount of time interacting with others; and lots and lots of exercise outside. I was in my zone—setting challenging goals, structuring my time with great discipline to achieve them, and interacting at an intense level with one or two people at a time. I cannot recall feeling any stress that year, so I know my underlying needs were met.

This was sheer bliss for me.

And that was the last time I was to feel that for more than 30 years.

In 1977, when I was completing my master's degree, I learned that the market was flooded with Ph.D. mathematicians. Many were "waiting" on tables while "waiting" to get academic appointments. I did not think

I needed a Ph.D. if I were going to wait on tables. And I did not have the competitive drive that I felt would be needed to compete with others for the few academic positions that might be available. This latter point, not having the competitive drive, turns out to be an important component of my personality, but I was oblivious to that at the time. I set challenging goals and compete with myself, but when it comes to competing against others, I shy away.

I did have a basic need that I was well-aware of: I needed money. I was unaware, however, about what was behind that need for money and why I felt such anxiety when the source was unknown. I assumed everyone had this need for security, but I was to learn that is not the case. In any event, I decided to scrap my plans for further graduate school and get a job where I could earn steady income. I settled on a job with the former Bell System as a telephone systems engineer in Charlotte, North Carolina. While it satisfied the need for steady income, the job was not a good fit for me. The work was very hands on, and I soon became claustrophobic as I was working inside central offices where there were no windows. I never saw the light of day. But I slogged through, did my very best to perform well, and just pushed deep down inside me just how unhappy I was doing this kind of work.

Was I successful? To the outside world, the answer was yes. I found niches where I could excel. I got recognition from my superiors and frequent promotions. But I was not interested enough to find ways to develop deep maintenance skills and knowledge. So when the Bell System broke up by court order in 1984, I looked around for someplace else to work, eventually moving north to work in the IT Department at DuPont. I worked there for close to 14 years. I had some good jobs, had some bad jobs, got steady promotions, but did not do much that I was hugely passionate about one way or the other. When DuPont outsourced its IT to CSC and Accenture, I joined Accenture.

One thing that I will never forget about my time at DuPont was a training course I was sent to in Hershey, PA. This training was designed to help new and mid-level female managers get in touch with their passions and strengths and to embrace them with more confidence. What I can remember vividly from that session was that I came face-to-face with the fact that I had no idea who I was. I had no idea what my ideal job was. I had lost any sense I may have had about what I was passionate about. I had no idea what my strengths were. When I felt stress, I assumed I was just not up to the task. Unfortunately, I failed to gain any clarity in that training. I went away quite depressed because I did not have anything to "unleash and embrace with confidence." So I quietly pushed it all down and continued to try to do what I could in whatever job I was in. I was not miserable. But I was not happy either. I was not a failure, but I knew I could have been more successful. I did feel stress often, but I was not about to let anyone at work see that.

So fast forward many years. Following another series of career decisions that were logical but based off no knowledge of my interests, strengths, or needs, I find myself managing large Business Process Outsourcing engagements for Accenture. Here is what I started observing. I was not the only one that did not know him or herself well. Many of my clients were less than happy at work. Some, like me, were just getting by and not focusing much on the fact that they were not happy. Some were flat out miserable. But I saw something else. Some of the unhappy majority were making changes to become happier with the assistance of coaches. What were the coaches doing? They were helping their clients get in touch with what made them uniquely happy and what their innate strengths were. Then they were supporting these clients in making a change to better pursue their interests and use their innate strengths. And here is the real kicker. Those that were becoming happier were also becoming more successful in their own eyes and in the eyes of those that observed them.

It was time I sorted this out for myself once and for all. What did I really love? What were my unique strengths? I still did not know. Did I need a coach? Fortunately, I was in a position that I could afford a coach, and so I got one. But the hard work of articulating the uniqueness of me was still to be done. With the help of a really good personality assessment, I was able to zero in on my unique interests, my strengths, my needs (and what stress I am going to feel if these are not met). With this knowledge, my coach supported me in making the career decision to retire early to focus on research, writing, and teaching. This is what I knew to be passions and strengths well over 30 years prior. My days now are much more joyful, and certainly, less stressful.

But a lot of people cannot afford a good coach. What can they do? I have learned that it is still possible to find out what is unique about you by following a simple 3-step process that I call the Know Thyself Process®:

1. KNOW. Get a little bit of information about your interests, strengths, and needs.
2. TEST. Share this with someone who knows and cares about you and who can help you think through what you can do with this information to increase your happiness, success, or sense of being understood.
3. GO. Take some action with this TESTed KNOWledge.

The trick, of course, is coming up with that little nugget of knowledge about your interests, strengths, and needs to get this process started. I think a good assessment is the fastest way to go about generating this knowledge, but here are a few things you can do on your own:

1. Your interests. These are the things you love to do on a day-in and day-out basis. Do you like the outdoors, as I shared about me? How much activity do you want? Do you like to work with your hands? Do you want to spend time directly helping or influencing people? Things like this. The best source of this information is yourself, and you can make a great start at this by just spending an hour writing down what you were doing when you believe you were the happiest.

2. Your innate strengths. What are you really good at? I find that the best way to answer this question is to ask someone else. My experience is that many people have a very jaded view of their own gifts. So ask someone who knows you, "When I was at my best, what was I doing and what strengths did you observe?" Keep quiet and just take notes.

3. Your motivational needs. I think this is the hardest component to do without an assessment, but you can start by examining every time you felt stress. What did you need when you felt that stress? For every answer you write down, ask "why" five times. You will begin to get at the underlying motivational need. (Example: To stay out of stress, I "need" a guaranteed income of $75K/year. Why? Because I need to live in a safe house, drive a reliable car, and get routine healthcare. Why? Because I worry about my personal safety and I will focus on that if I feel there is any risk to it. Why? Because I am not good at last minute problem solving and I need to do everything possible to prevent problems rather than solving them when they arise.)

With knowledge about you, your Road to Success can include satisfying the components of happiness and being understood as well as being successful. As I observed with my clients and experienced myself, when you get in touch with these three things that are unique to you, you will know what gifts you have to serve the world. And following this process can take more like 30-days than the 30 years it took me.

There is a reason they say on airlines, "Put your own mask on before helping others."

About Sarah

Sarah E. Brown, Ph.D., is leading the charge to revolutionize the self-help industry through the power of personalization. An expert on using the results of personality assessments and the author of the *Book of You*™, available at: www.bookofyou.com, she has created a way to generate a completely personalized book for each reader based upon the results of a quick, but world-renowned, personality assessment. A subsequent book, *Let Your Personality be Your Career Guide* is available on Amazon.com. This book contains a wealth of stories and exercises to help an individual quickly determine the key personality components that should be considered in choosing a career.

Following a very successful career in Corporate America, she retired as Managing Director at Accenture to devote herself to personalizing self-help advice in the form of customized books. With a Ph.D. in PsychoEducational Processes, 15 years of Talent Management experience, and skills and experience in scaling complicated operations, she is uniquely qualified to do so.

In addition to her writing, Sarah is available to speak or lead workshops aimed at building the self-awareness individuals need to be happy, successful, and understood in their various pursuits.

A native of Virginia, she now resides in Wilmington, Delaware, with her husband and standard poodle, Maharani. When not writing, researching, or speaking, she can be found rowing on the Christina River or chasing Maharani through the woods.

You can contact Sarah at:
- sarah@bookofyou.com
- www.bookofyou.com
- 1-302-521-9739
- www.facebook/bookofyou.com

CHAPTER 25

HOW TO BE YOUR OWN BOSS?

BY VICTORIA CUPET

Why people keep living unhappy lives and do nothing about it? The answer is different for each person.

In my case, ten years ago I was living an unhappy and unfulfilling life while trying to have a "perfect" life. I was doing my best to be a *perfect* wife, *perfect* friend, *perfect* employee, and so on. I was very busy performing my *perfect* roles, and, by the way, I was very successful at doing that. I was living a story which wasn't mine.

When I finally decided to break free from my fake life, it was a painful process on many levels. Beyond my emotional struggle, I had to deal with a lot of resistance from outside. All my family members, friends, and colleagues liked me being *perfect*. I needed to make a clear decision. Either keep my friends and family or step into the unknown and find myself in the middle. With the risk of being misunderstood and misjudged by other people, I took the chance to discover my true self. It took me a difficult divorce, after eight long years of marriage, and losing many friends, to finally find my freedom.

I paid the price for being who I am now: strong, happy and a free spirit. I am no longer living for others. I am no longer working for others. I am living my own dreams. I help other people to discover their life's purpose and be their own boss!

So how did it all happen? First of all, I asked myself the most important question: *Who am I and what do I want from life?* The answer I received was, *"I am a free spirit and I want my FREEDOM!"* In my particular case it was about freedom of choice. I wished to be able to choose where to live, whom to love, with whom to work or not to work, and many other choices in life.

The next step was to take 100% responsibility for everything that happened in my life in the past and will happen in the future. Full responsibility means accepting my failures and seeing them as my life lessons. There is nobody to be blamed for my decisions!

And the most life-changing step was to commit to deliberately create my own future. It means being conscious of my choices and acting upon my dreams. So I sat down with my diary and wrote my ideal life. Initially, it was a very general, loving relationship, fulfilling career, healthy body, etc. Later, I added many specific details and even financial figures.

I asked myself many questions and received many answers. It was my chance to have an honest dialog with myself. *I always say that my biggest pain was my greatest gift*! After becoming crystal clear about my ideal life, I started to see my dreams come true. My current husband asked me to marry him after only two months being together as a couple. We are happily married and have two amazing kids. Regarding my career, I am blessed to have everything I ever imagined. I am a successful coach, trainer, consultant, author and speaker. I have the freedom I always desired. I have freedom to travel the world with speaking and teaching engagements, freedom to choose clients to work with as a success coach. I have freedom of expression as a writer and artist.

So why is my story relevant to you? If you ever wished to live your dreams, then it's about you, not me!

I became a recognized world expert in my field, I acquired more than 20 International Certifications, and many awards. If I can do it, YOU CAN DO IT. If you wish to have more freedom in your life, if you want to be recognized as an expert in your field, if you dream of BEING YOUR OWN BOSS, then my story is relevant for you!

As a certified Law of Attraction coach and Neuro-Linguistic Programing

(NLP) trainer, I will guide you through a step-by-step process to make your dreams come true.

STEP 1: LOVE YOURSELF AND BELIEVE YOU DESERVE THE BEST

The first step is the most challenging. It is about loving yourself as you are and believing you deserve the best. If you already love yourself unconditionally, then congratulations. You can jump to the next step. If not, then allow yourself some time. Since the process of falling in love with yourself requires time, be patient!

Start by accepting yourself as you are right now, in this moment. Nobody is perfect and there is no need for you to be perfect! You are as you need to be at this particular time in your life. Forgive yourself for everything that happened in the past. Everything that happened in the past are lessons you needed to learn to be who you are in this moment. We learn through our failures. *Our most difficult lessons in life are our greatest gifts!*

As for any love relationships, the honest dialog is the most important. Be honest with yourself. Have a dialog. Ask questions and allow answers to come. Be grateful for your story!

As an exercise to help you build a stronger bond with your true self, use affirmations. It can be any kind of positive and loving statement. I personally use these: *"I love myself. I honour myself. I trust myself. I respect myself."* Use it daily as often as you can. Repeat it the first thing in the morning and before going to sleep. Set-up a reminder on your smartphone. Put some post-it's all over your place to remind you about these affirmations. How long to practice these affirmations? As long as needed to start believing in these statements. Your brain needs repetition to learn them and accept them as undeniable truths.

If you tried affirmations in the past and they didn't work for you, replace statements with questions. For example: *"Why do I love myself as I am? Why do I accept myself as I am? Why do I trust myself as I am?"* Our brain loves questions! When it receives a question it starts immediately searching for the answer (e.g., *"I love myself as I am because ..."*).

Have patience and build a strong, loving and trusting relationship with yourself. This is the base for all the other steps.

STEP 2: DREAM BIG!

This is the most creative step. Spend some time alone and ask yourself the question, *"How would I like my ideal life to look and feel like?"* The answers will come to you through pictures, feelings, or you can even hear the answer, or just know it. No matter how you receive the information, trust your intuition, and record the ideas without judging them.

One way of recording your ideas is using mindmapping. It is a very creative way of organizing ideas around a subject. In this case the subject is your ideal life. Start by drawing a circle in the middle of the page and write, *"My ideal life"* inside it. Then, draw some branches for each area of your life (e.g., love, relationships, career, finance, health, etc.). For each branch, draw additional smaller braches to add new ideas to it. You can expand each branch as much as you need, until you have the feeling of completion.

A vision board is another tool to record your ideas. It is a collection of images and pictures which reflects your desired outcome. You can have a vision board for any period of time (e.g., three months, one year, ten years, etc.). You can do a physical vision board by cutting images from magazines and newspapers. Or you can create an electronic version of it by searching for images and pictures online.

Let's say you finished your mindmap and your vision board. What next? Next you use it as a visualization tool. If you make your vision board and then put it on the shelf, there is no real benefit of doing it at all. Similar to the affirmations, a vision board is a powerful tool only if you are actively using it.

You can put your physical vision board on the wall of your bedroom, so you can see it before going to sleep at night and the first thing in the morning. If you have an electronic version of your vision board, place it as the wall paper on your smart phone, tablet, or your desktop computer.

A vision board act as a light house. It helps you see "the light" of your desired outcome during "stormy" days.

STEP 3: ACT

Many people create a vision board, do the affirmations and then wait for miracles to happen. It doesn't work like this. If you want to have results in this physical world, you need to do physical effort. This doesn't mean you need to have a detailed plan of each step you will take to bring your desired outcome into your life. It means we need to do our part of the job and let the Universe do its part. It is a joint venture. You show the Universe what is your desired outcome. The Universe brings you the opportunities in life. Your part in this play is to act upon them!

Sometimes acting means stepping out of your comfort zone. Nothing new or exciting is inside your comfort zone. Learn new skills, meet new people. Challenge yourself. Expand your limits.

Working in partnership is like dancing with the Universe. You do one step, then the Universe does a step. Then it's your turn to react. Then the Universe offers you new opportunities. Then you take the challenge and advance closer to your dreams. Enjoy the journey!

STEP 4: HAVE FAITH AND BE READY TO RECEIVE

Let's stick to the same metaphor of the dance. In the process of dancing, you surrender yourself to the flow and have faith and trust in your partner. Would you enjoy dancing if you would constantly doubt your partner and his or her movements? I would definitely not enjoy it at all.

The same is true for partnering with the Universe. When you create the vision board, you show the Universe the direction. When you act on the opportunities you receive, you show you are ready for the next step.

What happens when you start doubting the process? First of all, the Law of Attraction and Quantum Physics says, *"What you focus on expands."* When you put doubt and fear into this process, you attract more events, situations and people, which will amplify these feelings. When focusing on doubt and fear you are attracting more doubt and fear.

It is like dancing on a surface with lots of stones on it. You are losing the feeling of the flow and focus more by avoiding an accident or injury. Would you enjoy dancing in this setup? I would not. I prefer to trust my partner and enjoy the process.

How can you avoid doubt? By visualizing that you already have the outcome you desire to have. By feeling like it is already yours. By seeing it next to you or in your hands.

Also, you can use the affirmation *"I am ready to receive ... in my life right now"* or alternatively the question, *"Why am I ready to receive ... in my life right now?"*

STEP 5: BE GRATEFUL

Last but not least, be grateful for everything you have in your life. Be thankful for your past and present gifts. Remember, all the challenges we have are our lessons to learn from.

Gratitude has a very high vibration rate. When you focus on gratitude you attract even more things to be grateful for!

I am grateful to the Universe for letting me share my story with you. I am grateful to you for allowing me to guide you to live your dreams and be your own boss.

Love your story. Honor your story. Be proud of your story. Make your own story. Be your own boss!

About Victoria

Victoria Cupet is a certified coach, trainer, and consultant, a passionate artist, author, and speaker, as well a loving wife and mother of two boys. She has vast experience in professional fields such as business analysis, process management, and project management, as well as in the personal development area.

As an expert, Victoria has a key role in promoting business analysis on a local, regional and international level. In 2015, in her role of President of IIBA Romania Chapter, she received the *President's Award (Tier 2)* and the *Innovation Award* offered by the International Institute of Business Analysis™ (IIBA®) at IIBA® Chapter Awards. To achieve her purpose of contributing to the growth of the business analysis profession, Victoria was also a member of the writers' team for the new version of the *Business Analysis Body of Knowledge® (BABOK® Guide) v 3.0*. In 2016, Victoria was recognized as one of America's Celebrity Experts®.

For many years Victoria has attended international events as speaker and workshop facilitator. In 2015, she was the keynote speaker at the *Balkan Business Analysis Conference* (BBA2015) in Belgrade, Serbia.

Victoria's deep knowledge and strong commitment are proved by more than 20 international certifications. In the business area, some of her credentials are: Certified Business Analysis Professional™ (CBAP®), PMI Professional in Business Analysis (PMI-PBA), Project Management Professional (PMP), among others.

Beyond her vast consulting background, Victoria is recognized as a certified *Business Trainer*, a trainer for *Neuro-Linguistic Programing (NLP)*, and for *Personal Development Programs*. In these roles she supports professionals to advance their careers, by helping them learn new skills, as well as to successfully prepare for various certification exams.

As a coach, Victoria guides her clients in defining their success stories and supporting them in having it all! Being a *Law of Attraction* Certified Coach, she helps her clients to apply universal laws and principles to create successful careers and businesses, loving relationships, healthy bodies and abundant life.

As an author and motivational speaker, Victoria empowers her audience to believe in their true potential and DREAM BIG!

You can connect with Victoria at:
- www.victoriacupet.com

- www.facebook.com/victoria.cupet
- www.twitter.com/victoriacupet
- www.linkedin.com/in/victoriacupet

CHAPTER 26

CRYSTALIZE YOUR SUCCESS WITH THE DIAMOND METHOD™

BY MARY MESTON

You are, at this moment, standing, right in the middle of your own 'acres of diamonds.'
~ Earl Nightingale

What is your vision of success? What would you like to accomplish? What will provide you with a deep sense of fulfillment, joy and contentment? Is it clear? Does it sparkle?

Success is different for each of us. It might be that next promotion. It might be more time with your family, or making a visible contribution to your community or a cause you feel deeply about. And your vision of success may change over time. A close friend of mine's definition of success was to become a vice president of a manufacturing company, now it is something completely different.

As I have moved from student to corporate warrior to coaching, I've come to define success as: "Living from and into your full potential" in the direction you choose.

I've studied, applied, refined and polished what I call the Diamond Method™ for achieving success. It has worked for me, it has worked for my clients and it can work for you. Before you read on, take five minutes.

Grab a piece of paper and write this down and complete:

"I am (or will be) successful in my own eyes when I…. "

START WITH A POSITIVE MINDSET
You cannot have a positive life and a negative mind.
~ Joyce Meyer

What do you believe about yourself? Do you believe you can do great things? Or do you believe the deck is always stacked against you? Your mindset is your foundation for anything you want to accomplish.

Scientists have spent a lot of time studying what makes some people successful and others not. They studied people with similar backgrounds, upbringing and education and found a positive mindset improves income, health, creativity and productivity over 30% with greater joy and fulfillment! And lowers stress by 30% too! Success begins with getting and nurturing a positive mindset.

Our challenge is to develop a positive mindset isn't easy or natural. Our primitive brain is wired to protect us from threat – it works to keep us wary and on guard for real and imagined threats. Your decision to mindfully and consistently engage in mindset practices keeps our primitive brain from taking over. Your positive mindset is the crucible for creating your diamond of success.

Are you positive you know how to stay positive? Here are three of my favorite practices:

1. **Journaling** – is a good way to capture and pin down what you're thinking and feeling. Different than a diary, journaling allows you to record those fleeting ideas, thoughts and insights. It helps you control your mindset rather than letting it control you.

2. **Daily Gratitude** – Tomorrow morning spend five minutes reflecting on and writing down what you're thankful for and why. Even in my worst times, I could find a couple things. You'll find more, I promise. You will discover this five-minute practice will change the way you look at life for the rest of the day.

3. **Affirmations** – are short descriptions of who you are (even if it is something you are still reaching for). Recite these a few times each

day – and do your best to actually believe and "see" yourself as your affirmation describes you. It is a great way to jump-start embodying who you are and intend to be.

Clarity – The 1st Element

"Would you tell me, please, which way I ought to go from here?"
"That depends a good deal on where you want to get to."
"I don't much care where –"
"Then it doesn't matter which way you go."
~ Lewis Carroll, Alice in Wonderland

Take another look at the definition of success I asked you to write down earlier. How detailed is it? Can you . . . "see" it? . . . "touch" it? . . . "feel" it? Does it tell you who you are, why you want that success and what you will do to achieve it? Without the details, you are counting on luck and serendipity to lead you. It will be an "interesting" journey, but the chances you'll actually achieve your goals and dreams is very small.

Clarity is your starting point. Who? Why? What? Get these right and you'll have momentum to move through the other elements of the diamond method.

> ➤ WHO are you? What are your values, your non-negotiables, and your very core ideals? If you threw off the constraints of your environment and the expectations of your family, friends and co-workers, who would you be? Have a chat with the 5- or 6-year-old "younger you." That will give you a good idea of who you truly are.

> ➤ WHY do you want your success? Your WHY is your deep emotional reason you commit to something bigger than yourself. Remember the annoying little kid who continued to ask why? (I was that kid). Practice that to get to your true "why." Your first answer might be superficial, but asking about the why of your why six more times will – like eating an artichoke – will bring you to the heart – yours.

> ➤ WHAT are you going to do? It is the external manifestation of your WHO and your WHY. It maybe a new business, the birth of a third child, the next promotion, your new book, or simply eating well and exercising each day. Goals of all sizes, types and meanings are the "WHAT" you want to achieve. Many of us think we are clear, but in reality we only know the "WHAT" of our dreams without the deeper WHO and WHY.

Courage – The 2nd Element

I learned that courage was not the absence of fear, but the triumph over it.

The brave man is not he who does not feel afraid,
but he who conquers that fear.
~ Nelson Mandela

Now it's time to start. It is in action where you can achieve. Taking those first few steps can be scary. Remember the first time you tried to ride a bike or decided to dive off the high dive? Were you scared? Probably, but you did it anyway. And now you're fine.

Courage is not the absence of fear. It is taking action in spite of fear. I want you to feel the fear and move through it anyway. It has a huge impact on your likelihood of success. Try these practices my clients and I find helpful to foster courage, the second element in the diamond method.

> ➢ **Mine your fear**. What are you afraid of? Specifically? Don't let your fear be an amorphous blob engulfing you like the Sci-Fi monsters in B Movies. Fear distills down to three types. Is it fear of loss, fear of change or fear of actually achieving what you want? Shining a light on your fear gives you the advantage in planning how to face it and move on.

> ➢ **Size it**. How big is it, really? Is a lion chasing you? Did you get into a small fender bender and know your spouse isn't going to be happy? Are you afraid of you'll miss a few words in that important speech? Some things are truly life threatening, others aren't. Assessing your fear frees you to act appropriately.

> ➢ **Chunking**. Break down what you need to do into manageable parts and steps. Celebrate each step on your courage journey and develop momentum to continue on to success.

True courage can be mastered – it takes practice. The first time you take that leap, know it is going to be scary. But once you do it, once you experience your joy and fulfilment of facing your fear, your confidence and self-assurance will grow. And in the unlikely case you do fail, the outcome is going to be less "awful" than you imagine it and you'll grow from that too. As your courage grows, so does your competence. The most successful entrepreneurs, CEO's and leaders have mastered the practice of courage.

Competence – The 3rd Element

By stretching yourself beyond your perceived level of confidence you accelerate your development of competence.
~ Michael Gelb

Competence – in any area – is not something you are born with. You need to develop it—in any area. Competence comes from doing and is the third element. I'll bet you weren't "competent" the first time you rode a bike, did a long division problem or drove a car. And if you just read about how to ride, compute or drive, or even watched endless videos on the topic, you still wouldn't be completely competent. It is something that comes with practice. Learning, trying, adjusting, and repeating. You are not aiming for perfection, you are seeking to become competent. A client of mine used to be so shy she literally could not speak to a group of more than three people. She now routinely speaks to audiences of hundreds.

Can you see how courage fits in here. Are you beginning to see how the elements meld together?

Your skill and commitment to developing competence is developing your courage. As each of us grows in competence, we take effective action quickly and easily.

How will you build your competence?

> Seek out knowledge. Make it a goal to learn a new skill, talent or try a new experience. With the wealth of information available at our finger tips on the Web, it couldn't be easier. I bet you have watched a couple "how to's" on YouTube already. Make a weekly plan to take what you've learned each week and do something with it.

> "Practice, practice, practice." Just like location, location, location is the key to real estate value, practice is key to mastery. So go pull out that old sheet music or work on your metaphorical swing.

> Actively seek feedback. Think about your car's or smart phones GPS. It knows where you are, it knows where you want to go and it knows how to get you there. Best of all, it tells you when your location doesn't match what you need to do to reach your destination. Feedback from mentors, colleagues and friends serves as your GPS. Use it graciously.

Confidence – The 4th Element

When you have confidence, you can have a lot of fun. And when you have fun, you can do amazing things.
~ Joe Namath

Ok, write this down - on a scale of one to ten, how confident are you. In your work, in your social life, in your family life?

Now write this down – why are you confident or why are you not? What builds your confidence and what tears it down?

Confidence is – of all my elements –both a starting point and an ending point. Getting clear, mastering the ability to feel fear and move through it anyway and striving for your best, all combine to create high levels of confidence. That's the ending point. The secret is once you've arrived, you can use this confidence to go through another cycle of clarity, courage and competence. With that new-found or renewed confidence you now have created a new, higher foundation to launch to yet another level of success.

And any of you that scored yourselves an 8 or above – you're not challenging yourself enough!

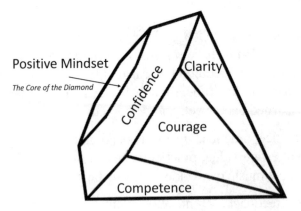

SUMMARY

So this is my Diamond Method™ – designed, refined and tested – to empower you to higher levels of success in any way you define success.

While it may seem simple, it is the simplicity that makes it so effective. Things don't have to be complicated to be effective. Embrace the four C's (elements) of my Diamond Method™. Practice them daily. You'll build clarity, courage, competence and confidence. And with that, you'll achieve success in reaching any destination you choose.

For the past 15 years, I have worked with individuals, teams and organizations just like yours. When they embraced the Diamond Method™, I've seen amazing accomplishments with people, teams and organizations just like yours. You can too.

You can always find another reason to stay in the same spot, see the barriers and do nothing. What treasure is beyond those barriers? What if you saw that clearly, overcame the rationalizations, reasons and – yes – the fear, and began your journey through, around or above them? What would you achieve?

Confucius observed that a journey begins with a single step.

I know you will take courageous action to reach your defined destinations with your new found competence and confidence.

Enjoy the journey and . . . don't forget to sparkle.

About Mary

Mary Meston helps her clients design and achieve their successes in life and do it in a way that is enriching, fulfilling and joyful.

Raised in a hard-scrabble small town in central Wisconsin, she learned early in life the need for, and value of, hard work. She leveraged that work ethic into a successful leadership career in a variety of companies across the spectrum – from start-ups to Fortune 500s, and in industries as diverse as footwear, utilities, software, biotechnology, pharmaceuticals and consumer products.

Along the way she learned the unpleasant truth that while working hard is a prerequisite, by itself it isn't enough to truly be successful. Often what prevents us from being successful are the barriers and blind spots we carry with us. That insight drove her to create a unique approach to finding and achieving personal success. After years of stressful, and unfulfilling, corporate life, her Diamond Method™ helped her to jettison the perceived safety of a corporate career. She tested it, refined it and tested it again on herself and those she worked with – until she felt it was ready to share on a larger scale.

In 2001, Mary left the corporate world to work with individuals, teams and organizations that wanted to develop the clarity, courage, competence and confidence to do great things. This approach continues to be the foundation for her personal coaching and organizational consulting practice. Mary's clientele spans the entire business map and ranges from small business owners and entrepreneurs to C level executives, professionals and leaders.

She founded **2SoarSolutions** – a coaching and consulting company established to further assist in her mission to end the continuous cycle of unhappiness, negative thinking and scarcity so prevalent in today's world. She knows that having what you want just out of reach is frustrating and disheartening. Far too many frustrated professionals settle for second best. It is important to not wait for joy, happiness and success, assuming it is just around the next corner. It is also important to know working harder doesn't necessarily mean you will get to your success. It is more important to put your efforts into leveraging a success method you know works.

Mary graduated with a Bachelor's degree in Psychology (with Honors) from Marquette University. She earned her Master's degree in Organizational Development at JFK University while actively consulting worldwide. She is also a Certified High Performance Coach (CHPC) with the High Performance Institute, an International Premier Success Coach and a featured speaker with eWomen Network events nationwide. She currently practices from both Cincinnati, OH and San Francisco, CA.

You can connect with Mary at:
- www.2SoarSolutions.com
- MaryMeston@2SoarSolutions.com
- www.facebook.com/mmeston1
- www.twitter.com/@MaryMeston
- Linked IN - https://www.linkedin.com/in/marymestonchpc

CHAPTER 27

THE #1 SALES HABIT

– SALES PERFORMANCE IMPROVEMENT WITH LEADING, LEANING AND LAGGING METRICS

BY NIK NIKIC, CEO AND FOUNDER OF SALES OPTIMIZER, LLC

Success and failure are both forged by HABITS.

The purpose of this chapter is to share the 4-step process for optimizing sales results by building a continuous improvement sales system. The key outcome is to develop the #1 Success Sales Habit to help you get maximum results with minimum effort. We've heard the saying that it's not about working harder but smarter. We think it's about working Smarter (process), Faster (tools) and Better (skills).

I read many sales and most of the best selling success books of all time and I found the latter are much better. My goal is to help translate those success principles, apply them to the sales profession and make it simple to execute.

I've tapped into some key concepts and created an executable sales improvement blueprint using three ingredients:

1. I started by extracting key principles from the best selling success books ever written and translated them to apply to sales.

2. I found a critical missing link in sales metrics; a Key Performance Indicator (**KPI**) concept we coined as **Leading, Leaning & Lagging KPI's**.

3. We tested this blueprint through practical application and learned from leading over 1,000 sales transformations.

Many companies invest, or rather waste, billions on training and tools to improve sales performance despite research showing that for the vast majority there is no tangible improvement. A 2015 McKinsey Global Survey of 1,713 executives noted that 26% say their transformations have been successful at both improving performance and sustain improvements over time. *That means a 74% failure rate.*

My objective is to provide a practical approach to ensure a near 100% success in your sales transformation.

The Sales Optimizer Story

After a ten-year successful corporate sales career, I spent eight more years in sales training before starting Sales Optimizer. During my sales training career, I worked for two great companies and we delivered excellent sales training programs without helping our clients realize sustainable sales results.

Getting an Electrical Engineering degree from Johns Hopkins taught me to think logically, simplify the complex and ask questions like *"why can't we deliver sustainable results and why can't we measure to prove— without a reasonable doubt—the ROI of our training?"*

When I started Sales Optimizer, I had the vision to develop a solution that would deliver sustainable sales results. The Sales Optimizer team has made enormous progress in perfecting the solution and we are now excited to share our findings with a broader audience, which includes you! The rest of this chapter is an overview of the 4-step process for building the #1 Sales Habit critical to predictable and measurable increase in sustainable sales results (see diagram on the following page).

Sales Success Habits – are the Key to Continuous Sales Performance Optimization

Success, failure, and mediocrity are all defined by HABITS or unconscious patterns of behavior, leveraging the power of our subconscious mind to power our success.

Albert Einstein defined "Insanity" as doing the same thing over and over and expecting different results.

Are your current HABITS helping you achieve your personal goals? No? Will you continue doing the same thing or will you develop a new HABIT to achieve your goals? What would prevent you from doing it? Old habits … because most of us have never "consciously and proactively" formed our current habits. Most of our habits just happened.

I am going to ask you to do something new, consciously and proactively follow this blueprint to design and execute a plan that in 15 minutes per day will develop a HABIT that will help you succeed beyond what you can currently imagine or believe.

- *We are what we repeatedly do. Excellence, then, is not an act, but a habit.* – **Aristotle**

- *Successful people are simply those with success habits.* – **Brian Tracy**

Companies invest a fortune in sales training and CRM systems, but get little to no value because they fail to convert that investment into a HABIT. Until new knowledge gets applied continuously for an extended period of time to become routine or a habit, it is essentially useless and even worse, it's a nuisance or distraction. We all know this but continue to blindly try new things only to see them fail over and over, because we are not willing to do what it takes to make them a useful habit.

In my experience, the only way to improve individual sales performance is to improve the **quantity** and/or **quality** of the **right activity**. I will layout a simple (but not easy) blueprint for developing the **#1 Habit** of increasing your personal and your team's sales productivity by 30 to 50% in 3-6 months by working less but doing it **Smarter, Faster and Better**.

As we all know, new habits are hard to form and old habits are even harder change. My favorite book on developing habits is *Mini Habits: Smaller Habits, Bigger Results* by Stephen Guise. Some key concepts that explain why habits are so hard to form:

- It takes an average of 67 days to form a habit, not 21 days.
- The brain is wired to protect you against BIG changes and will sabotage your efforts.
- Habits are like muscles; once you've developed a habit, you can make it stronger.
- Trying to develop more then 1-2 new habits simultaneously will lead to failure.

Amateurs become professionals by converting and perfecting conscious knowledge and skills to subconscious habits or routines. If you want to be paid like a true sales professional, take the next 90-days to develop one new sales habit using this sales success blueprint.

The 4-Step Process for Developing the #1 HABIT to Optimizing Sales Performance

In this blueprint, there are four critical steps that work together to develop the #1 Habit of a continuous improvement sales system. Poor execution on any one of these steps leads to failure.

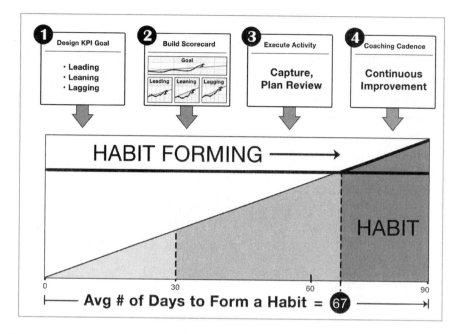

Step #1: Design the "KPI Goal"

One of my all-time favorite books is *The Goal: A Process of Ongoing Improvement* – January, 1992 by Eliahu M. Goldratt and Jeff Cox. This book does a fabulous job of describing the relationship between the right goal and the supporting metrics for continuous improvement in a manufacturing environment. My objective is to translate this to sales and make it practical for execution.

There are many books on the topic of setting goals; one of my other favorites is *Succeed: How We Can Reach Our Goals* by Heidi Grant Halvorson Ph.D. Great concepts but not practical or easy to execute. We have also found that thinking of goals and metrics separately is part of the problem. This section is about creating a killer "KPI Goal" that defines the relationship of a sales goal to KPIs to simplify the complex and enable better execution of the sales process.

> *Complexity is the enemy of execution.*
> ~ Tony Robbins

Moneyball: The Art of Winning an Unfair Game by Michael Lewis is a great case study in understanding the power of leveraging the right metrics. The basic premise is a hundred years of statistics wasn't optimized until someone started looking at them differently. They found the most important *Leaning* metric was **"on-base percentage."** Billy Beane, the manager of the Oakland A's leveraged this metric to try something different and with the second lowest payroll in baseball, he put together a team of misfits using this one metric to identify undervalued talent for his goal of winning without spending. The rest is history. That team challenged for the American League record for consecutive wins and changed baseball forever.

So what is a KPI Goal?

It is a simple way to anchor a sales goal to the right **Leading (L1), Leaning (L2) and Lagging (L3) KPI's**. The power is in the cause and effect relationship between these three levels of KPI's and the sales goal.

Let me illustrate by using the Moneyball example. The Goal: Win enough games to make the playoffs: The KPI metrics:

1. **L1** - # Of at bats
2. **L2** - On-Base %
3. **L3** - # Of runs/game

By improving those three KPI's, the Oakland A's went from last to first and into the playoffs.

In sales, I can give you dozens of sales KPI metrics, but I would be doing you a huge disservice. If you want to increase sales by 10% to 20% in 90-days and build a continuous improvement sales system, here is an example of great supporting KPI metrics:

1. **Meaningful Conversations**
2. **Deals Created**
3. **Deals Won**

In sales like in Moneyball, we have found the key to success is the **Leaning KPI** because it is the measure of the **quality** of activity.

Here is our definition of L1, L2 and L3 KPI's for sales:
1. Leading - activities
2. Leaning - outcomes
3. Lagging - results

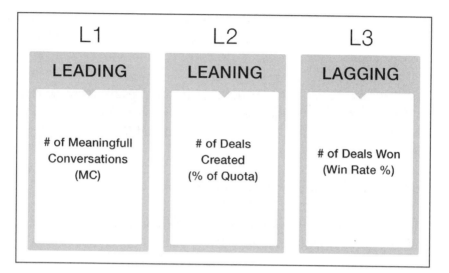

Note: This is not the only or the best but an example to guide your KPI Goal design.

"KPI Goal" example:

Sales Goal—Increase sales in 3 months by X% from Y to Z
- **L1 KPI**—Increase # of meaningful conversations by X% from Y to Z
- **L2 KPI**—Increase # of new qualified deals by X% from Y to Z
- **L3 KPI**—Increase win rates by X% from Y to Z

The ONE Thing: The Surprisingly Simple Truth Behind Extraordinary Results by Gary Keller and Jay Papasan is an excellent book that supports this concept of developing a laser like focus on one goal and KPI's.

Most people don't understand the power of compounding. This is especially true in sales. Here is the power and magic in choosing the right KPI's: How much do you think you need to increase the L1, L2 and L3 KPIs defined above to achieve a 15% sales? **The answer is 1%.** If you are like most people, you are saying, **"No Way!"** I say, **"Yes way!"** Let me show you how.

KPI Name	A Starting KPI Value	B Conversion Ratio	C Desired % Increase	D Target % (Column B+C)	E Ending KPI Value	F % Cum. Increase
1. # Meaningful Conversation	100		1%	1%	101	1%
2. # Of deals Created	10	10%	1%	11%	11.11	11.10%
3. # Opportunities Won	3	30%	1%	31%	3.44	14.80%

If you focused on only one **KPI Goal** for 90 days, can you increase performance on by at least 1%, like win rate from 30% to 31% (Columns B & D)?

If yes, you would realize a 15% increase in sales. A 2% increase results in 31% more sales. A 3% increase equals 47% more sales. Please do the math. During workshops, I ask this question and 99% are shocked by the answer.

Step #2: Build a Sales Success Scoreboard

A CRM is critical for optimizing sales performance. Over the past decade we have helped hundreds of companies deploy salesforce.com with our award wining sales performance Apps that make it easier and faster to enable the sales process. One of those apps is Sales Performance Optimizer, which was designed for this specific purpose. It was developed to simplify and automate the process of managing KPI Goals and helping sales people develop the right habits. Below is an example of a Sales Success Scoreboard.

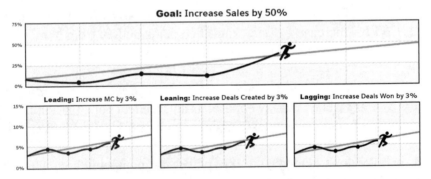

Like the latest technology we use to get fit, the key to an effective scoreboard is making it simple and easy to use. We need a way to easily capture and provide a real time display of our KPI's using our mobile devices. It's a way to display our L1, L2 & L3 KPI's contributing to the achievement of our sales goal. Additionally, salesforce.com "Wave" analytics engine can leverage these KPI's to analyze and transform entire sales organizations.

My favorite book on this topic is *The 4 Disciplines of Execution: Achieving Your Wildly Important Goals* by Sean Covey, Chris McChesney, and Jim Huling. In this book, they refer to how a scoreboard is critical to a sporting event. It engages the fans while providing the participants a summary of the key KPI's. It should be simple, easy to understand, easy to access, instantly tell you if you are winning or losing against your goal and what you need to do to change the outcome.

Step #3: Execute Activity

Success is the sum of our skills and habits, which are both formed by activities. The paradox is skills and habits are developed with activity but activity is hard to do without habits. Consider successful people you know, look at their skills and the activity it took to develop those skills and habits. Elite doctors, lawyers, athletes, professors, politicians and sales people all have developed skills through repetition of the right activity.

Developing a Success Sales Habit starts with execution of the right activity and then:

1. **Capturing the key activities and outcomes** – to improve, you must be willing to measure what matters. This is where CRM's are invaluable in easily capturing the key activities and outcomes. Capture only what matters, your meaningful conversations and opportunities. That's it.

2. **Process, review and plan your next steps** – every day, process what you did, review your scoreboard to see the impact of your actions, all for the purpose of planning your follow up activities or next steps.

3. **Read and Review your KPI Goal** – every day, read your KPI Goal out loud. This is the most critical step. You must be willing to burn into your subconscious mind your most important KPI Goal. The longer you do it, the stronger it becomes as your subconscious mind takes over converting your goals into reality.

These three steps take a total of about 10-15 minutes per day and are the critical foundation for building your #1 Sales Habit but it takes step #4 to make it a continuous improvement system.

Step #4: Coaching Cadence

Chris is my sixteen-year-old son with Down syndrome. He was born with a hole in his heart, has had dozens of surgeries, has a 70 IQ and could not walk until he was three.

Every morning at 6:00 AM, Chris gives me a big hug, says, "I love you, Dad, can we go to the gym?" Often enough, I want to say "no", but I always say "yes." You see, I helped Chris develop the habit of exercise and now he is my accountability partner.

I am my son's accountability coach, but I do hire specialists to help, like a coach to prepare us for a sprint triathlon, someone who is an expert on all three legs (swimming, biking, and running). Chris was born with many obstacles, but through great success habits, he is doing amazing things. We have learned that the right habits overcome all kinds of obstacles.

Coaches do three things for us:

1. Motivate us
2. Teach us
3. Hold us accountable

Weekly Coaching Cadence

As a coach, you must invest thirty minutes with your team, to create a culture of accountability to the execution. Each person gets five minutes to display their Scoreboard and answer three questions:

1. What did I do to move my metrics?
2. What did I achieve?
3. What I am going to do next week?

This is the single most important meeting of the week for building a continuous improvement sales system. Nothing should ever get in the way of this meeting.

About Nik

As Founder and CEO of Sales Optimizer, LLC, Nik Nikic brings over twenty years of experience to his clients by helping them execute their sales transformation in order to achieve measurable sales results. By using three levels of KPI metrics—Leading, Leaning, and Lagging—Sales Optimizer is able to deliver one cohesive solution that is supported by change management and powered by CRM market leader salesforce.com. Sales Optimizer made the INC 5000 fastest growing private companies list five times—an impressive and rare achievement.

Prior to forming Sales Optimizer, Nik was the EVP of sales and program development for Richardson, a premier skills training company, and before that a Sr. Partner with global sales methodology leader OnTarget (aka The TAS Group), prior to it being acquired by Siebel Systems, the global CRM leader.

Nik is a graduate of John Hopkins University, where he earned Bachelor of Science degrees in Electrical Engineering and Computer Science. His core competency is helping companies design, build, and execute successful sales transformations. And what does he bring to the table? A commitment to transform sales training from training events to a profession that builds sustainable improvements in measurable sales results validated by a pay-for-performance compensation model.

As a sought out keynote speaker, Nik has spoken at national sales conferences for United Technologies, CSC, Universal, Toshiba, Xerox, Deloitte, PTC, Gartner, Imagistics, Kodak and many others. He is an author of many white papers on optimizing sales performance, and a co-author with Jack Canfield in the book *The Road to Success*.

In Nik's personal life, he is grateful for his wife, partner and the love of his life for thirty years, always supporting and encouraging him to pursue his goals. He is passionately involved with his son Chris's Special Olympics endeavors. For his daughter Jacky, he has enjoyed being part of her life journey and her passionate pursuit of success in school, basketball and now her business.

CHAPTER 28

TAKE YOUR INCOME PRIVATE! A FINANCIAL LEMMING NO MORE!

BY PETER HIBBARD

Very early in my financial career I happened across a book by The Brookings Institution called *A Voluntary Tax?* It changed the direction of my career. This book reviewed studies of wealthy families in an effort to try and understand how the use of sophisticated estate planning can help these families avoid the estate tax in an era of relatively high estate tax rates. The conclusion was there are many tools available that account for eliminating or at least reducing the amount of estate tax paid. However, the true advantage to these families was the use of a special breed of legal and financial advisors who not only knew about the tools to be used, but more importantly had the ability to time, combine and sequence them to implement the tax reduction strategies.

As my career evolved, I wondered why the same result could not be accomplished relative to income tax at the personal level and corporate level as well. As I worked on this goal of reducing or eliminating income tax in retirement planning, I developed the proprietary TCS Process (Timing, Combining and Sequencing). The reason I became more passionate about this goal was our clients' painful experience regarding their taxes. As I learned more and developed my process, it was clear they needed relief from the taxes they were paying. Now here's my question. Do you think tax rates are going up in the future, or will they remain the same or will they decline? Most people when asked this question think tax rates will move up. At the writing of this piece, the USA is over $19 Trillion in debt and increasing. If you have the stomach for it, please go to: www.usdebtclock.org.

The USA has over $59,000 in debt per citizen and over $160,000 in debt per taxpayer. Few people can tell how this debt will be managed. But the real scare is in the amount of Unfunded Liabilities. Unfunded Liabilities are the sum of those benefits the USA, State and Local governments have promised to pay in the future. The problem with Unfunded Liabilities is that little money has been set aside to pay them. When looking at the debt clock you can see the unfunded liabilities amount to over $101 trillion dollars. If you're like me, you see no way to handle all of this unless the government takes more from its citizens in the form of taxes or confiscated assets. I'm not trying to be an alarmist, I just want you to think what your future or your children's future might be in a more highly-taxed world. Your retirement would be much less secure than it is today.

So how does one go about building a more secure future and protect it at the same time? The very first step is to see the danger, break from the pack, and DO NOT follow the other lemmings over the financial cliff.

The Wall Street casino and its penchant is to counsel you that you must risk your money to make money. The Wall Street casino, using its brokers and advisors, have told you that the general market has averaged about 9-10% over a long time period. With 2-3% of that return being dividends, the balance of 6-7% comes from appreciation. Therefore, you can conclude that over time 6 to 7 percent is the average growth rate of the markets.

That may sound all good and well, but it's a Wall Street half-truth and it's a misleading statement. If I put $1,000 in my investment account and it had a negative 50% return and positive 50% return the following year, I will have averaged a 0% rate of return. Let me ask you this, what would my account balance be? Many people are shocked when they do the numbers and see the answer is $750. When I tell my friends I averaged a 0% return over the last two years. They would logically assume my account balance stayed the same when in reality it went down by 25%. I would have told a half truth. There are periods of time when the markets go up greatly and other volatile times when the markets go down significantly. Actual returns and average returns (what Wall Street boasts) are never the same if there is a negative return in the years being measured. Negative returns distort the discussion and humble us all. The only way to have average return and actual return equal each other is when you never have a loss in your portfolio.

Avoiding losses is much more important than trying to grab all the gains you can get. Using the average rate of return ignores one of the biggest retirement risks which is the Sequence of Return. How would it feel if you had been age 65 in 2008 and you planned on retiring the next year? Many people experienced a 40% to 50% loss with a corresponding reduction in their account balances. They were devastated and many had to put retirement off for many years. As Warren Buffet said, the first rule of making money is never lose money, the second rule is not to forget the first rule.

So playing in the Wall Street casino is taking a big risk most are not willing or should not be willing to take. The second risk to going over the cliff is to let people and institutions leverage off you. The two best books on leverage are Eric Lofholm's book *Leverage* and Robert Kiyosaki's book *Retire Young, Retire Rich*. So what is leverage? In his book he defines leverage as the ability to do more with less. Robert Kiyosaki says this: "Leverage is the reason some people become rich and others do not become rich... Because leverage is power, some use it, some abuse it, and others fear it." – *Retire Young, Retire Rich*, p. xiii. He goes on to say: "The reason less than 5 percent of all Americans are rich is because only 5 percent know how to use the power of leverage. Many who want to become rich, fail to become rich because they abuse the power. And most people do not become rich because they fear the power of leverage." Finally, he says: "People who only work hard have limited leverage. If you're working hard physically and not getting ahead financially, then you're probably someone else's leverage." – *Retire Young, Retire Rich*, p. 33. My corollary to Kiyosaki's statement is you need to stop others from leveraging off you.

I believe the Wall Street casino leverages off you as noted above. They want you fully invested so they can make their fees and other forms of compensation from your assets and investment mistakes. They keep you in the game by keeping you positive. Ever hear the comment from your broker or advisor: "hang in there, the market will come back, it's only a paper loss." Financial advisors make their living by taking fees from your account whether it goes up or down in value. If they can convince you to keep giving them your money and you're lucky enough that it grows in value, they want to keep you in the game so they can make more money from your larger account. They want you in the game your entire life.

Who else leverages off you? How about your state and federal government in the form of taxes and fees? Probably the greatest destroyer of wealth is taxes. You pay tax on your income, tax on your dividends and tax on your gains. Retirement plans like IRAs, 401(k)s, 403(b)s and other pre-tax plans are only tax-deferral mechanisms. These government-controlled plans have regulations to force you to take money out so the government can get their slice of it. In the old days, you maybe had a chance to retire into a lower tax bracket. As I discussed above, in today's fiscal climate with all the debt and liabilities our governments have, it's more likely than not you'll retire into a higher tax bracket. The result is you deferred money in a lower tax bracket only to be taxed in a higher tax bracket. So look around and see who's leveraging off you.

There is a solution to this Gordian knot. There is a way to retire richer and sooner. The proprietary solution I'm proposing works for you as Joe Bluecollar or Pete Whitecollar. It also works extremely well for business owners and professionals. Wall Street wants you to grow your assets, but that is not the ultimate solution. Accumulating assets for retirement is necessary, but no one lives on just assets alone. You and I will live well with less anxiety if we know we cannot outlive our income. What if you had income that continues regardless of the balance of your assets? Our parents and grandparents planned on a three-legged stool for retirement. Social Security retirement income and old fashioned employer pensions are the best examples of income for life. The problem is most employer pensions plans have disappeared. The third leg of the stool was personal savings. Today we're left with a two-legged stool. One leg is Social Security and it has its problems. The other leg is personal savings and investment. So to retire with confidence and security we must stop letting Wall Street and Government leverage off us.

There is a solution. A strategy that will let you grow your money tax exempt, similar to an IRA or 401(k) retirement plan. However, the money in this strategy grows tax free for the rest of your life. Would it be of interest if it could provide you a tax free retirement income for life? You are taking your money private since pulling money out of the Strategy is not a reportable tax event if done properly. When you take your income private you are taking income off the 1040 tax form.

The strategy will let you take money out almost any time without regard to retirement plan regulations that penalize you if you take the money before age 59½ or if you don't start taking a minimum amount of your money out by age 70½. If you're fortunate enough to have money in an IRA or a 401(k) plan, the strategy, as a companion, can work in tandem with the pre-tax money to insure it never runs out. The strategy will allow you to fund any amount you can reasonably afford. In many cases, we can bring OPM (Other People's Money) to the table to help fund this strategy if your income and/or net worth are enough to warrant such an option. We partner with the finest financial institutions in the world in bringing the strategy to the market.

With this strategy you are no longer following as a Financial Lemming going over the cliff. The Strategy gives you these opportunites:

1. Over a lifetime, it's the least expensive method of savings when compared to the cost of taxes and fees taken by Wall Street and the government in any other saving or investment strategy providing similar returns. Yes, there are fees associated with the strategy and they are lifetime fees. The total fees of the Prestige Strategy will be approximately 75% less than the other saving and investing methods.
2. No income taxes are due on the earnings in the Prestige Strategy.
3. You will never have a loss on the money in the Prestige Strategy product.
4. The interest you earn is tied to market gains. The interest crediting methodology gives you upside potential and downside protection that halts decreasing market returns at 0%.
5. The Strategy let's you earn money like your banker. Banks have forever made money on arbitrage. You deposit money with a bank and what will they pay you on a CD? You'll earn less than 1% in today's interest environment. What the bank pays you is their cost of money. Now that the bank has your money, what do they do with it? They lend it to others at 5% or more. That's the bank's opportunity on the money. In other words, the bank's cost of money is always

less than their opportunity on the money. That's called arbitrage and in the bank's case it's always positive arbitrage.

As you may have guessed, this strategy uses institutionally priced life insurance. There are many insurance companies that say they have products that do all the things I listed above. That is not entirely true as there is but a handful of quality companies that do this well. Only a handful of companies have all the right contract provisions and financial strength to make this strategy work.

About Peter

Peter Hibbard has been in the financial services business since 1971. In 1978 he founded Columbia Benefits Consultants, Inc. DBA CBC Retirement Partners, Inc. (CBC) which is an independent consulting firm advising clients and their advisors on the advanced tools and techniques needed to create total financial and retirement security. CBC brings a unique series of services that holistically assists business owners and their employees to achieve their retirement goals. CBC may be engaged to provide actuarial, administrative, recordkeeping and advisory services for companies to establish and manage quality retirement plans for its employees. In addition, CBC's retirement income and compensation planning divisions help clients design their compensation systems in a way that properly aligns the owners and their key employees' vision of their future to grow the company profitably.

Following graduation in 1967 from Rutgers University, Pete was commissioned and served as an officer in the United States Marine Corps. During the Vietnam War, Pete was an infantry platoon commander and was decorated for his leadership in combat. He is also the recipient of a Purple Heart. He is a member of The Forum 400, the Society of Financial Services Professionals, American Society of Pension Professionals and Actuaries, The National Association of Actuaries and Consultants, and the Association for Advanced Life Underwriting. He has earned the professional designations of Chartered Life Underwriter (CLU) and Chartered Financial Consultant (ChFC) conferred by the American College, Bryn Mawr, PA. He speaks nationally to organizations of tax and investment professionals.

Pete and his wife Beth have two children and four grandchildren and reside in Columbia, MD. His daughter, Kerri, is a busy mom of four boys. Pete's son-in-law, Tim, is CBC's President, a registered investment advisor and plays an integral part in the firm's compensation planning, exit planning, and wealth transfer planning work. His son, Jamie, joined the firm as a financial advisor and is involved in all the planning needed by our clients. Pete also serves on the board of directors or chairs the finance committees of several local charities including Howard County General Hospital Foundation, a member of Johns Hopkins Medicine. He is also a member of the Board of Directors of First Financial Resources, a firm comprised of some of the top financial advisors from around the nation.

For more information on the Prestige Strategy, please email us at:
- info@columbiabenefits.com

You can connect with Peter at the following:
- phibbard@columbiabenefits.com
- www.columbiabenefits.com
- www.cbcdaily.com

CHAPTER 29

FULL HIP REPLACEMENT SURGERY WAS NOT A DEAD END

– HOW TO TURN LIFE'S CHALLENGES INTO A GREEN LIGHT FOR SUCCESS

BY RENATE PRANDL, MA, CHPC

Life's a **JOURNEY**. You encounter ups and downs, turns, dead ends, roadblocks, stops, new experiences. Exciting, and sometimes scary, it's up to you what to see and focus on.

As a *Feldenkrais®* Educator and *Certified High Performance™ Coach*, I help people who are aspiring to get to the next level of success in their life to achieve higher states of performance and potential – so that *they can make those obstacles into stepping stones*, enjoy their life's journey, and achieve their dreams.

Have you ever been excited about a job or new position, but then it turned out to be the same old lame routine and you lost focus, efficiency, and influence? Well, me too. After teaching at a commercial high school for 15 years, I changed my environment, went on leave and moved to another country. I was no longer passionate at the level I demand from myself to deliver the best possible performance. It was time to change direction and take a different route.

Have you ever been in a situation where you trained for losing weight, getting rid of back pain, preparing for a skiing trip, or just leading a very active healthy life, when suddenly something gets thrown in your way? This could be a stroke, cancer, broken bones, or some knee or hip surgery, anything that interrupts your journey and brings life to a standstill. Sounds familiar?

Imagine how these events can help you re-calibrate, look for new ways of moving or thinking, and bring the spark back into your life.

I encountered one of those **roadblocks** last year when I opted for **full hip replacement surgery**. I had been dealing with growing pain in my hip joint for a while, but eventually even simple movements like walking or getting out of a chair became difficult. I decided that "enough is enough" as I was afraid of seriously damaging other joints and my spine. I immediately contacted my surgeon overseas and we set the date for surgery within a few weeks.

I wanted to be back on my feet as soon as possible. I was scared, no doubt about that. Any surgery is a risk, bones are cut, muscles and nerves could be damaged. You get the picture. And some piece of metal in my body did not sound too exciting either. I frowned thinking of all those metal detectors at airports!
So I did what you do when you get on a long road trip into unknown territory – **prepare**.

I read medical reports, went on blogs to check what others who had been in the same situation had to say, read more medical articles, and made a list of questions I wanted to ask my surgeon. And I did. I wanted to know what kind of material, what type of techniques he had in mind, pros and cons, and also if there were any special exercises I could do to get into even better physical state for the operation.

I strongly believe that getting into the best shape like a sportsperson preparing for competition is vital. Surgery was the competition I was training for. Daily. *With focus and discipline, you will be successful - in every area of your life!*

My surgeon was not only very experienced, he also understood where I was coming from, the importance of sport for me, not just as a private person, but also professionally. It takes two to tango and I definitely found the surgeon I needed.

Clarity of what you want to achieve afterwards is crucial. Know where you are going to go to, know your goals.

By actively participating, the recovery period gets shorter and healing is much faster. This not only works for surgery, but also for ailments like back pain. The common response to injury and pain is that people stop moving, which creates even more problems for their physical and emotional health. These obstacles slow you down, no doubt about it. You may get frustrated and impatient. Solution: do the work, consistently, daily if possible.

I encourage you to see the positive aspect as well: You have time to get to know yourself better. *Increased awareness* of how you function, how you walk, how you sit, how you deal with problems help you identify unhealthy habits and initiate change. Looking at details lets you improve the quality of the movement (and your thinking process, too).

How did I do it? Whilst walking on crutches I noticed how different my shoulders moved forward and backwards, with one way more forward movement than the other. Despite doing daily Feldenkrais® exercises to bring my body into balance, this poor habit had slowly crept in. I slowed down moves and exercises to detect where I was using unnecessary effort. As I was advised not do full sports for three months, I did a lot of movement in my imagination. Not imagining the movement, but doing it in my imagination.

Like every journey it takes time to get to where you want to go to, to reach your destination. My *short-term* goal was walking the red carpet in high heels six weeks after surgery, my *mid-term* goal was skiing in less than three months, and my *long-term goal* was and still is to lead a vibrant, active life. So I did what I had to do – I trained every day starting small, no impact, little impact, and eventually lots of work on the cross-trainer. This was the closest I could get to running without the pounding or impact. PICK WHAT WORKS FOR YOU. More things are possible than you can imagine. It takes courage and hard work, but it can be done.

You know why I was scared at the beginning of my journey? Everywhere

I had read that my favorite sports – tennis, skiing, jogging – should not be pursued any longer. I kept checking the latest research and guess what I found:

The new shafts of the implant have different shapes, are longer for more stability, and newer materials (titanium) are much harder wearing. Proper exercising and having strong muscles keep the ball in the joint and you can do all these sports.

In Austria, there emerged a new "trend" this winter: pediatric surgeons go skiing with their implant patients. They even encourage taking up this activity after hip or knee surgery if you had done it before. No problem, even off-piste is possible with the proper preparation. You would prepare anyway, wouldn't you? All the people asked said that there was NO PAIN, only pleasure and fun.

My TOP FIVE TIPS to emerge from surgery with more power, awareness, energy, and vitality:

#1. Do your RESEARCH:

Often patients take their doctors' words for granted, sometimes with too much "obedience" and blind belief. I am not a doctor nor do I want to discredit them, but I like to know about various options and their pros and cons when my wellbeing is at stake.

When we buy a new car we check specs, compare different models, ask for advice, get second opinions, read expert reports, etc. When it comes to surgery it looks like we give all the power away too easily without asking too many questions.

People often tell me "But Renate, the doctor is so busy and does not like these questions." "If I ask too many questions the doctor does not want me as a patient." I have heard these and many more from friends, clients, and most recently, from my own family. I still like to know.

Knowing what to expect helps you get back on track faster, you have more realistic expectations, and you can prepare for life after surgery. Yes, it is your body we are talking about, and yes, it is your responsibility to take good care of it.

#2. PREPARE the best you can:

Ask your surgeon for *specific exercises to do BEFORE surgery*. As you will be on crutches for a few weeks your muscles will shrink fast.

If you are overweight, use this as a turning point. *Lose weight* to reduce impact on your joints, opt for low-impact exercises like biking or swimming.

Limit carbs, reduce fats and sugar, add lean protein and veggies. Healthier nutrition prevents or reduces inflammation to aid the healing process.

Find a support team. A "driver" and someone helping you with daily chores is very useful, so that you can focus on your recovery program.

#3. The "right" REHAB:

Make the person you work with understand what your aspirations and goals are. You can opt for a "one-size-fits-all" movement program, or you can opt for a more specific program helping you with what you want to achieve specifically. *Be clear about your goals.*

I went for two rehab sessions, but the program wasn't for someone like me who wanted to have an active sports life afterwards. I had two options – look for someone else or do it myself. I opted for the latter, since sports and movement re-education (Feldenkrais®), are my fields of expertise. I also added NLP strategies to work on the psychological side of recovery –imagining me doing all those things I love.

"Welcome" and accept the implant as part of your body, not as something alien. Sounds weird, but it helps you move smoother.

#4. Breathing and movement in your IMAGINATION:

Being sidelined and on crutches often leads to drawn up shoulders and flat breathing. Sufficient oxygen is necessary for your organs, muscles, and your brain to function at their best.

Here is an easy breathing exercise:
Close your eyes, breathe in fully, inflate your belly (yes, stick it out), then breathe out through your mouth, let your belly sink in as you exhale, and bring focus, intention and attention to your injured area – it is like breathing life and energy into the joint.

Movement in your imagination creates a neurological response and neurons fire to activate the muscles. This helps you delay atrophy.

#5. Manage your MIND:

Be mindful of your internal dialog, especially when you are tired or a little frustrated because the healing takes too long. Remember that this is a journey giving you immense opportunities to re-learn and improve some movements, to lengthen, stretch, de-stress. It is an amazing opportunity to rejuvenate, to be open for different ways of learning and addressing the challenges of life.

Visualize the time after recovery, pick an activity like walking or running or whatever it is for you. *Be specific.* Who else is in the picture? What colors, tastes, smells, sounds can you detect?

The more senses you activate, the more vibrant the picture, the more real the scenario, the more likely it will happen. The more likely you will stay committed to your rehab program and not quit. And guess what, all your discipline, focus and dedication will be worth it.

DO'S AND DON'TS

Here are some common mistakes and how to avoid them.

You have a roadmap, a plan, companions for the journey, and then these people who promised to be there for you quit. Or they focus on all the negative things, reinforcing them, instilling doubt, fear, and frustration. Best advice – stop listening, stop them doing it!

They are suddenly "the experts" in the field and give you advice – and trust me, it is mostly about other people who had been in a similar position and all the things that went wrong. Stop them doing it!

Trust in the process, it's a journey, it takes you to your destination where you will eventually do all the things you planned. Enjoy the detours and stops along the way. Enjoy all the little successes and surprises.

Put dates like when stitches get removed, when to put full weight onto your leg, and when to start full sports activities into your calendar.

Every stage will provide different experiences, challenges and a different pace, but this roadmap will keep you motivated and on track.

Enjoy the ride!

About Renate

Award-Winning author Renate Prandl, M.A. is a personal development trainer who helps her clients overcome obstacles and roadblocks to become successful high performers in their careers, relationships, and their health and fitness by applying cutting-edge, proven, no-nonsense methods.

For over three decades, Renate has influenced and empowered individuals to take action to improve their lives and achieve sustainable high levels of performance.

As a professor at a commercial college in Austria where she was born and grew up, she was always pushing her students to strive for more than they thought they could do. By instilling self-belief and good work ethics, opportunities are created to achieve goals and dreams.

As a Certified High Performance Coach™ (CHPC), she not only applies very high standards of excellence for herself, but her private and corporate clients as well.

Renate and her husband moved to Singapore in 1996 where she set up her health consulting business – "Body & Brain" – in a completely different cultural environment.

She was a pioneer offering a holistic approach to personal training and was the "go-to" person when nothing else worked. Renate added NLP, imagery, acupressure, and kinesiology to the training sessions with great success.

Renate studied in Vienna and Salzburg and holds a Master's Degree (M.A.) from the Paris Lodron University in Salzburg/Austria, majoring in English and PE and with a minor in Psychology. She studied with Gary Yardley to become a Certified NLP Practitioner.

A 4-year training program in the USA under Donna Ray and the late Mark Reese followed, and made Renate one of only a handful certified Feldenkrais® Movement Professionals in Asia.

Her client base includes people of different nationalities and backgrounds, from pop stars to CEOs to actors, TV personalities, runners and homemakers.

To provide her clients with even more proven and cutting-edge applications and techniques based on the latest research in physiology and psychology, Renate became a Certified High Performance Coach™ in 2014. She has been studying with one of her mentors, Brendon Burchard, for years.

Renate grew up in Austria and has lived and worked in Europe, USA and Asia. She loves to work with multi-cultural clients and understands how to deal with challenges based on different cultural backgrounds.

Whether you want to lead an active, vibrant life after surgery, walk again after a stroke, be more confident, persuasive and productive in business, more present in your relationships, Renate listens and challenges you to find your personal best and succeed. She strongly believes that every person has the power to improve.

Renate has completed two Singapore marathons and enjoys playing tennis and off-piste helicopter skiing in exotic places. She turned the roadblock of hip replacement surgery into a stepping stone to ski even better than before. She loves and collects art and enjoys healthy food and good wines.

You can connect with Renate at:
rprandl@icloud.com
http://about.me/RenatePrandl
www.twitter.com/BodyNBrain

CHAPTER 30

ARE YOU STRONGER THAN YOUR CIRCUMSTANCES?

BY MARY ELIZABETH MCGUINN

We all have a pathway to healing despite the adversities our life may bring.

I would have never described my childhood as traumatic, but it wasn't until much later in life that I realized the impact that it had on me. *A lot happened that was out of the ordinary for most kids growing up, and while I'd thought I managed things reasonably well, I came to realize that I also had some things that I'd never come to terms with. It was these situations that really helped identify the path that I would take in life and where I would end up today.*

When I was little, my family moved to New Jersey. We lived in a nice neighborhood and had a pretty modest split-level house in a very nice town—the type of town that many families would love to live in. Life was pretty great and I was a kid just like any other, running wild with my imagination, learning new things, and endlessly curious. Then I had a setback.

At the age of seven, I got really sick and it instantly changed me both physically and emotionally. It happened fast and it was very debilitating. I had Endocarditis—inflammation of the heart—and it was serious enough that it required that I be hospitalized for several weeks just to get it under control. *As a child that was terrifying, of course, because my awareness as a child wasn't equipped to manage such an event.* I could only have visitors for one hour per day. It was so tough, because I was scared and lonely and the busy medical staff hardly had the time to offer their young patients much comfort for those other twenty-three hours in a day. *No TV and No getting out of bed for the restroom.* To add an extra challenge to my plight, I was not allowed to have a button to press when I needed a nurse. The mentality was that kids would play with those buttons constantly. So, I had to yell. I was weak, and remember, also shy. This was not easy to do.

One night I just couldn't take any more. My Dad had come to visit me and I broke down crying, unable to console myself. *I remember him holding my face as the tears streamed down my cheeks.* He said, "We only live around the block—not far away." His words were meant to comfort and he'd offered the best he could, but to me there was no difference between a block and a mile. It was far.

Finally, weak and wobbly, I was able to go home.

My skinny little legs could barely support my tall, thin frame, but I was so glad to be home. I'd had moments where I thought it would never happen. Slowly, life became "normal" once again. I had a best friend, was enjoying school and activities, and felt that flow of a nice childhood taking place. Then sickness struck again.

My new sickness was just as tough as the old one had been. I'd contracted Rheumatic Fever out of all things. How? I had no idea, but I was a ten year old who had it.

I remember thinking, am I going to get this sick every three years?

That time it was a special day when I was admitted into the hospital— my parents' anniversary—and I was in a room with one other bed. *At first I was hopeful that there might be someone there that I could maybe talk to, someone who would fill that loneliness that I remembered all too well, but such wasn't meant to be the case.* The other bed had an oxygen tent and in it, a few infants came and went over the weeks I was there. *My same fears and shyness were still there and my medical condition was even worse—something I never would have thought was possible. Oh! how many times I wished my mother was there to stay with me.*

And I had major restrictions. I could not leave bed because I had to rest to regain strength. I had to get blood tests done daily. My veins finally collapsed, unable to handle the extensive blood draws. The problem— they still needed the blood. *I'll never forget the angel that helped me get through that first, rough experience.* After the lab technician had grown frustrated, she decided it best to call a couple of nurses in to help. This nurse with a soft voice and comforting expression said, "Mary Beth, just squeeze my hand as tight as you can, with all your might. Don't focus on anything else, okay?" I shook my head, fear still showing in my eyes and the all too familiar tears streaming down my cheeks, but I did it, and it worked. By focusing on the squeezing it lessened the pain.

This was an important lesson: If I found other things to focus on I could control my pain. Also, being kind to anyone who is sick means the world to them.

In the end, penicillin had been my saving grace from the Rheumatic Fever, and it became a necessity for my well-being in the future. If anyone in my family or that I spent a lot of time with got sick, I had to take penicillin—just in case. Needles to say, I took a lot of penicillin and this all happened in a time where they did not realize the long-term effects on the patient's body. Today, I'm allergic to it. That says something!

New boundaries due to my "at risk" health were also put into place. I couldn't go camping or do outdoor activities with my Girl Scout Troop. I even had to consider a different school, as the one I went to had stairs and they believed that I was too weak to take them. *But finally, things got back to what I'd hoped they would be.* I was able to be like other kids, growing older and going full out into my teens with the same issues they had. And better yet—I had been able to keep up on my grades, so I didn't get held back due to missing so much school. Feeling good and more confident ended up bringing about my next challenge. Change was on the horizon.

Fracture: a crack or a break.

I received news that no young adult who is in the middle of their senior year of high school wants to hear. This was the onset of the fracture of my life. At 17 years old, this would be the end of me living with my parents, a time in which I had to mend my issues and do what seemed best for me. My Dad told me that his job was requiring that he transfer from New Jersey to Chicago. Understandably, I did not want to go. I had already missed part of grammar school with my friends playing and having fun. *I wanted to stay right where I was and finish out what I'd started and worked so hard to get to, my diploma.*

I talked with my parents about it, nearly grown daughter to reasonable adults, and we reached a conclusion. I could stay with my aunt and uncle and cousins to complete high school. My aunt worked at the high school and they seemed glad to have me. My cousin and I were silly, and we did not have sisters, so called each other siscons (sisters/cousins).

My parents left, my life resumed, and I became more attached to a boy, who I met three months before my parents moved. And as different as we were, we seemed compelled to be connected to each other in some way. This started in high school and lasted even when I went to college, and by the time I was nineteen, we were engaged. Our upbringings were different, but we each seemed to need someone else and were there for each other. Maybe it was confusing to some and not perfect to many, but to us, it made sense.

> *It takes more than a good intention to improve issues*
> *and eliminate obstacles.*
> *Through my marriage came my greatest growth.*

My life went on and I became a mother of two and a wife to a man that I was so very different from. *I tried. He tried. We tried.* It took a long time to acknowledge that a parting of ways was necessary—twenty-nine years. I'd already gone back to school to get my under-graduate and then my Master's degree. In my gut, I knew there was a deeper purpose for why I went through all my circumstances. Like that angel of a nurse, who knew how to assist me, I could do the same for others.

Plus, I'd had another health crisis during graduate school. No, they never happen at an "ideal" time. Remember those childhood illnesses? They contributed possibly to an autoimmune disease—Fibromyalgia, which is thought to come from trauma, certain infections or genes. **That's when I learned about Myofascial Release Treatment.** It was a lifesaver and a technique that has offered me just as many physical and emotional rewards since learning it. *Better posture. Less pain and a new healthy daily regime of stretching and yoga.* It was wonderful! That's why so many people use these principles today in their pursuit of better health, in general.

Without fully realizing that I'd just found a way to make it happen, I found myself in a new and better situation. An internal revolution had begun that directly impacted me professionally. Helping others was what I was meant to do. I could help them find the place where they could become stronger than their circumstances.

I was exhausted from insanity and uncertainty, but now so invigorated and optimistic. For so many years, every day had been filled with nuances that I wanted to avoid, but had to manage. Wow! Had those things taught me a lot and I was far more resilient than I ever thought I was. Up until then, I'd still been looking into the mirror and not seeing the woman I'd grown into. It was time to take what I'd learned and apply it to my new career—that of a therapist who owned her own practice.

Today, my professional practice is very aligned with my personal philosophies of how to create the change you want to see in your life. It all starts with our gut instincts. We're all born with this instinct, but many of us lose it due to neglect and avoidance. But it's never lost forever!

> *"The wound is the place where the light enters you."*
> ~ Rumi

Here's how we work to get it back:

- Reconnect with spirituality—or find it for the first time—so you can trust your gut instincts more easily.
- Find your purpose in life - don't be afraid to reinvent yourself.
- Acknowledge your pain, as well as the pain of others, never withholding love or compassion.
- Gain the knowledge and art of just "being." Mindfulness is important because it can give clarity to your situation.
- Explore different ways of connecting to feelings and emotions. For me, EFT (Emotional Freedom Technique) was very impactful. I learned this practice of tapping on meridians and using positive psychology to bring anxiety and depression down a notch–when my father passed away. Now, I show it to clients who need to come to terms with the pain in their lives.

- Learn about Chakras—knowing our energy sources and how they can impact our physical and emotional health can lead to steps that clear your channels for solutions.
- Keep a journal so you can write your thoughts down, better understand them, learn patterns in your thinking to improve your well-being.
- Acknowledge that we all have tough situations at times and we can build our resilience to navigate them beautifully, while learning important lessons. And keep in mind—we cannot always control when the lesson comes to us.
- Recognize that if others blame you for their problems that doesn't mean you are the problem.
- Communicate—listen with your full heart and mind and speak from a place of honesty and compassion. Do not be afraid to reveal your authentic self.
- Realize that none of us know when something will come into our lives at just the right moment. Always pay attention and believe with all your heart that things happen at the right time and for the right reasons—even if they are ten years later!

By focusing on these ways to truly change your life and the aspects of it that trip you up you can overcome anything. *If you are in a situation or from a family where addiction, abuse, and other tough circumstances are a part of what you've lived, don't deny those things or run from them.* Create boundaries that allow you to safely explore those circumstances, to learn, and then grow from the experience.

We all have a lot to live for, joy to spread, and an ability to be stronger than we may have ever imagined before. The time to explore this is now – because "What you seek is seeking you."
~Rumi

About Mary Beth

Mary Beth McGuinn is a seasoned therapist and the "go to" person when one is suffering with relationship issues and personal limiting beliefs. She uses her expertise from over 20 years in a therapeutic practice to guide clients to be able to manage their lives, have less anxiety, and foster confident relationships at home and at work. Mastering techniques to take things down a notch, clients leave sessions feeling like tension has been released (like air being released from a balloon that was filled with too much air). Mary Beth has shown people of all walks of life that worry, depression and anxiety are often a consequence of something deeper. She works with her clients to help eliminate the feeling of being disconnected and unloved, which causes one to feel powerless and unable to make confident decisions.

Pairing Energy Psychology with traditional therapy and coaching, this integrative approach allows you to not only clear negative thoughts, but can possibly release tightness in your body. Mary Beth's eclectic approach draws from Psychoanalysis, Gestalt, Cognitive Behavioral Therapy and Grief Recovery Work, which gives her a unique ability to bring healing to her clients.

In addition to receiving advanced standing at Adelphi University, she has done post graduate work at the New Jersey Institute for Training in Psychoanalysis and a certification from the Grief Recovery Institute. She is also a member of the Pi Gamma Mu Honor Society, and member of the Association for Comprehensive Energy Psychology, NASW and the NJ Society for Clinical Social Work.

If you would like to contact Mary Beth, please call: (201) 493-1271.
Her Website is: www.marybethmcguinnlcsw.com
You can also find Mary Beth on: PSYCHOLOGY TODAY.COM

CHAPTER 31

COMMUNICATING ON THE ROAD TO SUCCESS

BY LEWIS DENBAUM

INTRODUCTION

On your journey down the road to success, you will encounter many people—parents, siblings, teachers, friends, spouses and business colleagues. Your ability to communicate with them will determine the speed, comfort and richness of your experience. This chapter provides practical techniques to improve your interactions with anyone.

AWARENESS

Awareness is the basis of everything we undertake. We operate on a continuum of awareness. If we're sleeping, we are almost totally unaware. At the other end of the continuum, people facing dangerous situations experience time slowing down and their awareness heightened. However, we usually operate somewhere in between these two extremes. What we don't realize is that with attention and intention we can live with more awareness.

CHOICE

Life is a series of choices. With greater awareness, we are able to see more choices. With little awareness, there is insanity – where we see only one choice and that choice is not palatable. This may be a choice that you've been making over and over again, getting the same unacceptable result. With expanded awareness, there is freedom--where we see a multitude of choices and we are free to pick the most desirable choice. More awareness more choices more freedom and power.

AWARENESS AND CHOICE IN COMMUNICATION

What do awareness and choice have to do with communication? Let's consider awareness. To improve our communication, we have to be aware of what is going on inside of us, what do we want, how do we want to obtain it, what have we already tried and with what result.

Let's consider choice. To improve our communication, we have to examine our choices. To whom do we need to talk? How do we listen? What words do we choose? What is our attitude?

Below are several approaches to better communication using awareness and choice:

100% RESPONSIBLE

We are 100% responsible for our communication – not 50%, 100%. Maybe that statement requires an awareness shift for you.

Why do we communicate? When we open our mouth to speak, we want something. It may be that you want someone to go on a date with you. Maybe you want someone to know that you love him. Maybe you want a raise in salary.

If we cannot communicate effectively, we don't get what we want. You may say: "It's not my fault if the other person doesn't understand me. I spoke clearly and he just doesn't get it." That may well be. However, it is you that wants something. Therefore, it is up to you to continue communicating until the listener understands you.

Think of communication as a maze puzzle, the objective of which is to find the right pathway to the exit on the other side. You try one path, dead end. You try another path, dead end. What to do? Don't give up. Keep trying till you get what you want—the path to the exit. Play the communication game. Keeping altering your message and delivery until the listener understands you.

I was once on a conference in the German-speaking section of Switzerland. I wanted a bone for my presentation. A colleague of mine and I decided that we could get a bone at a butcher shop. We located a butcher shop and walked in. I asked the man behind the counter if we could buy a bone. He only spoke German and answered us in German, probably saying something like "I don't understand what you're saying." Of course, we didn't understand what he was saying either.

In my stupidity, I did what many people under these circumstances do – I started repeating the word bone— "bone, bone, bone." Then I started saying it louder—BONE, BONE, BONE--and then more slowly--bbooonee, bbooonee---thinking that saying it louder or slower would magically make him understand English. I became frustrated and was ready to walk out without the bone.

My friend, however, understood that it was our responsibility to communicate to this butcher if we wanted to get what we came for. My friend lifted his arms and hands up by his shoulders, imitating a dog begging and started barking. The butcher started laughing and nodded his head. He walked to the back of the butcher shop and returned with a nice size bone on a piece of paper for us. I took out my wallet to offer him some money, and he just shook his head and would not accept any payment. Mission accomplished.

This story illustrates how being 100% responsible for our communication helps us get what we want. Many years ago, I learned from the Rolling Stones that "you can't always get what you want," but if we take 100% responsibility for our communication, we increase the likelihood that we will.

ASK FOR WHAT YOU WANT

Now we know that when we communicate we want something. We must be aware of what we want and choose to ask for it. But sometimes, we avoid asking directly. There are many reasons for this, including fear of rejection, feelings of unworthiness and protecting our pride. People are not mind readers. When we want something, we have to ask. And yes, you may not get what you ask for, but at least if you ask, there is a much better chance you'll get it.

Here's an example. One night after a hectic day, I wanted to chill out and spend some time with my wife Diane. I went online to find a movie I could stream over my computer. I was excited that I found one that I thought my wife and I would both enjoy. My wife was reading a book in the living room. I peeked my head in and said, "Hey honey, I found a fun movie on Netflix." She replied, "Great, I'm so happy for you," and continued reading her book. That was not the response I wanted! I felt disappointed.

Buried inside of my statement to Diane was a hidden want. I wanted her to watch the movie with me. To be more effective in getting what I wanted, I should have been clear and specific, saying "Honey, I found a really good movie on Netflix that I think you and I would both enjoy. I would love to watch it with you tonight. Would you like to do that?" Now she knows exactly what I want, and she can choose to continue to read her book or to join me in watching the movie.

Here are my suggestions for asking for what you want.

First, start your sentence with the word "I want" or "I would like." It is hard to miss that there is a request being made when the sentence begin with those words.

Second, express your request clearly and specifically. If my wife says, "I'd like to have a nice evening out with you," that isn't specific enough. What does a nice evening look like to her? How do I fulfill that desire for her if the only clue I have is the word "nice?" To me, a nice evening out might be going to the gym and pumping iron for a couple of hours. I doubt that's what she has in mind.

Finally, say what you want, not what you don't want. For example, don't say: "I don't want the memo to be too long." Instead say, "Please keep the memo to under ten pages."

RESPONSIBLE SPEAKING

You want to avoid blaming and shaming the listener at all costs. Saint Augustine said, "Love the sinner, hate the sin." Of course, it is laudable not to disparage anyone solely because that is the right thing to do. However, it is also a wise technique for communication. If, as we have said before, we are communicating because we want something, how likely are we to get what we want if we blame or shame the person to whom we are I'm speaking? Not very likely.

The best way to avoid blaming or shaming the listener is to use I-statements. Simply put, an I-statement is either a sentence that begins with the word "I" or has the word "I" as the subject of its independent clause. Here are two examples: "I feel sad that you are going away," and "When you drive over 65 miles per hour, I get nervous."

Blaming and shaming may feel good temporarily, but it is counter-productive in the end. If my intention is to enlist your cooperation in keeping clothing off the bedroom floor, which of the following two approaches do you think would work better?

- "You are the biggest slob I've ever seen; your clothing is all over the floor."
- "When I walk into our bedroom and see your clothing all over the floor, I get angry."

In my experience, the first sentence will result in an argument and a messy floor. While the second sentence is no guarantee of a clean floor, it's a good entrée into a discussion with the other person.

INTENTION VS IMPACT

When we speak, we have an intention and our words have an impact on the listener. When our intention matches up with the impact on the listener, we have perfect communication. If we are aware, we can determine from the listener's facial expressions, body language and words whether the impact was as intended. If we see that the impact was not what we intended or if we are unsure of the impact, we can ask the listener how our communication landed on them. Then we can clarify our intention for the listener.

Here's an example, Mary and John go on a picnic. Everything starts out fine. However, after a while, John becomes quiet and distant. Mary says, "What's wrong with you? Why are you so quiet?" John becomes annoyed and snapped back at her, "There is nothing wrong." If Mary's intention was to see what was up with John and to comfort him, her words and probably her tone did not have that impact on John. Her choice of the word "wrong" was blaming. In addition, questioning him with the word "Why" was accusatory. To correct the impact, Mary could say something like, "When I noticed you being quiet, I was concerned. I intended to see if there is anything I can do for you."

Be aware. Seek to bring the impact into alignment with your intention.

LISTENING ACTIVELY

"God gave us two ears and one mouth so we would listen twice as much as we speak." Furthermore, if I am talking, I am not going to learn anything new; if I am listening, it's possible I'll learn something.

Communication experts agree that active listening is the most important skill.

Listening is not a passive activity. Listening takes the utmost awareness in the form of attention. The more aware we are, the better able we are to take in the speaker's message. We need to have the intention to understand the speaker's viewpoint.

How do we listen actively? The first step is to focus on the speaker. Put away your cellphone, food and beverage.

Maintain eye contact. When you look at the listener, they know you're paying attention. Unfold your arms. Crossed arms convey that we are closed or we don't like what they're saying. Lean forward toward the speaker. Be aware of the speaker's voice, tone and body language. Don't interrupt You can ask questions later.

Now here comes the biggest challenge; avoid thinking about what you're going to say in response. This involves clearing out all of the noise inside of our mind and paying attention solely to what is being said. If I start thinking about what am I going to say, I'm no longer listening intently. I'm missing what you're saying because I'm thinking about something else. Stay focused, pay attention to that person and don't worry about what you're going to say. Our subconscious mind will take in the tone, facial expressions, gestures and body language. This will add additional content to what our ears are hearing.

The second step is called feedback. After you've allowed them to speak for a while without interrupting, you have to indicate to them that you're following along. How do you do that? Feedback in your own words what you've heard. This demonstrates to them that you're following along. If you've missed something, they'll let you know.

You'll be amazed how effective active listening is. You'll experience a deeper, richer level of appreciation for your partner.

CONCLUSION

With greater awareness and the recognition that we always have choices, we can improve our communication, Be 100% responsible for your communication. Ensure that the impact of your communication aligns with your intention. Use I-statements to avoid blaming and shaming. Be specific and clear when you make requests. Finally, become a master at the art of listening.

About Lewis

Lewis Denbaum is a "full contact" personal development coach who provides a firm but caring nudge towards a fuller destiny with an emphasis on pragmatism, compassion and knowledge gained through direct experience.

Lewis has a multi-faceted background. He is equally at home with right brain and left brain environments. He has been an attorney and accountant for over 30 years, He has been involved in meditation for 45 years as both a practitioner and as a teacher.

As a communication expert, Lewis helps people improve their relationships whether they are dating, in a committed relationship or part of a business team.

Lewis is a Canfield Certified Success Principles Trainer.

After suffering his second painful divorce, Lewis devoted his energy towards figuring out which way is up in love, marriage and relationships.

His efforts paid off in 2006 when he married the love of his life Diane. Taking what they learned from mistakes made in their previous marriages as well as relationship lessons learned since, Lewis and Diane co-authored a book, *Madly in Love Forever: A Guide to True and Lasting Love.*

Inspired by this new direction in his life, Lewis went on to become a Certified Singles and Couples Coach through the Relationship Coaching Institute. Lewis and his wife Diane teach relationship readiness workshops for singles who want to prepare for a better dating experience and relationship enhancement workshops and coaching for couples who want to improve the communication and intimacy in their relationships.

Since 1994 he has been deeply involved in men's circles and work through the likes of Justin Sterling, David Deida and The Mankind Project. As an important fulfillment of his own life mission, he applies his teaching and coaching skills in workshops specific to men and men's issues, and is passionate about helping men discover and live their mission, and balance mission and relationship.

Lewis lives in Scottsdale, Arizona and Fairfield, Iowa. He is married to Diane Denbaum. They have a blended family of five adult children.

Lewis is available to speak at your next company or association event.

Lewis can be reached via email at Lewis@LewisDenbaum.com His toll-free number is 800-639-4505. Visit his websites:

- LewisDenbaum.com
- MadlyInLoveForever.com
- MensTelesummit.com
- DenbaumCoachingForMen.com

CHAPTER 32

THE SECRET TO FINDING YOUR WAY

BY IRENE TITERA

My son Christian and I were invited to stay in the home of some generous new friends who lived near the medical center in Houston, where we needed to report daily for a couple of weeks for Christian's cancer treatment. It was a lovely home in an upscale neighborhood. We parked our car on the street so we wouldn't block the family's cars from access to their driveway. One night some kids went through the neighborhood on a destructive binge, slashing the tires and keying the sides of cars parked on the street, including ours. That was a demoralizing sight. I was worried about getting to the clinic and concerned about paying for the damages. I blew out a huff of air, decided staring at it wasn't going to help and turned to go make some phone calls.

A van I didn't recognize pulled up at the curb behind us and as the door opened, I thought "That looks a little like Amber, Christian's friend." But of course she must be at home, four hours away. Then she and another girl came over and hugged him, and a big smile spread across his face. Amber's Mom got out and told me that Amber had the impression yesterday that they needed to come visit us. She further felt that they needed to borrow a friends' van instead of driving their little car, so our search for a ride to the clinic was over. Amber's impression saved our day! Later I found out the slashed tires were covered by our road hazard warranty. The deep scratch across two doors and two panels was eligible for insurance coverage, but there was a large deductible.

As it happened, the deductible was almost the exact same amount that a family with three boys had donated to us to help pay for Christian's treatments. It was unthinkable to spend that amount to fix a scratch on a car after they had sacrificed their college funds to help us. So I decided that every time I looked at that scratch, I would think of the Peppers and how they showed us love. It would be a monument to their generosity. And it was. It made me smile to celebrate their sweetness whenever I noticed the scratch again, for several years. It still does when I think of it. I think that experience was when I realized that I can choose to celebrate. Sometimes it's easy. Other times are more of a challenge, but *there's always a reason to celebrate!*

That has kind of become my theme song in the years since then. Some of the people I love have had much shorter lives than expected, which caused a seismic shift in my outlook. I want to celebrate every day. I want to enjoy my time with my loved ones. And all those projects I was going to do someday? Someday has arrived!

So I turned my mind to focus on using my time effectively and achieving success. In visualizing the road to success, I imagined my GPS guiding me to the nearest freeway. I would roar up that entry ramp and glide on over to the fast lane. Of course everyone has heard that the fastest way to success is via SMART goals (Specific, Measurable, Attainable, Realistic, Time-bound). Just choose the smart goals, race up the road and celebrate upon arrival at success, right?

Or was it right? I had a lot of strong, hard-to-define impulses with deep roots. I knew I wanted to help people overcome adversity. I wanted to celebrate and bring joy. Yet I didn't really know how to do that, or know how long my learning curve would take. Trying to quantify things in a specific way and time was frustrating, because I couldn't even guess at how long something would take when I wasn't sure of how to do it. And it seemed like waiting for that distant day of final achievement to celebrate might make it less likely to ever happen. So I started to wonder if maybe the smart goals were not right for me, at least in this application. I wondered if I should stick with what I know works for me.

Mark Morgan Ford (of Early to Rise and The Palm Beach Group) says it is better to be vague about the big ideas. He says that to tie them to a specific outcome or time-frame is to court failure. If we wait until we can more reasonably figure out the outcome and/or a sensible time-frame to get started, we've wasted time. And more likely those aspects will never become clear unless we take that leap of faith into the dark unknown. It is only as we immerse ourselves in the effort that we start to grasp a little more of what needs to be done. At first we may not even know what we don't know. So how DO we figure out what to do, when, and how? How did Amber know to come visit us in a van at just the right time? It seems like Amber, as a good friend, had already decided to do whatever she could to be there for Christian, so she was attuned to the inner promptings that showed up in her mind, and she acted on the impulse when it came.

We have to make a commitment with very little to go on—just the stirrings of that inner voice. Mark said there's a big difference between *wanting* and *deciding*. As soon as he made that shift and decided that he was going to "get rich", everything he did in that direction made him feel rich already. He didn't have to wait until some arbitrary time arrived to celebrate. He could celebrate all along the way. I like that idea. It fits with my philosophy of celebrating.

Since that kind of shift from *wanting* to *deciding* is a commitment that stems from following your inner voice, it seems the first shift into deciding mode should reasonably be the decision to pay attention to your inner voice. **In fact, perhaps the most important decision you will ever make is the commitment to follow your inner voice.** That seems like the smartest goal to me. The formulaic SMART goals may not be the best approach for our *greatest* aspirations. In fact, Brendon Burchard jokes that we should have DUMB goals, because we shouldn't limit our dreams to the reasonably attainable, we should be stretching out even past what is considered possible. He is serious about his replacement goal description; they should be *Dream-driven, Uplifting, Method-friendly and Behavior-driven.*

Simply put, for really big ideas we may have a passionate, but vague concept of what we want, yet have no discernable plan for how to get there, and that's ok. No quantified plan is often the main characteristic of our biggest aspirations. Here's why: Our biggest goals are often the reaching toward abstract inner longings that may be hard for us to even articulate. Be a light... Give back... Help children...Save the environment... Go to Heaven...etc. We don't really know all the parameters because we haven't been there. But SOMETHING inside of us knows it is a worthy and personal objective. I'm going to call that something your spirit.

When I held our firstborn son and gazed into his eyes, I felt like they were windows of wisdom, like he had so much to tell me. I watched him breathing as he slept. Such a tiny body for a huge soul!

Thirty-two years later, his body reposed in a satin-lined box. The essence of life was gone. The vibrant smile that could so easily engage connections was here no more. That hum of energy that seemed so boundless – his spirit – was not in that box.

He was here for thirty-two years, but he did enough living for three lifetimes. He taught me *so much* about following his inner voice wherever it took him. I celebrate that I will see him again someday.

Your spirit, that essence of life in *your* body, hears an inner voice. You may call it intuition, your conscience, your subconscious mind, inspiration, divine guidance or all of the above. My take on that is: everything on the list is a gift from the Creator, so it is all divine guidance in some form. No matter what you call it, there is an inner voice available to you.

I always knew that to some degree, but certain life experiences have expanded and strengthened that awareness. When dealing with life and death issues, it suddenly becomes achingly clear that there is no other ultimate authority. It becomes absolutely necessary to consult with the source of life, and to get answers. When the ability to listen to that inner voice is so compounded by need, it's like instant Olympic training. What I didn't figure out as instantly, is that it doesn't only apply to those situations. It applies to all of life. Why would it only work in a crisis? What I do daily, the small things, is what makes me who I am. It is how I accomplish the larger mission and purpose. So I need to pay attention to that inner voice *all the time*!

SMART goals and other time management systems can be great ways to organize and implement plans, but *nothing else is as valuable to success as following that inner voice*. When we do follow it, we can celebrate all along the way, trusting that as the plan fully unfolds, those inner longings will be fulfilled.

I've heard that Steven R. Covey used to have his audience close their eyes, and then have everyone point to North. Then, while still pointing, open their eyes and look around at the wildly different directions people were pointing. If the objective is to get everybody to the magnetic true north, we have a tool for that, a compass that can bring everyone to the same place.

What if that is not the objective? What if everybody's North is different? I believe that since we all have access to an inner voice to guide us on our own journey, the better we are at paying attention to that inner voice, the more successful we will be at fulfilling our mission and purpose on earth. Truth is not subject to personal tailoring; we are all subject to the same physical and spiritual laws. But circumstances and opportunities vary. Our choices determine direction. The difference between *wanting* and *deciding* is the difference between *belief* (an awareness or acceptance) and *faith* (knowledge that becomes a driving force). It's the difference between *I would like that to happen and I am going to make that happen.* Your inner voice helps you make that decision, and then helps you find ways to move forward on that path.

About a year and a half after that time in Houston, I was sitting in a hospital room next to Christian. He was in a coma. Although we had experienced amazing success at shrinking what we had been told was an unshrinkable brain tumor, other health issues had necessitated a pause in the successful treatment and now the tumor had come roaring back. As I sat there, mulling over the situation and praying for help, I remembered back to a time years earlier, when I caught myself praying that my baby would be a little girl—but I was already pregnant! I had realized suddenly how ridiculous that was, because I knew the sex of the baby had already been determined. So I mentally backed up and said "Oops! Sorry Father! Never mind! Help me to give this baby all the love it deserves and to enjoy it. When I recalled that prayer, I wondered if I do that all the time—I'm in the middle of some plan in gestation and I pop up with an alternate request. I thought of how we say, "Oh, either sex is ok, as long as it's healthy!" And what if it's not healthy? Do we love it less? Will we decide not to be happy?

I wondered if it made sense to put a lid on my happiness that way. It seemed like it would be better to accept what is and find a reason to celebrate. The IV machine started beeping, bringing me back to

Christian's bedside, and I wondered, "If this is his birth into the next life, can I still find reasons to celebrate?" Even in times like that – maybe *especially* in times like that – our inner voice is a valuable resource. It is through our inner voice that we can receive comfort and manage to recover from life's pitfalls.

Steve Jobs was famously fired from the company he created. Much later he could say it was the best thing for him, but it was very painful. He was the commencement speaker at the Wharton Executive MBA Graduation I attended. With my own graphic design background, I found it particularly interesting that he dropped out of the required college classes and when he enrolled in classes he was drawn to, one was a calligraphy class, perhaps the best one in the country at that time. He immersed himself in typography design: serif, san serif, font design, irregular spacing, etc. He said it had no hope of practical application in his life.

He then told the story to Stanford students: "But ten years later, when we were designing the first Macintosh computer, it all came back to me. And we designed it all into the Mac. It was the first computer with beautiful typography. If I had never dropped in on that single course in college, the Mac would have never had multiple typefaces or proportionally spaced fonts. And since Windows just copied the Mac, it's likely that no personal computer would have them. If I had never dropped out, I would have never dropped in on this calligraphy class, and personal computers might not have the wonderful typography that they do."

Steve Jobs urged the students: *Don't let the noise of others' opinions drown out your own inner voice. And most important, have the courage to follow your heart and intuition.* (Stanford Report, June 14, 2005.)

There are efforts in this world that you are uniquely suited to make. There are ways that your life experiences have prepared you to serve. You have access to the impressions, promptings, gut feelings, tingly sensations, and warm peacefulness of your inner voice. This is your time on earth.

Celebrate the road, highway, or meandering path that is your own.

About Irene

Irene Victoria Titera is an artist, designer, writer and speaker who says her greatest desire is to draw beauty and joy into the lives of those around her. Readers and listeners find her profound yet approachable. Fans of her art describe it as inspiring, tender and uplifting.

Irene has a Master of Arts degree from the University of Houston at Clear Lake. She is the CEO of LifeIsDelightable.com, which has appeared in *USA Today*; an inbox magazine exploring the science of celebration and promoting positive psychology.

She is an accomplished artist and author of books for adults and children. She has produced an annual limited edition Christmas card drawing with accompanied poetry for over 20 years. Her paintings adorn the walls of patrons throughout the Dallas/ Fort Worth area, as portraits, watercolors, limited edition prints and murals. She maintains that her greatest creative efforts were the raising of her five sons. She admits that she was selected as the Betty Crocker Homemaker of Tomorrow in her high school, which honor she still deserves because she would always rather clean her house tomorrow.

She has enjoyed working as a designer of luxury homes, restaurants and commercial recreational facilities. As a home stager her superb mastery of décor, design, and human psychology consistently resulted in faster, higher-priced sales.

Irene, a national speaker, has spoken at Universities, Women's Conferences, women's organizations, and churches. She has appeared on television in New York, Texas and Alaska. She addresses overcoming adversity in an upbeat style that moves the audience from laughter to tears and back again, but there's no question that she has walked the walk. Her ideas about celebrating are like the perfect birthday present— they get opened up and used right away.

Contact Irene at:
- LifeIsDelightable.com
- www.facebook.com/IreneVictoriaTitera
- www.twitter.com/IreneVTitera

CHAPTER 33

GOING FROM "CORPORATE COMFORT" TO PASSIONATE ENTREPRENEUR
– TURNING THE TOUGH LESSONS INTO TRIUMPHS

BY KYLIE HAMMOND

They've always said that life is a journey. Well, so is business.

I've been that person that many people are today—the frustrated employee who was craving to break free and create their own opportunity. For fifteen years I stayed in the corporate world and endured the struggle that came along with the "security" that working for someone else should offer. My industry was IT, and what I offered was in demand. There were some pretty fantastic things that I got to experience, including traveling around the world. As someone who has always loved travel, that was excellent. However, there was a downside.

Travel was hardly enough to fill me up and give me the satisfaction that made me believe that I'd found the place I should be—that place of passion and purpose that just feels right. With a bit of ego and some proven knowledge, I struggled because I felt that I could do many of my managers' jobs better than they did. I know that I was hard to deal with and my "outside the box" thinking and lack of fear to state what I would best describe as "the obvious" didn't make for a good relationship. I was just so frustrated!

I'd walk into performance reviews, rolling my eyes to the heavens and already loathing the bureaucracy that came with the process. It just wasn't for me. Why were so many people content, even grateful, and I was anything but? Aside from my paycheck, I felt like I had nothing to fill my cup.

I reached my turning point and it all became abundantly clear.

There had been a time when I wanted to become a partner in a consulting firm. I'd worked hard for it and when the opportunity finally came, all I could think was, *are the next five to ten years working in a professional services firm what I really want? Is it worth it?* No, it wasn't! So I quit.

The one thing that had always resonated with me was to open up my own recruiting business. I'd worked with recruiters before, and I had a lot of knowledge on how the process worked, plus a lot of connections. The bases were covered, right? Wrong!

Here are four quick lessons that I learned, each one making me second guess what I did. Harsh lessons, to say the least.

1. *I was under-capitalized.* I never would have realized how much money you had to have in your resources to cover your "ramping up" period.
2. *I spent more money than I was making.* In the corporate world you are used to spending a certain amount of money to get certain results. When you are self-employed, once you spend the money it's gone!
3. *I was too focused on infrastructure.* I wanted my business to look professional and good so I invested heavily in a great logo, expensive business cards, a high end website, stationary, etc. Well, I looked good, but all that expense made my bank accounts look bad. None of those things brought clients or income in the door.
4. *I hired the wrong people and had poor advisors.* Here's a somewhat embarrassing truth about recruiters—we are masters at thoroughly screening hires for our clients, but not nearly as in depth at hiring our own staff and advisors. For me, I just assumed they were on my page. Bad assumption!

My lesson was learned: *you need fiscal discipline and strong business practices in order to be successful in business.* Without it, you are more likely to sink than swim. Did all the other entrepreneurs just know this? What had I missed?

When we hear success stories we often don't realize that they had failures first.

I knew my core values and thought that other people would buy into the vision that I shared if they also shared those same values. As a result, I hired employees and advisors on my gut instincts, and they failed me miserably. These values were good in theory, but somehow didn't transcend into the work culture. They included:

- A positive, energetic attitude
- A strong work ethic
- A bit of humor

When I found out that these core values, although stated, didn't spark people to have the same vigorous passion for my business as I did, I had a tough time. People didn't want to work like I did and weren't as inspired by my vision as I was. The results were costly mistakes that further displaced me from success. Hiring the wrong employee is an expensive mistake. Loss of clients, continuity, and reputation are costly mistakes. Add to the mix employees that learn from you, make some connections, and then move on to start up their own business, or work for a competitor – well, it's a recipe for disaster – the fast track to failure!

A new lesson was learned: *follow the recruitment principles when hiring someone.* This includes lots of interviews, extensive reference checking, and making sure there is a thorough understanding of the job's duties and responsibilities. For me, this meant talking about just how hard it was and how much work was expected. No more sugar coating!

Sometimes we find that it's our own mindset that is really holding us back.

My business challenges extended beyond the poor hiring choices and fiscal decisions I'd made. I was prone to thinking negatively and I worried non-stop. It consumed my thoughts for the better part of the next decade. I worked constantly and everything was intense. I basically surrendered my social life and everything I did was focused on business. I was so isolated, basically abandoning my friends and the people I'd grown up with. I was a business woman on a mission. Eventually, I'd find that success. There was no turning back any more than there was any potential to happily return to the corporate world. Then came the global financial crash. And boy did I crash.

Basically overnight the clients I relied on for business stopped using recruitment services. This had such a major personal impact and I was in dire financial straits. Being broke isn't great for anyone, but being broke in a large city like Sydney is particularly taxing. I lost everything that I had worked for and was really down and out.

What I was experiencing was the type of thing you read about happening to other people. It's never supposed to happen to you. My eyes were wide open. Depression set in and I really struggled to have faith in the universe that I was going to come back from the situation intact. Despite being embarrassed and struggling on such an intensely emotional level, I began to read self-help books. I read and read, trying to find a place of comfort and a spark of hope for the future. I thought about family who had invested in my business. It was so stressful knowing that my loss was also their financial loss.

But determination and persistence is something that I have, thankfully. I worked hard to find ways to keep money coming in enough to avoid becoming homeless.

The lesson was profound: *if we give up on ourselves, there is not going to be any reason for others not to give up on us too.* I had many skills that could earn me an income. I just had to think outside of the box. For me, that meant offering career coaching and resume writing services. It was a start! Within 3 years I had rebuilt my career, business and bank account, heading up a thriving multi-million-dollar international coaching and mentoring business.

Worry is such a useless emotional state to be in, but worry is crafty and it can trap us if we're not careful.

Worry stifles us and makes us unproductive—at all the wrong times! Yes, I was experiencing all these failures and set-backs, but at my core, I still had a great desire to find my purpose and true passion in life. This is what I did:

1. *I developed a millionaire mindset.* Only after I believed that I would make more did it start to happen and my mindset became my reality.

2. *I was grateful for the evolvement of my business.* With lots of life lessons learned—and finally embraced—I did things smarter and stopped investing in areas that didn't show a more direct return than what I'd previously done.

3. *I surrounded myself with the "right people."* Surrounding myself with fabulous advisors was key. I began gravitating toward successful people who have made a lot of money and have also made their share of mistakes. I wanted to learn it all. One mentor, Siimon Reynolds—a known marketing and advertising guru—helped me learn ways to avoid making small and big mistakes alike.

With the right conversations and questions, you can gain a wealth of knowledge in a short amount of time.

A good mentor provides you with an intangible experience if you allow their expertise to sink in! I became a sponge and wanted to take advantage of all the golden advice I could find. I began to:

- Approach high profile industry veterans who gave me rare insights into business. This helped me to refine my business strategy and mission.
- I began studying more and became a voracious reader of all things related to business and personal development.
- I realized that many of the challenges I was facing had come about through a bad mindset and limiting self-beliefs. This had to change!

I began to actively work on developing a positive mindset and started to apply it in a small way to cash flow issues in my business. Money was a major source of stress and concern for me. You need positive energy that the money is going to come; however, you cannot just sit around and wait for it. You've got to do your part. Expecting checks to fall out of the universe just doesn't happen. The effort you put in is what you get back.

You ask, "What do I need cash flow for this month?" Then you focus on your steps to get it and go to work. This is when the right person, client, or opportunity appears.

A lesson of amazing value: *when you are in good energy and surrounding yourself with good energy, positive things start happening.* Links, connections, introductions, and opportunities happen at all the right times when you do this. It feels a bit like magic…you're amazed and thankful.

Always operate from a place of gratitude and acknowledge the universe.

After you get positive energy and begin experiencing it, you don't just "level out." You keep moving forward, pushing your energy level up and you begin giving back out of gratitude for what you've been given. Knowing this is a good way to be living mentally, because it will carry you through what you are doing to make your dreams, goals, and passions happen. And if you sense a negative mindset creeping in, act quick and change your thought pattern in the most efficient, quick way possible.

I evolved with time and so did my business.

In 2015, I launched Director Institute. This is the place where my passion and purpose have finally met. During my recruiting career I realized that I worked with senior level management and CEOs quite extensively, and I had very candidate-centric business practices. One common thread amongst all these various people was their desire to eventually serve on a Board of Directors. It's the next logical step after a successful corporate life. I began to help recruit Board Directors and the results were really favorable—businesses grew more successful quicker.

For far too long, Board of Director hiring decisions have been based in old world methods. It's who you know that gets you the position. Today, the world has shifted and business demands are not what they once were. There's a separate set of skills required of Board members so they are contributing a positive impact for the company they serve.

Executives who want to be on a Board of Directors need a pathway to become "board ready." It's exciting for me that Director Institute has quickly become one of the fastest growing director networks in the region. And we are expanding. Our focus has made a noticeable impact on the market, assisted thousands of businesses across industry and provided talented board directors an opportunity to apply their skills and talents in the boardroom. Having a diverse boardroom is highly effective. Challenging the status quo is necessary. I've always liked to challenge that proverbial status quo, almost as much as I've delighted in challenging the old school networks that many boardrooms are currently comprised of.

Ten areas of focus that we help connect executives to in order to become "board ready" are:

1. Spend time developing their unique Board Director brand.
2. Teach the importance of having a good Board resume and LinkedIn profile.
3. Know where to target board opportunities to secure a first appointment.
4. A focus on how every Board appointment helps to build experience.
5. Showing the value of earning your stripes in unpaid and volunteer positions when you start out.
6. Helping to find ways to fast-track Board experience, such as working with start-up businesses.
7. Learning how to conduct the due diligence necessary before accepting Board Director roles.
8. The preparation involved for investing time and effort into a Board career, particularly with effective business networking.
9. Don't go it alone—seeking help and advice from more experienced Board Directors.
10. Not being romantic about Board offers—parking the ego at the door.

These few simple strategies and steps help executives align themselves with their future goals of serving on Boards. The concepts are ones that Director Institute effectively uses with our clients.

Our success helps businesses and individuals succeed.

A healthy business environment provides benefits for everyone. People like to reference that it all starts at the top, so why not make the top—the Board of Directors—better prepared to contribute to the businesses they serve. Knowing that I've found my calling through this inspires me to continue giving back to the world that has offered me so much. And the results that have revealed themselves thus far are a great indicator that we are on track to something big...a meaningful new approach to better business.

About Kylie

Kylie Hammond is the Founder and CEO of Director Institute, a world-class management consultancy specialising in board search, board career management and CEO mentoring. Kylie is passionate about building businesses, developing leaders, and connecting the two. She has spent the last twenty years coaching and mentoring thousands of Australian and International CEOs, senior executives, entrepreneurs and board directors, to visualise and achieve their goals.

Regarded as Australia's #1 Board Search Consultant conducting thousands of board director appointments each year and a leading 'career guru', Kylie brings unique experience and extraordinary levels of passion and commitment to each and every engagement.

Working in partnership with top CEOs in the Asia Pacific region, Kylie's career management support has helped executives execute highly confidential career moves. She has implemented career portfolios of employment and business activity, secured non-executive director and director-level board appointments, and combined this with not-for-profit, public speaking, coaching and mentoring engagements, creating fulfilling and exciting career pathways for senior executives.

With many years of experience leading human capital management and performance management programs, Kylie has worked as a trusted advisor in global corporations – including Cisco Systems, Oracle, Gartner and Deloitte. She is a certified Human Resources Practitioner, Career Development Association of Australia Practitioner, Fortune100 Executive Coach and is certified to implement 360-Degree Assessments & HR Performance Services leveraging industry best practices, knowledge and experience.

Kylie has a Bachelor of Arts, majoring in Industrial Relations and is an accredited Australian Small Scale Offerings Board Sponsor enabling her to assist high growth companies raise essential capital by connecting them to investors.

Kylie Hammond is regularly asked to comment on issues related to leadership, mentoring, career management, business and governance and has been interviewed and featured in a variety of publications that includes *The Sydney Morning Herald, The Australian, The Financial Review, Business Insider* and *Company Director.* She is a co-author of *In the Spirit of Success: Inspiring Stories from Entrepreneurs Around the World, Millionaire Coach* and has written two books, *The Executive Candidate's Survival Guide,* published in 2012, and *101 Career Mistakes and Solutions,* published 2015.

You can connect with Kylie at:
- Email Kylie@directorinstitute.com.au
- LinkedIn https://au.linkedin.com/in/kyliehammond
- Twitter www.twitter.com/directorinst

CHAPTER 34

COME ON NOW, LET'S GET REAL

BY JEWELL SIEBERT

Remember sitting in high school English class trying to decipher William Shakespeare? I sure do. I found his plays were much more powerful when I could actually see them onstage and fully grasp the emotions of his words. But even without seeing Shakespeare's plays, he shared plenty of wisdom easily gleaned from the written word alone. Heck, you could probably write an entire self-development book based on his quotes. (I call dibs!) My personal favorite is Polonius' advice to his son in Hamlet, "This above all: to thine own self be true...." It's a much more eloquent and poetic way of saying one of my personal mantras:

The fake you is a waste of time and energy; go do you!

How I lived a Fake Life for 18 Years

Today, I am living the life I was meant to live. And I love it! I have never been happier, healthier, more successful, and well...FIERCE. But this wasn't always the case for me. I spent much of my life trying to be someone I wasn't. Most notably were the 18 years I spent in a career that wasn't aligned with my innermost desires.

Ever since I was three years old, I had big dreams about becoming a marine biologist like Jacques Cousteau. I was obsessed. But then along came college application time, and even with scholarships, everything was so expensive. I was terrified of being broke and in debt. Instead of being excited about getting into the colleges I wanted, all I saw were bills.

But on a whim, I had applied to the US Military Academy at West Point. I had never thought about being in the Army, but the idea of serving my country was incredibly appealing. When I got my acceptance letter, I couldn't believe it. And neither could anyone else (except for my mom, of course). Most people discouraged me from going. My school counselor sought out my mom to tell her I shouldn't go because I was too gentle. Another teacher said I shouldn't go because they do push-ups in the Army, and I wouldn't be able to make it. Going to West Point meant that I was giving up my dream of being a marine biologist. But it also meant free tuition (in exchange for five years of service on active duty). It also meant proving all those people who said I couldn't do it wrong. In hindsight, I probably should have picked a means to do it that better fit my personality.

But I decided I would attend West Point, and I faxed in my acceptance letter at literally the last minute before the deadline. After the fax transmission completed, I immediately burst into tears. See, our bodies have ways of telling us when we're on and off track. Getting a sick feeling in your stomach, excessive fatigue, or crying at what should be a joyous and exciting time...these things are all flashing neon signs to turn around and do something else. I should have listened to my body, but I thought that I knew better.

Truth be told, I did love many things about my time on active duty. So much so that I stayed in for 14 years after graduation. But at my core, I knew it wasn't the right fit for me. I wasn't living my life purpose. And the repercussions were palpable.

While I kept up the appearance of always being happy, deep down, it was quite the opposite. I was so drained, unfulfilled, and lacked confidence. I felt like something was missing, but I couldn't figure it out. It just didn't make sense. I had a fantastic husband, a steady job with great benefits, awesome friends, a beautiful home, my dream car, wonderful vacations... but all that isn't enough if you're not living the life you were meant to live. The life that's aligned with your true desires. The life you miss out on if you let fear and worry get in the way.

Even with the feeling that I was living a life that wasn't a good fit for me, I planned on staying on active duty until retirement, another six years. Luckily for me, I got a big kick in the butt to get me back on path. When I had my baby, I realized that I was no longer available to live a life that didn't truly fuel me. I wasn't going to work long hours and be gone for a year at a time for a job I didn't truly love. And furthermore, I realized my decisions would have a ripple effect on this tiny perfect human who stole my heart. I knew I needed to be true to myself for both of us, so I made the decision to leave active duty in order to live a life that I loved and be a role model for my daughter.

At first it was really hard. I didn't know what I wanted or what I was going to do. My husband and I were both unemployed after we both left active military duty, so that was another layer of stress. But then I found some coaches and mentors who helped me identify my passion, and what really lights me up inside. They helped me rediscover my authentic self. As a result of dropping my fake life and embracing my true self, I'm so much happier. I'm more present with my family, my relationships are so much stronger than they've even been, and I feel unstoppable, no matter what obstacles show up.

So, I didn't become a marine biologist, but I did find my true self and launch my company where I help people discover their life passions and live the lives of their dreams.

Who even has Enough Energy for This?

You give up an awful lot when you're not being authentic with yourself and choose to fake it in life. Let's face it, faking it in life is more consuming than the black hole that ate Matthew McConaughey in *Interstellar*. Spending all your time and energy maintaining a fake life doesn't leave you with enough energy to pursue the things you truly love. It dampens your creativity. It takes a massive amount of effort, and doesn't allow you to be as successful as you otherwise could. It's remarkably draining both physically and emotionally. And for what outcome?

Living a fake life is doing a serious disservice to yourself and those around you. By doing so, you are subconsciously telling yourself that you are unworthy, and that my friend, is not the case! I truly believe that everyone has a special beauty, love and worthiness. But when you try to fit into a mold that is untrue to your authentic self, you are robbing yourself of vital energy and the world of that special light that only you can shine.

Waking Up is Sweet

Like I eventually learned and I continue to share with my clients, trying to fit yourself into a life that doesn't fit has a plethora of negative effects. But once you decide you're going to bring your authentic self into the light of day, life is fantastic. Of course there are still hardships, quarrels and overslept alarms. But overall, when you're on the right path for you and you stop filtering your truth, things are good. Plain and simple. When you stop denying that the inner you is a person of worth, you are free to devote your full energy into achieving your goals. You can find your creative spark. You can be more successful. The universe lines up blessings and gifts to help you live your purpose. I know all this, because it's now my reality. I wouldn't give up my past for anything, but I'm so glad I learned how to be true to myself when I did. And it's not too late for you to do the same.

Jealousy isn't Always Bad

While I firmly believe that one should live a life of complete authenticity, jealousy - in healthy doses - can act like a signpost and be a powerful motivator to help you get where you want to be. If you notice what you're jealous of, you can take that information and identify your innermost wants and motivate yourself to accomplish your goals.

For years, I was jealous of my old college roommate. In a nutshell, she's perfect. She is literally the woman from the movie, *Bridesmaids*, who has it all together and is even a pretty crier. Not that I've ever seen her cry, but you get the picture. She's brilliant, a successful surgeon, incredibly kind, funny, athletic, confident and beautiful. You know, basically all those things we mere mortals aspire to be! Now, I can't even watch an episode of *Grey's Anatomy* without holding my hands over my eyes, so there's no chance that I'm going to try to live her life. That would be a serious waste of time. But you'd better believe that I use her myriad of positive qualities as motivation! That's healthy jealousy. I use my friend's life as motivation when I really don't feel like putting on my tennis shoes and taking the jogging stroller for a spin. And you know what? It works!

Because I used my friend as motivation, I'm that much closer to living the healthy lifestyle that I genuinely crave.

How to Stop Faking It and Live Your Own Fabulous Life

There is no way I would have been able to truly love myself and be content with my life until I learned how to pull a Frank Sinatra and do it my way. And hopefully, by now I've convinced you of the importance of living a life that's authentic as well. However, you may be wondering how the heck do you do that? I hear you. After years of living a life that was based on "I shoulds," I didn't have a clue on how to figure out my "I want." That, my friend, is a muscle you have to keep flexing if it's going to stay strong. But never fear, we can get you back on track and enjoying the life you were meant to live in no time flat.

FIVE SIMPLE AND EFFECTIVE STEPS TO HELP YOU GET REAL

1) Inventory your environment.

Take a look at your life right now. How do you feel when the alarm goes off in the morning? What is your body telling you? Are you living the life you dreamed about when you were younger? Do you change yourself to fit what others deem acceptable? Do you feel unworthy and unlovable being the authentic you? Are you doing things you "should" instead of things that bring you joy? Take an honest look at yourself and answer these questions. I recommend daily meditation and journaling to get everything out. There's something wonderful that happens when you put pen to paper and let the words spill out. You'll find your truth.

2) Clarify what you want.

Now that you've figured out where you're faking it and where you're being true to yourself, it's time to figure out what you really want in life. Everyone says they just want to be happy. That's awesome! That's fantastic! That's incredibly vague and not a course by which to navigate your life. Get specific as possible. Make a list. It's deceptively simple. If you can't figure out what to write, start by vocalizing it to your spouse, partner, dog, cat, pet turtle…whomever. Just get the words out. Once you put it on paper, share it. Lou Holtz did this with a list he made of over 100 goals, and his friends and former players have helped him achieve most everything that was on it. What do you have to lose? If you're worried that people will hold you accountable to actually go out and do the things you've said, well, that's kind of the point.

3) Practice being uncomfortable.

No one likes being uncomfortable. I make a big production about getting into a chilly pool because I hate being uncomfortable. The thing is that being uncomfortable is a part of changing from what you DON'T want to what you DO want. When you start living a life of authenticity, it's probably going to feel a bit odd. You've been out of practice. It's ok. I promise it will get easier. And I guarantee you'll actually start to enjoy doing those things that are aligned with your purpose once you realize how liberating and natural they are. So start small. Try a new food. Ask a coworker to join you on an outing. Ask for a raise. Climb Everest! Ok, maybe not the last one, but you get the idea.

4) Mantra it up.

I love visualizations and affirmations and I use them daily. These are positive feeling statements you use as mantras and meditations. They're fantastic for getting your subconscious mind on board and speeding up that whole transition out of discomfort. An easy way to do this is to set alarms on your phone with titles such as "I am worthy," "The real me is perfect," "Living an authentic life brings me success," and "Go do you!" You can incorporate these into your daily visualization practice as well.

5) Savor, rinse, repeat.

What good is creating something if you don't take time to really enjoy it? I like to say, "life is meant to be savored" as a reminder to slow down and really be present in the now. As you're creating the life that's authentic to you, really pay attention to what's happening. Enjoy what you're doing. Truly invest yourself in your conversations. Look for the gifts in the everyday. In doing so, you'll get positive reinforcement that your efforts are worth it, and you'll also quickly see how much better life is now that you're being true to yourself.

IN CONCLUSION

These are the steps that I took to get real. Now I share them with my clients who are stuck in lives that they don't love and are working to find their passion and I'm sure these steps will work for you too!

Remember, this isn't a dress rehearsal, my friend! We only get one shot at this life, so make it count. I keep a note on my desk that says, "This is it." It's my reminder to myself to be present, take big risks, and most of all, to live authentically. Only then can you reach your full potential.

About Jewell

Jewell Siebert is a life coach and Certified Canfield Trainer in The Success Principles. In her coaching practice, Jewell helps people make their lives Boldly Better. She helps them create the life of their dreams by helping them to rediscover their passions, find their ideal spot in their work/life balance and increase their level of happiness in both their personal and professional lives. Jewell believes that life should be savored and she reconnects her clients with their true desires in order for them to live lives that they can truly enjoy.

Jewell is a graduate of the United States Military Academy and Saint Mary's University. Prior to launching her coaching business, Jewell served in the United States Army for fourteen years, first as an air defense officer and later as an intelligence professional. During her service, she enjoyed extended working vacations at scenic locales in the Republic of Korea, Iraq, Afghanistan, and Texas. These intense experiences have fueled her desire for an amazing life for herself and her family, and a passion for helping other women in pursuit of happy, harmonious, and thrilling lives themselves. Jewell's current project is practicing American Sign Language with her daughter, Amélie.

You can connect with Jewell at:
- jewell@thefemmebrulee.com
- www.twitter.com/jewell_siebert
- www.facebook.com/thefemmebrulee

CHAPTER 35

THREE WAYS TO REDEFINE TRAUMA AS A TRANSFORMATIONAL CATALYST

BY KRYSIA BROUGHTON

I am the phoenix rising from the ashes of trauma. As it has cracked me open and obliterated former ways of being, I have consciously chosen to redefine trauma as a transformational catalyst.

Prior to 2011, my definition of personal success was deeply rooted in my role as elementary school teacher and literacy coach. I described myself as a well-educated overachiever who had a passion for facilitating the education of young hearts and minds. The classroom was my lifeblood and heartbeat. I took great pride in my well-developed expertise to plan, execute and then reflect upon educational goals. In my philosophy of life, I had my "ducks in a row" or a feeling of ultimate control over my daily work and, in a larger framework, over my own destiny.

All of my meticulously executed groundwork for success came to a violent halt on January 7, 2011. It started off as a routine drive home in my Honda Civic. Music was gently playing. A major Toronto highway was filled with vehicles rushing to diverse destinations. Day was overcast. Roads were clear. In a split second though, I entered into my own personal nightmare. I'll never forget the onslaught of excruciatingly loud screeches that felt like my car was being shredded apart while still in motion. These violent soundbites corresponded to the metal on metal contact as a tractor-trailer truck collided with my car. To this day, these ear-piercing sounds are my only recollection of this segment of the accident. These are the sounds of my trauma.

From the force of the collision, my car spun sideways on Toronto's busiest highway, the 401. Clinging to the steering wheel, I was now screaming with terror and dismay, for I saw that a second collision was inevitable. As if by slow motion, I helplessly watched the grill of the truck, jutting out in triangular metallic fashion and high above my Honda Civic, coming closer, closer to me. This is the face of my trauma. As the grill of the truck collided into my driver's side door, I feared for my life. I thought that the truck's cold, metal steel was going to slice me into pieces. I had nowhere to hide! Screams of terror and shock vibrated through my body. Heart pounding and yelling, I remember gripping the steering wheel with white knuckled hands. Being pushed sideways down Toronto's major highway was the ultimate terror! I thought I was going to die!

But then, I felt myself drifting out of my body and floating on the roof, still inside my car. Looking down on myself, I witnessed my physical body in terror. Yet, at the same time, I felt the liquid-like pulsing of inexplicable serenity through my spiritual being. A human being is actually capable of experiencing extreme trauma and spiritual peace at the same time! This otherworldly peace of the Divine was accompanied by angelic intervention.bI saw a group of majestic, powerful angels literally holding me and my Honda Civic together! It was a life-altering display of magnificent Divine mystery and it reassured my spiritual side that I wasn't going to die that day.

It was a miracle! I had survived an accident with a tractor-trailer truck! The frame of my body was intact! All limbs were accounted for and nothing was severed!

Post-accident, I just assumed that, with a little recovery time, I would return to my road of success, as I had previously defined it. After all, I had miraculously "survived" the accident. What actually happened was the onset of some devastating health issues including chronic pain, fatigue, flashbacks, nerve damage, grieving cycle emotions (shock, denial, anger, despair, depression), overwhelming anxiety, and a strong urge to hibernate, etc. Eventually, I was diagnosed with post-traumatic stress disorder (PTSD).

PTSD is like living in a parallel universe in which your inner core of being is shred into teeny, tiny fragments, while you look "perfectly fine" on the outside. Although I looked like the same person living in the same world, the trauma of my car accident had silently propelled me into a parallel universe where my life was completely unfamiliar.

Post-trauma life consisted of mind, body and spirit being locked in a disabling fight-or-flight response pattern. I was either in emotional fighter's mode with defenses sky high or I was pretending that my trauma only existed as a fragment of my imagination. Perhaps, if I exerted enough effort, I would ignore and outrun the trauma! The fight-or-flight response created a pattern of continual struggle with the trauma itself. This struggle caused more layers of excruciating pain. My life spiraled deeper and deeper into despair.

In the midst of the darkness, I was drawn to visionary Jack Canfield, and his book, *The Success Principles*. I courageously committed to Principle #1 by claiming 100% responsibility for my life. For me, taking responsibility meant stopping my continual inner war against trauma. When war is declared, its energy becomes larger than life and viciously devours everything in its path. Have you noticed, for example, that the war on fat has only created more obesity? There is no peace in struggle and war. In order to use trauma as a transformational catalyst, I began to let go of the struggle mentality, one moment at a time, in favour of a surrender/embrace continuum of empowerment.

1) Surrender the analytical mind. Embrace the intuitive inner voice.

"Stay away from that truck!" That's what my inner voice screamed at me, seconds before the accident. Did I listen to my inner guidance? No! Instead, I gave permission for my well-educated, analytical mind to drown out my inner guidance system. The next thing I knew, that truck had violently invaded my space.

Choosing to follow my intuition while it is still in the whispering (not screaming) mode was my first, and most important, life lesson from the accident.

Following the numbing stage of post-accident shock, my analytical mind kicked into overdrive with an overwhelming abundance of questions. "How do I...?" and "Yeah, but..." indicate that your mind is in supreme control. On the other hand, the inner voice is a strong knowing that flows through your core of being. Its timing is always perfect. It may not follow the norms as defined by society, religion, education, culture or family. Your inner voice is your own personal brand of wisdom based on the essence of who you truly are. Being still and listening to my breathing helps access my inner voice. Gentle walking, especially in nature, also strengthens my intuition.

My inner guidance has become my compass for all decisions, from choosing nourishing foods, to following strong urges to start post-accident journaling (my most transformational therapy) to knowing which treatment plans align with my personal values.

Trauma is complex and so are human beings. We are all unique based on our DNA, experiences and responses to our experiences. While there are many standardized tests to diagnose the severity of trauma-related symptoms, each person's journey is distinctly personal, thus defying all labels. This is why listening to the inner voice is so powerful. It is your personalized compass. It is your individualized transformational tool, just for you!

When the mind is put in service to this inner knowing, the forces of personal transformation are unleashed and echo in the world through moments of synchronicity.

2) Surrender the Fear. Embrace the Visionaries.

After trauma invaded my existence, fear became a constant, intimate companion. This fear spread out from the actual "face" of the trauma (in my case, the grill of the truck) to every aspect of my existence. The overwhelming perception of post-trauma fear is that life is unsafe. I responded by hibernating for days, weeks, even months at a time, barely going beyond my four walls of my home, thus transforming my environment into a claustrophobic prison of anxiety. Fear, indeed, has a torment like no other.

Surrendering fear can be done one moment, perhaps one microsecond, at a time. Support is needed. My psychologist not only guides me through the traditional Cognitive Behavioural Therapy (CBT) but also a powerful form of Energy Psychology called Emotional Freedom Technique. EFT enables you to intimately observe your emotions without becoming imprisoned by them. Combining these two diverse forms of psychology is truly visionary.

Visionaries are spectacular, compassionate human beings who are passionate for their fields of expertise, have unparalleled visions of empowerment for humanity and no tolerance for excuses. They educate, not label. Visionaries operate on the belief system that, no matter the circumstance, life ultimately has your back.

So where are your visionaries? Start by looking in the mirror. You are the biggest expert on you! Honestly, in the depth of my post-trauma brokenness, I thought I had absolutely nothing to offer myself, so why interact with those who embrace the transformational possibilities in challenging circumstances? In your empowered reality though, courageously facing post-trauma life, one moment at a time, gives you a red carpet of personal qualifications. You are your own superhero! Where others have claimed victimhood, you are persevering through the darkest night of the soul.

If you truly show up for yourself as visionary for your own life, then it is inevitable that magnificent support will materialize. Whoever and whatever you need is right in front of you. In my own experience, visionaries are found in clusters of networks so once you connect with one who resonates deeply with you, other inspired beings are nearby.

It was my family doctor who referred me to my chiropractor, the visionary who continues to have a profound impact on my healing journey. Did you know that chiropractic adjustments facilitate the body to heal itself naturally? As the adjustment gently re-aligns the vertebrae, it removes interference to the nervous system which controls and regulates every cell, tissue and organ. During an adjustment, I visualize health and vitality spreading through my nervous system highway into every single cell of my body. Chiropractic care transforms at the cellular level.

Ultimately, you are the centre of your own support system. Having the courage to ask questions and then allowing yourself to receive support deeply acknowledges your own self-worth and creates a fertile foundation for personal transformation.

3) Surrender the "ducks in a row" philosophy. Embrace the present.

"Here ducky, ducky! Where, oh where are my ducks so I can place them in a neat and tidy row?" Much of my depression was caused from my inability to force back together the pieces of my life as clearly defined by my pre-accident existence. I have learned that the transformational journey through trauma follows the pathway of your own true essence so this will be anything but a straight, predictable line. The very nature of trauma is inviting you to stop trying to feverishly control your outer circumstances and, instead, go inward. For the overachiever, it is just as painful to stop "doing" as the actual trauma-induced pain. I realized that I had thrived on a false sense of security based solely on a continuous routine of taking predictable actions.

It requires great courage to just "be" in the present for it is defined by a massive amount of question marks encompassing every aspect of life. Embracing the present involves three spectacular ingredients: extreme self-care, unrelenting gratitude and unparalleled self-gentleness. By focusing on one moment at a time, something revolutionary has occurred; my perception of the question marks has dramatically changed from menacing obstacle-focused creatures to graceful dance partners gently guiding me in my transformational journey. Surely, there is no greater road to success than courageously choosing to dance with the ambiguity of challenging times, gently moving to the beat of your authentic self.

Redefining trauma begins with the conscious choice to shift your awareness from struggling to witnessing, without self-judgement, your own rhythm of surrendering and embracing elements of the present moment. As you truly honour your experience, you empower yourself to transform, one moment at a time.

About Krysia

At the age of eight, Krysia Broughton had a clear knowing she had the heart of a teacher. After being inspired by her Grade 3 teacher she set her sights and goals on becoming an educator. She more than realized her dream, in a successful career of achievement and accomplishments teaching in public and private educational institutions. Having received multiple Awards of Distinction for innovative and visionary teaching, she truly answered the call to make a difference in lives.

For Krysia teaching is a sacred profession of educating hearts and minds and she thrives in the joy of seeing the connections that teaching can provide. She is passionate in helping others see the light of possibility turn on, and assisting students know what the next step is and to take it. She cherishes her role as literacy mentor and coach to other teachers helping them re-vision teaching and apply a transformational approach to learning. A car collision with a tractor-trailer truck stopped her in her tracks and challenged all of her beliefs.

Krysia, an inspired writer and published author, has become an important voice in redefining trauma and success. Now, she is an educator to all of us as she boldly continues in her commitment to be an inspiration and as a catalyst for living courageously and successfully in the classroom of life.

Krysia has a B.A. from the University of Guelph and a B.Ed. from the University of Western Ontario. She has been a member of the Ontario College of Teachers since 1996. Krysia currently resides in Toronto, Canada.

You can follow Krysia on her blog: www.traumaredefined.com.

CHAPTER 36

A TIME FOR EVERYTHING — A TIME TO HEAL AND A TIME TO SUCCEED

BY FAI CHAN

I do not consider my life before forty a successful one. There were setbacks. Even my successes (sometimes) were short lived. I used to wonder if life was a choice or it was predestined. I had tried very hard, but circumstances took the upper hand of me.

I am an immigrant. I was born in Hainan, China, and grew up in Hong Kong. I moved to the States because of my marriage when I was 30. I was nowhere, and did not know what I wanted to achieve here. I worked as a clerk in a Christian bookstore, and started to write Chinese articles for the monthly newspaper there. In six months, the head of the bookstore wanted to offer me the manager position. However, my husband's job required him to move to another state. That meant my dream vanished into thin air....

During my stay in Dallas, I was also the secretary of the Ikebana Club (Japanese floral arrangement), and then someone offered me to be the first Chinese to serve on the board of the International Women's Club – perhaps those opportunities were not the ones that God prepared for me. It was really a hard decision to make as I had to forgo those golden opportunities.

What was worse was that my mom got liver cancer when I had just moved

341

to Dallas. Life was like that . . . my husband used to be a joyful person, and I was a person of pessimism. I still remember when my mom had just passed away, there was a night when he was watching a talk show laughing . . . but I was crying in the bedroom.

To tell the truth, I had acne during the onset of puberty, and my face was full of scars. It made me a bit rebellious in character, and sometimes I gave myself excuses to rebel because God owed me something in life.

Luckily, I met a dermatologist from Yale, who helped me to heal. All my acne was gone... leaving the scars. However, with the technology of micro needling, my face returned to normal. I was so determined to heal completely, as I needed to go forward and pursue my dream of being an aromatherapist. After abandoning myself as a complaint to God, I finally awoke!!

I learned aromatherapy because I wanted to earn money by myself and not to rely on my husband totally. Deep into my heart, I wanted to tithe with my own money, not my husband's. I always think that being able to tithe is an honor for me. I based it on this reason, and set up my own company.

I seldom planned in my earlier days. But, I planned ahead this time. I took all the necessary courses to get my certification and membership with related associations. I met Andrea Butje, who is the teacher and mentor. I got my clinical certification there and successfully become a clinical member of the world famous and renowned aromatherapy association called AIA (Alliance of International Aromatherapists).

My interest is in writing. While I was studying with Andrea, I started to write and submitted articles for publications. Luckily, I got my first publications while I was still a student. My first article was seen at Lab Aroma, then AIA. I then pursued writing further by submitting articles to international journals like Aromatherapy Today. Articles in Aromatherapy Today are translated into Chinese in Taiwan, and my articles can be read by Chinese. My work can be searched through academic search engines like EBSCOhost.

Marc Gian, who is an acupuncturist and essential oil specialist, offered me a coaching course. With this coaching, I was very clear what I really wanted to achieve. He also helped me to release the guilt that I had for my mom, for not being able to accompany her when she died. I even coauthored an article by combining Aromatherapy and Traditional Chinese Medicine (TCM) in a UK aromatherapy magazine.

After a year and a half working in the field of aromatherapy, I was offered a directorship of AIA (2016-2017) by the president elect, Nancy D'Angelo. In fact, I was still very green at the time she offered me the Director's position. I did not know what would happen but wanted to take this rare and precious opportunity to grow. And I got that position. I also joined the Publication Committee, and am the Chair of the Publication Committee now.

As a Chinese, I thought I should do something for the Chinese community in Greater China. I set up a webpage in weibo – the largest Chinese social media – to educate people about aromatherapy. It turned out to be a success for me. My posts keep becoming hot picks ever since I have started my writing there. I helped the industry and those aromatherapists to translate their work and post them there, so that their work can get promoted. I also have my own aromatherapy journal in Chinese called *Aroma Search*, which is still a digital copy at this stage. To ensure the quality of the articles submitted, I set up an advisory board. People are more confident if there are experts on the board. By the time that I wrote this chapter, I had two books published in China.

As you all know, aromatherapy is an alternative protocol of healing, as many people believe. However, Madeleine Kerkhof-Knapp Hayes, an authoritative figure in using aroma care in the Netherlands, changed my point of view. She termed aromatherapy as a complementary protocol, which works side by side with conventional medicines. As a clinical aromatherapist, I do not feel inferior because of how people think. I have applied what I have learned to help people live a better and healthier life. As a therapist, it is always a joy to see people free of constraints, free of restraints, and free of limitations. They are not a slave to their ailments, be it physical or mental. I admire her work on helping people in the end-of-life stage to live peacefully, and I have planned to take her intensive course this year. Deep inside, I know the reason behind — I feel relieved by helping those people to compensate for what I have not done for my own mother in her end-of-life stage.

The turning point in my life came after I took Gabriel Mojay's class on emotional issues and aromatherapy through the use of acupoints. My expertise got refined and I am able to handle cases with complications on emotional issues. People began to recognize the significance of my knowledge even within the healthcare professional industry. I then started to raise my fees and my status was elevated too.

After the induction of my director's position in AIA, I was eager to find some good outfits to wear. I met a guy (Marcus) in Gucci. He has been working hard on getting me the items that I wanted to order. This was my first encounter with the top fashion brand, excluding the online experience. I learned from my experience that it is so hard to get items that I want, I needed to wait in line for quite long time, without any guarantee that I would get them. Since I wear a small size, it is doubly hard to get them since I have to compete with celebrities. After a few encounters, I became their VIP, and they threw me a party. I received gifts at Christmas and Chinese New Year. Since then, things became much easier....

I went to Hong Kong in Jan 2016, and visited the Gucci store there. I was so glad that I was also treated like a VIP there. People there watched me having my dessert....

Since I am their VIP, they are interested in my work in aromatherapy. The regional director asked for my articles, and he shared them with the head of regional directors. Who says that aromatherapy is an alternative protocol, and aromatherapists are having an inferior status? As a matter of fact, Burberry and Tiffany also want me to dress myself using their items.

My dentist, Dr. Chris Kimball, once told me after reading my articles that he thought that I had an exceptional future in aromatherapies without knowing what happened in my life. After his "oracle", opportunities kept pouring in. And now I am coauthoring this book with Jack Canfield. I also get the chance to be featured in *The Wall Street Journal*, and be interviewed on TV show(s). I will speak at UN Headquarters in June 2016.

I was not born into a rich family. I used to be a lazy person and depended a lot on my parents. I was able to find my husband because of the hard work of my younger brother and his wife. I used to be a watcher, watching people enjoying good stuff in their lives; but now, I am watched by others…. I don't feel that I am happier, but the big changes do bring me sorrow of life. When asked what kind of life that I want to live? I just want to have a stable life without any ups and downs.

Life does have a predestined element, but when I changed my attitude towards life, I was able to turn crises into opportunities and enjoy success. My happiest moments in daily life are to debate what I have observed with my husband. I enjoy that kind of intellectual discussion. I cannot thank him enough for being so supportive in my life, even helping me to finish my homework, to edit my articles and to do the household chores for me. Even if I fail in other parts of my life, I am still a winner with him being my husband.

Sometimes, I think God loves to shower gifts to me… I have so many good things in my life. I begin to treasure them in my mid-phase of life. Everything does have its time — a time to heal, and a time to succeed. If what you have is not what you want, then you may need a little patience to wait for the right time to come.

I am very happy that I can contribute to my industry. Money is not the most important thing in my life… spiritual richness is more important to me. My first book in Chinese topped first on the Best Seller's List (fictional and non-fictional short stories) of my publisher several times. My publisher is the largest online book seller in China and is listed on the New York Stock Exchange. My second Chinese book, which is the sequel of the first one, was a Best Seller (fictional and non-fictional short stories) on my publisher's list several times. I am working on my third Chinese book (fictional) which incorporates aromatherapy into the storyline.

I am also working with a renowned author, Elizabeth Ashley. I am so glad to be able to help other less well known aromatherapists to promote their work. If everyone pursues self-interests in their life, who is going to take care of the bigger picture?

My deepest longing is to become a "Christian nun" so that I can serve God wholeheartedly forever. People may envy what I have now, but I can abandon them to pursue my dream. I started my company by hoping to tithe; I chose aromatherapy because God loves fragrance. I have been working hard to master it so that I am qualified to work as a "Christian nun" in God's temple. People may laugh at my decision and choice of life, but who knows if it is because of my pure heart that God rewards me so abundantly?!

About Fai Chan

Fai Chan started her career in 2014, and by now, she has published 10 articles in international journals. She has recently published two books in Chinese in China, and she is the publisher of the digital journal – *Aroma Search* – a Chinese aromatherapy journal. One of the largest Chinese publishers is very interested in her work and would like her to write for it.

Recently, Fai signed a contract to write a chapter in Jack Canfield's forthcoming book – *The Road To Success*. He is the co-author of the *Chicken Soup for the Soul* series. Fai will be inducted into the National Academy of Best Selling Authors, and plans to attend the award ceremony in Hollywood in September.

The Wall Street Journal is arranging an interview with her. She will also appear in the TV show(s) for an interview in Hollywood in the second half of the year. Since she started posting on weibo (the largest Chinese social media), her posts have been hot picks.

Fai Chan serves on the Board of a world-leading aromatherapy association called AIA (Alliance of International Aromatherapists). She is also the chair of the publication committee there. She is a clinical member (CMAIA) of that association.

The two books she wrote in Chinese hit the No. 1 spot on the Best-Sellers list. She is also helping renowned aromatherapists in her industry to translate their work into Chinese and helping them promote their books. She is also co-authoring books with them.

Some of her work can be found via Academic Search Engine EBSCOhost.

Fai Chan's company, Deli Aroma LLC, is dedicated to holistic healing protocols. Her specialties are mainly in the healing of emotional issues with aromatherapy. Based on a Traditional Chinese Medicine (TCM) framework, with the synergistic effects of combining the therapeutic approach with chemistry, her remedies are very effective. She takes joy in knowing her clients personally, and gives them personalized care. She puts a lot of time and effort in doing follow-ups. She asks a lot of questions and firmly believes that, when they get healed, they will thank her for that.

When you are sick, you may not know the best treatment. As a therapist, she is very clear what works best.

CHAPTER 37

CONQUERING YOUR FEARS OF PUBLIC SPEAKING

BY GRACE CHIVELL

I grew up in a happy and vibrant European family in Adelaide, South Australia. I was the youngest of three girls. However, it felt like I grew up as an only child, as there was sixteen years between me and my sisters. They had already left home by the time I was nine years old. So for me, I felt I had all my parents' attention. At an early age, I was lead to believe that it was not to my advantage to voice my opinion. If I had something to say, my mother would always say that it was best to be quiet and not voice your opinion or rock the boat. Both my parents were very loving, yet in my mother's mind, she felt she was protecting me from the outside world.

There were so many times at primary school where I would respond to a question, but was given a negative response from the teacher that my answer was irrelevant or incorrect. There was one particular teacher who did not give me any encouragement at all, and I would also hesitate in answering for fear of being humiliated in front of the class. I would always dread the day I had this particular teacher.

So there it began – my fear to speak my mind in all areas of my life. This also extended to speaking in a group or having to do a presentation in my working life.

As a child I was very shy, especially in primary school when the teacher called on me to answer a question. I remember one day, we had a debate to present and we were put into groups for the presentation. I was so afraid. My body was shaking and this heat took over my body. Then it came to me. If I made out that I have lost my voice, I won't have to participate in the debate. I felt so bad doing that, but it's the only thing I could think of to avoid the debate. In High School I gained a little more confidence, but I was still very shy. I felt very afraid to converse in a group, go into a shop to buy something, asking for directions, and speaking up in the classroom. I was the quiet achiever.

When I began my working life at sixteen, we had already moved to Melbourne, so there was the added pressure of being in an unknown location and not knowing my way around. My two sisters were instrumental in me getting to know my new surroundings as they were already living there.

My banking career helped me substantially in dealing with people and learning how to interact with them. Even though the first six years I was not in a customer-facing role, I was engaging with new colleagues and experiencing the different personalities and behaviours. My colleagues would never have known that I was so shy because talking one-on-one, I was very confident. Once I was placed in customer facing roles I gained more confidence and learned many interview techniques. However, this was still in a one-on-one basis.

I believe that my love for learning has assisted me in all facets of my life. I have acquired so much knowledge over the years that I just wanted to share it with everyone I knew. The ability to run success training workshops and seminars has for many years been one of my life goals. It would give me great pleasure to be able to share my knowledge to help others to find their purpose in life and go on to great things.

I was a Bank Manager for many years, and in that time I was still very shy and did not think that my thoughts or opinions were valued by anybody in the room at our meetings. I was confident with my staff in our weekly meetings, however, in the managers' meetings my participation was non-existent. I had a lot to say and opinions to put forward, but never did.

At Christmas time one year, the group of us went out for lunch to celebrate. We all had to bring a Kris Kringle present of a certain value. I always looked forward to this even though the colleague had no idea who was providing this gift. After lunch, we decided to call out the names and give out the presents. As I unravelled the paper, I saw a toy bear. This was not just any ordinary bear. It was a famous bear on a nationally televised children's show in Australia.

This was the turning point for me. You see, the bear in the television show never spoke. He only communicated through hand gestures and body movements. My heart sank. I felt so hurt. I put on a brave face when everyone looked at it, but I didn't acknowledge that I knew what the meaning was. The gifts we gave were supposed to be funny. I didn't find it funny at all. I went home and thought hard and long about it. How could this person publicly humiliate me like that? Why would they think it was funny? Is this what everyone thought of me?

Several months later, after going over it many times in my mind, I realised that this was the opportunity for me to take action once and for all, because the only person that could do anything about it was ME. I needed to change. Not to change who I was and what I believed in, but change my mindset. During my recent training with Jack Canfield, I realised that what I had decided that day was actually what he teaches – that it is your response to the situation that will change the outcome.

I never found out which of my colleagues gave me the gift, but if I ever do, I would tell them "thank you" because even though I was very hurt at the time, I have let the feelings go, and that the gift changed the way I thought of myself and others from that day forward. So I took action and decided to use my love of learning to my advantage. I knew that my mind was like a sponge that required constant and consistent information on a daily basis to function. I knew that the more knowledge I could acquire on the subject, the more successful I was going to be.

Even though I was a good learner I was not necessarily an avid reader of books. I knew that if I was going to be successful at this, I needed to have the knowledge behind me. I had to balance my work and home life to achieve this goal of conquering my fears. Visuals assisted me immensely. Vision boards, sticky notes and photos are required to be part of my environment to ensure I see these things daily to remind me of what I want to achieve. This will be important for you too. Some of you may prefer to listen to a motivational CD in your car instead . . . we all learn in different ways.

Reading has helped me so much to understand the mind and how we think and perceive things that happen around us. Around this time is when I decided to go back into the education system and graduated in the subjects that were close to my heart. I became more confident with my presentations.

By 2015, when I was attending the Flight Centre Travel Academy, I was looking forward to putting together presentations with my group but especially my own presentation. I couldn't wait to get up there and speak about my topic. I noted that most of the classmates were very nervous about doing a presentation in front of the class even though there were only ten of us. I thought to myself, that's how I used to feel.

There was a pivotal moment after my own final presentation, where the facilitator gave us feedback about our presentation skills and content. She went around the room and when she got to me she said; "Grace, you were the only one that showed more enthusiasm about your topic, that was a great presentation. You must do this in your work?" Wow! Was she talking to me? I couldn't believe what I was hearing! For a facilitator to say that to me was a wonderful compliment.

That's when I realised I was ready to do what I have always wanted to do:

- Run my own successful training and coaching business
- Keynote Speeches
- Tell my story and for my audience to know that anything is possible
- And most importantly, to work with the education system to teach children that they do have a voice and to let them know to follow their dreams and that anything is possible, by showing them ways to accomplish this, for example, how to set goals for themselves

The five steps to conquer your fears:

S tart -- small and present in front of a family member or friend, use a subject that you are knowledgeable in.

P ractice -- until it becomes second nature, maybe in front of a mirror, you may want to record yourself (This may be a little confronting, however it is an important step in uncovering any areas for improvement).

E ducate -- yourself in what interests you and in what interests your audience, as well as your subject content.

A spire --   to reach new heights, set even higher goals once you have achieved your current ones, know that it's possible.

K nowledge -- is the engine that provides the power in everything that you do and everything you want to achieve in your life.

Start small. That's what I did. Just take one step, then the next and so on. Think about when you were first learning how to drive a manual car. It felt uncomfortable. Now you don't even have to think about it. Every day we are learning even if we don't realise it.

Get your audience to encourage you and give you feedback on what they think you could have improved on. Feedback is a wonderful tool. It continually helps you improve on your presentations skills, content, use of technology and so many other things that you may not have considered if not for the feedback provided to you. Think of it as "positive engagement."

You may also want to attend an event that has a public speaker. The topic of this event is not important, but here are some of the things to take note of:

- How well did they introduce themselves?
- How well are they presenting their content?
- Do they seem confident with their content?
- Is it easy for you to understand the content?
- What type of technology is being used?

There is so much information that can be taken away from observing someone that you want to learn from.

Many of you may be thinking:

- "I get nervous speaking in front of a lot of people"
- "They're all looking at me"
- "They're judging me"

What you need to remember is that no matter how many people are looking at you during your speech, they are not judging you. They have come to hear you speak. Yes, they are looking at you not necessarily smiling, but they are actually listening intently to what you have to say. Never assume to know what they are thinking. That is not important.

What is important is the message you want to convey to them and how you present it.

We all had to learn to crawl first. It is the same in our adult life as we learn new things. We become nervous about learning something new and start feeling uncomfortable. If it is something that you have always wanted to do, and you are starting to feel uncomfortable when you begin, trust me when I say, you're doing the right thing, you are on the right track. You are moving out of your comfort zone. You also need to know that when you display confidence in your presentation, your audience will feel the same confidence in you, they are your "mirror image."

It is unfortunate that I did not have a mentor. But with everything that I have learned up to this point, I am confident that one day soon, I will mentor someone to many great achievements. Helping just one person will be a wonderful accomplishment for me.

Just imagine for a moment, if we could all help just one person achieve their vision and goals, what a happy and beautiful world it would be.

Remember, your knowledge is your Power! Go for it!

About Grace

Grace Chivell has always had a great relationship with her clients. Building rapport has always been very important to her. She has a great ability to assess their financial position so that the right decisions are made. This has ensured her repeat business on a consistent basis. Her fascination with numbers began at an early age when she attended a business and accounting course in High School. Grace was born in Adelaide, South Australia. Her parents migrated from Italy to Australia in 1954 to build a better life for themselves and her two sisters. Grace was born 9 years later. Her family affectionately called her "The Kangaroo" of the family.

Grace was immediately employed in the banking industry after leaving high school. From the beginning she was known by her colleagues as The Poet. Grace has a great sense of humour. She would often write comedic poems for colleagues who were leaving the bank, with anecdotes of their working life, and then present and read the poem to them during the farewell dinner celebrations.

Throughout her career she received many Banking and Finance achievements, and acquired a total of 36 years' experience in various areas of the Banking industry, serving for 18 years as a Bank Manager for various branches across Melbourne, Australia.

Grace's career has always been centred on face-to-face interaction which she feels is the key to communicating and building great rapport and trust with her clients which has ensured her continual repeat business. Grace is a life coach and personal development trainer servicing both individual and corporate clients to achieve their highest potential.

Grace is a graduate of the Victoria University in Melbourne majoring in Business and Accounting. She is also a graduate of the Flight Centre Travel Academy due to her love for traveling the world, majoring in Travel and Tourism as well as Events Management. Grace also enjoys volunteering at various Travel Expo and charity events throughout the year.

Grace also has a successful online store selling various small and unusual items. To assist her store to achieve great success, she is utilising her vast knowledge of search engine optimisation to empower the site to receive as much traffic as possible.

More recently Grace has been certified as a Jack Canfield Trainer. Grace is the founder of the "Success Coaching and Training Institute," which facilitates personal development workshops and seminars for individuals and the corporate sector. The

Institute will now also be focussed on teaching Jack's principles for success. Her unique program has several different formats which is tailored for each individual client.

Grace is a mother of three girls and grandmother to four grandsons.

You can connect with Grace at:
- grace@successcoachingandtraininginstitute.com.au
- http://facebook.com/gchivell
- https://au.linkedin.com/in/gracechivell
- www.successcoachingandtraininginstitute.com.au

CHAPTER 38

THE THREE P'S OF FINANCIAL WELLNESS
– PURPOSE, PLAN AND POSITION

BY CHANTELLE L. MORMAN

Speaking in 2014 at the United Women's Conference in Ft. Lauderdale, FL, I revealed to the audience a simple truth that guides my work in providing economic empowerment and what I call "International Diversity Life Coaching." "Traveling the country," I said, "I have heard hundreds of stories from individuals and members of families who are in need of a better way. These and life's realities are what drive my passion for creating a different kind of motivational, educational yet mindful experience." All of the consulting services under the umbrella of Morman & Company, are geared towards helping clients reach their financial and personal potential.

Everyone we work with brings different problems and priorities to the table, but those are not the P's I am referring to in the title of this chapter. Rather, I have boiled down the road to success and financial wellness to three P's that help solve those problems and inspire a re-assessment of my clients' life priorities. These are PURPOSE, PLAN and POSITION.

FINDING MY PURPOSE

I wouldn't be able to help people all over the world discover their unique Three P's had I not been through a powerful journey of self-enlightenment myself. While pursuing degrees in Medical Systems and Business Administration, I was actually passionate about becoming a medical doctor. Having a young family to raise, however, I decided to shift my focus to the business world with belief in the wealth creation opportunities that an independent business could create.

My start began by launching a series of businesses in my hometown of Waterloo, Iowa, including a neighborhood convenience store, bar and barbershop. While getting those up and running, I was offered to branch out and become statewide director of a federally-funded outreach program that was focused on sustaining the health of families in Iowa's communities. Education and motivation ultimately inspired a career path I could never have imagined while dreaming of being a M.D. One of the things that fueled my "flames of service" was my exposure to the needs of the people, especially the importance of change and opportunities that were not accessible to most due to a simple lack of knowledge. I decided to become a "financial doctor," originally incorporating one of my firms as Health & Finance MDs. I have since dedicated my life to providing financial education and building generational wealth through customized financial planning.

My life's purpose changed as I discovered this need to help others, and I felt that I could be of better service being a money doctor than a M.D. Once I moved to Florida and began getting my licensing in health, life and annuity, I positioned myself by affiliating with the financial services industry, then followed the guidelines to incorporate that for my plan to be achieved. Obviously, the goal of starting any business is to help bring in revenue, but for me, it was important as an entrepreneur to succeed in something I love – and what I am most passionate about is helping others gain the knowledge that's needed for them to grow. Happiness for me is a journey, not a destination, and I'm blessed to be living my dream and passion in the service of others.

YOUR PURPOSE, YOUR PLAN, YOUR POSITION

So let me start by asking you:

- What's your Purpose?
- What's your plan to reach your Purpose?

Those two questions lead us to the bigger question:

- What Position are you in to achieve your Purpose?

I'll break those down very simply into three steps aligned with the Three P's.

Step #1 – PURPOSE

Knowing your purpose provides a reason for your planning and a GPS to the paths needed to implement a plan. Re-route to rethink if you find yourself off track! Sometimes looking into your past or your pain helps determine your true purpose. Think of those things you dreamed of someday doing when you were young, but got sidetracked from.

It's so easy to get lost in the day-to-day priorities and problems that we can get distracted from pursuing the true passions we once had. Likewise, many of us have been through painful experiences and as a result have a wealth of personal experience that can become a resource for others going through the same situations or physical and emotional traumas. Sometimes the things we thought were the worst things we could endure turn into the greatest blessings when we use them to help others.

Knowing your purpose provides a reason for your planning and the knowledge of your final destination. Sometimes, looking into your past, or your pain, helps you discover your true purpose. Think of those things you dreamed of someday doing when you were young, but got sidetracked from. Or the circumstances and individuals that inspired you. Discovering your purpose is the initial step to formulating your ultimate life-plan.

Many of us have lived through painful experiences of physical and emotional trauma, and as a result have a wealth of knowledge that can become a resource for others facing similar situations. Sometimes the things we thought were the worst things we could endure, turn into the greatest blessings, when we use them to help others.

Often in your life's story you will discover your purpose.

Step # 2 – PLAN

Planning for a purpose provides you the strength and knowledge of knowing that your purpose can and will be fulfilled. Identifying your purpose helps you formulate a vision and a roadmap to get to there from here. As you see with my story, sometimes it evolves in unique, unexpected ways due to outside circumstances. And sometimes, it's a matter of getting back to what you have always loved; setting aside time to formulate a step-by-step plan; and taking things out of the realm of "wishing" and into the realm of "doing." The world is changing rapidly, and as a result you must also make changes from within in order to fulfill your purpose. It's so easy to get lost in our day-to-day responsibilities that we can get distracted from pursuing the true passions we possess. Your plan is your GPS to the paths needed to fulfill your purpose. Re-route to rethink if you find yourself off track!

Step #3 – POSITION

Positioning yourself to achieve your plan requires you to pave additional paths. These new paths lead to the GPS route that guides you to the fulfillment of your purpose. Two of the keys to having the freedom to position yourself on to these paths are: (a) making your money work for you, and (b) turning your time into money. Many people prevent themselves from developing a larger vision for their life because their choices have left them in perpetual survival mode.

When you're trying to figure out where your next meal is coming from, you don't have time to create a viable vision for yourself. Some people have a purpose but no resources to achieve their plan. For those, I aim to provide a plan that aligns with their purpose, and positions them for those plans to be achieved. We can do this by introducing different resources to add additional income streams, eliminating debt and learning to invest in ventures that help money work for them.

ROADBLOCKS:

As we begin to think about reaching our purpose and realizing our plan we all encounter roadblocks. Here are some tools to use as your GPS to deal with the roadblocks and reach your destination.

MY GOALS WORKSHEET

Too many people never ask themselves what they want to accomplish in life. They're far too busy trying to keep up with everyday life demands, such as paying the bills and taking care of loved ones. There are also deeper reasons beyond daily "busyness" and stress. Maybe you've had some shattered dreams in the past. Or you've done "lots of doing" but with minimal or no positive results. All of these things can lead to low or no self-confidence, which can block motivation to break from your routine, set new goals and develop a vision for a more fulfilling life driven by purpose.

So how do you take control of your life and move forward? The answer is planning.

The first step in planning is setting goals. Goal setting is a major component of personal development. To achieve your goals, you must focus on them. Achieving your goals will give you a great sense of accomplishment! Goals can be divided into three durations: Short-term goals (Three months), Medium-term goals (Three months to a year), and Long-term goals: (One year or more).

First, think about short-term goals—those you can reach in about a three-month span. These might include saving enough money for the children's holiday presents, taking yourself to the beach for a day, or buying a new flat-screen television for your home. Simple enough, right? Then, consider medium-term goals that can be reached in three months to about a year. These might include trading in your car for the pickup truck you've always wanted, learning to sew your own clothes, or signing up for a class at your local community college. These are a bit more challenging, but still not too outside the norm. The long range goals that are more than a year away, however, may take you out of your comfort zone – but in an invigorating, potentially life- changing way. Perhaps you've always wanted to go back to school for a degree or certification, start or expand your business, or buy a home.

I have another memorable acronym for you – SMART. Remember to use the SMART system (Specific, Measurable, Achievable, Realistic and Time-bound). When you reach your first goal, re-evaluate and add new goals to your list. Then begin working towards accomplishing your next goal! Planning for a purpose provides you the knowledge and satisfaction of knowing your goal is being, or will be, fulfilled.

TOP TEN SIGNS YOU HAVE TOO MUCH DEBT

As a "financial doctor," one of my roles with clients is helping them identify the signs of having too much debt – and finding solutions to reduce or eliminate it, which opens doors of investment and opportunity.

Although a limited amount of debt isn't necessarily a bad thing, excessive debt can prevent you from achieving your long-term financial and personal goals. Some people don't even know when they're in over their heads in debt. Once you realize you're in trouble, it's important to know that there are things you can do to get out of debt. While the solution might not be easy, you can regain your balance and your future. The following are signs that you have too much debt:

1. More than 20 percent of your income goes toward paying of car loans, credit card debt, or other kinds of consumer debts.
2. You have to borrow money each month to pay off your debts.
3. You don't know how much money you owe.
4. You pay only the minimum amount on each bill.
5. You pay your bills late each month and sometimes even miss payments.
6. Creditors have to call you to get you to pay your bills.
7. Businesses refuse to give you credit.
8. You have taken money from retirement accounts and/or have used credit cards to pay normal monthly bills.
9. You write postdated checks.
10. You have to take an extra job to keep up with your bills.

I ask people the following questions: Do you have money left over at the end of the month? If so, go back and increase your monthly savings expenses to build financial security. Not enough income to cover expenses? Where are your spending leaks?

Make certain that you track your actual income and actual expenses for the month. How did you do? Are you on track? Do you need to make some adjustments? It's time to start the process all over again and create next month's Spending Plan.

Working through potentially crippling debt issues is an important step towards positioning yourself to achieve your plans via paving additional paths that lead to the ultimate route set forth to fulfill your purpose. It's important to figure out ways to make your money work for you and turn your time into money!

DECREASING DEBT

Sometimes debt can make you feel like you're living at the bottom of a deep well. The good news is there are many different ways to pull yourself out into the daylight of financial security. I suggest the following steps can help you get started:

1. Because interest on debt compounds over time, there's no time to get started like the present.

2. Cut your everyday expenses so that you can use more of your money to pay off your debts.

3. Work with a credit counselor to set up a debt-reduction plan. Although each company you owe will send you a bill each month, your best course of action is to send any extra cash toward the creditor that is charging you the highest interest.

4. Consolidate your loans by shifting higher-interest loans to a single lower-rate loan, and make sure that you're not running up new charges.

5. Limit yourself to one or two credit cards. Pay off any other cards you have, call those companies to cancel your accounts, and cut up those cards. Keep the final one or two cards in a safe place at home, where you won't be tempted to use them for frivolous occasions. You can even call the credit card companies and have the credit limit lowered on those last cards to prevent you from running up too much debt on them.

6. Earn the most money you can. Getting a second job or working overtime can be ways to increase your monthly income. If you have a family, however, it's best to decide whether your time is more valuable at home or at work.

7. Sell or trade items that you own yet never use. Instead of pawning items at a pawnshop, sell them yourself and use the money to help pay down debts.

8. When you pay off one debt, make sure you continue to set aside the same amount of money each month to pay off other debts.

9. Sometimes you have to be honest with yourself in order to make the best financial decisions. If you purchased a car but are having trouble making the monthly payments, you may be better off selling the car and paying off your loan rather than letting a creditor repossess the car. A record of a repossession will hurt your credit rating.

10. Join Morman & Company, where I and my team can help you learn of additional revenue streams that can move you from the red into the black.

THE DIFFERENCE IS YOU

Choosing the life we live solely depends upon us as individuals. Advisers, counselors, concerned friends and those who take the time to encourage us are wonderful, but in the end, the choices we make determine the ease or difficulties we have in moving closer to finding our purpose and achieving our plans. So it's always wise to, as I say, "Be Mindful, Not Wasteful!" And remember that if you do the same things you've always done, you'll receive the same circumstances or situations you currently have, or have had in the past. If you desire change, you must position yourself for it.

Persistence and Perseverance are the keys to this, but let's not forget everything my work is founded on – EDUCATION! It's the ultimate necessity in nearly everything we do! Continuing education has allowed me to conquer obstacles along my journey and live the life I've chosen. This is why I have made it my purpose to educate others globally on eliminating obstacles that exist, because people have not been exposed to financial literacy.

I hope you take my life experience and words of advice and encouragement to heart, and that this chapter helps you get started on discovering your own Three P's of Financial Wellness.

Ultimately, however, the difference is YOU, Your goals, Your effort, Your dedication to education and Your determination to change what you must to live the life you have long dreamed of.

About Chantelle

Chantelle L. Morman, a determined, driven, goal-oriented visionary, dubbed "The Financial Empowerment Guru", was born and raised in Waterloo, a small city near Des Moines, Iowa. Chantelle intrinsically understood that education was pivotal to her achieving success; as a result, she enrolled at the University of Northern Iowa, pursuing degrees in Medicine and Business Administration. Chantelle opened various successful service businesses within the community where she lived to enjoy the freedom derived from being an independent business owner. She believes, "Your health is your true wealth." Her professional experience, knowledge and personal triumphs in overcoming her own financial challenges has served and continue to serve as an asset for those she decides to work with.

As State Director of a federally-funded outreach program focused on sustaining the health of families within communities of Iowa, Chantelle was exposed to the needs of the community juxtaposed against the lack of opportunities accessible to most people due to their lack of knowledge, education and motivation. Consequently, she championed financial education programs aimed at building generational wealth through customized financial planning with a promise to leave no family behind. It was her ability to identify and develop the proposal for federal funding that made the program successful, financially viable and ongoing. Through this avenue, she was able to improve not only the physical health of patients, but a client's financial health using educational techniques focused on building generational wealth.

Chantelle is the Founder of Health & Finance MDs, whose goals are for all to achieve financial success by teaching that the difference is **YOU**, Your goals, Your effort, Your dedication to education and your determination to change what you must. The organization provides customized financial planning and education to individuals, families and businesses.

Chantelle L. Morman & Company was later created to challenge the status quo, to offer superior expertise, strategic advice, exceptional services and a competitive advantage while managing clients' measurable goals and expectations to reach their financial goals. She believes in partnering with, and employing people with the right character, values and positive personalities.

Ms. Morman is co-partner and COO of Paragon Financial, where she oversees operations and manages the group's financials to ensure they are operating according to the state of Florida's regulations. She has been a developer of innovative products to strengthen people financially. Staying true to form, she developed partnerships and programs in Fort Lauderdale and Miami, Florida, and has spoken at numerous conferences across the country on her models. Her experiences have taught her how to identify non-traditional funding sources such as, organizations, foundations, corporations, private funds and individual funds, partnerships and sponsorships to support her goals.

Chantelle, a National Speaker, Certified Financial Educator and Author has received notable accomplishments such as: featured in *Forbes* as a Trendsetter, HFA-Family Assessment Worker Training Coordinator, Maternal Health Depression Trainer, Prenatal Health Educator, Plan A Abstinence Facilitator, Strengthening Families Educator, Health, Life and Annuity Licensed.

You can connect with Chantelle at:
- Chantelle@MormanAndCompany.com
- www.twitter.com/CLMorman&Co.
- Facebook.com/MormanandCompany

CHAPTER 39

7 SECRETS OF THE "ONE CALL CLOSE"

BY: DEAPHALIS SAMPLE

Growing up as an inner city kid, Jean always aspired to be someone great. She was the fourth child of seven kids seeking the Road To Success at a very early age. She knew she was different from her siblings and friends because she always seemed to never quite fit in. She was physically smaller than most her age, and couldn't explain to others why she ended up with a birth defect. She would attempt to make friends, but would somehow find herself being the victim of what she had no control over. Her eyes would always tell the story every time she looked at anyone.

Jean had become an astounding athlete – becoming a cheerleader and making the cut on the track team. She felt as though she always had to prove herself, but suddenly realized she had been bottling up words, conversations she had been having within herself. Deep inside, she always wanted to become a writer. She started to express these conversations through poems, and short stories. For the first time in her life, she felt a burning desire to bring to light how she felt after she was molested. Her thoughts and emotions expressed on paper would open her up to new opportunities. Suddenly realizing this would change her life forever, she could finally free herself from the rigorous chains of bondage that held her mind captive. She began to write about the struggle of being held bound in a place of freedom.

In her final year of high school, Jean hit another road block. She got pregnant and had to face the humiliation and embarrassment of having an unplanned child. The feelings of insecurity, inadequacy, and loneliness, among other negative feelings, would creep through her mind and set up residence there. Jean knew if the baby was going to survive, and even if she was going to make it in this world, she had to overcome what she felt, and tell the last person she ever wanted to know or let down, her Dad.

She would go home later that day after telling her boyfriend she was pregnant. He decided at that time he wanted nothing to do with the child. Now, it was time to face her Dad, the man she feared the most. Upon telling him, he blew his top with anger which made her feel even worse. She wrestled with all these feelings, emotions that depleted her self-esteem and self-worth. What would she do now? How would she ever accomplish anything in life now that she had a child to raise? When would she even find the time to write and participate in all of those other things she really loved to do? Nine months went by, and her first child was born – a new addition to her family was now a baby girl. Shortly after, she would go on to finish and graduate high school.

A few years later, she found herself married to someone who accepted her daughter and ended up having two more kids. She soon discovered that working and saving all of her money wasn't enough to get what she really wanted out of life, which was true success. Fifteen years passed, and Jean was then at another crossroad in her journey of life - Divorce! That was the turning point that caused her to change the way she thought about how productive she had been with her own life. Now she was sick and tired emotionally. She had enough of settling for less, barely making ends meet with just enough to get by. She knew making excuses was not an option, and made a decision to move out because she was previously told by someone she respected that doing the same things over and over expecting different results was insanity. Jean found a new place to live on the other side of the city. She remained in her current position as a marketing representative for a very popular food chain restaurant.

One day she received a phone call from a lady she met five years earlier that offered her a position in sales. Jean knew the income potential was greater than what she was making now, so she decided to accept the new position.

After several months on the new job, she met a nice, tall, handsome, very successful businessman that began to admonish and admire her. He would encourage her about things she really could do. Suddenly, a flame of joy and excitement ignited between them and they began to date. They would read self-help books, travel, study, go out and spend hours upon hours together until after one year of dating, he decided to ask for her hand in marriage. She responded with tears of joy and faithfully said yes. She knew that life for her was now beginning to look in such a way that she could dream of one day becoming a famous writer and speaking to millions of people through the books she would write.

Jean began writing again, networking with others, talking with God, and members of her church. Her husband would mentor her on those negative qualities she picked up as a child that stunted her professional growth. He first started with her mindset and initiated a systematic program that made him very successful. He knew he needed to shift her way of thinking. He would show her how she could literally close anybody in the sales industry and receive instant gratification from doing it. He began sharing principles with her that he had sought out through practical psychology. He knew that would give her an edge over the competition. He would deposit little nuggets of wisdom that changed her life forever. He began sharing the 7 secrets of the One Call Close with her. They went to a nearby lake and sat beside the still waters. He began talking with her about the Success Principles he researched and implemented in his own life -- that brought him much success.

Secret # 1 - People follow people would be the first thing she'd began learning. He would say things like the power to define is the power to fulfill which caused her to seek out the ambiguity of what he said so she could simplify the principle. She would begin to see that people follow people was true because he taught those profound techniques in the business they started together that led to their success. As Jean absorbed this concept, she saw the dynamics of this displayed on TV commercials, as an example he shared with her. Every time a TV commercial would air, there was almost always a person in it, or whenever she'd attend a professional sporting event, she noticed the crowd wearing T shirts of the most famous people playing in the game. She even observed the attendance of the game was also predicated on who was playing in it as well. Wow! she thought. People really do follow people.

Secret # 2 - People follow purpose - she remembered the words he said about the power to define is the power to fulfill. So she went to the dictionary and looked up the word purpose. She discovered from the definition the reason WHY people do what they do. She read that purpose was the reason for which something is done or created or for which something exists. Now she understood why businesses, churches, organizations, fraternities, sororities, non-profits, etc., exist today. She would see this in the company they were building because they started with the purpose of why they wanted a business.

Secret # 3 - People follow pleasure - she got really excited about this step like most do. He would tell her to pay attention to how people chose to gratify themselves through pleasure. As she observed this principle, she noticed this was a belief that most people in life thrived on to reach their level of success. This principle gripped a person's emotions so closely until this is the make-it- or-break-it principle that requires management. He would go on to explain that people who could manage their pleasures are the people who win big in the end. He also stated, "the problem with most people is that they don't manage this emotion and it causes them to live a life beneath their potential." She began to think about the conversation they had when he talked about how society has been slowly moving the world to feed off of instant gratification. It's become so vast that people will do anything just to get it, he would explain. People will make superman suits, jump off the top of a mountain, fly through the air and risk their own lives to receive this pleasure. Jean knew this was true even in her own life when she began to realize how many pairs of shoes and purses she now owned. Her level of awareness was heightened and she begins practicing the principles that always existed but never paid much attention to.

Secret # 4 - People follow phobias. Wow! Really, she would say. Yes, he stated. More people are motivated by the fear of loss rather than the possibility of gain. Most people go to work because they don't want to lose their house, their car or their possessions. She thought again about the statement and how true the principle was for people who worked for others. She reflected back on her very first job at a fast food restaurant and how hard she had to work just so she wouldn't lose the small amount of possessions she had accumulated. She wanted to hear more and he would say of all the motivators in the world, fear is the biggest one. Jean knew this was true because it worked so well in sales. The more she forecast danger, the more she would experience those same people making buying decisions.

Secret # 5 - People follow provision would be the overarching principle that governed successful people's lives. This would give Jean an altitude view of how she needed to be thinking about her own life. What was her vision? She'd ask herself. She discovered this principle was one of direction and knowing where she wanted to go. He shared a scripture from his favorite book, The Bible, which stated, Where there is no vision the people perish. It would remind herself of how she read about the most successful companies were great at communicating vision. She knew she needed one for her own life so she sat down and wrote out a Vision Statement. It became the mantra she would live by. She could now get people involved in anything she was a part of, because she became a master at communicating her vision. Two more secrets to go, he would say, while still sitting beside the lake. He picked up a rock and threw it in the water and they both watched the ripple effect layout across the lake.

Secret # 6 - People follow posture is a conscious mental or outward behavioral attitude he would say. Jean would ask him to clarify this a little more because she knew there had to be more. He went on to tell her that people who possessed the confidence in their body language and tone were projected and perceived as being strong. Posture is more than just a mindset he would say, but rather a skill set she could develop if she was ever going to become that writer that possessed the qualities that others wanted to follow.

Secret # 7 - People follow persuasion - is a deep conviction or strong belief. This was the last secret but also the most powerful of them all. Jean didn't understand why he stated that at first, so he decided go in depth with the psychology of this secret. This is the one secret that encapsulates all the other secrets. He would tell Jean, the Greek philosopher Aristotle listed four reasons why one should learn the art of persuasion:

1. Truth and justice are perfect; so if a case is lost, it is the fault of the speaker
2. Persuasion is an excellent tool
3. A good rhetorician needs to know how to argue both sides to understand the whole problem and all the options, and
4. There is no better way to defend one's self

Her husband would say that persuasion is more about leading someone into taking certain actions of their own, rather than giving direct commands. Suddenly a light went off in Jean's head and she said, "So it's making a connection with people." That's exactly right, he would say. The connection is to affect how different people view certain products or services knowing that most purchases are made on emotion. Sometimes, you may recall a memory from a certain smell or sound. The objective of advertisement is solely to bring back certain emotions to prompt you to make a buying decision. Repeating the message will cause the person to more than likely purchase the product, because they've already connected with a good emotion and a positive experience.

Jean felt exhilarated after learning the secrets. She immediately studied all of them in depth and implemented each one in her everyday life. Jean excelled at their company and surpassed her husband for the first time in sales numbers after the second year. The world around her was different now, because she would see everything from a different point of view. Jean finally finished her own book and was nominated to co-author a book with one of the top 10 motivational and sales speakers in the world. She had finally reached the pinnacle of where she wanted to be with her life. Jean and her husband would go on to build a very successful business together, and she continues to write books. Jean is now able to travel, give back to her favorite charity, and volunteer her time to teaching others what she learned about the 7 Secrets of the One Call Close. This launched Jean's career even further, and she would find herself sitting on the Board of Advisors of the Millionaire Mastermind Group.

Jean finally lived the life she always wanted to, because she overcame fear of failure. Jean and her husband reside in the Houston, Texas area where they are heavily involved in their local church and community. She is a highly sought after motivational speaker and sales trainer. She attributes her success to her new way of thinking now that she has encountered the 7 Secrets of the "One Call Close."

About Deaphalis

Deaphalis Sample, the Master of the "One Call Close" brings to the business owner and entrepreneur the practical psychology of closing the sale the first time with his addition to this book *The Road to Success* with bestselling author Jack Canfield. A must read for the person looking to break away from the traditional follow up in sales for instant gratification. He has helped thousands of individuals and business owners achieve exceptional levels of success in sales. He has also received numerous awards and brings more than 38 years of marketing and sales experience along with him.

Deaphalis is a bestselling published author and has been seen on ABC, CBS, NBC, and FOX affiliate networks around the country for his business expertise. His new and upcoming book the *7 Secrets of the One Call Close* has catapulted him into the top 1% in the marketing and sales industry.

A highly-sought after speaker, Deaphalis speaks to many small business owners, networking groups, churches, community events and non-profit organizations. He currently sits on the Board of Advisors Millionaire Mastermind group, and is a part of various organizations like ASTPS (American Society of Tax Problem Solvers), Michael Rozbruch's Tax and Business Solutions Academy, NAACP (National Association for the Advancement of Colored People), La Porte-Bayshore Chambers of Commerce, and many others including City Mark Church in League City, Texas, Jimmy Evans Pastoral School for Pastors and Leaders certification, and a certified marriage counselor from Marriage On The Rock.

Deaphalis and his lovely wife have built a multimillion-dollar tax resolution firm, and he's coined the phrase: "We're making a difference and changing lives one person at a time." In his spare time, he loves spending time with his wife and kids along with helping people by giving them practical tools to use to become successful.

CHAPTER 40

THINK DIFFERENTLY BE HAPPY

BY CHRIS MYNETT

[This chapter is dedicated to my Mum and Dad who never got to see their son achieve all that he has so far, and to all the people that have inspired me along the way, also to my business partner and colleague Julie, for being the next step in my evolution.]

At the age of 54, I have come to realise that the best part of my life has been all about thinking differently. Born on a cold November morning my mother refused to get into the ambulance until she had sorted her hair, so she proudly told me. At 8:10 a.m. on the 10th of November 1961, Christopher Mynett was bought into this world. Life gave me the opportunity to be different from day one, flaming red hair and a bad dose of eczema made sure of that. I cannot remember the number of medical checkups I had as a child and into my early teen years— potions and lotions were the order of the day, and being experimented on was no great fun.

As an eleven-year-old boy I was extremely lucky to have been taken to the British Museum to see the first ever visit to the UK of Tutankhamun's death mask and its exhibition. It left a lasting impression on me for the love of all things Egyptian and mystical. I took to reading Eric Von Daniken books and started to wonder about life, the universe and everything in between. My teen years were as normal as teen years go, and passed with all the girls, music, and usual drama that teenage years have.

My mother passed away at age 47 in 1985 when I was 24, and I got married the year after. My thoughts of life were replaced with thoughts of working long hours in a Rank Xerox warehouse, being promoted from the warehouse to run the load planning department of the company, replacing my boss when he was nearly killed by a drunk driver and was too seriously injured to return to work, decorating and renovating houses and keeping my wife happy by keeping on the move. So, after five moves in six years or so, and with the help of what was then a good friend, my wife then decided that babies were next on the agenda. The house was a complete shambles and only just starting to take shape; my view was let's wait till the house is complete. Unfortunately, she did not want to wait, and instead struck up a relationship with my good friend and that was that. What followed was a messy divorce and the rest, as they say, is history.

Little did I know then, in the depths of depression and looking through the bottom of a whisky bottle, that Jack Canfield would be the light at the end of the tunnel. My doctors wanted to medicate me and Jack wanted to motivate me. I chose to be motivated, that was in 1989 and the "How to build High Self Esteem" became a very much listened to and worn out tape in my car.

I went on to do various jobs – auditor, logistics, warehouse work – until I was introduced to being a trainer on this "new thing" called the Internet. That was in 1994 when the Internet in the UK was predominantly an academic tool and CompuServe only had numbers for email addresses. That was in Central London. Whilst there, the owner treated us to a weekend session of NLP, and my thought processes were being challenged again. I stayed with that company for 3 to 4 years then moved to a local company in Letchworth as I was living in Stotfold at the time and was starting to develop an Internet Training business, when out of the blue an opportunity to join a small company in Beaconsfield called OpenText presented itself, and all for the want of asking a friend of a friend if they wanted or needed a trainer – and a whole lot of using the "Law of Attraction." I was dissatisfied in Letchworth and had started to think about working for a larger Company again.

Life changed back into being focused and talking to people about the many aspects of Document Management, Business Process Management, Records Management and lots of very technical stuff. I used this opportunity to bring Jack's thoughts into the induction classes we were running, so E+R=O and the "poker chip theory" were well practised and repeated phrases. That was the way of the world for 2 to 3 years. When I left, I was Head of Training for EMEA. I went on to head up the training division of another software company and onto another company to head up the Consultancy team, but that did not work out and I was finally made redundant late in 2002. After many applications and having picked up and re-studied NLP and re-listened to Jack's Work, I finally decided to take 100% responsibility for my career and decided to become self-employed. With the shift in mindset, "Thanks to Jack" I set about creating my vision of what I wanted to do – to "teach software" and all that Jack had taught me came into being, and I started my company, *Here's How To, Ltd.*

I re-mortgaged my house and went off to get a formal qualification in Training. As I was doing the qualification an opportunity presented itself to tender for some work, "Oh what the hell, go for it anyway!" was my mantra, having learnt it from Jack and his reference to Susan Jeffers. How much should I charge? Will they like me? The fears came flooding in but my mind kept thinking E+R=O, so I put on my best positive mind and succeeded in getting the contract which led onto more work. After about two years of working with this company, I had a thought that I was good at doing this training thing and loved talking and meeting new people. I took the decision to go back to OpenText and ask if they needed a contract trainer, was I surprised when they said yes. No, it wasn't once again the Law of Attraction had kicked in, they even offered me a job, but I declined in favour of being a contractor.

As such, that has been the status quo for nearly 13 years. I have travelled the world on the back of what I love to do for a living, I visited many beautiful places met many people and enjoyed many cultures. I lived in Australia for two years returning to the UK in October 2012. All I did was use the Law of Attraction and kept thinking I would not mind going to this or that country this year and sure enough they would pop up on my schedule to deliver training – from Asia to South Africa, across Europe and to the Middle East, Canada, America and Russia. The saying goes that travel broadens the mind, this is so true. I believe being happy is not about what you own; I have seen people with very little be happy and people with a great deal who are not. It is people that you learn from, not their possessions.

I have always thought I wanted to get into the Human Potential Training/ Coaching business, so in 2015 I signed up for Jack's Coaching Classes, I wanted to experience first-hand what the process was about. During the process Jack launched his on-line Train The Trainer course. I had no hesitation in signing up for it and am extremely proud to be one of the first twelve in the World to pass the certification, now I am a Certified Success Principles Trainer. I intend to diversify my company and expand it this year into being a Human Potential Training and Coaching Company, and as if by Magic, an old work colleague of mine, Julie Lane, who is qualified CBT Therapist has decided to come along for the journey too, between us we have a wealth of experience in many areas, we intend to offer our knowledge to anyone who is willing to listen.

Why the title "Think Differently Be Happy?" Well, that's because it's true, there are many people with many possessions who are not happy and strive to put more material things in their lives, and there are many people who have nothing, and are far happier that those who have plenty. My thinking has changed over the years and I firmly believe that to be different, all you need to do is to think differently and follow some basic guidelines – like those set out in the Success Principles and you too can do many things and achieve many goals.

1. Take 100% Responsibility
2. Meditate or practice relaxing
3. Practice the art of valuing all around you – especially yourself
4. Do five things a day to move your goal forward
5. Create and keep affirmations close to you
6. Review your day
7. Write your ideas down as soon as you have them, as they disappear as quickly as they appear
8. Get your life into balance
9. Think Differently
10. Be Happy

I have studied, read and listened to a lot of Human Potential material, I have become an information sponge and I love it. Without doubt, it has allowed me to look into the Prism of Human Potential Training with all its facets and cast a light on the elements that work to make individuals transform themselves into whatever it is they want to be, do, become, or achieve. For me, this has been something of a journey and I am enjoying its continuation. I can think of nothing more inspirational than to see someone develop and change their thought processes and to see the change in their approach, it is truly magical. I continue to learn and am signed up to a long life of learning, we never stop changing and nor should we; we never stop thinking, but thinking differently definitely leads to being happy.

Ever since first hearing Jack speak on "How to Build High Self Esteem" many years ago, I have wanted to make Human Potential Teaching my full time job and I am not far from achieving that goal, this is very exciting for me and my career as a trainer. My heartfelt gratitude goes out to Jack and his team for producing material that makes the difference and his work has inspired hundreds of thousands if not millions of people to make significant changes in their lives and achieve wonderful goals. His vision of having a million Certified Trainers in my opinion is an admirable one and one that is very achievable.

I possess neither a degree nor a doctorate. Many years ago I used to look on that very negatively, but having self-studied and been certified in the craft of Training and using Jack's Company to help me achieve this, I no longer feel under-educated.

I remember with fondness and often recite the "Golf Ball Theory of Life" – My knocks and scrapes have enabled me to fly to my true path, and have helped me put the past where it needs to be "behind me." Live in the now and plan for the future.

I have a passion for learning and a thirst for knowledge. "My vision of me is to be the happiest person I can be by teaching and coaching people to be the most productive they can be by living a life of self-empowerment by assisting them in the way they think." It is one of my goals and one of my affirmations that I use every day to remind me of what I want to achieve.

As I look forward, I can see opportunities to assist others in being empowered, all I can ask is that I remain humble and grateful and appreciative at all times for the opportunities I have had, the journey I have been on, and those things that are yet to come.

The journey continues!

About Chris

Chris Mynett has a background in many different careers, from Logistics, Auditing and Sales to his longest being an early adopter in teaching people how to use the Internet. He subsequently moved on to open his own business in 2003. A former certified member of the Learning and Performance Institute, he has taught thousands of people all over the world in some of the top ten thousand Corporates from Asia to India and South Africa, Europe to America and Canada. Chris has a passion for communicating complex ideas and making them simple to understand, taking the Tech out of Technical and putting a smile into simple.

Chris is proud to have been one of the first 12 people in the world to have become an Online Certified Jack Canfield Coach. This year sees Chis embarking on developing this area of his business in the autumn of this year along with his colleague. Between them, they share some 50 years combined experience in helping people develop themselves and change situations in their lives. It is Chris's ambition to share his knowledge of the Success Principles and other methodologies to help people who want to make a change to their lives in a positive way.

CHAPTER 41

THE WOMAN WHO SOLD HER DIAMONDS: MY VOYAGE TO LOVE AND SUCCESS

BY BILLUR SUU

[Divorce? Suicide? Finding a new lover? Staying in bed forever? Jolted between the light and the darkness, she considered these options for a year. Feeling defeated by life and betrayed by her soulmate, she had gone from being a cherished wife and adored mother to someone broken in pieces. A sudden onset of andropause had turned her husband into a skirt chaser and a human being she could not recognize. Facing her own menopause, she felt herself thrown into the garbage. She had hit the invisible wall felt by millions of other women. That woman was Billur Suu.]

Coming from the specks of dust of the cobblestoned streets of Istanbul, I had almost no chance in life. I was a girl, thus a second class citizen. I was born in a Muslim society imposing a strict code of behavior. My parents' life vision was limited to survival needs. I was doomed to be a married woman with three children before my 30s. In my circle, success meant to keep the windows of my home as clear as Billur crystals and obey the husband and his relatives. Everyone expected a woman to dedicate or rather martyr her life for the sake of children. Period. No questions asked or encouraged.

But I was asking questions as early as I remember myself. One day when I entered a local mosque with my brother and was guided to the back where girls were supposed to be, I asked why. I was only 6 years old. Then I started asking bigger questions like "what is the meaning of life?" or "was I here on Earth to make myself happy or others happy?" As a freshwoman at the Journalism Faculty of Istanbul University, I vowed to be happy no matter what! I was awakened. I had to leave the country I was born in and take my life in my own hands.

Back then, I did not know Jack Canfield or his famous first rule of success: Take 100% responsibility for your life. When my family refused to send me to England to improve my language skills after the university because they had spent a fortune on my brother's lavish wedding, I registered as a community service volunteer for a year and left. "I will not return one day early even if I die" I said to myself. And I came close. I was almost killed in a women's shelter in northern England. Then, I found myself in New York with $5 in my pockets. But nothing changed my resolve. I marched steadily on my way to success.

A decade after following my heart, I was the happiest woman alive. I had it all: a Ph.D. from Columbia University, a dream job of empowering women for the United Nations, a six-figure income, a soulmate who respected my freedom and encouraged my explorations, and the best gift I received from the Universe, my beloved daughter.

Then on a sunny day in Central Asia where we worked to bring safe drinking water to thousands of marginalized villagers, my dream life shuttered. This was in 2005. My Beloved's broken childhood lurked into our "happy life" and I lost all my beliefs about life and love. Determined to decipher the roots of his betrayal and its meaning for my life, we delved into our wounds and healed each other.

When the second crisis hit last year, I was not prepared. This one hit harder and deeper than the first one. Nothing calmed my 65-year-old husband who was now acting like a rebellious teenager. As Rumi said, "I was raw, cooked and then burnt." I was raw and innocent and thought love would conquer all. With the first crisis, I was cooked. The second one burnt me until the last cell.

I waited for my soulmate to change and empathize with the pains he caused in me and in our family. I pleaded. I wrote him love poems when I woke up in tears each night. I stayed strong insisting to see his light, for the sake of our love, our family, our special bond. Then one day Gandhi's words vibrated in my soul, "Be the change you seek in the world." I desperately needed to make sense of life in my own terms, in my own heart and soul. Decision was clear, back to the same rule again: Take 100% responsibility for your life.

Rumi said, "Travel brings power and love back into your life." I believed that it would. My 50th birthday was around the corner and I decided to make a tour around the world in 50 days. I sold my diamonds to finance the journey. As women, we do not buy Ferraris or leave all behind to be a monk. I had a teenage daughter, a family to care, a School of Happiness to lead, and a life time commitment to another human being. Even though I could not recognize my partner and all his humanly qualities during the last year, heading to Himalayas to live in cave was not an option for me.

I chose five spiritual places that I had never been before: Bhutan, Ayers Rock, Tahiti, Machu Picchu, and Santa Fe. This journey was not about settling, but rattling my life…it was about connecting the dots of the drama. I needed a room of my own…to be me again…without any responsibility…cry as I wished, laugh as I wanted. Desperately needing a re-birth, I gave myself a new name: woman who sold her diamonds. The only brilliance I needed was the light of my soul. But my light was barely alive, flickering in the hands of my Beloved. I had given him my heart, and it was time to take it back.

> I take my power back
> I gave you all I could
> You took all you could
> Left me like an orphan
> Like a disposed garbage bag
> In a dark alley
> But you forgot
> One's garbage
> Other's treasure
> You overlooked
> Who I was
> What I was
> How I was
> A firebird
> A Phoenix

A voyager
A light
A woman
A love
Eternal…

These were my feelings before I left for my travels. I called my journey "Voyage to Love" because for the first time in my life, I did not love who I had become with this drama. And I knew what was important in life. What Harvard University found after 75 years of research, I knew it all along in my heart: that love matters, and quality of our relationships is the biggest happiness maker or breaker in our lives. Health, wealth, and success all depended on our love vibrations.

Fifty days around the world nurtured me beyond imagination with thrills, spiritual lessons, adventure, and enchanting encounters.

I share a few moments with you from my journal:

Bhutan: A new kind of divinity or a new kind of love? On a sunny September afternoon, I land in the heart of Himalayas, the majestic and mystical happiness country. I discover a country a thousand miles apart from the overly-romanticized tourist photos. I meet with monks young or old glued to their smart phones. I strike up conversations with divorced single mothers or witness the dilemma of youth squeezed between material reality and spiritual upbringing. But most importantly, I learn that divinity is about accepting our materiality, our humanness without resistance or labeling or judgement. No separation. If you apply this rule to love and relationships, there is no you and I, no lover and loved, we are all one.

Ayers Rock: Wholeness or timelessness? It is a living temple that emerged over 900 million years ago, not a rock! I am fascinated staring at the ruby land of Anangu people; colors and people are enticing. I learn how to do a dot painting from an aboriginal elder woman and paint my future. As the sun set in with thousands of colors, I take my seat at the Sounds of Silence restaurant. We are instructed to stay silent. Energy changes around …silence …like death …like life …deep silence envelops all of us. I lift my head to stare at the Milky Way from the southern hemisphere. I feel myself between earth and heaven and I let go. When I return to my senses, I feel that for the first time in my life, I am not missing anything or anybody. I had carried my loved ones in my heart, in my thoughts, in my conversations with myself for the last two weeks. Silence had seduced me, they all had disappeared. After years of meditation, a moment of eternity touches me. I sleep well that night discovering that detachment is the best gift we can give to ourselves and our loved ones.

Tahiti: Am I still beautiful? Coldest days in the history of Bora Bora. It is raining, windy, I hardly sleep in my beach bungalow. Nature is roaring. In a little beach shack, I see colorful, home-made rum bottles. I drink some, get warm, and let the ocean wash away my sorrows. I feel even a deeper shift here. I do deep breathing exercises on the beach to take the beauty inside. The majesty of nature, colors just swallow you ...breathe in ...breathe out ...some days I stay in silence, listening to the wind, waves, birds. My inner voice is softer. Without realizing, I am re-born, reconnected to the depths of my soul. I feel beautiful, inside and out.

Peru: Which path to take? Following the Inca trail at 10,000 feet high, one single concern of my soul: Which trail to follow and what trail to leave behind? How to let go of the past? How to find harmony again within me and with my circle of love? In Cusco, I find a spiritual center and join them for a sunset meditation. Our guide says. "This meditation is causal, ask all your questions and you will get your answers." The next day, I skip lunch and climb the mysterious Machu Picchu twice. I gaze into the Lost City and stay until the guards gently accompany me to the exit. And I receive three magical signs or responses to my one essential question. I am perplexed but not surprised. My heart is still open to welcome the guidance of the Universe. My path is as clear as Billur waters.

Santa Fe: What does it take to be yourself? *How Georgia Became O'Keefe* is one of the books that fascinates me. How do we find ourselves or create ourselves? A trail blazer, a loner in the desert, a painter, a woman like no other. Along with Frida Kahlo, O'Keefe is one of my idols ...women who dared to live authentic lives. Exposed to overly sensual interpretations of her paintings, she took shelter in Santa Fe's red rock energy. I drive from her museum to her home to her studio to her ranch. Freedom is in the air: freedom to be yourself. This is the gift I receive on the footsteps of O'Keefe. I dare here; a different kind of courage is shining in me. I know that my silence has come to an end. I need to speak up, share, help to heal broken hearts ...cause relationships may be dysfunctional, but love never is.

If you ever find yourself in the same or similar drama or darkness as I did, here are few pearls of wisdom which emerged from my voyage to love:

Silence heals. How? It puts you in touch with your inner heart as Bhutanese say. You can only listen to your heart if you are empty within. When you face a life crisis or drama, take a few days off to stay in silence. Walk in nature, sit under a tree in a park, climb a mountain or watch a sunrise. Silence will create a space between you and the drama. It will become easier not to take the other person's deeds or hurtful words too personally.

Find an outlet for your pain and suffering and fill that space in you with new experiences, sights, visions, and energies. Poetry saved my life; travel filled me with wonder, awe, and beauty. ...A short cut to connect with my spirit.

Put a time frame to end this dramatic exchange of energy. Share this idea with the person involved. Nothing lasts forever, good or bad. A time frame will give a signal to your unconscious mind as well as to your partner's to find a solution.

Clean out the debris from your hearts by organizing a ritual focusing on heart connection, ...to put a full stop to what happened, closing the window and opening a new one. It will clean your energy fields and will bring out the shift of consciousness needed.

Conduct a tree exercise to allow you to see the drama and the other person free from illusion so that understanding gives way to compassion, and compassion to forgiveness. A tree exercise is easy to conduct and helps you to discuss how a drama is a product of a particular past or life experience.

Write your own Manifesto, liberating your soul and allowing you and your loved ones to connect with your values and life vision again. Invite your partner do the same.

Honor the creative being that you are, give birth to yourself, …be a Phoenix. We all have the ability to die and to be reborn before our death. My Phoenix poetry is a gift for those who choose to live from the heart.

I am not the smoky fire
Hovering over you
Little by little
I am the bonfire
Burnt herself completely
For your love
In your love
And
Reborn from her ashes.

About Billur

Billur Suu -- Voyager of Love, Poetess, Author, Soul Doctor, Awakener

Billur does not walk on water but paints on water. At the age of 6, she realized that she was born to be happy but felt squeezed by her religion, gender, culture and social obligations of Turkish society. At the first opportunity, she spread her wings and flew away in search of the meaning of life and purpose of her existence. United Nations gender equality expert, Ivy League professor, women's rights specialist, poetess, writer, lover, mother, wife, soulmate, yogini, spiritual awakener, are just a few roles she played for the last five decades. Describing herself more of a student of life than a teacher, she founded Cannes School of Happiness to help other women to live authentic lives from the heart.

Billur shares her wisdom, inspiration, and lessons on love, life, and relationships during spiritual discovery retreats she organizes in five continents. She also conducts small group courses and individual consultations. Voyage to Love, Rebirth, Silence in Cote d'Azur, Healing with Water and Heart-Full Living are Billur's signature programs providing guidance to fellow voyagers of light and love.

Called a "soul doctor" by her students and love circle, Billur is a unique spiritual teacher who integrates ancient wisdom with modern-day scientific knowledge. Billur's Healing Circle lectures empower her audience with practical tools, creative solutions and insights from her own life around the world. She is the guide you need when you feel broken by a relationship. If you need to stop a drama or discover who you really are, Billur is the best person to help you.

Billur's success and unique approach to soul-full living stem from her own life experiences. In 2015, a life-changing relationship crisis gave Billur an invaluable opportunity to practice what she teaches. She sold her diamonds and bought herself an around the world ticket with a hope to make sense of disheartening events in her life. That ticket molded her into the exceptional teacher that she is today.

Passionate about helping other women and sharing her amazing transformation from darkness to light, Billur wrote her second book, *The Woman Who Sold Her Diamonds and Became a Voyager of Love in 50 Days around the World.*

Billur has a B.A. in Journalism and Public Relations from Istanbul University. She studied Gender Equality at the School of International and Public Affairs at Columbia University graduating with a Master of Public Administration degree. She later obtained a Ph.D. in Social Policy Analysis from Columbia University where she was awarded many prestigious fellowships such as the Fulbright, IREX and Burns Scholar Awards. She was listed in Who's Who in the World 2009 edition for her work on empowering women in Central Asia.

You can explore Billur's diverse and enriching spiritual, personal, and professional accomplishments and her three decades of dedication to making a positive difference in the lives of women at: www.schoolofhappiness-cannes.com or www.billursuu.com

You can reach Billur at billur@billursuu.com or billur@schoolofhappiness-cannes.com and follow her inspiring journey on Facebook and other social media.

CHAPTER 42

MOVING UP FROM VICTIM TO WINNER

BY ISABEL HARKINS

Wishing you all the success you deserve. First of all, CONGRATULATIONS! If you are reading this book, give yourself a congrats, for you are ready to take your power and life back in your hands, and set your true self free. Thank yourself for taking the step and starting out on the road of transforming your victim into your winner.

I will share with you my journey from victim to winner. Everyone wants to feel good, to live care-free, happy and have an easy life, to fall in love and to be loved, to have an ideal abundance and to be accepted. We wish for VALIDATION, and here is where the victim gets lost.

We spend our entire life seeking acceptance either from ourselves, other people and even animals; that is the struggle that propels the human race to do all that we do. And then, there is the choice to shape our internal power to be our true identity, not the one that is shaped by external influences or second-hand opinions—this is our divine GIFT.

WHERE IT BEGAN

I was born in Chile. Growing up, I had quite a few reasons to adopt the victim role for my life structure. I experienced what in my perception was extreme abandonment from a mother that I later found was going through her own challenges, who wanted to provide me with the best according to her perception at the time. In the process, she left me with different caretakers, in different homes, where I didn't have a room or place that I felt belonged to me, that kept changing quite often. So, needless to say, I grew up with no sense of security.

She decided to place me with Andrea, an Indian mama that my mother trusted up in the Peruvian Andes, she was what you call a Shaman healer, half-Mapuche and half-Quero Indian. I had an incredible journey growing up with her, we frequently went into the Amazon jungle and I learned different cultures and a healing tradition that now is called Shamanism. So far so good, right? Well, for a child that meant I didn't belong anywhere, I was not good enough, and many other negative kinds of self-programming.

I didn't have a kid's room or common toys, etc., so once I got back into the city, I really didn't have much in common with kids aside from totally not fitting in. Now looking back, I realized through my life that these experiences were great opportunities that I *shape-shifted* to the **GIFT**. I can live anywhere and adapt, I can have a lot of material possessions or very little, and I am great in both places. I learned to connect with the Earth and to love and respect all its beings, I learned to think globally since I was very young. For me, we are all one. I always include the planet in anything I do.

And here is where the victim in me found its role, and, without consciously knowing it, that role shaped my future for a long while. That was until I developed a deadly Cancer, which was the turning point when I decided to stay and work on my perception.

In the Shaman upbringing, I learned that you can change your reality if you shift your perception–we call that *shape-shifting*. In the process I learned about the Victim and some of its best friends: sabotage, judgment, self-pity, manipulation, etc. Once I acknowledged that I was victimizing myself for a living, and if I didn't change my perception and transform the victim, I wasn't going to make it.

THE VICTIM

When the victim rules our life we give our power away.
We seek validation from the wrong people and material gain, everything outside ourselves (I call this second hand validation), addictions are

subconsciously invited into our lives – it can be over eating, drugs, alcoholism, abusive relationships (that is a common one for a victim), etc. Victims are consistently attracting punishment and some sort of pain, failure and all those "poor me" situations; one other "quality" of the victim energy is **blame**. Not only do you blame yourself, but you also blame others for anything that your victim perception feels is out of control. *The interesting part is that the victim is never in control.* It (the victim) seeks external control, so it can be in its role as victim. If the victim is truly in control, who will be to blame?

The common belief is: *Well, the victim needs to take responsibility.* Unfortunately for that concept, victims don't know much about responsibility due to the fact that they don't believe they deserve or can have the right to a positive quality. Their control comes from external sources, not from their own. Their feeling is, "What's the use? It won't work anyway." Or, "What about if I am wrong or people laugh at me for trying?" and blah-blah-blah. I find it better to suggest to get our power back – even victims don't like to know that they are powerless. **The victim accepts this concept of regaining power better; it starts the process of recognizing the power of making conscious choices.**

One of the tools that helped me and still does when I am having a pity party for myself is GRATITUDE. There is no space for the victim here. I practice that throughout my day. I have a gratitude journal and I write at the end of the day what I am grateful for, and give thanks even for challenges.

Challenges are gifts in adversity, and when we start acknowledging these gifts, our victim transforms into our winner by *consciously allowing ourselves to transform a negative (victim food) to a positive (Spirit food).* When we are in **Gratitude**, we connect with **Love**, **Compassion** and our **Source of Creation**.

At the core of all human behavior, our needs are more-or-less similar in many ways. The positive experiences are easy to handle, but the challenges are the ones that give us the opportunity to grow and use the tools that cannot only help us, but that we can access when other beings are in need of them also. That is how I have transformed the so-called negative moments into my very precious gifts, and as I am writing here and you are reading, your life and mine will never be the same again.

That is my wish for you – that one of these gifts can become yours and that you may share it with the ones in need – making a difference one transformation at a time. **Together we can create a powerful healing web that will grow stronger every moment and one that can be accessed by many.** And I pray and meditate every day to have the tools, energy, health and an open compassionate heart to make a difference.

In a lecture I attended, the teacher asked us how long do we wish to smell something rotten? How long do we want to keep something that has spoiled in our mouths? Not very long, right? So, the question here is why do we drive our lives through the rearview mirror, always in the *poor-me* past? Do we want to dig in the trash to make our dinners or do we want to start afresh?

One very helpful step to move through is to keep ourselves in check. When the victim shows up to sabotage, we must ask ourselves, "Does this feel good?" "Does it make a positive difference in my life or the life of others?" Can this help me grow or is it just a perception that I can release to free myself and just observe it as a contrast? . . . And find the gift in it. Obviously, embracing the victim doesn't work, it never has. It was just what we thought we deserved, and the reality that we lived from morning to night and is now free.

THE WINNER

I Practice Self-referral – this means that our internal reference point is our own self, and not our external perceptions.

I suggest here what has worked for me. Checking in has been a really good tool. Because when you check in with the motives of your actions, you have a reference from where you are coming from. By that I mean, "Am I doing it because of self-validation (my own approval) or second-hand validation (external approval)?

It helps me connect with my true motive. And this is where the field of all possibilities resides. When you are in this space, you can manifest anything you truly are passionate for, because here you are coming from your source.

Another tool that I use is Detachment (not to be confused with disconnection). So what is detachment? What I learned is that in detachment lives the wisdom of uncertainty, and in uncertainty lives the freedom from the past conditioning, the unknown of the present, and perception of the future, in other words, the POWER OF NOW. When we are willing to step into the unknown, which is the field of all possibility, we surrender to our true source, where all is possible. Anything can be manifested through detachment because here is the source of the unquestioning belief of your true self.

Let's check the quality of Attachment. Attachment is based on fear, insecurity, hopelessness, needs, trivial concerns, silent desperation, non-faith, lack of laughter and lack of trust, just to mention a few. These are all transitory riches, which lead to poverty of consciousness and spirit.

There is no evolution in that. When evolution is not present, it is stagnation, disorder, stress, mediocrity, lack of freedom, and powerlessness. This is food for the victim. When we are in this place we shut out our true possibilities. We lose creativity. And here we create a rigid framework which interferes with our whole process of *shape-shifting*. When you understand the Law of Detachment, here is where we free ourselves from the stale repetition of worn out memories.

Coming from detachment, we can go into that space of all possibilities and I access that place through meditation. A suggestion here is to practice detachment in small things every day.

The victim will hijack our biochemistry through fear, self-punishment, living in uncertainty all the time, feeling threatened and powerless. In other words, a passive state of stress where our nervous system is flight-or-fight at all times. Our immune system is depleted, our nervous system is compromised and our health deteriorates.

A good recipe for this is to practice acceptance of self and everything around us. Just start in small steps, this is a challenge for victims, due to the fact that non-acceptance supports the victim. So pay attention to second-hand validation here, where the non-acceptance resides and turns your attention to self-validation where true acceptance resides.

Another good practice I find is meditation and communion with nature. Spending time in nature in silence and just connecting on how nature just is. Nature doesn't try to be perfect, it just is, and is perfect on its own. That combined with meditation will begin to transform the victim.

A useful exercise is to make a list of contrasts.

For example, write the victim's negative talk next to the positive talk. By doing this exercise, you *shape-shift* your perception and you will change your reality. I am suggesting giving you some of the tools I used, but here is a great place for you to source your own, and by that come from your own power.

Here are some examples:

Victim Qualities	**Winner Qualities**
--Low self-worth	--High self-worth
--Procrastination	--Proactive
--Impatient	--Patient
--Insecure	--Confident
--Indecisiveness	--Self-assertive
--Feeling inadequate	--Self-acceptance
--Resentful	--Expressing what we feel

Accept the negative with humility. AND REMEMBER THAT WE ARE NOT ABOVE OR BELOW ANYONE. One very important action is to check in with our motives. To make sure we come from a place of sincerity not manipulation. Sincerity comes from spirit. *Now you can transform your social mask and play your true role in life without it – as the winner that you are.*

A few good questions I use for self-referral in meditation are:
- Who am I?
- What do I really want?
- How can I use my unique gifts to help others and make a difference?
- How can I be of service?
- And a very important one, What am I grateful for?

Silently hear the answer, don't force it, the answer is always there!

I wish for you to find you own ways to use the tools that are available to all of us when we stop coming from the "poor me," "everyone is so bad to me," and all the other stale programming tools that we have used and that no longer work. Does it make sense? Maybe not so much right now but as you enter the road from victim to winner you will love the ride, trust me, your spirit has been waiting for you your entire life – it deserves the honor.

One thing that I got from studying the Law of Attraction is that there is only one roll at a time. By that I mean, when you have a strong drive or feeling, that is the only thing that the universe and your higher self brings forward. So, if we are in a victim role, we cannot be in winner mode simultaneously. They are opposite energies with opposite feelings, so the Law of Attraction manifests what we put energy, focus and attention on. It is our choice to decide what we want.

Let's strive to raise our standards. Absolutely love what you do, associate with high-minded individuals, be truly fulfilled, always continue to make progress, always offer excellency, give your best without expecting in return – that is true giving and service. Create win/win relationships that means no attachment, make decisions that can deeply affect change, love yourself through you not other people, when the going gets challenging look for leverage, make sure that your activity is always connected to a high level of purpose or it won't work, stay flexible and always willing to enjoy change because one of the guarantees in life is IMPERMANENCE is less suffering when we accept this.

I wish to express my gratitude for the chance to write this chapter and for your presence and attention to it.

With love, gratitude and respect.

About Isabel

Isabel Harkins was born in Santiago, Chile and grew up in the Peruvian Andes, where she learned ancient healing ways by the Mama that raised her. Isabel knew at a very young age that she wanted to make a difference in the world – she grew completely connected with the earth and its beings. She always sensed that all people were connected somehow and never doubted it—that is how energy works!

When Isabel's birth mother returned and they moved to the north of Chile to live together with her adopting father, she began to learn that the simple ways of the Indian life she had learned in the Andes, was not the same in the city. Working with her adoptive father, who was a diplomat, she was exposed to many different cultures and ways of life, and again, fell in love with the multicultural ways of life and the connection to all.

During Isabel's struggle to fit in and adjust to this new life, she manifested a deadly cancer that forever changed the trajectory of her life. She applied her training and upbringing in *shape-shifting* to start the journey of changing her perception of the world around her. And during the process many years ago, she learned the tools she now shares with thousands.

In the years to come, she married and moved to the USA and she went to work in the film industry in make-up and special effects. Now, with a career of over 40 years, she has worked with stars like Lucille Ball, Barbara Streisand, Jared Leto, John Travolta and many more. She has also been a part of many, very successful, award-winning shows and films. She attributes her success to what she was able to learn at a very young age, something many people don't discover until they are adults.

As time passed, she always kept investing herself in the healing arts and in mentoring services. Isabel has worked in that capacity in many different countries that she has lived in. She has shared the stage with Wayne Dyer, Gary Young and many other inspirational speakers. Her commitment to service is her drive. She always finds the time to lend a helping hand, mentoring people to access their own tools.

She believes that there are certain spiritual laws which are available to all of us, and when we follow them we can accomplish anything we set out to do.

You can connect with Isabel at:
- isabelsbeautyblog@gmail.com
- isasbeauty@yahoo.com
- www.facebook.com/isabelsbeautblog

CHAPTER 43

REVERSE MORTGAGES 101 – THE BASIC STRATEGIES

BY LARRY MCANARNEY

In my 17 years of reverse mortgage experience, I have had the opportunity to meet with literally thousands of people who have had many questions about how a reverse mortgage works. Many times I get questions about common misconceptions that are simply not true, but most often the questions come down to, "How can I benefit from a reverse mortgage?" This is the reason I wrote this chapter. I want people to know that the reverse mortgage is not a one-size-fits-all program.

In my conversation with clients, I inform them that a reverse mortgage is a financial tool in their financial tool box, one they may not know is even there. It may or may not be the right tool at this time, but it is important for them to know that they have this tool and how it works. I have been very fortunate to have been able to help so many seniors in a very positive way by using this program. I truly love what I do. I educate people about the powerful strategies that the reverse mortgage program offers, many of which are covered in this chapter.

This chapter is written for senior homeowners, their families, and financial professionals, so they may have a deeper understanding of how a reverse mortgage works and the financial benefits it offers. It is my hope that by reading this chapter you will be able to answer questions that others may ask you about reverse mortgages. As baby boomers move into retirement at a rate of about 10,000 per day, it will become even more important to understand the strategies outlined in this chapter. But before getting into the details let's start at the beginning with a brief history of reverse mortgages.

HISTORY OF REVERSE MORTGAGES

The history of reverse mortgages dates back to 1961 and has evolved dramatically over the last 55 years. Nelson Haynes was a young loan officer from Deering Savings & Loan in Portland, Maine. He designed a very unique type of loan for Nellie Young, the widow of his high school football coach, so that she could stay in her home after her husband's sudden death and loss of his income. Since Nellie had very limited income, the loan was structured in a way that did not require her to make monthly payments. The idea of using housing wealth as a source of income without a mandatory monthly mortgage payment was born, today known as a reverse mortgage or HECM.

The Reverse Mortgage Stabilization Act of 2013 was signed into law on August 9, 2013, which introduced new policy guidelines to better protect eligible non-borrowing spouses. It also ensures that borrowers have sufficient financial resources to continue paying property obligations such as real estate taxes, insurance, and maintenance expenses. Because of these changes, many financial advisors, mainstream media, and the retirement planning community in general have endorsed the HECM line of credit program as a viable and important retirement income planning tool. Many financial firms have started researching how housing wealth can create liquidity and be utilized as a tax-free fourth leg in retirement income distribution planning.

Reverse Mortgage Basic Requirements

- Borrower must be 62 years or older and, if married, only one spouse need be 62 or older

- Must be legal owner(s) of the home at application

- Must be the primary residence (no second homes or investment properties)

- 1 to 4-family, HUD-approved condos, and manufactured homes (land home) are eligible properties

- Maximum loan amount is calculated based on the age of the youngest borrower, expected interest rate, and home value

- Lender requires 1st lien position

- No monthly mortgage payments are required, voluntary payments are permitted

- Fixed rate and adjustable rate line of credit programs

- No defined loan term (the HECM becomes due when the last surviving spouse, who is on the HECM loan, leaves the home permanently)

- Property must meet FHA appraisal requirements

- Federally-insured loan

COMMON REVERSE MORTGAGE MISCONCEPTIONS

If I do a reverse mortgage, will the bank or government own my home?

I am often asked the question about who owns the home in a reverse mortgage. The answer is: *the homeowner retains full ownership of their home throughout the life of the reverse mortgage.* Just as with a conventional home mortgage, the lender places a lien on the property to ensure the bank is covered for any money that is borrowed. Many people, including bank officers, attorneys, CPAs, and even some financial advisors think that the bank or government takes ownership of the home and that the borrower has basically sold their home to the lender. This is simply not the case and to this day remains the biggest myth about reverse mortgages.

Can I have a mortgage on my home and still qualify for a reverse mortgage?

Yes, you can have a current mortgage and qualify for a reverse mortgage, however, the reverse mortgage loan requires the lender to have 1st lien position. Therefore, any liens, including a current mortgage, must be paid off with either proceeds available in the reverse mortgage, private funds, gift funds, or a combination of all three.

Are reverse mortgages only for people who are desperate?

No, in recent years the use of housing wealth through a reverse mortgage has become an excellent financial planning tool to complement and enhance retirement income planning by increasing monthly income. As you will learn in this chapter, there are several powerful strategies for using housing wealth in a coordinated financial plan.

RETIREMENT INCOME STRATEGIES USING A REVERSE MORTGAGE

Using housing wealth and converting it to tax-free guaranteed lifetime income is a very powerful strategy and will greatly increase the survival rate of a retirement income plan. Adding monthly income to any retirement plan will increase the probability of success that the retiree will not run out of money in their lifetime. Of course, the biggest concern for retirees is running out of money in their lifetime. The strategies outlined below show various ways the reverse mortgage can complement and supplement a comprehensive financial plan. The HECM line of credit is very versatile and flexible as changes in the distribution of proceeds can be made at any time, unlike many other financial products. Michael Kitces, Partner & Director of Research at Pinnacle Advisory Group says, "The bottom line to all these strategies, though, is fairly straight forward: reverse mortgages may work far better when they're done not as a last resort, but as part of an ongoing retirement plan."

A good friend of mine and bestselling author, Jim Fox, president of Fox Financial Group, Ltd., has encouraged the use of a reverse mortgage to his clients for many years as a way to free up other assets and dramatically increase their retirement income distribution options. He says, "You can lower your debt and increase your income. How awesome is that."

Strategy 1 - Standby Line of Credit / Deferred Monthly Income

Many top financial advisors refer to the *reverse mortgage standby line of credit or deferred guaranteed monthly income* strategy as the program of choice for liquidity and emergency reserves. The idea behind this strategy, as with most of the strategies using a reverse mortgage in a retirement portfolio, is that the available funds in the HECM line of credit has a growth rate which will compound in the borrower's favor.

As a hypothetical example; a homeowner has $200,000 available in a HECM line of credit. The $200,000 available balance will grow at a rate equal to the index, plus the margin, and the HUD annual rate. For sake of this example and simplicity, let's assume the rate remains constant at 5.0%. If the growth rate remained at 5.0% for 1 year, the available funds in 12 months would be $210,232. In 20 years the available funds would be $542,528. This is because of the 10th wonder of the world, which is compounding. In this example, compounding is working in the borrower's favor to defer use of available funds until needed. At any time, funds can be accessed as needed by the homeowner, converted to lifetime monthly income, or both.

The longer the HECM line of credit is allowed to grow and compound, the greater availability of future funds and greater guaranteed lifetime monthly income. It should be noted that any money that is borrowed will accrue interest at the same rate and the loan balance will increase if no monthly payments are made.

Another amazing aspect of the HECM line of credit is that no matter what happens to the economy or housing market, the growth in the line of credit will continue and cannot be cancelled, frozen, or reduced by the lender as long as the terms of the HECM are met, which were covered earlier in this chapter. Since the HECM line of credit growth rate is tied to an index and not the housing market, it is truly a hedge for both a declining housing market as well as a hedge for inflation.

Strategy 2 - Deferral of taking Social Security

This is similar to the *deferred monthly income* strategy except its purpose is to provide monthly income to the homeowner so that social security income can be deferred until age 70 or a future date. For most married couples, delaying benefits for at least the higher wage earner makes sense if they can afford it. For each year you wait to claim social security past your full retirement age, you receive an 8% retirement credit. If you wait until 70 to take social security, your benefit jumps 76% more than taking it at 62. Assuming income is needed during the deferral period, using the reverse mortgage to provide monthly income needed for living expenses, while allowing for a greater lifetime social security benefit through deferral, could be very beneficial. The borrower can choose to stop the monthly payments from the HECM at any time and begin taking the increased social security benefit, or continue with both monthly income sources. It's their choice.

Strategy 3 - Payoff a current mortgage with a Reverse Mortgage

There are two possible strategies with this option; 1) Refinance the conventional mortgage with a reverse mortgage, freeing up the monthly mortgage payment obligation. This increases the monthly household income because the homeowner never has to make a monthly mortgage payment to the HECM, so long as one eligible borrower remains in the home as their primary residence and meets the terms of the HECM loan. 2) Refinance a conventional mortgage with a HECM line of credit, but continue to make voluntary mortgage payments to the HECM line of credit. Making voluntary payments to a HECM line of credit is essentially the same as making a deposit into your HECM line of credit, which will then continue to grow and compound as described earlier. At any time, this can be converted to guaranteed lifetime monthly income or drawn in a lump sum (some first year restrictions apply). Remember, no monthly payments are required in a reverse mortgage, so any payments are optional. However, by making payments to the reverse mortgage, two things are being accomplished simultaneously; paying down the mortgage and increasing the growing line of credit for future retirement distribution options. Ask a banker about that and if see if they understand what you are talking about. They won't.

Strategy 4 - Reverse Mortgage Purchase Strategy

Most people, including most realtors and builders, either aren't aware or don't understand that a reverse mortgage can be used to purchase a new or existing home. Normally, as homeowners get older and their children start their own lives, the house may be too big and upkeep too much. They choose to sell the house and purchase a smaller home that requires less upkeep and maintenance. Usually this involves using the cash from the departure home and paying cash for the new home. In the *HECM for Purchase* program, approximately 50% of the purchase price of the new home can be financed with proceeds from the *HECM for Purchase* program. This allows for more money from the sale of the departure home to be retained and used for retirement income instead of tying it up in home equity on the newly purchased property. Some seniors choose to increase the purchasing power of the new home by about 50%, in effect doubling their purchasing power.

Believe it or not, many seniors who understand the power of this program choose to have more buying power and upsize in home value and amenities rather than downsize. Example: new home purchase price is $200,000. The *HECM for Purchase* provides approximately 50% of the $200,000 purchase price or $100,000. The borrower comes to closing with $100,000 and retains the other $100,000 for retirement income instead of paying $200,000 cash for the new home and tying up the entire $200,000 in the new home. Either way there is no required monthly mortgage payment.

WHAT HAPPENS AT THE END OF THE REVERSE MORTGAGE?

The second most commonly asked question I get is, in the event of death, how long does the family have to satisfy the loan balance? Upon death or permanent departure of the last surviving borrower, the HECM loan becomes due. This means that as long as one eligible borrower or eligible non-borrowing spouse remains in the home, the loan is still in effect and is not due and payable.

Once the home is unoccupied by a participating HECM borrower, the "due and payable" process begins and is very simple. The clock starts ticking the day the last surviving spouse no longer occupies the house as their primary residence. The heirs have six months to pay off the loan with up to two three-month extensions, for a total of one year. These extensions are not automatic and must be applied for through the lender. The payoff balance is the amount borrowed, plus accrued interest, plus government mortgage insurance, less any optional payments that may have been made.

HECM loans are non-recourse loans, *meaning that the borrower, their heirs, or their estate cannot be held personally responsible for any shortfall.* If the loan balance exceeds the value of the home, the difference is paid to the lender from the FHA insurance fund. In a reverse mortgage, the lender is prohibited by HUD from seeking a deficiency judgment and looking for other borrower assets to make up the shortage. In a conventional mortgage loan, the lender will usually enter into a short sale agreement and then seek the remaining funds through a deficiency judgment to try and mitigate the loss through other borrower assets.

I hope this chapter has given you a basic understanding of the reverse mortgage program and a few basic strategies that can be used in a coordinated financial plan. I often hear that this is too good to be true, and it probably is, to some extent. As with any financial product, changes can and will occur to the HECM program. However, borrowers' who initiate or already have a reverse mortgage are contractually protected under current rules. Before making any changes to your financial plan, contact your financial advisor.

About Larry

Larry McAnarney; CSA, NMLS ID 21059:

- Member of the Society of Certified Senior Advisors since 2006
- Board of Directors, Financial Planners Association of Illinois, Oak Brook Council
- Member of the National Association of Insurance and Financial Advisors
- Volunteer, AARP Representative Payee Program
- Volunteer, Illinois Department on Aging Representative Payee Program

Larry McAnarney has specialized in reverse mortgage lending and providing his clients and partners with the education and information needed to make informed financial decisions since 1999. After researching several white papers published in 2005, he has incorporated the protective power of housing wealth in a coordinated retirement income distribution plan for financial advisors and their clients. Knowledge is power, and educating financial professionals and clients about the proactive use and retirement income strategies of a reverse mortgage in a comprehensive financial plan has become his career focus.

Beginning his career by taking out a home equity loan to fund their start up mortgage business, Larry and his wife, Linda, worked very long hours to establish themselves as financial leaders in their community. For the first few years their employees made more money than they did as payroll and bills had to be paid, but eventually persistence paid off and today Larry is nationally recognized as a leading authority in the reverse mortgage industry. "My father taught me that without honesty and integrity, you really don't have much to offer anyone. It may sound like a cliché, but in business, the customer and their needs come first and everything else is second."

As a Certified Senior Advisor, Larry helps seniors fundamentally understand the dynamics of the reverse mortgage program. He supports the conservative use of housing wealth and promotes responsible lending principles. Larry strives for collaboration among industry leaders and financial advisors who are investigating the proper role of housing wealth in retirement income planning. Larry's passion and client reviews clearly show his interest in helping others. He currently has a 98% verified customer approval rating and doesn't understand why it's not 100%.

Larry has been featured in *Bloomberg Businessweek*, *The Reverse Review*, *Illinois Realtor Magazine*, and is a contributing author in a best-selling book on retirement income planning. His experience is broad and deep in financial services dedicated to senior households. "I am truly passionate about this industry because it allows me to have a very positive effect on my customers' at this most important time in their lives."

When Larry is not busy helping others he enjoys spending time with Linda, daughters Kali and Kacey, son-in-law Josh, and grandchildren Kinzie, Evelyn, and Dax. Being an outdoor enthusiast and adventurist, Larry enjoys travel, hiking, skiing, and four-wheeling. In his younger days he enjoyed cliff diving, but at this point in his life that might be a bit over the top.

Larry can be reached at:
- 815-703-4745
- HECMinformation@gmail.com

Or online at: www.ReverseMortgageIllinois.com

CHAPTER 44

THE HEALTH BUILDS WEALTH CLUB

BY LINDA EVENHUIS

My road to success started whilst growing up in Alkmaar, near Amsterdam, the Netherlands. I grew up in a typical middle class family. My dad owned a barber shop. My mum ran the barber shop and took care of my brother and me. Growing up as a child in a small business taught me many valuable lessons and instilled some key behaviors that have lead me to success.

We had loyal customers from all layers of the society, from the waste collector, constructors, successful entrepreneurs and nationwide soccer players who grew up in the neighborhood. My parents taught me that it does not matter what profession you have, we all have a place and purpose in society. So as a child, I felt comfortable interacting with people from all layers of society. Moreover, they encouraged me to go for my dreams and figure out what I wanted in life. They also taught me manners, on how to behave in a professional environment. And humor was a key ingredient!

So I adopted this "way of working" throughout my professional career.

I also started to open up to my "inner voice." I was working in the banking industry and enjoyed my roles in Sales and Business Development because there was a lot of human interaction and you get concrete results by contributing to building a business. However, the "juice in life" for me was when I empowered others on their personal journeys. Listening, providing advice, sharing my best practices proved very fulfilling for the other person and me.

I found my life's purpose, I want to empower others to be at their best! Whatever that means for them, it can be a balanced life working part-time or reaching for the stars. I want people to become who they WANT to be – not what society or anyone else expects from them. I love guiding people in their transformational journeys, as I know how it feels. I have a clear roadmap, am truly motivated and then I start driving and find out that there are roadblocks and fears.

Am I willing to pay the price to chase my desired lifestyle? And I am not even sure if I will achieve this! What will others think and say about me when I chase my BIG dreams? The disapproval and fear of rejection was one of my biggest blockers to get ahead in life! Achievers and top athletes focus on the prize at the end of race. Incredible how just one letter in a word can make a huge difference in one´s life!

So I started to figure out how I could become a Trainer. I read lots of books and attended one of Anthony Robbins´ seminars in London, a game changer! Listening to his motivational CD´s got me right on track of taking massive action and that was how I found out about Jack Canfield´s *Success Principles* and *The Secret*. Have you ever had that feeling that you deeply felt: THIS IS IT! The *Success Principles* are for me the fundaments for a solid road to success. I am deeply grateful that Jack Canfield arrived in my life, as he provides for me a road map to get to a wonderful destination together with like-minded people.

Let´s get back to my career… I got a wonderful chance of becoming a Retail Trainer at one of the greatest and coolest international sports brands at the world, Adidas! How did I achieve this? When you switch careers, you need to make sure that you have a USP to outperform the rest, as you have much less experience in the playing field you apply for. My USP was my "transferable knowhow": International Sales and Business development and I can conduct my trainings in five languages. As a result, together with my previous boss, we won the Emil "Inspiration" 2013 award for the area Germany, Austria and Switzerland, recognition for co-designing and executing a physical "Retail University" program at the Adidas headquarters in Herzogenaurach, Germany.

I was proud of my success and at the same time, I was physically exhausted. So I thought to myself: well, there you are Linda, you are doing what you love and are grateful for the results, however you are not managing your own health! You are not on the road to build health and wealth. As a working mum, I also had to focus on my daughter. I paid a price for being successful in my career. I was out of shape and weighed twelve kilos above the World Health Organization (WHO) standard for optimum health. Ever had the feeling of knowing you need to work out to feel better but are just too tired to do anything? My focus had been to establish myself as a trainer, not on staying healthy in the meantime.

I also had to look at my food intake. Regarding diets, I tried several and personally I got confused. So many contradicting opinions, each diet appears to hold the "Holy Grail." I was sick and tired of that and had to find a better road. **I started looking at the energy process in my body, listening more to my body.** Does this particular food provide me energy or does it take my energy away? I do not stick to a specific diet; I *feel* better when I eat an alkaline/paleo diet supported with alkaline water and have my "comfort moments," enjoying my sugary treats once in a while. It is all about consistency, not perfection. I need to feed my inner child too, to stay grateful ;-).

The universe gave me a "breakthrough goal": become the co-facilitator for our *Fit to Lead* program, a first time People Manager program. The title inspired me. If I want to conduct this, I need to make sure that I practice what I preach: GET FIT LINDA! So I embraced a healthy sporty lifestyle, lost twelve kilos and changed my food and water intake. And as a result, I co-designed and conducted the new internal *Fit to Lead* "Health" Module. And that is where the magic happens, you will start to work towards your goals not based on a "to do" list, but fully aligned with your life purpose.

I base my decisions on my life's purpose – does it bring me closer or further away from that? It makes it easier to make decisions, however sticking to it can be a challenge and that is where you need to adopt the "athlete's mindset," focus on the prize that will be amazing and worth growing towards as a person. I learned so many difficult life lessons through this, it hurts, and at the same time, feelings come and go, the positive results will have a rippling effect to even greater things. I walk through life trusting in the universe.

I currently work as a Senior Manager Learning EMEA markets where I continue to build a solid reputation as an in-house Trainer and maintaining excellent relationships. I am known for taking my job very seriously and going the extra mile, wanting to make a genuine positive difference in people´s lives and the company´s business direction. Through team building, I work together with internal, international (cross functional) teams to build high performance teams.

Simultaneously, I currently work on a private project called the Health Builds Wealth Club, another "THIS IS IT" moment! I am optimizing all the knowledge and passion that I accumulated during my career: my sales, business development skills and training skills. I am uniting both worlds.

Alone you can get a lot done and be successful. However, understanding that together with your network, you can accelerate your success and achieve much, much more! I go through life embracing diversity and finding win-win situations with like-minded people that tick different in the approach on how to get there. They open up my mind to be flexible and show me roads to success and possible danger zones I had not even thought about. I am teaming up with champions, people who are successful in their own "health builds wealth" area and are just as passionate as I am.

So what does the **Health Builds Wealth (HBW) Club** stand for?

- HEALTH is for me a vibrating energetic body, mind and soul that are conceived by daily Success Habits.
- WEALTH for me is to be grateful to have a healthy functioning body and mind, have financial security AND being able to realize all the great dreams in your life.
- HEALTH and WEALTH are clearly connected together in order to lead the lifestyle you desire. Based on a Healthy lifestyle you are building your physical, mental and financial Wealth.

Being part of any Club, it empowers you and keeps you on track of your goals. At the HBW Club, the focus is on uniting like-minded people who want to achieve their next step in a healthier Body, Mind and Finance. I offer to connect with people who are ahead of the game in order for you to step up your own game and break through any limitations that have held you back up until now. There is also a community where you can connect with like-minded spirits and build a powerful network or act as a source of inspiration, depending on where you are in your **Health Builds Wealth** journey!

I am offering a platform where a successful team can empower people to turn any dreamed life style into reality by offering a road to success in health and wealth. The events, trainings and workshops on this platform will focus on a healthy body, mind and finance. My blog has a weekly focus on how to build your (part time) business to generate passive income, another "THIS IS IT" moment in my personal Health Builds Wealth journey, thanks to the lessons I learned from Robert Kiyosaki and his "Cash Flow game."

There is a road to success that can lead you faster to health and wealth.

The Cambridge Dictionaries Online describes the fast track as: "The quickest route to a successful position. She/He is on the fast track to success." It is also a great parallel for the sports industry and the people I work with. There are many lessons I learned along the way, these tips helped me to get faster and more efficient to my destiny. Get on your fast track by joining me in becoming a continuous transformer, stepping up your game in your journey for lifelong health and wealth.

15 TIPS FOR YOUR – "HEALTH BUILDS WEALTH FAST TRACK"

1) Map out your road to success and execute your plans with an athlete mindset.

Live by the Success Principles and use the power of visualization; gold medal winners apply this technique.

2) Take your time seriously.

As you are becoming more successful, you will be asked to support more people and projects. I train bigger groups, become more virtually present, and build a business system. Work smarter, not harder AND keep the human connection.

3) It is a marathon, not a sprint.

I am very impatient and want to get to my destination fast. However, along the road there are valuable lessons waiting for you; take your time to learn these and avoid making the same mistake twice. It is about the journey, not the destination.

4) Listen to your inner GPS and act upon it.
No matter how uncomfortable something is or hurts, feelings come and go. Results stay. Stand for who you WANT to be. Pick your battles wisely too.

5) Surround yourself with champions.
Learn from people who are better than you. Play sports with people who are a challenge to beat! The same goes for business, who is already better at what you want to master? Get in the game!

6) You are warming up.
Study your competitors on the playing field and offer your uniqueness.

7) Protect yourself against possible injuries.
Understand what it takes to set up a (small) business. Register your domain name, your brand etc. Make sure you implement the right terms and conditions for your website.

8) Get a Coach and use feedback to your advantage.
Each athlete has a coach that will empower you to stay on track and get better. Listen to others when they provide you feedback and decide to act upon it or not. Someone is just giving his/her perception of a situation.

9) Build a High Performing Team.
If you want to be successful, you need to build a high performing team. Do you need to pull your team over the finishing line or are they so inspired that they are engaged to reach the vision? Make sure you lead by example and foster a culture of trust and healthy conflict, meaning you can have a conflict with positive intent. You both want to get to a desired result and then you can move on without grudges. Clean up any misunderstandings.

10) The right fuel for your race: Nutrition and Hydration.
Listen consciously to your body and eat foods and liquids that are good for YOU, not what an expert recommends. Try out new intake for thirty days and feel the difference, I got my energy back in a way I did not expect, by drinking ionized water!

11) Fill up your mental gas tank.

Music connects me to my envisioned goals, I dance in my office when I prepare for my trainings and when people see me walking around at work wearing my head phones, they know that I am in the "zone", focused on the business results I need to deliver.

12) Get back quickly on your feet when you get punched.

How fast are you to recover from your mistakes? It is ok to get side tracked and take a break for a moment, but then get back on your feet. By sticking to your *Success Principles* system, you are back on the highway in no time.

13) Recovery.

On my list of incompleteness, I had scheduled a minor operation last year. However, I got back too quickly and did not have the full energy to keep up my busy lifestyle. This was a good lesson and now I schedule in much more relaxing time – enjoying going to the sauna and getting a massage.

14) Have fun along the way and celebrate your wins!

I find it essential to enjoy what I am doing. One thing I got better at is that I celebrate my wins, and not just tick of a box...

15) Health and wealth are interconnected.

By building your mental, physical and financial health, you are building your wealth. Step-by-step I am transforming my life, in order to achieve life-long health and wealth by scheduling time to take care of my body, mind and finances.

About Linda

Linda Evenhuis empowers others to be at their best by designing and conducting trainings, workshops and motivational talks for the Adidas Group and the Health Builds Wealth Club. She fosters a culture of positive empowerment and unites people in order for them to reach their highest (health and wealth) potential and meet their business goals.

She was brought up in a family that owned a small business where client loyalty, joy, open-mindedness and respecting each individual's life purpose was the foundation. The milestones for Linda's road to success were hereby defined.

Linda has a Bachelor's Degree in International Business and Languages and communicates in five languages: Dutch, English, German, French and Spanish. To unleash her passion for Business Development and Relationship Management, she started her career as a global player working in the Fashion and the Banking industry. International Business, Account and Relationship Management positions were her main domain, where understanding and communicating clients' products, marketing, operational and financial needs were her key focus.

Moreover, she over-watched that contract compliance, negotiating payment terms, and ensured that payment, lending, investment and securities business is run efficiently and effectively. Conquering new territories through cold acquisition was another passion that fully goes with her determined and positive character, always looking for the win-win in a situation and entering unpaved roads to success.

Whilst on this career journey, she noticed she had a natural talent for empowering others and fostering a positive, goal-oriented driven culture. She started as a Retail Trainer at the Centre of Excellence Talent at the Adidas Group for Germany, Austria and Switzerland, where she could combine her business and training skills.

There, together with Stephanie Dust, she co-designed and co-facilitated a new business demand-led Retail University program; an in-depth weekly Training curriculum based on her specialization in Emotional Selling, Customer Service, Brand Loyalty and Values. This was recognized with the Manager of the Year "Inspiration" 2013 award.

She was then promoted to Senior Manager Learning EMEA markets at the HR Talent Department, where she continues figuring as a key point of contact for the HR Community to build and deliver trainings and workshops. Custom made team buildings are co-designed with Matthew Stone. Linda is also part of the leadership team of the Adidas Women's Network where she advises on the Training and Development curriculum.

The "Fit to Lead" program is one of her core responsibilities. Inspired by her own health journey, she successfully initiated a new Health Module focused on movement, nutrition, burnout prevention and a healthy mindset.

With her acquired business acumen, creativity, and passion for people, she pursues her road to success by managing her private business, the "Health Builds Wealth Club." There she focuses on a curriculum based on a "healthy body" through the alkaline lifestyle and ionized water in conjunction with running champion Gesa Bohn. A "healthy mind" is conceived by the Success Principles and "healthy finance" teaches how to build a passive income with ionized water and developing your own business.

- Linda@healthbuildswealth.com
- www.healthbuildswealth.com
- www.kangenwasser.de
- info@kangenwasser.de

CHAPTER 45

FINANCIAL SUCCESS FROM A TO Z
– SAVING TODAY FOR A RICHER TOMORROW'

BY LINDA J. LEVESQUE

You are on the road to success by reading this book. Financial Success is really as easy as learning your ABCs. In this chapter I will give you the basic overview of the tools you need to get on the financial road to success.

Because you are reading this book, and in particular this chapter, I am assuming you need information to get you to where you want to go financially. The first piece of advice I can give you is to get **A**dvice from the experts. If you don't want to pay for the advice or you think you don't have enough money to get professional advice, then you can always ask people who are financially successful to share some insight with you. Most people are willing to help if only you ask.

Having a **B**udget and sticking with it is one of the hardest things to do, but really is one of the most important things you can do. The reason a budget is so important is because you need to know where you are spending your money. I have had clients do a log of their expenses for a period of time to see where money was being spent, only to discover a large part of their monthly expenses was going towards discretionary spending. Discretionary spending is within your control.

Do you find sometimes there is too much month at the end of your money? You make a decent income but the <u>C</u>ash flow just doesn't seem to be there. Without positive cash flow it is hard to save. Planning to have a positive cash flow at the end of the month is important in achieving financial success.

Drowning in <u>D</u>ebt is not a great way to be financially successful? There are good debts and bad debts and you need to know the difference. Good debt is when you purchase a home, get an education or possibly start a business. Bad debt is where you run up your credit cards and have nothing to show for the debt incurred. Unfortunately, you can go deeper and deeper into debt and find yourself drowning if you do not get your debts under control. Having good debt will help you achieve your financial goals.

Having an <u>E</u>mergency fund is like having a lifesaver when you get caught off guard with a large, unplanned expense. Many people find themselves in this situation at one time or another. Having money set aside allows you to cover the expense without having to use your credit card or get a bank loan.

What does your <u>F</u>uture look like? Is it something by design, or are circumstances dictating your life. We all have the power to choose what kind of life we want to live. All you have to do is decide what you really want out of life. You can start by setting some <u>G</u>oals for yourself.

Most successful people set goals. The difference between a wish and a goal is that one is written with action steps and the other is a dream. Something you hope for but with no real plan to achieve it. Having written goals that are specific, measurable, actionable, realistic, and time-bound make for smart decisions on your part. What actions can you take each day to work towards achieving your goals? You must review your goals on a regular basis. Start getting into the habit of doing at least four or five action steps daily.

Everything we do can become a <u>H</u>abit if we do it long enough. I have read that change can happen in as little as 21 days. If this is the case, wouldn't it be nice to start some daily actions that after 21 days just become a habit. A habit is something that you are now doing that you no longer have to think about, but you just do. It is like brushing your teeth every morning. No thought needs to go into it, you just do it. The challenge you will have is making sure you develop good habits that help you get closer to achieving your financial success. As easy as it is to develop a good habit, you can also develop bad habits if you are not careful in the actions you are taking.

When you think of people that have already achieved financial success, you might not realize that part of the plan they have put together for themselves is what happens if something unexpected happens. I am talking about putting your family at risk of financial disaster by not having adequate **I**nsurance coverages. Everyone likes to believe they are immortal. They are not going to die. They are too young to die. They are too healthy to die. Then out of the blue, something happens like an illness, accident or whatever. This happened in my own family. My father was a very healthy man up until he got cancer and died. My father died leaving our family at risk of losing everything. My father was the bread winner. I am the middle of seven children. How do you think my mother felt losing her husband and now having to deal with how to feed her children? Part of the plan of being on the road to financial success is having adequate coverage for all the foreseen things that can and sometimes do happen. Don't put your family at risk.

There will be times when people marry and they have not openly discussed how to manage their money so financial goals can be achieved. If you are in a relationship with someone that has different values towards money than you, then having **J**oint bank accounts may be setting you up for financial infidelity. Joint bank accounts work when you both have the same end goal in mind. When you are both starting with practically no money, then joint accounts may work. When I was first married, it worked having the joint accounts. Over the years working in this business I have found that each having your own bank accounts works far better. This is in part due to the fact that there are a lot of second marriages, and it is easier with less arguments about where money is being spent with your own bank account.

Having the **K**nowledge needed to make the right decisions will get you closer to achieving what you set out to do. The road to success is all about getting you closer to your ultimate goal, whether financial or otherwise. Get the knowledge required. It is all out there. It just takes time and effort to find it.

Sometimes you may need to **L**everage to bring your ideas to fruition. Using other people's money in the case of starting a business is a good idea. With a proper business plan, many people have become very successful using the bank's money instead of their own.

Financial success will be different for everyone. How do you know what you want and how to achieve the level of success you are looking for? **M**editation practiced on a daily basis is probably one of the secrets to success that no one ever told you. Meditation helps you to relax and lets the ideas come to you once you have quieted all the noise around you. Just a very minutes every day can make a world of difference in speeding up the process towards your financial success.

At this point, what is your **N**et wealth? Your net wealth is the measurement of what you own less what you owe. Working to increase the bottom line figure to the number that you set out in your goals is what this chapter is all about. What is your number? Knowing your number you now have to figure out how to get there. Remember your goals. When working towards increasing your net wealth you have to see the **O**pportunities as they present themselves. Sometimes the opportunity is staring you right in face but you are not looking at the big picture. Remember to open the mind and use knowledge to help you recognize the opportunities when they are there for the taking.

I find the most financially successful people are frugal. Some might call them a **P**enny **P**incher or cheap. I would have to disagree. I have spent most of my life clipping coupons and taking advantage of sales. I love to save money wherever I can. People with money have money because they pinch pennies. I grew up with the phrase, 'take care of the pennies and the dollars will take care of themselves.' I like that phrase and consider myself frugal not cheap, because I do penny pinch even though we really don't have pennies in Canada.

Have **Q**uestions so far? There are no stupid questions when you are looking for the knowledge to get you closer to your goals. Just don't be afraid to ask. Most people will help if only you ask. If they don't it is no big deal, just move on and ask someone else.

Part of the ultimate goal in reaching financial success is so you can have the lifestyle you want right into retirement. **R**etirement planning must start today because before you know it, it will be right around the corner. Achieving financial success is for your whole life, not just while you are working. There is no real success unless you do your retirement planning along with it.

This will mean that you need as part of your plan to start paying yourself first. Who is more important than you? If you are wondering how much to save, you can start with **S**aving 10 percent of all you make. This is a great starting point for anyone. It can be gross or net of your earnings. Gross is definitely better but net is better than nothing. Stop making everyone else rich and forgetting to pay yourself off the top. This is just another habit you need to do for yourself and your family. Also remember the savings is for long term, not a new car or whatever else you decide you want but don't really need.

In looking for ways to help you save, you can always find out what programs your governments have as incentives to save **T**axes. There are always programs out there that your government has that could help fund some of your lifestyle if only you took advantage of them. Ask an accountant or other professional what is available to you that you have not so far been using.

You may have already achieved your level of financial success or it may be right in front of you and has been **U**ndiscovered up to this point. Take notice of your surroundings or it may go undiscovered all along.

Having clarity about what it is you want and using **V**isualization to see it in your mind may be the second secret to financial success you have been missing. Use a vision board so you have real pictures to look at that will feed into your subconscious to speed up the process of your financial success.

Remember **W**ealth will be a fantasy or reality depending on what actions you take to accomplish your goals. Take a good look inside your own situation. I mean really go deep like you were giving yourself an **X**-ray. What do you see? Where do you need to go? What do you need to do? How will you do it? When will you get it?

Now is the time to take up something new like **Y**oga to enjoy good health to go along with your new wealth. You will not have a **Z**ero net wealth following these principles. That will be other peoples' problem, not yours.

All the best on your journey to success!

[This chapter was prepared solely by Linda Levesque who is a registered representative of HollisWealth® (a division of Scotia Capital Inc., a member of the Canadian Investor Protection Fund and the Investment Industry Regulatory Organization of Canada). The views and opinions, including any recommendations, expressed in this chapter are those of Linda Levesque alone and not those of HollisWealth. Levesque Wealth Planning is a personal trade name of Linda J. Levesque. ® Registered trademark of The Bank of Nova Scotia, used under license. HollisWealth is a trade name of HollisWealth Insurance Agency Ltd. Insurance products are provided through HollisWealth Insurance Agency Ltd.]

About Linda

Linda J. Levesque has been helping families 'Save Today for a Richer Tomorrow' for over 25 years. Linda understood very quickly the value of saving money when her father took her to the bank to open up her first savings account. That's when she learned you need to save or money eventually disappears if you keep spending it.

Linda is the author of *Financial Success from A to Z: Saving Today for a Richer Tomorrow*. In the book she credits her father's financial savvy for her own success in achieving her financial goals. Growing up in a family where her father had to stretch a dollar, on a miner's income, in order to provide for his large family was a major influence in Linda's life. Not feeling deprived as a child was the driving force behind wanting to help others do the same with limited resources. Look for the e-book on *Financial Success from A to Z: Saving Today for a Richer Tomorrow*, for buying and reading this book.

Linda is a CERTIFIED FINANCIAL PLANNER® professional, public speaker, author and Sr. Investment Advisor with HollisWealth under her own banner of Levesque Wealth Planning. She has a team of specialists that she calls upon to help her clients with whatever financial challenges they face. Linda's clients include doctors, dentists, professionals, retired clients, and their families.

Linda is known for her dynamic presentations to audiences large and small; she uses humor, knowledge and stories to get her points across. A featured guest on Sirius Satellite Radio, she has written a chapter in the Trusted Authorities' book on *Single Again: Wealth Planning on One Income*. Linda uses the *Success Principles* in conjunction with her teachings on Financial Success.

As a CERTIFIED FINANCIAL PLANNER®, Linda specializes in meeting the needs and protecting the accumulated wealth of the conservative investor, and is an independent thinker who offers independent products. Everything Linda recommends is geared to the individual's needs and goals. She rarely follows the crowd but takes the initiative to lead.

Linda regularly takes continuing education courses to help stay abreast of new and changing trends. This has helped her to successfully plan and transition clients' lifestyle changes throughout their lives and throughout the various stages of retirement.

Linda J. Levesque CFP®, FMA, FCSI
Director, Private Client Group
Sr. Investment Advisor
HollisWealth, a division of Scotia Capital Inc.
HollisWealth Insurance Advisor
HollisWeatlh Insurance Agency Ltd.
Levesque Wealth Planning

You can connect with Linda at:
  linda@levesquewealthplanning.com
  www.twitter.com/levesquewealthp
  www.levesquewealthplanning.com
  https://ca.linkedin.com/in/levesquewealthplanning

CHAPTER 46

SHARKS DON'T WEAR BRACES

– HOW TO SELECT THE BEST INNOVATIONS FOR YOUR CUSTOMER

BY REGINE C. HENSCHEL

Many business owners and salesmen currently use a lot of time to highlight their own abilities and possibilities. The website shows awards and grandiose products, but what is the value for the customer? How can the customer recognize what he benefits from? And this becomes especially difficult in the case of new topics and innovative projects that are brought for the first time to the market, for which there is no "proof of concept." As an "innovation communicator" you need special skills for this task. The good news: they can be learned and implemented with a little practice, so that any technical start up may result in a long-selling product and not in a false start.

I take myself as an example, because I myself made a mistake for a long time, presenting the great innovations of our company TAO-Group in a solid and "colorful" way on our web pages. Based on my experience as a science editor and public relations manager, I presented the various products such as seasonal energy storage, green batteries or towel-large seawater desalination plants in colorful pictures and beautiful texts. The people addressed were suitably impressed, but they were still a long way from becoming customers! Many guests visiting our labs and testing facilities were impressed by the diversity of developments and ideas.

They had never before seen so many innovations and ideas in one place. *But they did not order or purchase anything!*

"That can't be true!" I thought. It must be clear to all that we have just the solution for their technical problems and that we are the ones able to solve their problems. But although the visitors went home with a thank you for our many inspirations - we did still not get a contract.

One evening, I was sitting with a glass of wine in front of the TV watching a documentary about sharks. They swam through the sea, did their own thing and looked scary, but they did not care about it. As a public relations manager, I would classify these sharks as being resistant to consulting. Due to daring camera shots, I could see the impressive throats of these marine predators and their mighty teeth. I thought for myself: such crooked teeth, actually they have to wear braces. But hey! . . . this is a shark, why should a shark need braces? The shark does not care whether or not their teeth are crooked. For the shark, the main thing is to get along down there in the seas and catch some fish. He will never take part in a beauty contest! Those sharks, being resistant to consulting, never will buy braces. Eureka! . . . that's it!

I turned off the TV, took a package of plain white paper, my favorite pen and began to sketch our own communication tools in the company. We have always focused just on ourselves, our enormous efforts to provide customers with the best possible energy calculations and ideas. But we overlooked what the customer actually wants and needs. Where are his problems that he needs to have solved? Where is his position in his business plan in five years? And what are his visions for his company?

After years of innovation-communication in our company, I recognized the central question: What can TAO do so that the customer feels better about our products? This change of focus brought about enormous success. This simple question influenced our entire presentation and dealing with customers. It revolutionized everything and seems so self-evident. Of course, it is great that we have received international, prestigious awards and good references, and referring to this on our website. This gives trust to the customers to give us a first call and to talk with each other. But ultimately, our customers needed someone who solves their problem, who gives them a hand and paves the way to their goal. And the crux was that they sometimes could not even explain their problem. This means that a high degree of empathy and conversational management know-how has to be introduced into the talks in order to understand the customer. This means we are the problem-solving analyst for the customer.

At this moment, two things helped me perfectly: First, my experience as a journalist, and the associated curiosity about people and issues. And secondly, my analytical thinking from my nearly-forgotten philosophical studies. And because I've already learned to offer the best possible solutions in a short time to my clients and readers, I grasp and combine twenty years of study, TV journalism and corporate management together into a few proven parameters – which catapulted our company, our customers and ourselves to the top. Let´s start!

Nothing connects you with your customer as much as real interest. If you really want to know how he is thinking, then just ask him. Ask him what he wants and what his goals are for his own business. It's like a good interview in front of a TV camera. Start with general questions about the profession and education, perhaps questions about hobbies and travel, so that the interview gets "warmed up." Then go deeper and ask what goals he still has in this year. And even this question will be answered in the course of a comfortable conversation. Design your own questions for the initial consultation. Make your notes, but be wary of offering a solution immediately.

Because here the second component comes into play: the analytical reasoning. Clearly, we are trimmed by putting everything said into a box, to label and to form an own opinion immediately. That's not so good. Because the experiences and early assignments obstruct our path as to what really lies in what has been said. Write down the wishes of the customer, think about them and describe feasible solutions in the form of visions (if you can't hold them back), but collect as much information as possible - and do not make a judgement on them.

Do as much research as possible on your customer. You would not believe how many people go into conversations unprepared. There is no excuse for poorly-prepared meetings. Your time and your customer's time is precious. Imagine that your client is a date. You would surely give everything to make a good impression. You would find out where your heart partner went to school, what hobbies he has, what he likes to eat.

Your customer is your long-awaited date, your soul mate and you want to enter into a long-term, happy relationship with him - and not only once an order.

So, look at the websites, which products and services are offered? What is the history? Were there any breakthroughs, developments, changes, turning points that have affected profound impact on the company's activities? Who are the partners or stake holders? And what values represents your client? Slip into the shoes of your customers. Walk a little way in his shoes. Where is the problem? Invest empathy for the needs of the customer. Yes, that is quite valuable in these days of Facebook and individualism.

After detailed analysis of the company, you may research further: In what business is your customer working? Which developments are already in sight in the foreseeable future on the horizon? Are there strong developments he must keep up? How can he make sure not to lose the connection? Or even better? If there were a possibility to be a leader or to occupy a new gap? And can you help him? Find out if there is new business in this area – whether it is the construction sector, financial services, horticulture or whatever. Be curious like your young niece. Engage your employees. We have an interdisciplinary, international team of engineers, aviation and space professionals, chemists, philosophers and marketing people with diverse knowledge and background. This means that our innovations arise from the interesting topics that form the basis for solutions for our customers as well as joint discussions.

The research is done, you know a lot about the business and now you examine which are the short and medium-term solutions you can provide to your customers with your projects and innovations? Does it make the customers richer, more beautiful, more intelligent? Or is it a sustainable innovation with true demand for job security, secure income and green technology of the future?

Here's a story for example. We have developed a fantastic new seasonal storage, which receives heat from the sun via collectors in summer and stores the energy inside. In this way, a house can be heated in the wintertime without energy loss. The storage material is inexpensive, nontoxic and beautiful: Silica. As we also received an award for the polar-bear-storage and were invited on television in prime time to introduce the energy storage, the success was unstoppable - we thought. After the broadcast, which took place on a Saturday, the following Monday morning the phones rang hot. From the numerous requests, ultimately 60 serious customers remained. How many energy storage units were sold? None!

What went wrong with the best PR on TV you can imagine? In short, we could not adjust to the individuality of the prospective customers. These prospective customers owned old houses which had to be renovated. Other consumers wanted to heat a farm. We had swimming pool owners, laundries and more. Each request was so individual that it exceeded our time and personnel capacities. The breakthrough for our storage came by teaming up with a partner from industry, producing the storages, and installing the storages individually with customers. Thereby, the industry partner secured an added value from a new, environmentally-friendly technology in the short term, and in long-term, the market leadership and the satisfaction of customers. Their environmental awareness is taken seriously and implemented in a product for one's own home. And we support the project as a technology and gain further innovations from the project.

Back to you: Have you found the best innovation or service for your customer after thorough considerations with which he can raise his business to a new level? Are you enthusiastic about your idea and do you expect an order after the presentation next week? And you can get it! Congratulations!

For those who do not get a contract the first time, there is no reason to be frustrated. Because now it goes further: Up to now you know all about the customer's business. You also know, of course, its competitors. What could be better than getting in contact with the competitor and ask for a conversation or a presentation on the spot? I have found that the number 2 or number 3 in an industry is always awake and loves to get the chance to be number 1. Help the competitor with your knowledge you have gained through intensive professional elaborations and discussions about this business with your employees.

This is a win-win situation:
  a.) You've worked as an expert and all knowledge is available on an actual basis.

b.) The number 2 in the sector will receive a fantastic opportunity to ascend with your support. So you will find the number 2 as your customer since you could not succeed with the number 1.

Study the website - and go to a new one. You will win!

To convince a shark in 7 steps:

1. Don't think about yourself as being very important, rather prefer genuine interest for your customers.
2. Leave your sales goals aside and ask for the customer's wishes and needs.
3. Consider your customers as "dates" and search everything about his hobbies, his company and his life.
4. Get into the shoes of the customer. Where are his problems? Feel empathy!
5. Can your customer become a leader with your help or be successful within a market gap?
6. Find out with your team what are the short and medium-range values for your customer in working with you.
7. Adjust the best possible innovation or service to the needs of your customers and present your "Proof of concept."

I wish you success!

About Regine

Regine C. Henschel, MA is an "innovation communication officer" and a CEO who has a lot to do. She works with the TAO company. TAO means Trans-Atmospheric Operations GmbH and this contains all research activities in the atmosphere between earth and heaven for eco-friendly and humane technology. Many of the TAO-Innovations such as the seasonal polarbear-storage, the new Green Battery or the high altitude platform for telecommunication out of the stratosphere have to be presented clearly and in an interesting way for both customers and investors. Regine together with her business partner, Prof. Dr. Bernd Kröplin, founded the TAO Group in Germany.

On the one hand, this is public relations, if the new technology is presented to the customers without being too detailed and too much in love with the impressing technology. On the other hand, a partnership between innovator and customer with a common goal has to be arranged: optimal transfer and realization of the technology for a short and long-term benefit for the customer.

Therefore Regine developed a new innovation-communication-strategy with a road map and a questionnaire. The innovation has to "fit" the customers like a good suit. A specific search and strategy are needed. For innovation communication, you need extra skills if the projects are unique worldwide and not made on an assembly line. The good news: you can learn and execute these skills.

Regine was trained in her analytical mindset during her academic studies in philosophy at the University in Göttingen/Germany, which helps her today to put the overwhelming technology in a nutshell. She worked seven years as an editorial journalist for renowned television channels in Germany like ZDF, Deutsche Welle and Arte. She was keen on producing her own stories and themes for television about sciences, research and architecture like she does today for her company. She loves everything that is "humming and flying," so she worked also at the Institute of Statics and Dynamics of Aerospace Structures at the University of Stuttgart/Germany for a year and a half.

Regine wrote and published five books and more than 250 articles for newspapers and magazines like the renowned *Süddeutsche Zeitung* and the engineering news *VDI*.

"You don't have to sit in the front row to be successful." – is her credo. With her experience and PR-support, a young movie team could win an Oscar for their animation movie in Hollywood.

After all these professional experiences with different topics, she operates internationally in Europe and China with the TAO Group.

In Asia, it is necessary to apply a different behavioral pattern, and the ability to communicate is diverse, too. Chinese are different-minded, but they have a high demand for innovation and have a high conversion rate. Regine learned how to change the European mindset into Chinese thinking and built, together with her business partner and their team, valid and successful business contacts.

The TAO Group got the "Top 100" award in 2016 for one of the most innovative companies in Germany. Regine shares her knowledge about innovation communication in lectures and in selected consultations.

You can connect with Regine at:
- henschel@tao-group.de
- www.tao-group.de

CHAPTER 47

HOW TO HIT A PUBLIC SPEAKING HOME RUN: USE SIX SPECIALIST COACHES

BY RICHARD DEAN

Here's how to knock it out of the park on your next presentation: Take a leaf out of the Major League Baseball coaching manual and use not one coach but SIX specialist coaches – plus a manager to set the game plan.

How? The bad news is that one of your coaches (Aristotle) died 2,500 years ago, while hiring the others would cost the price of a small house. The good news is that they've given away their secrets in countless books, blogs, seminars and talks, available online free or for just a few dollars. Simply do as they say.

Right, now it's time to meet your team. Together, their advice will transform your public speaking. Like specialist baseball coaches, they're niche experts in their field:

#1. Message
#2. Persuasion
#3. Storytelling
#4. Slides
#5. Pictures
#6. Delivery

But let's start with the boss. . .

MEET YOUR MANAGER:

Who: Bert Decker
Claim to Fame: Creator of The Decker Grid™
Words of wisdom: "Prepare in half the time"
Further Reading: *Communicate to Influence* (2015)

The manager's job is to set the game plan, and when it comes to public speaking, Bert Decker is the master planner. He developed the one-page Decker Grid™ 35 years ago and it remains the gold standard in presentation structure.

The unique magic of the Decker Grid is its four-part template for opening and closing a speech. Here's a quick recap of the opening gambit:

a. Start with a S.H.A.R.P. That's an acronym Decker uses to describe emotional content that grabs attention and builds rapport. The S.H.A.R.P.s are Stories, Humour, Analogies, References, Pictures/Visuals.

b. Tell your audience your P.o.V. – your point of view. Be bold.

c. Tell your audience what to do – the action steps they should take. Be specific.

d. Tell your audience the benefit of taking that action.

S.H.A.R.P.	Point of View	Action	Benefit

The Decker Grid then follows a fairly classic speech architecture for the main body, covering three main points in a bit more detail. It concludes by repeating the opening gambit, with a couple of tweaks.

Now go away and... Use it.

#1 – MESSAGE COACH

Who: Nancy Duarte

Claim to Fame: Created the PowerPoint for Al Gore's Oscar-winning *An Inconvenient Truth*

Words of wisdom: "Your primary filter should be what I call your big idea: the one key message you must communicate."

Further Reading: *Slideology: The Harvard Business Review Guide to Persuasive Presentations* – TED Talk.

Duarte isn't alone in telling public speakers to have one – and only one – key message. All the greats seem to agree on this, from Cicero in ancient Rome to Steve Jobs ("Today Apple Reinvents the Phone" at his 2007 iPhone launch). Duarte's genius is to give us a foolproof, three-step formula for crafting that one message.

The technique is best illustrated with an example: Al Gore's one sentence message for his Oscar-winning, *An Inconvenient Truth*, which is essentially a movie of the PowerPoint presentation Duarte helped create.

Step 1: State your unique point of view. Al Gore does this in the first part of the sentence: "Global warming is real, man-made…". The best points of view are ones that people can disagree with, and Gore certainly ticks that box.

Step 2: State what's at stake for people who do - or do not - adopt your point of view. Gore does this with the second part of the sentence: "…its effects will be cataclysmic if we don't act now."

Step 3: Write these elements in a complete sentence. Gore pulls it all together in this one sentence that summarizes his key message: *"Global warming is real, man-made and its effects will be cataclysmic if we don't act now."*

One big idea gives you clarity, focus, and an attention-grabbing headline. Most presentations are the polar opposite: vague, wishy-washy and aimless.

Now go away and… Use the three steps to write your next presentation title around one big idea.

#2 – PERSUASION COACH

Who: Aristotle
Claim to Fame: Father of Western Philosophy; pioneer of rhetoric
Words of wisdom: "Ethos, Pathos, Logos." (Character, Emotion, Logic.)
Further Reading: *On Rhetoric* (c.322 BC); *You Talkin' to me: Rhetoric from Aristotle to Obama* (by Sam Leith, 2011)

For Aristotle, public speaking was all about results. In Ancient Greece, that meant two things: persuading judges in court or persuading voters and politicians in public life. "Rhetoric," he wrote, is "the available means of persuasion."

Aristotle's greatest contribution to public speaking can be summed up in three words: **ethos, pathos, logos,** the so-called *Three Modes of Persuasion* that he outlined in his classic book, *On Rhetoric.*

Ethos is the integrity of the speaker. "Persuasion is achieved by the speaker's personal character," wrote Aristotle. Put simply, you must be an expert in your field and of good moral standing to persuade people. Pathos is emotional appeal. In Aristotle's words, "awakening emotion in the audience so as to induce them to make the judgment desired." He particularly liked metaphors, stories and a passionate, energetic voice. Logos is logical argument - the facts and figures that appeal to the rational side of our brain, and the thread of logic that links them together.

Now go away and... Strike a balance. Too much pathos makes you superficial, too much logos makes you boring.

#3 – STORYTELLING COACH

Who: Chip Heath
Claim to Fame: Stanford Professor; co-author of *Made to Stick* which has been translated into more than 25 languages
Words of wisdom: "Stories and Examples are the Building Blocks of a Presentation. If you use only one tip, this is the one."
Further Reading: *Made to Stick* (2007)

Made to Stick begins with a casual observation: some ideas survive while others die. It then asks 'why'? The answer, it turns out, is that some ideas are 'sticky' not because they're better, but because they're better presented. Abstract, theoretical ideas whither; concrete evidence such as stories flourish.

Chip and his brother Dan illustrate their point with countless examples, including this one from the documentary *Sicko* by left-wing filmmaker Michael Moore about the failings of US healthcare.

> Rick is a carpenter: an archetypal American lumberjack with broad shoulders, a big beard and check shirt. One day disaster struck – Rick accidentally sawed off two fingers – but like many Americans he had no medical insurance. When he went to hospital, with both fingers wrapped in tissue paper, he had to choose which one of them to have sewn back on because he couldn't afford both.

Chip and Dan use Rick's fingers to demonstrate the power of real examples in driving home important points. "He [Moore] doesn't make conceptual points about the healthcare system," they write. "He makes his case through the stories of individuals."

Now go away and... Use more stories and examples. Chip and Dan conclude: "Most people communicate with, say, 3 parts exposition to 1 part example. That's exactly backwards."

#4 – SLIDES COACH
Who: Edward Tufte
Claim to Fame: Barack Obama's data design guru; Yale Professor; "The Leonardo da Vinci of data" *(New York Times)*
Words of wisdom: "Eliminate Chartjunk."
Further Reading: *Visual Display of Quantitative Information* (1984)

Tufte has a tough message for presenters who use slides: get rid of EVERYTHING that isn't vital to your message. He even invented a word for superfluous gridlines, legends, labels and numbers: chartjunk. "The interior decoration of graphics generates a lot of ink that does not tell the viewer anything new," writes Tufte. "Regardless of its cause, it is all non-data-ink or redundant data-ink, and it is often chartjunk."

Most famously, Tufte argues that chartjunk may have contributed to the

2003 Columbia Space Shuttle accident, which killed seven astronauts when the shuttle broke up just before landing.

Here's what we know: the explosion was caused by damage sustained during take-off two weeks earlier. Space experts spotted the damage instantly and gave a PowerPoint presentation to NASA bosses – but buried their warning at the bottom of a cluttered slide with 20 lines of bullet points. The Columbia Accident Investigation Board concluded: "It's easy to understand how a senior manager might read this PowerPoint slide and not realize that it addresses a life-threatening situation."

Could better PowerPoint have saved the astronauts? Maybe. Some engineers argue that had NASA bosses fully understood the seriousness, they could have sent a second space shuttle, Atlantis, on a rescue mission. We'll never know.

Now go away and... Remove everything from your slides that isn't essential. Be ruthless.

Seth Godin, author of *Really Bad PowerPoint*, has this advice: "No more than six words on a slide. EVER."

#5 – PICTURES COACH
Who: John Medina
Claim to Fame: Neuroscientist, bestselling author
Words of wisdom: "Burn your current PowerPoint. We are incredible at remembering pictures."
Further Reading: *Brain Rules* (2008)

Prof. John Medina, author of *Brain Rules*, urges us to use pictures instead of words wherever possible. "Professionals everywhere need to know about the incredible inefficiency of text-based information and the incredible effects of images. Burn your current PowerPoint presentations and make new ones."

His research reveals that if we hear a piece of information, three days later we'll remember 10%. Add a picture and we'll remember 65%. "We are incredible at remembering pictures," writes the neuroscientist.

Psychologists have spent decades studying the so-called 'picture superiority effect'. Newspaper editors and advertisers have known the power of pictures for a century; today science can explain how it works. Indeed, researchers at MIT have shown that we can recognize pictures in as little as 13 milliseconds, or 76 images per second.

Elon Musk's 2015 launch of the Powerwall battery is a great use of images in a classic problem/solution presentation. The tech billionaire opens with the problem: a string of photos of dirty, coal-fired power stations billowing thick black smoke. Next he presents the solution: an image of the sun, a source of limitless energy. Then the punchline: another picture, this time a map of the US with a tiny blue square in the middle. The square, reveals Musk, is the amount of land needed to convert the US to zero carbon electricity generation, mainly from solar power.

Now go away and... Think about images that will grab attention and drive home your point.

#6 – DELIVERY COACH
Who: Amy Cuddy
Claim to Fame: 2nd most watched TED Talk of all time; Harvard Professor
Words of wisdom: "Fake it 'til you become it; strike a Wonder Woman power pose."
Further Reading: *Presence* (2015); TED Talk.

Amy Cuddy has a cure for stage fright: strike a pose like Wonder Woman. It sounds ridiculous, but she's a Harvard Professor and she's done her homework.

Previously psychologists assumed that feeling confident led people to strike so-called power poses. Cuddy's research discovered that the cause-and-effect works in the opposite direction too: striking the pose can make you feel confident. It's a subtle but massive difference. In her words: "fake it 'til you become it."

Here's what you have to do it you're feeling terrified before a speech, job interview or first date. Strike a pose like Wonder Woman, the iconic 70s TV superhero: hands on hips, icy stare with feet planted firmly on the ground, shoulder-width apart.

Cuddy got the idea from painful, personal experience. A car accident as a teenager rocked her confidence, making her too nervous to speak in class at college. She was about to drop out until a teacher convinced her to simply pretend to be confident – and over time it worked.

To understand how it worked, and whether the lessons could be applied to others, she tested the hormones of two groups – the first group struck power poses, the second group weak poses, such as sitting with arms and legs crossed while hunching forward. Saliva samples taken before and after revealed that in the power group, cortisol fell 25% (lower stress) while testosterone rose 19% (higher confidence). The weak group reported the exact opposite effect.

Now go away and... Strike a power pose. But recognise that glossophobia, the fear or public speaking, is as real as fear of spiders or flying and should never be trivialised. Power poses may work for you, but be aware that you may need other assistance, such as a psychologist.

About Richard

Richard Dean is a journalist, broadcaster and public speaker. He's spent two decades interviewing and sharing a stage with with business leaders, politicians, royalty and Oscar-winning actors including Sir Richard Branson, Tony Blair, Malcolm Gladwell, HH Sheikh Ahmed bin Saeed Al Maktoum and Sir Ben Kingsley.

Richard began his career as a reporter, writing for *The Economist*, Reuters and *The Financial Times.* For the past decade he's worked as a broadcaster for Bloomberg Radio in London and Dubai Eye 103.8FM, where he presents the UAE's leading daily current affairs show, The Business Breakfast. His first book, *Sink or Swim*, analysed the real estate crash that hit Dubai during the global financial crisis of 2008-09.

As a professional MC, moderator and keynote speaker, Richard speaks at about 50 conferences a year. He gave his first TED talk in 2016, at TEDxJESS in Dubai.

Richard is known as "the three degrees" for his university honours in history, economics and communication. Born and raised in the UK, he now lives in Dubai with his wife and two young children.

CHAPTER 48

THE EXHALE FACTOR

BY MELISSA VEESER

They told me diamonds were a girl's best friend….

I sell diamonds. Not the pretty kind that would grace your fingers, ears, or neck. (Because that would feel awkward and look desperate and silly. I know, because I tried it.) I sell industrial diamonds. The kind used to make vascular wires, eye glasses, armored plates for our military, and more. I love being part of the creation of an end product being used in heart surgery, eye glasses to improve someone's vision, or armored plates that offer our men and women protection. I love the people we work with and their dedication and desire to improve over their current situation.

When I first entered this industry, I was unaware of all the various operations and areas that diamonds were used in. As we continue to grow and assist our clients, we are learning more every day of new territory and areas to implement new ideas. I am fortunate to know someone who has a wealth of knowledge in the diamond industry and is innovative and proactive too. *(Important: choose your colleagues wisely!)*

I knew nothing about the industry. *Nothing.* I welcomed the challenge (and I had bills to pay….and I like to eat foods other than ramen noodles and beanie weenies). I had no choice but to make it. I didn't pretend to know their business or processes. I asked a lot of questions. The 'meat' of the technical side: they taught me. To lighten my obvious lack of knowledge, I would pass out antacids and aspirin to them and say, "You will need these as I will have a lot more questions." They laughed it off, until my continued questions started, then they were chewing on them like skittles. They would show me beautiful pens their current supplier gave them. I was on a budget, so I would take a Sharpie marker and write my company name on a twenty-cent pen and give it to them with promises of magic markers if they stuck with me. And stick they did. I am thankful and blessed and really enjoy them and what we accomplish every day, they truly are wonderful!

What I lacked in industry knowledge – I had a sincere interest *in the person* and *their* needs and concerns. This can't be forced or faked. If you have the desire and determination with *everyone's* best interest in mind – you *will* be successful and have fun in any industry you are in.

I believe that all areas can be improved in some way. Regardless of what we sell, or our occupation, there is always room for making it better, for them and for ourselves. This is where it gets exciting because: *this is where you can help everyone shine!* Creativity kicks in and everyone's energy starts vibrating at a higher frequency. The juices start flowing, people feel the shift and amazing things happen.

Selling and consulting is an 'emotional' thing. Yes, business is business, but no one wants to look foolish or feel played (emotion of embarrassment, frustration at making a misguided or poor decision). People are under stress, have deadlines and budgets to meet, people to answer to, things going on in their personal life, etc. A little humor can go a long way. Everyone we meet has 'schtuff' going on. This is where that human element of emotion comes into play. Trust, credibility, and knowing the *Exhale Factor* you can provide them. More on the *Exhale Factor* later on.

Ask questions, and follow up with more questions. Make notes – hear what they are saying, as well as what they're *not* saying – this is key. Not everyone wants to lay it all out – it's still in the vulnerable stage, emotions are present and guards are up. Remember, they feel they have heard it all before but have agreed to meet with you because something is missing in their current situation. You need to show you're credible to build the trust. Are they guarded in what they are telling you? If yes, that may be an area they are having difficulty in. Listen to what you are *not* hearing.

If they are an open book – be thankful! That is a Gift! Any time a prospect or current client has a complaint, there is a request behind it. What are you going to do to fix it for them? What improvements will you implement? Is it a billing issue? Fix it. Is it a delivery or quality issue? Fix it. Whatever it is, it is a Gift because it is telling you to hone your skills and those of the people in your circle involved in your business. By honing yourself with expectations of the same from everyone, you are cultivating a work environment of success and growth. You stay ahead of your competition because you are stronger, and sharper. Some may groan with irritation, and complain, "Why do I have to do this? We have been doing it this other way for years…" You remind them: "Because, just like your socks, change is necessary on occasion." Always look on your business or position with fresh eyes from time to time. Like it's your first day. Step back, look at your habits, the processes, and the industry you are in . . . and change your socks. Always. Please….

THE DIMMER SWITCH & VULNERABILITY

We all have a 'dimmer switch.' I think we are amazing beings and start out shining bright. Due to our environment, the light may or may not last. As we go through life we all encounter the 'dimmers.' These are people, who due to their own unhappy circumstances, dim the light of others around them. The person you are sitting in front of or on the phone with: may need an adjustment on their 'switch.' You don't have to know *what* or who dimmed their light. Instead, keep your light bright and focus on *them* – turn up their dimmer switch! You want them to shine bright like a diamond. You want them to feel better and lighter after talking or meeting with you.

We have a belief at my company: When you interact with someone, via phone, email or in person, you want them to feel lighter and better than prior to that interaction with you. Implement this in all areas of your life, even on a challenging day or with a challenging person – especially then! You do this, *you will build credibility and trust with them.* This works in all areas of your life, even simple interactions at a grocery or department store. You can do this through humor. There was a long hair hanging off of my face which was from my blush brush. I hadn't noticed it until after the appointment and I was back in my car. I had to call them, I was embarrassed! It turned out being a good ice breaker (a little self-deprecating humor can go a long way). There was an awkward silence

– like he didn't believe me. Like that 2-inch boar hair was attached - and mine. So I blurted out I needed his business so I could buy a new razor to shave my face. He laughed. Nervously, but he laughed. They have been a client for years and we never talked about the disturbing 'boar hair' incident again. *Every time you turn up someone's dimmer switch, yours goes up!* Make it about them and they will listen, they will share. *Exit:* Fear. *Enter:* Trust.

MUSHY LIMA BEANS

Everyone has a mushy pile of lima beans 'on their plate.' That pile of yuck they want to go away, but keep nudging it around with their fork. (Disclaimer: If you are a lover of mushy lima beans, I apologize, and want to assure you no lima beans were hurt in the writing of this chapter.)

That pile of mushy lima beans you see on their plate represents the 'what-I-am-not-telling- you' as well as your findings after reviewing their current circumstances and/or environment when you visited. This is 'hearing' the 'unspoken' I mentioned earlier. Now it's time to remove the lima beans without telling them you are removing them. Don't embarrass them or make them feel stupid because they didn't chuck them in the garbage sooner. (Hey, we've all had mushy lima beans on our plate.) Instead, offer solutions. Offer things way better than those nasty lima beans! Remember, you want to offer it to them as *their* ideas, not yours. Give them the credit, thank them for sharing and guiding you so you can better serve them. Let them know you appreciate them for working with you on this. You just turned up their dimmer switch a little more.

This is where the lima beans turn into your proposal of cheesecake and tiramisu. It's effortless, and done with ease. Removing the issues from their plate by replacing it with the solutions. Share the wonderful benefits and proactive ideas that will be implemented. This is your nobility coming through for others.

Here is how you do it:

Everything you are sharing with them, you have tailored to their needs based on information you have gleaned. Examples: *They* helped *you* create a new order processing program, streamline their inventory control process, and implement a periodic reassessment. It's collaborative.

Whatever industry you are in, apply these improvements in your offerings to them. *You want to ease the stress and fear away, and see them slowly exhale.... all is well....*

This is part of the *Exhale Factor.*

THE EXHALE FACTOR

- Don't fake it until you make it. Fresh eyes and ears are an asset. Be up front and open when chartering new territory or challenges and you will earn their trust and gain credibility. Their walls come down and they exhale.

- Thank them for helping you help them. With their openness and guidance, you can accomplish great things together. Let them shine! Remember, it's *about them.*

- By removing those mushy lima beans off of their plate, you are reassuring them they made a sound decision. Show them what they co-created with you to improve their current situation. This will keep both of you excited about what you do. Exhale, it's fun again!

- Introduce humor. (Telling the elusive prospect that 'you have been unable to get a hold of them after many attempts...only to see their face on a milk carton that morning' doesn't work.) Trust me on this one. There are better ways to lighten the moment with humor.

- Ask yourself: How can I make it better? Touching their spirit is noble and beautiful. Many lose track of this over the years. This is true strength!

Keep your dimmer switch up. Raise your level of energy and vibration in various ways:

- Volunteer. It is fun and fills the heart and lightens your spirit. Your spirit needs to be fed too...continuously. Ideas: nursing homes, homeless shelters, etc.

- Eat 'clean.' Cut back on processed and fast foods. Take small steps and you will feel the difference and increase your feeling of self-worth because you are doing more for 'you.'

- Move. Do some type of activity or movement. Thirty minutes is just 2% of your day. I know you are worth more than 2%. My mother Jeanie has had MS for over 45 years. She has survived a heart attack, multiple strokes, broken hip and is in a wheel chair. She does her PT five days a week and is such an inspiration for me to: Move! She takes care of herself inside and out!

- See yourself and others as already whole. We all have times where we feel broken. When someone sees us as whole, it lifts us up. It heals.

- Keep your independence and don't sell out for the proverbial carrot. Being independent removes limitations and mediocracy. This also assures your clients you have their best interests at heart. When you do this, you raise the bar of your company, suppliers, and everyone involved in your business circle. (Do this in your personal life as well!)

- Inspire. Inspire others with your light, humor, and expertise. Be an example of 'being limitless' and you will inspire yourself as well!

You will create amazing things! Exhale…all is well.

Love, light and success to you! ~ Melissa

About Melissa

Melissa Veeser is a business owner and does distribution of industrial diamond products and consulting for manufacturers in the ophthalmic, vascular/medical, military/defense, aerospace and technical ceramics industries. She has worked in the manufacturing field for over 20 years and has clients worldwide. She named her company after her mom Jeanie, with the hope this would elevate her to 'favorite' child status.

Her business belief and practices are based on focusing on improving her client's current operating procedures with high quality diamond tooling and implementation of operating cost-reduction programs and inventory management.

She is a self-starter with a love for helping people and belief that every person she works with is an important 'cog in the wheel' which supports a collaborative relationship that reveals the amazing gifts we all possess. Every person is a diamond-in-the-rough, sometimes we just need a little polishing! The key is focusing on everyone's strengths – recognizing the areas for improvement – and stepping up to help assist in those areas. Doing this also helps herself and her company to continue to grow in the services and solutions they offer.

Melissa currently resides in Minnesota. She has completed her first inspirational and humorous hand book for her clients and will be releasing another book at the end of 2016. Jack Canfield will be tweeting out when it's released. She also enjoys long walks to the fridge, her steak medium, and a good movie…wait…

You can reach out to Melissa via email:
• Melissa@JeanieDiamondTooling.com

Or find her on LinkedIn.
Her website is:
• www.JeanieDiamondTooling.com

CHAPTER 49

CHANGING THE HEALTHCARE CULTURE

BY DR. SHIRLEY WATSON

I have been in the Alternative Healthcare field for over 30 years, and during that time I have experienced through my patients and my own personal health issues, the brilliance as well as the foibles of the allopathic medical system that in many ways is failing us.

The brilliance I refer to is in the arena of acute trauma. There is no better healthcare system for a broken bone, a burst appendix or almost any other physical trauma. However, in long term health issues like cancer, autoimmune diseases or the myriad of psychological issues we are facing, this medical system falls short.

Let me tell you a personal story that will bring this more to light for you. It did for me.

I have taken up Kayaking over the last five years and I go on an annual trip with a group of very interesting women. The oldest is 87, and I'm the pup at 67. This year only three of us could go on the trip to Shoshone Lake in Wyoming.

IN THE WILD

Shoshone is the largest wilderness lake in the U.S. A wilderness lake is one where no motorized vehicles are allowed, no fires and you carry your waste out. In order to get to Shoshone Lake, you have to kayak across Grant Lake then portage your kayak for about a mile-and-a-half up a channel, because the water is too shallow to paddle. The day we set out was amazing, the sun dappling on the water gave me a sense of infinite possibilities. We had just crossed Grant lake, we took a rest and had a small bite to eat and then started up the channel pulling our kayak's behind us. It was maybe a mile in when I slipped on a mossy rock; I was only in the water about 30 seconds. But when I lifted myself out my left inner arm started to sting like I had been stung by something vile. As I ripped off my life vest and then my long sleeve shirt I envisioned a swarming angry wasp or the like flying out but nothing came, as I closely inspected the inner belly of my left arm I found two little holes. I did not think much of it; I put bite ointment on and set out again on our trek.

About an hour later we arrived at our first camp and unloaded our gear, had a meal, set up our tents and hung our food from the 15-foot pole provided to keep the bears out of our food. By dusk I was feeling weary, but wrote it off to the altitude, we were at 8,000 ft. I slept fitfully that night but the next morning, while a bit weak, broke camp and kayaked for two hours to the next campsite. By the time we arrived I was totally spent. I crashed on the beach with my bear spray in hand while Jay and Susana went back to find a couple we had passed on the shore. By this time, they were suspecting I might be in trouble.

During that second night I awoke to intense internal shaking from deep within my body, I knew I was in trouble and contemplated that this may be my last night on this beautiful earth. You hear the stories of near death experiences where people see the light and their life passes before their eyes; well been there, done that. I knew there was no way my friends were going to be able to get me out of the remote backcountry in time; yet I experienced a deep inner calm. I hesitate to even say what came next, but it is the truth so I will share it.

As I was contemplating my life, amid abject darkness, gradually in the upper reaches of my inner vision I saw a muted light, it looked like there were two silhouettes leaning over the opening encouraging me toward them. I found the distance between me and this light getting smaller, I knew I was not actually moving but the space was contracting. As I came closer I realized that this was it, once I got to the light, life, as I knew it was over. I felt very calm and accepting, there was no fear. I was more inquisitive to tell you the truth. I had almost reached the light when 'swish' it was gone; it had vanished in an instant. The trembling in my body had ceased and I fell into a dreamless vacuum of sleep.

The next morning, I awoke in amazement that I was still alive! Once my friends realized my predicament they moved into action. It was 28 degrees and "no fires," so Susana waited until the frost burned off and she could safely get into her Kayak and go find that couple. She arrived with only about ten minutes to spare; they were on their way out; it took about five hours for them to reach the ranger station.

The rangers arrived by Canoe; remember no motorized craft in the backcountry. They put me into a rubber type suit and zipped it up. It was very claustrophobic. By this time the winds had come up, which is a daily event, making the trip out rather exciting to say the least. I was just grateful to be moving in the direction of medical help. When they got to the channel they had to get out of the boat and actually push and pull the canoe along with me in it. I remember being so full of gratitude enjoying the dappling light of the sun on the water, incredulous that I was still here to enjoy it.

Once we traversed the channel, there was a speedboat waiting to take us across the second lake, the driver of the boat was also the paramedic that came with me in the ambulance. My breathing was very labored, so they were looking for heart problems, not paying much attention to the bite on my arm. By this time my arm had about a 5" by 3" intensely red area and the entire arm was red and swollen, they put me on IV fluids, I was dehydrated. EKG, and anything else they could think of was performed. I had to change ambulances halfway to Jackson Hole, and eight hours later I arrived at the hospital.

JACKSON HOLE

The first thing out of the ER doc's mouth was snakebite.

They admitted me, put me on IV antibiotics because cellulites had developed and was moving rapidly. They continued me on a total of four IV fluids. I started to feel better almost right away, however, that may also be because I no longer felt like I was going to die.

Jackson Hole hospital is like staying at a resort hotel, with private room, my own shower and amazing care. I had a menu by my bed that I could order from any time. In the morning after my first good night's sleep in three days, I ordered a mushroom, provolone, spinach and avocado omelet that tasted fantastic, with hash browns and turkey sausage. Everything on the menu was organic.

Many of the nurses and even my doctor were refuges from larger hospitals in big cities. They each had their story of escape and their inability to really care for patients in these larger hospitals.

They were sending me home the next day with antibiotics. Because I was checking out just before lunch, the chef in the kitchen came in and said she would make me a bagged lunch to go if you can believe that. She brought it to my room just as I was leaving; a spinach salad the likes of which you would find in any good restaurant, Pellegrino and two homemade chocolate chip cookies to boot in a beautiful handled bag with the hospital logo on it. When I checked out the receptionist gave me a loaf of homemade banana bread. Wow! Maybe healthcare had changed!

 My friend picked me up and I spent the nine remaining days of my vacation sleeping with brief interludes of energy. I got winded very easily so I stayed low. I assumed that once I got out of the altitude my breathing would return to normal, unfortunately that was not the case.

Just barely strong enough to fly home, I landed at LAX twelve days after the bite, I took a cab home and fell into bed. I only had a few more days on the antibiotic.

BACK IN LA

I finished the antibiotic and to my horror the symptoms returned. I immediately phoned my MD in LA, he called in a prescription for Bactrim, the antibiotic they use to treat MERSA. I was glad to get it, however after about five days on it I developed severe pain over my liver and the labored breathing intensified.

I called my doctor's office and asked the receptionist to have my Dr. call the hospital to admit me so I wouldn't have to wait hours to get in.

The receptionist insisted that I had to see the doctor first. I drove myself there, and after waiting 1/2 hour to see him, he asked me why I had not gone to emergency, I told him his receptionist had told me that I had to come in. Well that was not the case. A friend picked me up and drove me to the hospital.

When I got there my Doctor had not admitted me nor did he contact me the entire two days I was in the hospital. In fact, six months later as I write this, he still has never contacted me. Needless to say I am finding a new doctor.

I waited hours in emergency before they took me in, once in they ran a myriad of tests, mostly focusing on the heart because of my labored breathing, all were negative. Because they were running tests, they would not let me eat or drink and except for the initial intake, they never gave me IV fluids.

During the brief time I was on IV I had to go to the bathroom, I called the nurse and told her, she said she would send someone in; no one came. I had to get up, connected to the IV, push the bed next to the door and call out for someone to come. The nurse who heard me said it was not her job.

Finally, someone released me from my agony.

The doctors decided to keep me overnight. I assumed they would check me into a room. Instead they took me to a "Holding" room with about 15 other patients, each in a very small cubicle surrounded by only a curtain. Each patient had a TV that was on all the time, the lights were never turned off and the nurses never stopped talking across each other. The food was outrageously poor and I knew I was getting dehydrated again.

When I got a headache they offered me a Norco, this is an opiate. I said I just wanted an Advil. They told me that this Norco is what they had and it was a light dose and not to be concerned. OMG.

RECLAIMING MY POWER

In the meantime, I began to suspect the antibiotic was the cause of my symptoms. I began to refuse the antibiotic, this caused a huge commotion, and the nurse said I had to take it. Once off the antibiotic I began to feel a bit better. When I discussed this with the fourth doctor that saw me, he said it was possible. He was one of those condescending guys, unlike the other three I had had when I first arrived.

By this I was starved, dehydrated and sleep deprived. Any food I got was poisoning me, it was so bad. I had had enough. I called the nurse in and told her I was checking out. She told me that the doctor had to release me. My experience with this particular doctor was less then encouraging, his arrogance got in his way. "Well then, get him on the phone please, because I am leaving." They finally reached him and he released me. Some friends came and picked me up and took me home.

As you can see, two very different experiences.

Once home I put together a team of forward thinking doctors who have been amazing – a chiropractor/nutritionist, a dentist who saw the bigger picture, an acupuncturist and a biochemist that understands detoxifying poison from the body. They actually check in on me, offering me help that I was not able to get through our very broken healthcare system.

I was reminded of what I already knew; relinquishing power to the health care system may not always be in our best interests. I offer some suggestions for you if you find yourself in a similar situation.

#1. Have an advocate – someone who can speak with authority for you when you are not able or capable to do it for yourself. That may be a family member, a friend or a professional – someone who will keep your best interests in the fore.

#2. Build a relationship with your doctors – be they MD's or Functional medicine doctors, Chiropractors or surgeons. Make them aware of each other, and work with specialists from many fields that are willing to work together for you.

#3. Don't be fearful of questioning your healthcare providers – If they discourage this, find another doctor.

My experience in the LA hospital felt like the medicine of a different era, one that is out of step with the new innovations in health and healing.

MD's are not the enemy, don't get me wrong; I am very grateful to the team in Wyoming, they saved my life. But, like the hospital in LA, many work within an outdated infrastructure. They have become myopic, unable to see the bigger picture, grasping tightly to the standard of care of the past. This is not a new problem; each generation confronts this as they attempt to grow into the new thinking in medicine.

There are among us, leaders in our amazingly-innovative culture blazing new trails in the field of health, envisioning new ways for our children to experience more natural and soul healing approaches to creating and sustaining health. These leaders are researchers, Chiropractors, Naturopaths and opened-minded escapees from our archaic system who are forming groups of health care providers from a multitude of disciplines that offer real alternatives in medicine.

Our culture is screaming, just as I was screaming inside as I lay in that small, windowless cubicle for a nurturing of the soul, for a humane way back to vibrant health.

The change that is burgeoning in healthcare comes in small steps, but it is the new vision for those of us who wish to see change in an outmoded, dark and disconnected experience of medicine.

About Dr. Shirley

Dr. Shirley Watson is a QRA practitioner, a CCN (Certified Clinical Nutritionist) and a Doctor of Chiropractic specializing in nutrition and wellness. She is in private practice in Culver City, CA and has become a go-to health practitioner for those with chronic ailments. Many of Dr. Shirley's patients, who have suffered from low-grade to high-intensity pain with symptoms including irritable bowel, arthritis, headaches, constipation, chronic fatigue, sleep issues and hormone imbalances, have spent years visiting large numbers of medical and health professionals before finally arriving at Dr. Shirley's front door.

The secret to Dr. Shirley's success? While she works extensively with the physical manifestations of ill-health, she is also a firm believer that "ill health is the soul's voice wanting to be heard." As such, she has a three-pronged approach to reestablishing wellness in the body. In addition to her QRA practice and the use of ERT techniques, she uses a specific and self-styled form of lifestyle coaching to help her get to the emotional, physical and spiritual drivers behind the ill-health a patient presents.

Much to the initial chagrin but eventual gratitude of many of her patients, Dr. Shirley's practice isn't for the faint-hearted nor those looking for a one-pill-prescription fix-all. She works in partnership with her patients, offering innovative tools and health practices, while encouraging hard work and the removal of limiting filters and beliefs.

In addition to her extensive practice, Dr. Shirley is a published journalist who has written monthly health columns for magazines and newspapers. She has been published in numerous professional journals including the *Journal of the America Chiropractic Association*, and has also been a featured guest on national radio programs.

Often referred to as a health professional ahead of her time, Dr. Shirley wrote the American Chiropractic Association's position paper regarding Genetically Engineered Food over a decade before the current understandings of the dangers of genetically modified foods had entered the mainstream. Dr. Shirley's findings encouraged sustainable crop practices and the labeling of genetically engineered foods.

Dr. Shirley teaches nutrition for continuing education to Doctors, with a focus on healing the body, mind and spirit.

In addition to teaching, she is a dynamic and entertaining speaker helping to empower those who feel disenfranchised by our current health care system, teaching a way of healing that puts the 'buck' back in the lap of the individual.

If we do not take responsibility for our own health and then turn our recovery over to a system that does not address the underlying causes of disease, we cannot then blame the system. What we eat, how we live and what we believe — all contribute to our health challenges and to our recovery.

CHAPTER 50

THE HEART OF HEALTHCARE: PEOPLE-BASED PRACTICES DELIVER RESULTS

BY LOUIS KRAML, FOUNDER OF KRAMLKEYS.COM

We rise by lifting others.
~ Robert Ingersoll

My first introduction to healthcare was at Garfield Park Community Hospital, in Chicago. As the story goes, I was delivered by C-section late in the night, very premature and very small. The nurse placed me in the hand of my father, a bricklayer, who remarked, "He looks like a drowned rat; is he gonna make it?"

The nurse said "no" to the oxygen tent, telling my parents that I would be kept warm and they would blow some oxygen past my face, and if I made it through the night, I'd probably be strong enough to make it through life. My mother died of cancer shortly after I was born, and I stayed in the hospital for quite a while to get "fattened up."

That time in the hospital must have made an impression on me.

In my profession as a turn-around and growth CEO, I have followed my gut when it comes to the way I envisioned that a hospital should serve its community. My motivation was simple–I deeply wanted a family's dear

Grandma to be home enjoying one more holiday with her loved ones. It was from that place that I was able to go into small hospitals and change a worried and wondering team into a thriving culture where patients felt the difference from the moment they parked the car.

It was so clear. You walk into the hospital, perhaps nervous and afraid of what's coming next, and the person that greets you is someone you know and trust. Fear begins to melt away and is replaced with a confidence that you will be well cared for. You're not just pointed in the right direction; your guide accompanies you and your loved ones to your service and reassures you that you're in the best possible hands. Every team member understands the hospital culture and that you are cared for as a neighbor and friend.

This picture of caring service doesn't always happen on its own. The key is to provide ongoing education with clearly-established standards and regular evaluation. It ensures a consistent, inviting entrance to this patient-centered healthcare system.

My vision has always been for people to know immediately that they were walking into a different kind of hospital – one that saw their needs and comfort as a top priority.

I've always been a believer that when we focus our decisions in healthcare on how it will benefit our patient, everybody wins. Through this philosophy, I've helped hospitals who were not reaching their full potential to achieve success in the eyes of their patients. Those are the eyes we are all accountable to in the end. When they look at us, do they see and feel that their outcomes are something we truly care about? Are we able to quantify our success?

The key is that the best doctors, nurses and staff are in place, and what makes up the rest of the patient experience is of an equally high caliber. Creating this connection is my specialty. The key is that it's the little things that really matter and make the biggest difference.

When you arise in the morning, think of what a precious privilege it is to be alive—to breathe, to think, to enjoy, to love.
~ Marcus Aurelius

As a young Hospital Administrator, I was a man of many hats, doing what it took to create a culture within the business that was distinctly different. It was a matter of respect for one's self and accountability to achieve the hospital mission. I called it the "Kraml Touch."

The key here is anything that contributes to the greater good should be done with pride. Patients and their families take notice of these things.

As I matured in my career, my goals expanded. Staff understood the "Kraml Touch" and what it truly offered the patient. Patients saw a caring professionalism in the staff, which inspired them to know—without a doubt—they were receiving the best care.

The next key was to focus on the unique business opportunities for hospitals:

- Smaller hospitals are often less expensive because they have less overhead.
- Smaller hospitals are more agile and create quicker solutions that meet patients' needs without unnecessary red tape.
- Smaller hospitals offer a balanced life for physicians and staff that help attract high quality care givers.
- Smaller hospitals can create partnerships that bring many joint venture opportunities.
- Smaller hospitals can offer the newest innovations that directly impact positive cash flow.

If you capitalize on the advantages in small and rural hospitals, you can easily compete with larger, regional facilities that erode your market share. Patients no longer have to travel for general medicine services. They receive excellent care right at home. It's not about how small, how poor, or how disadvantaged we are – it's a new, positive way of thinking. And it works!

Reflection is looking in so you can look out with a broader, bigger, and more accurate perspective.
~ Mick Ukleja and Robert Lorber

Fast Forward To Today ...

Helping hospitals, one at a time, is wonderfully fulfilling for me. To take the pulse of a hospital, I can walk through its hallways and feel what is going right, and what is going wrong. I can feel what the customer, our patient, actually feels. I double-check my gut by discussing with staff just how they perceived the patient experience–because oftentimes a process needs revision. We work together to find solutions. The key is to do whatever it takes to have our hospital provide both a quality service and loving experience to our patients, families, and the community.

I make decisions based on a philosophy of trust, then verify. And in the case of an individual patient, family, or staff member, I always know "the look" and it identifies that the correct decision was made. You know "the look" – unexpected, unanticipated surprise, almost shocking, followed by gratitude, then happiness. Like when you present an engagement ring to the one you love.

I'm a fortunate man, because I absolutely love what I do. I don't just like it. I work to surround our patients and customers with a team that also loves their individual professions. It is much easier and more invigorating to effect change with those who are proud of what they do.

If you, as a CEO, want to have a successful organization, one that follows your mission statement, with teams that are competent and secure, just go around your shop and strive to get that "look" from a few different people each day. And if you're respected and admired, your team will enjoy getting that "look" from you. For a leader, that's where everything starts and ends well.

Today, I see a way to share my insights and proven turn-around abilities with a larger audience of healthcare professionals.

Now, I focus my passions on the hospital industry and reach Administrators and key personnel with concepts, ideas, and solutions that will help them turn the tides of how business is done inside their walls. My mission to serve is not over – it has shifted.

It's better to be in charge of change than to have to react to change.
~ Roger Ailes

I once had a mentor who always carried a large pocket knife. He didn't speak too often, but when he did, it was thoughtful and pertinent to deriving the solution to most every serious conversation. And in case you weren't necessarily paying close attention, he would take out his pocket knife, open it with a subtle flair, and work on his fingernails. That was the signal that he meant business. He would gently repeat himself, and most often he was correct in his assessment and suggested solution. He called it, "cutting through the bull." I attribute my personal mission statement to him:

If you love what you do, are respected for your contributions, are happy and work well with others, you will remember, understand, and live by his credo: Quality drives volume, and volume drives profit.

The quality of care that we offer patients comes from the content of our characters, the services we provide, and the way we help them heal the conditions that bring them there. If all you think about is quality, patients will feel it. They will go home and tell their neighbors, families, and doctors all about their great experience. The word gets around, and your volume increases. If you continue to always drive quality, God will bless you, and the money will come.

Today, I have launched: www.KramlKeys.com. It is a forum for mutual learning and a valuable resource for:

- Hospital Leaders
- Doctors, nurses, and other medical professionals
- All employees of departments who provide direct and ancillary care

In its essence, Kraml Keys is built to help you save time and be more profitable by unlocking the secrets to your success.

My role is as a mentor and consultant to hospitals who want to create a substantial turn-around in their approach to patient care. With www. KramlKeys.com, we have a new venue for dialogue and teaching. We share real life scenarios and solutions.

As I move into the future, I find that I am also changing the "consultant role" for hospitals that choose to look outside for answers from people who sometimes may not have the breadth of experience necessary to effect change. It's a powerful, down-to-earth connection to have a seasoned veteran with proven success walk your hallways with you. That's what I do, offering individualized solutions for:

- Physician recruitment
- Revenue enhancement
- Development of new product lines
- Leadership and staff team building
- Integrate best practices into daily operations
- I "take the monkey off your back"

Success begins with the power of belief.
It ends with what we do to prove what we believe in.

The opportunities that exist for the healthcare industry to put the focus back into the heart and the patient are extensive. Working with key staff to find better ways to create a hospital culture that celebrates people-based practices will lead to its ultimate success. If you create this type of hospital, the community will find there is no place they'd rather be when they are looking at you, wanting to know that they are more than just a patient, knowing their wellbeing is your business.

In grateful appreciation to
my Mentors, Physicians, and Colleagues.

About Louis

Louis Kraml is a Chief Executive Officer in healthcare. His experience has been centered around organizational vision and leadership – turning under-performing rural and community hospitals into high quality and highly profitable health systems. Louis recognizes strengths in communities where others may believe growth is long gone. Physician recruiting, retention and advocacy are one of his many passions. He has recruited and signed well over two hundred doctors in specialties from Family Practice to surgical super specialties, all relocating to small towns.

The Kraml's are a construction family by lineage, and even though Louis does not use bricks and mortar, he is a builder by heart. He is capable of seeing opportunities, developing plans for achievement, and with education, encouragement, timelines and continuous evaluation, the Kraml Teams have been recognized regionally and nationally as "the Best in their Field." Staff says: "If you can think it, you can do it at our hospital!"

Being born and raised in Chicago, Louis attended the U.S. Navy for six years, trained in hospitals, then was awarded the privilege of receiving a Master's Degree in Health Care Administration. Louis Kraml was not raised or educated around the farm, but as a start-up, first to market, new service-line administrator, some say: "He can make just about anything grow and generate income." The rest is hard work, dedication to quality, and loyalty to the team that worked to get to the goal. Louis enjoys transforming older facilities into boutique patient-centered systems.

Kraml states emphatically: "I just don't like what I do...I love what I do!" He surrounds himself with great professionals, and along with taking really good care of patients, they also learn to look for things that support a community's growth and wellbeing. Installing baseball fields for regional teams, providing computers for schools, and supporting many programs that enhance community pride, are all components of a small hospital's obligation to serve.

Louis has been a CEO for non-profit and profit-centered hospitals, Joint Venture partners with many physicians, surgery center start-up and management companies, nursing homes, clinics, doctors' offices, and other projects that are too numerous to mention. He is also a bestselling author of the book *The Road to Success* co-authored with Jack Canfield. His latest decision is to broaden his base of knowledge and teach the keys that unlock the secrets to success in healthcare through his website (Kramlkeys.com), speaking engagements, and conferences. With experiences we can relate to, and a down-to-earth style, he will share the stage with other specialists to educate and dialogue "the keys to success."

Louis Kraml believes that multiple and mutual "wins" are the first secret to success in healthcare.

Louis says: "Stay tuned as we learn from each other how to achieve the dream of having neighbors go home from our facilities much better than they arrived! Best wishes to you and your loved ones."